IMPARTED WISDOM IN TROUBLED TIMES

MAKING SENSE OF THE SENSELESS SITUATION

MY MINI SERMONS OF 2017

PASTOR STEPHEN KYEYUNE

authorHOUSE®

AuthorHouse™
1663 Liberty Drive
Bloomington, IN 47403
www.authorhouse.com
Phone: 1 (800) 839-8640

Published by AuthorHouse 06/29/2018

ISBN: 978-1-5462-4695-4 (sc)
ISBN: 978-1-5462-4694-7 (e)

Library of Congress Control Number: 2018907028

Print information available on the last page.

Any people depicted in stock imagery provided by Getty Images are models,
and such images are being used for illustrative purposes only.
Certain stock imagery © Getty Images.

This book is printed on acid-free paper.

CONTENTS

ABOUT THE AUTHOR

Pastor Stephen Kyeyune is currently the senior pastor of the Multicultural Family Fellowship Church at South Bend Indiana, USA. He is the author of several books including The New Generation of Worshipers; The Spirit is the Crown of the Heart; The Acts of the Holy Spirit; When God Calls a Man; The Legacy of a Hero; A Miracle at Prairie Avenue; Devotional Journal Living: Nuggets of Wisdom for Practical Living; Common Wisdom to Proper Understanding; Inspired Wisdom for Progressive Living; Imparted Wisdom in Troubled Times, Making Sense of the Senseless Situation; A series of books> Shaping the Society.

You may contact me on the address below:
Pastor Stephen Kyeyune
2029 South Michigan Street
South Bend Indiana 466613
<stephkyeyu@hotmail.com>

FROM MY DESK

This book contains a series of my mini-sermons as posted daily on my wall. I want to talk directly to thousands of my friends on Facebook. We are friends but utmost I feel we are Facebook dysfunction family. Ironically, we don't choose our family, we are related to them by nature, but we can choose our friends. Thank you for accepting me as your friend. Thank you for reading my posting and for sharing your postings.

When you add someone as a friend, you automatically follow that person, and they automatically follow you. I highly esteem my Facebook friends. Also, there are people who follow my updates by following me on Facebook without being friends. These are followers who chose to follow my activities on the Facebook site even though my posts do not appear in their news feed. They can see my posts, even though I don't see theirs. Often, they opt to like or comment on any of my postings. They respond to my posting without requiring me to respond in kind. It is sort of like a one-way friendship. It's an easy way for fans to follow celebrities or public figures. I am not a celebrity but I have a sizable number of followers. Although these followers are not accepted friends, they are potential friends who have interest in my postings. It is the right step in the right direction because knowing me begins with understanding me.

The bottom line is that you write your life story by the choices you make, including the friends you choose. I want to say explicitly that we are not friends by coincidence but by the divine appointment. Friendship is the greatest gift which life can grant to us, and I have received it. Friends are like balloons, when you let them go you will never get them back. So I am going to keep you tight to my heart so that I never lose you.

Interestingly, some of my youthful old friends are now friends on Facebook and we chat occasionally to reminisce about the past. One of the blessings of old friends is that you can afford to be stupid with them. "The biggest lesson I have learned is that no one is really your friend or truly loves you until they have seen every dark shadow inside you and stayed." My old friends know my ugly past but they chose to love me in spite of me. Certainly, to be with old friends is very warming and comforting. Whenever I receive a friend request from an old friend, I'm very excited because they are the most faithful mirror to reflect on my past. The reality is that you can't make old friends; you either have them or not.

The story of life continues until your last breath. Life is like a moving train with many stops. You will meet many people in your journey of life. The thread of our life would be dark if it were not intertwined with great friendships, heaps of laughter, entertainment, love, and compassion.

We were created for each other. God created and shaped each one of us differently, with such awareness that we are all bearing different perspectives and all of us essentially contribute to the development of our communities. We are of the same package but wrapped differently, and we can use our differences to complement each other. We need each other. A lonely life is a painful life; we will all need a shoulder to lean on at some points in our journey of life. Remember we are all something, but none of us is everything. Jesus plus nothing equals to everything. God created mankind of one kind like Him; which means a kind of man to appropriate His grace. We were created to perfect His holiness by loving each other. "When our life in Him is healthy and vibrant, we do not only ache to keep sinking our roots down deep in Him, but we also want to stretch out our branches and extend His goodness to others."

Life is the most precious gift. Life is short. The story of life is quicker than the wink of an eye. People will do anything in their ability to live. Yet it is tough to live. Success is a reserve of those who are willing to make a sacrifice. Heroes represent the best of ourselves, respecting that we are human beings, and respecting others. "Hard times don't create heroes. It is during the hard times when the 'hero' within us is revealed."

Expect disappointments when dealing with people because our nature is not perfect. Make friends but never find your happiness in people. The reason is that you will never feel sad when they decide to leave. There is nothing as painful as when somebody whom you expected to be your friend disowns you. Never feel bad when a person decides to leave you, it simply means their chapter in your life is over. There are purposes and time limits for everybody you're meeting in course of this journey of life. Some are for a season, while some are perennial. Some are blessings, while some will be lessons. Some are coincidental, while some are for a reason. Some will make you, while some will break you. Some are sent to assist you to accomplish a specific task and leave, while some will be part of your life for duration of time. Some you wish they never leave and some you cursed the day you meet them in life.

Love many but trust a few. It is possible to have so many fair-weather friends who can't afford to face a single storm with you, and worse is when some of them happen to be the very perpetrators of your storms. If a normally kind, agreeable person makes an enemy of you, you ought to ask yourself why. Some people are friends only when they benefit from the friendship. Remember the friends who stuck with you when they thought you had nothing. "There is no such thing as a fair-weather friend. Pay attention to those who are there for you in your time of need, and those who are not. Some people are only there when skies are sunny. A fair-weather friend is not a friend. Give your time and energy to those who care about you, who love and respect you. Find those types of people to be friends with. Friendship is reciprocated, respectful, honest, and loyal."

It takes patience to keep friends. Be an example of what you expect others to be. Respect yourself; if you don't others won't either. Hold yourself to a high standard of grace, integrity, and elegance. Transparency, authenticity, and accountability are the keys to a healthy relationship. Truth is the single most important ingredient in the recipe for transparency. A true friend is not afraid to tell the truth, no matter how bizarre. True friendship has the capability of growing into mutual friendship. Most good relationships are built on mutual trust and respect. "I am in you and you in me, mutual in divine love."

The currency of harmony is selflessness. Share your soul and conscience with people and show them that you care. Looking for the good in all people is the secret to living in harmony and a key to happiness. The image of Christ in us must be attracted to the image of Christ in others. Give, and it shall be given to you; the measure you give will be measured back to you. Don't think you will be vulnerable by being generous. Remember that in Christ, we are all winners. In the kingdom of God where Jesus reigns, everyone is necessarily a hero of his own life story.

The Internet has created a one world order. It is widely believed that he who controls internet controls the world. Most economic transactions are now carried out on the internet. Most political wars are won on the internet. As somebody said, "If you are looking to create an information weapon, the battle space you operate in is social media. That is where the fight happens."

Our defenses are controlled by the internet. Cyberwarfare involves the battle of space use - targeting of computers and networks in warfare. It involves both offensive and defensive operations pertaining to the threat of cyber attacks, espionage, and sabotage. Although cyberwarfare generally refers to cyber attacks perpetrated by one nation-state on another, it can also describe attacks by terrorist groups or hacker groups aimed at furthering their goals or of the particular nations. The increasing global interconnectivity and growth of digital technologies have amplified exposure to cyber risks and threats, making cybersecurity an emergent public good. Governments are looking to protect their citizens, data, communications and critical infrastructure through national policies, laws, and strong institutions. The required security involves going out and engaging with the enemy, rather than passively waiting for them to show their hand. There is the need for measures for proactively hunting down and neutralizing threats on our networks before they materialize. It involves the use of external threat intelligence, internal telemetry, and other data to uncover adversaries who have the intent, the ability, and the opportunity to do harm.

On the positive side, the availed new technology in communication helps to connect and create the social cohesion. Social media avails us various opportunities to exchange information at a lightning speed. Social media extends to us multiple opportunities to catch up on events and to follow the latest developments in this small world. We know a little bit of everything going on the planate. But without God, we know nothing at all.

Facebook is a place where we practice our reading and writing. Ironically, the majority of people do read Facebook memos and other insignificant tales like celebrity gossip. I suggest that you read purposely to be informed. Reading is the main brick by which civilization is built.

Reading is a requisite to knowledge. Reading is important because if you can read, you can learn anything about everything and everything about anything. Reading opens up the world to you taking you to places you have never been. As somebody insinuated that the beauty of reading is that I can be here and there at the same time. "The more that you read, the more things you will know. The more that you learn, the more places you'll go."

Reading sharpens the minds. The mind is a collection of thoughts, patterns, perceptions, beliefs, memories, and attitudes. The brain can be trained to behave, and even gradually evolve, based on the activities of the mind. "The mind can use the brain to perceive itself, and the mind can be used to change the brain." The brains are one of the most important and complicated human organ; far more complicated than the computers. For more than half a century psychologists, linguists, [and] neuroscientists have been asserting that the human brain works like a computer. But this just isn't the case. Computers process information from memory using CPUs, and then write the results of that processing back to memory. No such distinction exists in the brain. Our brains do not operate based on innate programming or create digital representations of stimuli. "They lack memory buffers or long-term storage, and they don't process via algorithms or "write" and "retrieve" data from neurons." The brain is a self-organizing system. Your brain has a kind of "built-in Google," in which just a few cues (keywords) are enough to cause a full memory to be retrieved. Of course, similar things can be done in computers, mostly by building massive indices of stored data, which then also need to be stored and searched through for the relevant information (incidentally, this is pretty much what Google does, with a few twists).

As I said, reading contributes effectively to the social comportment. Reading stimulates the minds. Thinking affects the way in which people resolve the impediment of moral dilemmas. Reading facilitates good communication. "Communication leads to community, that is, to understanding, intimacy and mutual valuing."

In the age of knowledge, ignorance is a choice. Reading eradicates ignorance. A library, therefore, is the hospital for the sick minds. Basically, reading is not an optional but a necessity. Reading is to the mind what exercise is to the body. Reading is the hub for the wheeled education system. Education is a progressive searching and a discovery of our own ignorance. In spite of the education school system in place, reading and writing skills are not faring any better. A new government report has accused teachers of training learners for only passing exams instead of equipping them with interpersonal, critical and vocational skills to deal with real-life situations. There is a need to adopt a better method of assessment instead of repeated tests which limit critical thinking. The education system should concentrate on securing an overall improvement in activities such as listening comprehension and oral passage reading.

I want to warn that as much as education is significant, increased knowledge apart from the wisdom of God yields to increased disorientation and worries. Life is a puzzle. The more you learn about life, the more you become worried about it. "The greatest enemy of knowledge is not ignorance; it is the illusion of knowledge." If you think that you know anything, God says that you know not as you ought to know. Knowing God is the beginning of wisdom. Foolishness is the immoral desire to be a god to yourself. The soul will never find rest until it finds its home in Christ (Isaiah 57:18:20).

Choose the right books to read. We become like the books we read. "When reading, we don't fall in love with the characters' appearance. We fall in love with their words, thoughts, and heart. We fall in love with their soul." Begin with reading the Bible. Study for knowledge and inspiration. Read the scriptures to understand to apply. "Study the Scriptures diligently and get knowledge; for knowledge of doctrine will help a great deal to confirm faith. Try to understand God's Word; let it dwell in your heart richly." The Word of God stands alone and preeminent as the bedrock of truth. I like this quotation: "The Bible is my textbook. Jesus is my principal. The Holy Spirit is my teacher. Temptations are my exams. Overcoming Satan is my hobby."

The books you choose to read stimulate your desire to read. A good book is something that challenges your perception and allows you to see the world anew from a different point of view, without disturbing your innate sense of what it should be about. Read objectively not to contradict and confute but to weigh and to consider. Look for important ideas and see how details relate to the whole.

Ignorance is not shameful but remaining ignorant is shameful. Reading demolishes the cartel of ignorance before it makes a home in your head. Learning is not attained by chance; it must be sought for with ardor and diligence. Learning and studying are byproducts of reading. Reading initiates knowledge and it is the way to practicing your knowledge capabilities; it contributes to more than intrinsic ability, it compensates for a lack of natural aptitude with diligence and discipline.

Reading is admitting that you don't know everything. Minimum reading contributes to forgetfulness. If you wonder why you sometimes forget seemingly easy things, like any of us, the answer is that there is probably nothing wrong at all with you but everything wrong with your inability to exercise your minds in particular when reading. For example, there is nothing worse than going to the grocery store and forgetting the most important thing you went in for in the first place. Such error could have been averted if only you wrote down everything at home before going to the grocery store. We write down things in order not to forget them. You can't forget what you are reading. This is when at the end of the day, forgetting actually becomes a natural brain process that might actually even make you smarter by reading.

Forgetting is considered to be a defect. But some psychologists disagree. They say that the people with the best memories in the long term usually forget details once they are no longer needed. So if you forgot the directions to that new restaurant, it's probably because you have more important things on your mind... literally! If you remember everything, you can have a hard time focusing and making decisions because you have so much competing data. A super intelligent person lets go of the data, their brain simply doesn't need any more, making it easier for them to think and make decisions.

The advantages of reading outweigh by far the leisure of not reading. You live several lives while reading. Books are the quietest and most constant of friends; a friend that always loves to sit on your lap. Somebody said that "Books are the ultimate Dumpees: put them down and they'll wait for you forever; pay attention to them and they always love you back."

The common excuse for not reading is lack of time. Life teaches us to make good use of time and time teaches us to value time. As somebody said "The bad news is that time flies, the good news is you're the pilot. Time is free but priceless. You can't own it but you can use it; you can't keep it but you can spend it, and once it is lost you can never get it back." Time abides long enough for those who make use of it. There should be no excuse for not reading. We all only have 24 hours per day to divide amongst our various activities. Redeeming time means trading it for something worthy. For efficiency, you need to reallocate value time toward reading and sharpening your brains. Every time is an opportunity to explore your talent. Always look out for an idea and work on it. Time invested in reading is time well spent. "Literature adds to reality, it does not simply describe it. It enriches the necessary competencies that daily life requires and provides; and in this respect, it irrigates the deserts that our lives have already become." ~ C. S. Lewis

Next time when confronted with a birthday of a friend or family member, remember that a book can be a really good present, too. A book is a gift you can open again and again. According to psychology, reading and books are fundamental to a child's language development, whether a first or a second language. It means that reading is first and foremost affecting young people's lives and reshaping childhood and adolescence. Storytelling through the classic fairy tales and inventive bedtime stories can effectively stimulate the children's minds. The Bible, in particular, has good bedtime stories for kids. I mean soft stories soothing the soul, which are usually told them just before the lights are turned out and they are left alone. The benefit of teaching them the Bible stories is that we are definitely learning alongside.

You probably won't be surprised to hear that a new report found that teens spend a lot of time watching TV, videos and movies, playing video games, listening to music and checking social media. I want to say that the impact of advanced technology in communication today has not diminished the significance of books. Reading has been simplified by electronics. The majority of the population does everything on laptops these days, so I positively believe that electronic books are a trend that's going to expand. Electronic books counter the challenges of the electronic digital era. It is very simple and easy to purchase and download ebooks through the Internet. It is exactly like purchasing any other product. The only difference is that after payment you will either be directed to a download page or receive the download link in an email. All you have to do is click on the link and the ebook will automatically download to your computer, to a folder of your own choice. So books will be ever relevant.

Somebody made the following comment: "Books conduce for wisdom, piety, delight and etc. Books break the shackles of time. Writing is perhaps the greatest of human inventions, binding together people, citizens of distant epochs, who never knew one another."

I am an author by accident but a teacher by calling. A good teacher is like a candle, it consumes itself to light the way of others. As somebody said, "Selfless acts of kindness lead others so much farther in life. If the world had more people that were not about themselves imagine how we could gain strength together; light one another up and strengthen the foundations of each individual just by saying, "hey- let me help with that burden and sacrifice a bit of my own life for yours, and you owe me nothing!"

Writing is an art, creating a story artistically should go along playing with words artistically. The major reason for writing is to pass out the intended message. I write while putting into consideration my audience. I except my words to itch at your ears till you understand them. I try to use simple words rather than complicated vocabularies which may be a turnoff. Chinua Achebe said that a good writer is the one who uses the 'is' and 'was' language". He meant that a writer is supposed to use the simplest words.

Writing is an exploration. You start from nothing and learn as you go. Your story of life began on your day of birth and continues as long as you are living. Tomorrow isn't written as yet; what would you like to write about you? Either write something worth reading or do something worth writing. Literature is the expression of a feeling of deprivation; a recourse against a sense of something missing.

Digital technology allows us a much larger scope to tell stories that were pretty much the grounds of the literary media. Social media provides a platform to practice writing. For example, one of the famous authors today started her writings by sharing and posting her brief life experiences: "I wasn't trying to write a book; it wasn't even in my vision. I was posting stuff online just because it made me feel relieved - as a way of getting things off my chest". Various stories from people who were not born with a silver spoon in their mouth; people who lived hard lives but still managed to reach the top of the mountain with their effort and sacrifice have a different effect on the readers. Usually, readers relate to your story, whereas some find it hard to believe because it sounds so spectacular. They read with wonder asking: "Were you there, really? Were you? How did you get there? How did you get out of there to become what you are?"

Social media improves writing by practicing. Even the people who don't read books regularly tend to read and respond to the posted messages by their friends daily. Volunteer to write the story of your life for the people to read. Write down even the dark chapters of your story. The part where God delivered you is what the world is desperate to read. Start to write by keeping a journal of your daily activities. Most people who are not professional writers find it daunting to sit down and tell their life stories. If you're literate, you can write about your own life, with or without some help. Hiring a writer can run into the tens of thousands of dollars – and you don't need one.

The goal of the biography is to convey the details of one's life. Your life is your story. Write well. Edit Often. Writing feels safer somehow. I can catch myself before I say the wrong thing. Never be afraid to offer the little you have. We learn by practice even when it comes to writing. In case you need help there are online free services that offer the tools and guidance you need to create and publish a book. Some also offer a paid option where a consultant will help you through the process.

"Writing your life story can be one of the most complex forms of storytelling. It could involve emerging themes, narrative flow, and re-creating dialogue from memory. Or it can be surprisingly easy and fun." Remember that your documented story outlives you. There is nothing much that people celebrate about us but they celebrate our work. Writing never ends because as long as you are still alive, your story is never over. Leisure is the time for doing something useful; decide to use leisure as a means of mental development by writing. "Nobody gets me like paper and pen".

This world is a small place. When you don't know something, there is someone who knows it. Communication is the key to an effective sharing of information. Communication efficiency means that you deliver your message quickly in a way that allows the receiver to hear it, interpret and make use of it as you intended. "The power of communication of thoughts and opinions is the gift of God, and the freedom of it is the source of all science, the first fruits and the ultimate happiness of society; and therefore it seems to follow, that human laws ought not to interpose, nay, cannot interpose, to prevent the communication of sentiments and opinions in voluntary assemblies of men."

Social media has tremendously improved on the inter-communication of the world. It is a place where we meet friends from all over the world. We connected with them just by reading their postings. Then we dig into the information shared perpetually to grow our relationship. We trust them to counsel and mentor us on face value. Social media is rejuvenating to all parties involved. Ironically, we are like patients with the same diagnosis sharing information to affect our healings.

Social media is not exempted from impediments; it has its good and bad sides. The old adage says "If you are interested in picking a rose, be prepared to handle the thorns." Often humility walks out through the window of social media. It is unfortunate that we have turned social media a wall to exchange insults. As Anthony said "Social media websites are no longer performing an envisaged function of creating a positive communication link among friends, family, and professionals. It is a veritable battleground, where insults fly from the human quiver, damaging lives, destroying self-esteem and a person's sense of self-worth."

There is a temptation to seek attention and to be victimized by pride. Most people who are addicted to Facebook are actually addicted to fame and attention seeking. Some of the postings are intended to draw our sympathy but it is not easy to sympathize with someone when all you have is one sided story, without having the other party's story. Generally, the messages posted give a vague picture because of the limited information provided. "Sometimes Facebook is like a book that you randomly open to pages and only get a tiny bit of the story – since you're not going to see a person's updates every time – and I get that. But then there are those who seem to do it on purpose. For example, such posting: "Just left the hospital." Were you visiting? Were you injured? Are you really going to make me ask?"

These attention seekers are ever active on social media, but it is a fact that many of these people do not really know that they have a personality disorder. At times these attention seekers post things just to draw attention to them but they end up hurting others. It is possible to post something for fun, but somehow your joke ends up rubbing someone the wrong way, or you reveal something you weren't supposed to about someone else, or you post something vague that someone somehow takes to be about them. Never trade respect for attention. Attention seekers are sadly the most coldhearted people because they neither show remorse for their actions nor take steps to make amends or have empathy for others. They are often selfish and morally bankrupt. One major influence on behavior is surveillance, where people change their behavior when they know they're being watched, in this case on social media. People tend to be a bit emotional once they don the anonymity cloak the internet provides. I think the most cherished and happiest moments in life occur out of public view.

On the public platform, Satan uses some believers to distract others from witnessing the saving grace. Watch what you post, please. Sometimes we post sensitive theological topics to invoke debate but we end up distancing the potential converts. I think we should be preaching rather than debating the Word of God on a public platform where many are lost. Debating each other on important doctrines pertaining to salvation is like giving the nonbelievers more reasons and excuses to doubt. They see the arguments and disagreement among us, and they don't want to be part of it. Some are on the verge of becoming born again but we end up distancing them from us instead of assisting them to come to us.

According to Jacquie Tyre, there is a protocol within the Kingdom that creates a safe environment for healthy discipleship and maturing together with others, and protects against the random discourse of opinions and pontifications of ideas that may or may not be beneficial or valid. Within the context of Kingdom discipleship and operation, when a person has been given the assignment to teach, that person has delegated authority and should be respected as such. If someone comes in and attempts to interject experience and knowledge to appear more than the teacher with delegated authority, that one is out of order and creates confusion and disorder in the spirit for the entire group. Such a person may know more, but projecting that to draw attention to yourself is pride and reveals dishonor, lack of a teachable spirit, and a lack of understanding of Kingdom culture. This type behavior is born of the flesh and is not according to the ways of the Kingdom. (As Dr. Don Lynch says, we have lost Kingdom culture and don't even know it...). Humility, submission, possessing a teachable and transformable heart, respect and honor are keys to living according to Kingdom culture.

The advantage of the Internet is that anyone who wants to express an opinion about anything can make their thoughts available to a worldwide audience far more easily than it has ever been possible before. A large and growing group of Internet participants have seized that opportunity. Narratives that work in social networks are the exchange of stories that are told well. However, it is not just the useful information that is shared but the harmful information also gets a free ride on social media. Lately, it seems a week doesn't go by without some new news about a Facebook-related security problem. Facebook is supposed to be a place where the heart can be open and loving with a sense of security. It must not be a place of fear. There are massive falsehoods circulating on Facebook. The impostor can easily set you up to steal your identity or valuable information from you that they can use to hurt you or manipulate someone else. It is a proof how much off track most people are!

High-speed internet has turned up to be high-speed temptation. Morality has been the major victim of freedom of speech and expression on the Internet. As I was writing this article, police were reportedly investigating the suspected gang rape of a woman after the attack was live-streamed on Facebook. An online witness said the victim had her clothes pulled off by armed men and was sexually assaulted before cops arrived and turned off the camera. According to Swedish tabloid Aftonbladet, three people have been arrested. In a separate incidence, three teenagers were arrested in Memphis, Tennessee, after allegedly raping a teenager and broadcasting the attack on Facebook Live. One of them is accused of recording the attack on video and posting it on Facebook Live. Officers recovered the footage from his cellphone. Welcome to our brave new digital world in which raping women is all fun and games!

It has become a very normal thing for young girls to exhibit their half-naked bodies on Facebook to lure men into a casual relationship. Social media is a place where nude and sex videos are leaked by the extortionists. The current levels of unemployment, moral decadence, and the trendy levels of technology are partly to blame for this growing vice of nudes and sex tapes. The institutions responsible for ensuring sanity have failed to counter the mischief even when the names, addresses, and photos of those involved in leaking these sex videos are known. This has created an enabling environment for the nudes to keep leaking.

There are predators on Facebook targeting our children. The predators exploit unmonitored internet access to target their victims. It is, therefore, your responsibility to guard yourself against such predators. No unfiltered access to the internet. Meanwhile, the governments of some countries are weighing in to rectify the situation. One high ranking African government official said, "Social media is not a garbage dump of sorts. Our country has a culture; the wrongdoers would be brought to justice." President Trump recently signed 'FOSTA' targeting online sex trafficking. The bill gives federal and state prosecutors greater power to pursue websites that host sex-trafficking ads and enables victims and state attorneys general to file lawsuits against those sites.

According to Facebook's rules and guidelines, the consumers reserve the right to block whosoever they deem to be unfriendly. To unfriend someone means that they'll no longer be able to see the posts you share only with your friends, and you won't be able to see theirs. You don't have to worry because Facebook never tells them that you've unfriended them. Finding out who's deleted you is often difficult due to privacy settings. The social media site's privacy settings mean it's tricky to determine if you've been blocked, unfriended, or if the other user has simply tightened up their profile for everyone. You can search for a person in your inbox and, if they're still on Facebook and haven't blocked you, their profile picture and name will appear under the 'More People' heading. When you block someone, they lose the ability to access your profile except through a friend's account. The people you have blocked lose the ability to start a Facebook chat with you. If you still have the option to message someone you're no longer friends with, you haven't been blocked, but unfriended.

Every citizenry is entitled to exercise their constitutional right to free speech. Free speech entails that the community be empowered more to access information. And the people who are giving out this information need to be more accessible. Social media promotes free speech but not without limitations. One of my friends posted the following disturbing article regarding how the system works: "Here is a post explaining why we don't see all posts from our friends. Newsfeed recently shows only posts from the same few people, about 25, repeatedly the same, because Facebook has a new algorithm. Their system chooses the people to read your post. However, I would like to choose for myself. Therefore, I ask you a favor: if you read this message leave me a quick comment, a "hello", a sticker, whatever you want, so you will appear in my Newsfeed. Otherwise, I don't need Facebook to choose who to show me. This is how to avoid hearing from the same 26 FB friends and nobody else".

There is an allegation that Facebook is cracking down on potential instances of what it calls "hate speech" by adding thousands of employees to delete offensive posts, the company announced in a blog post recently. "Our current definition of hate speech is anything that directly attacks people based on what is known as their "protected characteristics" — race, ethnicity, national origin, religious affiliation, sexual orientation, sex, gender, gender identity, or serious disability or disease," said Richard Allan, Facebook vice president of public policy for Europe, the Middle East and Africa. "There is no universally accepted answer for when something crosses the line. Although a number of countries have laws against hate speech, their definitions of it vary significantly."

Mark Zuckerberg, CEO of Facebook is confident regarding their performance. He said that "We've got over two billion users now, so it's never been more important to show them only what we want them to see while throttling to death of all content that we don't think they should be consuming for whatever reason," the Facebook chief said. "My days are longer than ever."

Social media is a fertile soil where hate speech flourishes. According to the psychologists, like violence, hate speech can also be a physical imposition on the freedom of others. That is because 'language' has a psychological effect imposed physically — on the neural system, with long-term crippling effects. Freedom in a free society is supposed to be for all. Freedom rules out imposing on the freedom of others. You are free to listen to your kind of music, but not to keep others from listening to their kind of music or even not listening to anything at all. Ironically, free speech is intended to force us to accept other people's contradictory views. Debates on sensitive topics should therefore not be labeled as hate speeches.

There is a systematic policy by Facebook to suspend or block people from posting what is considered to be the sensitive matters to the society. For example, some people claim that they were censored by Facebook for posting some conservative pro-life articles. Recently, a German Catholic Historian was blocked by Facebook for his comments on Islam. Facebook is accused of biased political censorship like initially shutting down of Chick-fil-A appreciation day page; blocking Trump supporters Diamond and Silk's page with 1.2 million Facebook followers after branding their page as unsafe to the community.

Facebook can block you without notification of why you are blocked. Some of the reasons you may be blocked are posting on walls in rapid succession; when you're sending too many friend requests; posting offensive updates and pictures; posting duplicated texts in too much messages; when you're poking rather too much; when your account is a potential risk to other Facebook users; affiliation with a Doubtful Organization or Page; when you have more than one account; posting copyrighted materials; getting reported by rather too many people. Whereas it is necessary to curb indiscipline, some people say that Facebook is broken by design. It will censor you to force you to pay for ads to reach your own subscribers and friends.

Generally speaking, politicians have been the primary violators of free-speech. Authoritarian leaders are fond of severing communications in a bid to hold on to power, and that tradition sadly isn't going away. Recently, the Democratic Republic of Congo's government has ordered telecoms to cut internet and SMS access ahead of planned mass protests against President Joseph Kabila, whose administration has continuously delayed elections to replace him. An attempt to sever internet and SMS access may make it difficult to coordinate, but a sufficiently angry public will still find a way to make its voice heard. Elsewhere, faced with an increasingly critical citizenry, the government of Uganda has slapped new taxes on social media platforms such as WhatsApp, Facebook, Twitter, Skype and Viber to stop what the President has called *olugambo* (gossip). "I am not going to propose a tax on internet use for educational, research or reference purposes... these must remain free. However, *olugambo* (gossip) on social media (opinions, prejudices, insults, friendly chats) and advertisements by Google and I do not know who else must pay tax because we need resources to cope with the consequences of their *olugambo*," Mr. Museveni wrote. Kenyan President Uhuru Kenyatta recently signed into law a sweeping cyber-crimes act criminalizing fake news and online bullying, with clauses that critics argue could stifle press freedom. The bill imposes stiff fines and jail terms for hacking, computer fraud, forgery of data, cyber espionage, publishing child pornography or sending pornographic content via any electronic means. Anyone found guilty of publishing false information that "is calculated or results in panic, chaos, or violence" or that is "likely to discredit the reputation of a person" can be fined $50,000 or jailed for up to 10 years. However, bloggers and media rights activists have expressed alarm over a clause which criminalizes the publication of "false, misleading or fictitious data."

Journalists have often fallen victim to the uncalled for harassment by the governments. They identified some of the threats as confiscation of equipment, theft, data leakages, fraud, surveillance, phone tapping and hacking. According to one of the journalists, "The attacks have created an atmosphere of fear among journalist some of whom have resorted to conventional reporting and abandoned enterprising, interpretative and investigative reporting".

Social media has turned up to be the main source of news. I love it except for the calamities caused by the fake news. Recently, a number of online news publications have mushroomed around the globe. Most of them have been in the business of "breaking news" although the majority of them have been running what can be described as fake news. "As the Internet of things advances, the very notion of a clear dividing line between reality and virtual reality becomes blurred, sometimes in creative ways." The funny thing about fake news is how mind-numbingly boring it can be. Not the fakes themselves – they're constructed to be catnip clickbait to stoke the fires of rage of their intended targets. The fake news is akin to a fake prophet preaching a fake gospel. And the only thing that enchants you is fear. Therefore, the circus of fake news which is maliciously circulated on the social media is ill-intentioned rumor peddled.

Zeeynep Tufekci eloquently argued that "The most effective forms of censorship today involve meddling with trust and attention, not muzzling speech itself." Ironically, some politicians have benefited from the epidemic of the fake news. We get subjected to all this intentional padding, applied selectively, to defuse debate and derail clear lines of argument; to encourage confusion and apathy; to shift blame and buy time. Bored people are less likely to call their political representatives to complain.

Social media is where we access splendid messages from a splendid people like you. Earnestness is the assumption. But people are increasingly becoming reluctant to take things at face value on social media. We are coming to a place where everything is not decidable by seeing or hearing due to the computer (lab) generated images. Rumors and accusations are backed up and constructed by the computer-generated images such that you cannot tell by seeing or hearing which is fake and which is real. There is a website where you can make somebody say what you want if you control their voices. Through this door of technology, people can destroy others' reputations by posting fake images.

Former US President Barack Obama personally urged Facebook founder Mark Zuckerberg to counter the rise of fake news on the social network during a meeting held shortly after last year's election, the Washington Post reported. The encounter reportedly took place on the sidelines of a meeting of global leaders in Lima, Peru on November 19, two months before Trump's inauguration and days after Zuckerberg had dismissed as "crazy" the idea that misleading stories driven by Russian operatives had made a major impact on the outcome of the vote. "Zuckerberg acknowledged the problem posed by fake news. But he told Obama that those messages weren't widespread on Facebook and that there was no easy remedy". The newspaper reported.

Facebook is blocking pages that post fake news stories from buying ads as part of its efforts to curb hoax articles on its platform. In a bid to curb the swift flow of fake news, Facebook said that the pages that make a habit of linking to bogus news stories will no longer be able to advertise at the world's leading online social network. The move is the latest shot fired by Facebook in its war against 'fake news' that is used to deceive instead of enlightening. "If Pages repeatedly share stories marked as false, these repeat offenders will no longer be allowed to advertise on Facebook," product managers Tessa Lyons and Satwik Shukla said in a blog post. "This update will help to reduce the distribution of false news which will keep Pages that spread false news from making money." The social network already didn't allow ads that link stories determined to be false by third-party fact-checkers. "False news is harmful to our community," Lyons and Shukla said. "It makes the world less informed and erodes trust."

Facebook may not be directly responsible for the circus of the fake news but the system is set up as an enabler. We've entered an era of digital connectivity and machine intelligence. Complex algorithms are increasingly used to make consequential decisions about us. "We're building an artificial intelligence-powered dystopia, one click at a time," says Techno-sociologist Zeynep Tufekci. In an eye-opening talk, she details how the same algorithms companies like Facebook, Google, and Amazon use to get you to click on ads are also used to organize your access to political and social information. "And the machines aren't even the real threat. What we need to understand is how the powerful might use AI to control us – and what we can do in response."

Facebook algorithmically arranges the posts that your friends put on Facebook, or the pages you follow. It doesn't show you everything chronologically. It puts the order in the way that the algorithm thinks will entice you to stay on the site longer. Open Graph is a technology first introduced by Facebook in 2010 that allows integration between Facebook and its user data and a website. The theory behind Open Graph as the business model is trying to get you to share as much information as possible so they can monetize it by sharing it with advertisers. Facebook came under fire recently, when 15 privacy and consumer protection organizations filed a complaint with the Federal Trade Commission, charging that the site, among other things, manipulates privacy settings to make users' personal information available for commercial use. Also, some Facebook users found their private chats accessible to everyone on their contact list - a major security breach that's left a lot of people wondering just how secure the site is. Last month, researchers at VeriSign's iDefense group discovered a hacker was selling Facebook usernames and passwords in an underground hacker forum. It was estimated he had about 1.5 million accounts - and was selling them for between $25 and $45.

Facebook faces what some are calling an "existential crisis" over revelations that its user data fell into the hands of the Trump campaign. It is said that the Trump-affiliated consulting firm obtained data on at least 50 million unsuspecting Facebook users. This information was used to target voters in the US, based on psychological profiling, with political adverts spreading disinformation. But while the Trump campaign used Cambridge Analytica during the primaries, it didn't use the information during the general election campaign, relying instead on voter data provided by the Republican National Committee, according to CBS News. Donald Trump's social media manager disclosed that they were using

Facebook dark posts to demobilize people, not to persuade them, but to convince them not to vote at all. And to do that, they targeted specifically, for example, African-American men in key cities like Philadelphia, and I'm going to read exactly what he said. I'm quoting. They were using "nonpublic posts whose viewership the campaign controls so that only the people we want to see it see it. We modeled this. It will dramatically affect her ability to turn these people out." What's in those dark posts? We have no idea. Facebook won't tell us.

In 2012, the Obama campaign encouraged supporters to download an Obama 2012 Facebook app that, when activated, let the campaign collect Facebook data both on users and their friends. The campaign boasted that more than a million people downloaded the app, which, given an average friend-list size of 190, means that as many as 190 million had at least some of their Facebook data vacuumed up by the Obama campaign — without their knowledge or consent. If anything, Facebook made it easy for Obama to do so. A former campaign director, Carol Davidsen, tweeted that "Facebook was surprised we were able to suck out the whole social graph, but they didn't stop us once they realized that was what we were doing."

Aleksandr Kogan, the University of Cambridge psychology professor who harvested data from Facebook and sold it to Cambridge Analytica, apologized for a tactic that has spawned the wrath of internet users worldwide. He said that he was "sincerely sorry" for assuming that everyone knew their data was being mined, but didn't care. He was the one who designed the personality quiz that granted access to personal data – location, gender, birthday and page likes for the person taking the quiz as well as their friends – on tens of millions of Facebook users. He said "Back then, we thought it was fine. Right now, my opinion has really been changed," he said." "If I had any inkling that I was going to cause people to be upset, I would've never done it."

Jim Mellon, the billionaire British investor, has predicted that Facebook faces "decimation" over the Cambridge Analytica data disaster. "The Cambridge Analytica thing is just the tip of the iceberg," said Mellon, who is typically bearish on big tech. "We're going to see the decimation of particularly Facebook and quite right too — it's a trivial use of modern technology and one that's rather sinister."

Facebook has resorted to a stricter privacy environment as counter offensive following an outcry over the hijacking of data on 87 million Facebook members by Cambridge Analytica. The new move could be significant for campaigns; Facebook appears to be making it harder to use software tools to automatically match members of the social network with other affiliations. Facebook's new focus on protecting private user data is likely to change the game for many campaigns, making it harder to deliver highly targeted, personal political messages. The new privacy effort could limit "microtargeting" using the social network, a technique used successfully by Donald Trump's campaign in 2016 and others. "Microtargeting is a big deal for campaigns, because they have to decide how they spend money and who they target," said Joseph Hall, chief technologist for the Center For Democracy & Technology. He is leading a research project on election privacy and security. "Any clamping down on data collection is going to have a large effect on campaigns."

Facebook has also promised labels and verification for ads on hot-button political issues which are not for specific candidates. Young Mie Kim, a University of Wisconsin professor who led research on 2016 Facebook political ads said that it may have trouble living up to that pledge. Kim said many disputed 2016 ads were "dark" posts by anonymous groups, shown only to small numbers of users without mentioning a candidate's name. "It is incredibly difficult to define an issue ad – even policymakers do not completely agree on this," she said. "Facebook will have a very difficult time defining what are political ads."

As per now, Facebook scans the contents of messages that people send each other on its Messenger app, blocking any content that contravenes its rules, it has emerged. The scandal-hit firm, still reeling from the Cambridge Analytica debacle, checks images and links for illegal or extreme content using automated systems. What you write in your messages may also be read manually if it's flagged to moderators for breaching Facebook's community guidelines. While the intentions behind the practice may be well-meaning, the news is likely to add to users' concerns over what the social network knows about them. Facebook is also facing criticism for collecting years of data on call and text histories from Android users.

Generally, the consumers are increasingly worried about discarding their privacy to the social media companies controlling the data. People are concerned about their right to privacy; the limits of their rights to privacy; how much they give away in the name of connecting them to the world. People have come to realize how easy it is to unwittingly hand over reams of personal information to companies and persons unknown. While a majority of users are aware that anything they post – essentially – becomes Facebook's property, and can be exploited in a variety of ways. Anything shared to the social network can be used to dig up an ever-more accurate picture of who you are, where you are, what you do, what you like, and who you know.

Mark Zuckerberg appealed to the consumers to gain confidence: "We've already stopped apps like this from getting so much information. Now we're limiting the data apps get when you sign in using Facebook. Finally, we'll remind you of which apps you've given access to your information — so you can shut off the ones you don't want anymore. We have a responsibility to protect your information. If we can't, we don't deserve it."

On the positive side, the stored data can be useful when tracking down criminals. For example, in Texas, authorities tracked down the suspect, identified as Mark Anthony Conditt, 24, using a combination of cell phone triangulation technology, surveillance footage from a FedEx drop-off store, store receipts, and combing through Google searches on the suspect's computer history. Austin Police Chief Brian Manley said in an early morning press conference that witness reports helped police identify the vehicle Conditt was driving. Manley said surveillance teams then tracked the suspect's vehicle to a hotel in Round Rock, Texas. Authorities say the suspected bomber died from a self-inflicted explosion as the members of the Austin police department SWAT team approached his vehicle. "The suspect detonated a bomb inside the vehicle, knocking one of our SWAT officers back, and one of our SWAT officers fired at the suspect as well," Manley said.

Meanwhile, social media is the single largest user base. During the month of July 2017, 135.6 million mobile users accessed the Facebook app. Facebook's Messenger app had a monthly mobile audience reach of 102.32 million users. The whole point of social media is continuity and continual engagement. It is estimated that each day 93 million selfies are taken each day in the world. Most of them are posted on Instagram and of course

Facebook. With 1.86 billion monthly active users – that's 25% of the world's population – it's clear that Facebook reigns supreme amongst social media platforms when it comes to overall global reach. Given the fact, according to the most recent study published on May 31st, teenagers and kids are rapidly abandoning Facebook. Instagram is used by 72 percent of teenagers, and Snapchat by 69 percent. 51 percent of surveyed kids age 13 to 17 said they use Facebook. In 2015 that number was 71 percent, and Facebook was the dominant social media platform.

I'm a little bit uncomfortable with the monopoly and arrogance of the "big players" on the internet (Google, Yahoo, Facebook, Craigslist, eBay, etc.). Since Facebook is the world's largest social network, they think that can do what they want. My advice is that do not put all of your eggs in one basket. Open up other accounts like twitter in case your Facebook account is compromised. No wonder WhatsApp's popularity has been consistently growing over the years. The timeshare on messaging with friends has now been divided to some extent between Facebook and WhatsApp, what was previously the monopoly of Facebook only. Teens and younger Millennials are increasingly moving away from Facebook to newer, trendier platforms – and Snapchat is a key player. Snapchat has 301 million monthly active users worldwide and has been consistently growing year-on-year. By the end of 2017, the app is forecasted to have 13.6 million monthly active users in the UK. However, as was in the news a few months back, Facebook saw more than a billion active users in a single day and has been clocking approx. more –than 1.86 billion monthly active users – that's 25% of the world's population active users a month, it does not seem to be going away.

The Church is always the victim of every wrong move made by the world. Recently, Facebook announced the goal to take the role of Church. Facebook founder and CEO Mark Zuckerberg just rightly identified a major problem with the Church today: people aren't going. And instead of wanting to reverse that, he wants to capitalize on it. At Facebook's first summit focusing solely on building communities, Zuckerberg said: "It's so striking that for decades, membership in all kinds of groups has declined as much as one-quarter," Zuckerberg said, as Lifesite News reports. "That's a lot of people who now need to find a sense of purpose and support somewhere else." Social media is increasingly becoming a replacement of church for the lukewarm believers. They go to Facebook for comfort, counseling, and to evangelize instead of actively participating in their home churches.

Decreased church attendance affects the secular institutions as well since churches are the main financers of charities. Zuckerberg downplayed the role of faith as the major factor behind charity. He told the group of community leaders: "People who go to church are more likely to volunteer and give to charity, not just because they're religious but because they're part of a community." Stimulating church attendance is not a product of rainbow illusion. "A church doesn't just come together," said Zuckerberg. "It has a pastor who cares for the well-being of their congregation, makes sure they have food and shelter. A little league team has a coach who motivates the kids and helps them hit better. Leaders set the culture, inspire us, give us a safety net, and look out for us." Zuckerberg shared his huge goal with the leaders: "We're going to change Facebook's whole mission to take this on." He goes on to say that "In the next generation, our greatest opportunities and challenges that we can only take on together, is ending poverty, curing disease, stopping climate change, spreading freedom and tolerance, stopping terrorism." It sounds to me like the liberal social gospel at its best.

Zuckerberg's remarks and revamped mission statement should be a wakeup call to the Church. We need to find a way to revitalize our community and our faith. Social media presents to us a golden chance to share the gospel but it is not the only means to share the gospel. We are called to use everything to reach out to the lost world. Preach the gospel in its simplicity. Never be ashamed or fearful to share with others what God has done for you! Tell them what He's delivered you from. Tell them how He's saved and restored you. They need to hear it!

Paul often went to the theatres, marketplaces, and synagogues to preach the gospel. The marketplaces, in particular, were known for hooliganism. But he went there anyway because that is where multitudes of people gathered. Likewise, we go on Facebook because that is where people are. We have the world at our fingertips right here on Facebook. The more we tell the people about Jesus the more the world will come to know Him. Occasionally, I have been contacted by Facebook to put restriction measures in place on my home page to restrict who sees and shares my messages. I declined because my objective is to share the gospel to the whole world rather than to a few chosen ones. Nobody has the copyright to the gospel.

JANUARY FOR PROSPERITY

2018 is knocking at the door. Quit making resolutions for the New Year; if you can't do it now you won't do it tomorrow either. Every day has 24 hours on your credit to use regardless of the numbers of the year. Every day has daytime and nighttime. You cannot rush the day into the night or the night into the day. You have to go through the twilight into the broadening day before the full sun comes. We cannot catch up with the past but the past is the beginning of the beginning (new). All that is (now) has ever been (past) and will be (future). Your glorious triumph does not depend on time and space but on the timeless and the unchanging God. The duration of life does not depend on what you have but on whom you know. Eternal life is the life of the soul. He, therefore, who neglects the eternal life, casts away the life of the soul. How long you live in this world is not as important as how you live because how you live determines where you are heading.

When God created the sun, He organized time into a working system for us. Today, physicists describe time as a function of matter. God numbered the six days of creating and the seventh day of resting; by virtue of dominion over all creations, Adam divided days into manageable segments of weeks, months and years. We don't know how long Adam lived in the Garden before he was corrupted by sin because eternity is not limited by time. Genesis 5:5 says Adam lived for 930 years in his corrupt nature outside the Garden. Judging by today's standards, this sounds impossible but to God, a thousand years is like one day. The fact that the recorded counting of years began after Adam was corrupted with sin implicates that the duration of years is a countdown towards the end (death). As per judgment, the natural life is not exempted from death. This life is not ours to grasp and to keep; we grow into death. Even when the gospel is preached and received, it brings death to this life first before it introduces the eternal life. Getting excited and enthusiastic about the New Year when you are not born again is, therefore, pushing yourself to the extreme.

Time changes; years come and go but the unchanging God is ever on the throne. Prayers change things. Praying is being honest to God by verbally expressing your feelings to Him, speaking the words within your heart to Him, and communing with Him having grasped His will based on His Word. Let your prayer be close to God's heart one day at a time. We cannot over-pray because God expects us to pray; He wants us to pray more than we do. The peace that averted you in 2017 will continue to avert you in 2018 until you embrace the Prince of Peace wholly heartedly. His peace surpasses human understanding. His truth suppresses the deception of the world. You must go beyond the constant clamor of ego, beyond the tools of logic and reason, to the still, calm place within the realm of the spirit in order to experience His peace. If your prayers were not answered in the past year, keep on praying. "Take courage, you who prayerfully work for Christ with only scant success—it will not always be this way; better times are ahead. Your eyes cannot see the wonderful future: borrow the telescope of faith; wipe the misty breath of your doubts from the viewfinder; look through it and behold the coming glory." My prayer is that everyone enters the New Year bowing down on their knees, for there cannot be a happy New Year without a happy New You.

Life is what it is: Every year that comes is a grind. Every day is a grind, and you've got to grind hard. You've got to pray and to work in order to get what you want. In case of failure, dust yourself off and move forward. Every minute lost is not recoverable. Squander your chances today and you will find yourself useless tomorrow. Spiritually, every new day is an opportunity to serve God. He who refuses to live for God squanders all he is and all he has. Whom God loves, He corrects. I want to be open-minded and an open reproof yielding to conviction. I want to count my blessings one day at a time, trusting in God because unmerited praise is the recipe of disgrace. I want to be a legacy of charity. I want to be a stepping stone for the lives in the present and future time. The only viable New Year's resolution is to get on my knees and pray. "Lord, my confidence is in you. Where I lack, you provide; where I lose, you compensate. Turn my hindrances into guidelines, humiliation into humility, adversities into advantages, and pain into gain. In the name of Jesus, I pray.

The past is history. We will never get the past year back. The good news is that the God of the past year is the God of the New Year. He never fails us; He goes ahead of us in the New Year, as He did in the old year. God is the same today, yesterday and forever. Therefore, for the people of faith who depend on what God can do, there is no past or future except as memory or anticipation in your mind. The Bible says that "For behold, I create new heavens and a new earth, and the former things shall not be remembered or come into mind (Isaiah 65:17). This was prophetic of the future time beginning with now. Regeneration is the effect of the creating power, of the mighty, powerful, and efficacious grace of God converting many souls by the gospel. A new race of people that is void of race, gender and ethnic is in place. We are new creations, and our thinking, behaviors, and desires are new: "Therefore, if anyone is in Christ, the new creation has come. The old has gone, the new is here!" (2 Corinthians 5:17). We are new, and our anticipations are new. "We are ever on the threshold of new journeys."

Looking behind at my life's voyage, 2017 has been a rough year but thank God we have prevailed. As we are anxiously commencing on the New Year's voyage, the real challenge is not acquiring new territories but securing the ground we are standing on. Every year has its positives and negatives. A new year means closing the past and beginning afresh. We are told to forget the past. Whereas shutting off the skeletons of the past year in the closet is rejuvenating, it is not easy practically because the mind has a reputation of recharging and bringing up the past regardless. But we can deny the past to influence our future by refocusing. I mean acquiring the new lens so that you can see things from the perspective of the Creator. Whenever we open our eyes, Satan focuses us on the kingdom of this world but God wants us to focus on the kingdom of heaven of which Satan has no influence. When you change your focus you change your thoughts and hence your priorities. Ego is nothing other than the focus of conscious attention. "The temptations of the devil assail those principally who are sanctified, for he desires, above all, to overcome the holy." Change your focus from the journey of life to the destiny of the living. Have a blissful 2018.

Commitment depends on how efficiently you manage your time. The discipline of the renewed minds helps you to avoid unconscious commitment to things which don't matter. God wrote His moral decrees in our conscience (Hebrew 10:16), where they cannot be escaped, destroyed and changed; they are true to all people of all generations. Naturally, we are different and we do things differently but we have the same standard of morality. When the heart is transformed, the conscience is cleaned and it becomes God's inward voice to guide us. Jesus said that the Spirit of truth will guide us into all truth. The conscience must be programmed in the Word (truth) In order to guide us into all truth. Jesus said "I do what the Father does" (John 5:19). The Son, being in the Father's bosom was privy to the whole plan of His works. The Son does everything in conjunction with the Father; with the same power, having the same will, being of the same nature. Jesus is the only person with the unchanging resume. Our commitment to Him moves us into action to follow His guidance. In order to do all things which God commands us, we must be fully committed to the person of Christ to sanctify us by His Spirit through the Word.

In the real world, success means public approval. Nothing is considered to be mind-blowing and amazing unless it resonates with the audiences. People would do anything to win the approval of others. Without absolute truth life is meaningless. It means just keep doing things hoping that it resonates with people. And if it doesn't, you keep on switching plans until you find the one that does. In such a situation, rational judgment is more likely to be based on instinct rather than overpowering logic. Anything that does not resonate with the public's views is utterly rejected. Also, it means no uniformity of the truth. I want to emphasize that all truth is God's truth. All truth has its base in God. God alone has the integrity to dictate to all people what is true. Because He is all righteous nothing inconsistent will come from Him. He can be completely trusted. Therefore, truth is that which conforms to reality as it is perceived by God. Any truth must, therefore, be traced back in God.

"A new year is like a blank book, the pen is in your hands. It is your chance to write a beautiful story for yourself. May you hold the smile, let the tears go, keep the laugh, lose the pain, look for joy and abandon the fear. Wishing you find happiness, health and success all year long. Happy New Year!" ~ Precious Aniede Partrick

"Great thanks to everyone who accompanied me throughout my 2017 journey sharing the good and bad moments, inspirations and disappointments and above all prayers. May the Almighty Lord reward you abundantly and grant you happiness and prosperity as we journey through 2018" ~ Patrick Kibombojja

Life, by its nature, includes movement and growth, and our inspirations come to help us move and grow. Most people have great ideas, but only a

few people turn their inspirations into reality. Many people also have life dreams and goals that remain tucked away in the backs of their minds. Spiritual people are especially prone to inaction. Some have excuses of still waiting for the divine sanctioning to swing into action, which is good, but God does not approve redundancy. The Bible says that "Idle hands are the devil's workshop; idle lips are his mouthpiece" (Proverbs 16:27). Some even wrongly think that God wants them to be full time in ministry without a job to generate income. They think that the spiritual world is superior and that the physical world should be ignored or avoided. The next time inspiration strikes, act on that inspiration immediately. Not acting on your inspiration is a kind of abortion or death to the ideas that God implanted in you to activate. Don't wait later, until it is late.

Life is like a book. Every day is a new page; every month is a new chapter; every year is a new series.

Life is like a game. You're only as strong as your next move. "Life's not about how hard of a hit you can give... it's about how many you can take, and still keep moving forward."

"Worry does not empty tomorrow of its sorrows; it empties today of its strength. Don't worry about your failures, worry about the chances you miss when you don't even try".

"If you can't draw strength from what life brings; you can't hold up to what it is yet to bring. The world is a merciless mixture of fortunes and misfortunes. The persistent and brave often beat up the resistance it throws in the path to their destiny." ~ Godfrey E N Nsubuga

Romans 8:28 – "And we know that in all things God works for the good of those who love him, who have been called according to his purpose." 'All things' means everything – good and bad. Every good thing comes from God. God is not the architect of our misery but evil cannot override His hedge of protection around us without God allowing it. This scripture is an assurance to those who are called by God, and who are actively pursuing what God called them to do that nothing will prevent them from reaching their divine intended destiny. God is the efficient cause that makes all things work together for His people's good. Therefore, don't waste your life into endless worries. Worries end when faith begins. Turn your worries into worship. "Those who leave everything in God's hands will eventually see God's hand in everything."

Matthew 6:33 – "But seek ye first the kingdom of God, and his righteousness; and all these things shall be added unto you." Heaven and God's righteousness are to be sought for in the first place, as the perfection of the saints' happiness. And all these things shall be added unto you: of the free bounty, goodness, and liberality of God, without your thought and care, and much less merit. If you chase Jesus as much as you chase the earthly things which you think you want, you will wind up with more than you will ever need.

"Until you love your job and you work hard to earn a living, to turn things around instead of complaining and griping, you will remain asleep and nonproductive."

"Money is a resource that everyone is after, but the secret which everyone isn't aware of, is that money don't just come. It is attracted by the environment one would have to create. Instead of pursuing money, pursue an idea. Why? Because money pursues ideas. Take a deep look at how money circulates from one person to another. If you do not have an idea you won't have money. Money doesn't stay in one pocket, on one person. Why? Because no one owns money, no one has the power over money. The only thing that has power over money is an idea. An idea is the power of humanity over money. When you have an idea you attract money but it does not mean to say you are going to have it forever. Keep improving, upgrading your idea because money is attracted to the best idea. That is why people believe that money comes and goes. When money leaves your pocket it goes to someone with a better idea than yours." (Posted by Kasoma Joshua)

Ideas are easy. Implementation is hard. "Being an entrepreneur is a mindset. You have to see things as opportunities all the time." ~ Soledad O'Brien

Every accomplishment starts with the decision to try. A little progress each day adds up to big results. Try when trusting God to fight for you. When God opens the door no man can shut it; when He shuts the door you cannot open it.

It pays to choose God's will even when there seems to be hostilities. God will take you through the fire and make you fire proof.

You can't become a new person if you keep to your old routine. Be innovative; push harder than yesterday if you want a different tomorrow.

Never allow the trials of life to deter your progress. Without the dark, we could never see the stars.

When the past calls, let it go to the voice mail. It has nothing new to say.

Memories play on the keyboard of the past. Revelation looks into the future.

"Anxiety does not empty tomorrow of its sorrows, but only empties today of its strength" ~ Charles H Spurgeon

"All the flowers of tomorrow are in the seeds of today".

"To walk a thousand miles, you have to decide to take the first step".

Don't ever give up. Our best stories will come from our struggles. The seed of our success is in our failures. Our praises will sprout from our pains. Bend if you will, cry if you must, but keep standing! We have never seen a storm that lasted forever. Seasons change, so does our life! (Love Lanie)

Winners never quit and Quitters never win! "You never really know the strength of the anchor until you're in the middle of a storm whether it

be in the natural or the spiritual. Regardless of the boisterous winds and heavy downpours that seem to be destroying and washing away all your hopes and dreams... hold on! Don't give in and don't give up!"

Failure is a detour, not a dead-end street. Never let a stumble in the road be the end of the journey. Remember that fortune always favors the brave who never quit, and never helps a man who does not endure and persevere.

Adversity is a better teacher than prosperity. For every one person that learns from prosperity, there are ten who learn from adversity.

When you focus on the problems, you will have more problems. When you focus on possibilities, you will have more opportunities.

When one door closes, another opens; but we often look so long and so regretfully upon the closed door that we do not see the one which has opened for us - Alexander Graham Bell

There are principles which you may violate at your peril; you violate them, you suffer the consequences. You will be most effective if you're taking care of your emotional, spiritual and physical wellbeing.

The Principle says: There is one who disperses yet is enhanced more, and another who keeps back more than what is upright yet ends only with lack.

"If we find ourselves with a desire that nothing in this world can satisfy, the most probable explanation is that we were made for another world." ~ C. S. Lewis

You should have a working capital set aside to be able to finance your business, pay your rent, staff and any other immediate costs. It takes time to break even. Whatever you start let it be a stepping stone to achieve more dreams in life. Aim high, and be encouraged. Not even Hell or high water can quell the stalwart Spirit.

"Entrepreneurship is living a few years of your life like most people won't live so that you can spend the rest of your life like most people can't."

Successful people are specialists. Arthur Miller said that, "You specialize in something until one day you find it is specializing in you." Specialization is the unrestricted access to knowledge, involving proper planning. "The kinds of nets we know how to weave determine the kinds of nets we cast. These nets, in turn, determine the kinds of fish we catch." — Elliot Eisner, Cognition and Curriculum

Opportunities don't happen, you create them. "If you fail to plan, you are planning to fail." ~ Papanie Turay

When God is your master, money becomes your servant. "Crave for a thing, you will go for it. Renounce the craving, the object will follow you by itself".

Do something and ask God to bless it. If you have nothing, God will not turn your nothingness into something.

Before the world was created, God had a plan in place for your life. God already did it when He nailed your problems at the cross. Failure to embrace the divine plan for you means that you are the determiner and terminator of the dreams and the plans which God has for your life.

There is no elevator to success. You have to take the stairs.

Successful people are unstoppable. Not because they didn't have failures but because they continued on despite of them. Success is legally a matter of holding on when others have let go.

"Nothing has more strength than dire necessity." Someone who is desperate will stop at nothing to succeed. Such a person has nothing to lose and everything to gain, so he or she has unmatched strength."

Successful people don't reach their goals alone.

Hard work pays, but it doesn't guarantee success.

The most important thing after setting a goal is taking action.

Success is a goal that will change you but not transform you!

Success begins by prioritizing lasting things over temporally things. "We all grow older and our eyes grow dim but the things we see with our heart will remain forever a thing of beauty."

The ingredients determine the goodness of the cake. Don't incubate with the failures because you will end up with defective results.

Hosea 4:6 - "My people are destroyed from lack of knowledge." Because you have rejected knowledge, I also reject you as my priests; because you have ignored the law of your God, I also will ignore your children." Knowledge is accessible to all because you can't reject something that is not available. Knowledge is essential because God will not help you with something you don't know. The last part of the scripture says that "I also will ignore your children." The reason is that we are supposed to pass on (impart) what we have including knowledge to our children. If you reject knowledge, your children are most likely to follow you in rebellion, and hence ignored by God.

"We must be discerning of those who enter our lives. We must not haphazardly make alignments, covenants, and even friendships. Who do you share your heart with?" ~ Tina K Baker

If it is important to you, you will find a way. If not, you will find an excuse. Procrastination is avoiding or failing to do what's needed in a given time. The best preparation for tomorrow is doing your best today. Sometimes we miss a move of God because we are afraid to move.

Life is primarily sensation; it is a compelling notion that we simply exist! I intend to live life to the maximum, not just to exist briefly as the life of the autumn grass.

Ideas pull the trigger, but instinct loads the gun. Sometimes the heart need more time to accept what the minds already know.

When God sends us to go somewhere, He goes ahead of us before we get there. God sends us in a straight line. But we go in zigzag because of the detours positioned in our way to our intended destiny.

Genesis 50:20 - "You thought evil against me; but God meant it unto good". I am talking prophetically to somebody who has been hurt by the evils actions of others. Don't be down cast. Take your focus from that aggressor and the circumstances surrounding you. The most devastating effect of evil is when you allow it to dash your hopes. God will not let evil diminish His glory in you. He is going to use the evil acts of others to make you a greater person than before. Faith brings hope. Hope is not wishful

thinking; it is trusting in the strength of God to deliver what He promised regardless of the circumstances. Be encouraged and make optimism a way of life to activate your faith. At the end of the day you will prevail.

Life is a mystery. The potential for success depends on your attitude. Consult not your fears but your hopes and your dreams. "The potential God sees in you is not the potential man has for you!"

"Indecision is also decision. Inaction is also action. Omission and commission both have consequences." The choice is yours.

Nothing in the world is more common than dreamers without authentic plans. All dream but the ones who are crazy enough to pursue their dreams can change the world. "If all wishes were horses, even beggars would ride".

Five people you want to surround yourself with: The inspired, the passionate, the motivated, the grateful and the open minded. Avoid the negativity. A negative mind will never give you a positive life. Miracles start to happen when you give as much energy to your dreams as you do to your fears.

"Close your minds and imagine the best version of you possible. That is who you really are; let go any part of you that doesn't believe it".

Risk and failure are parts of our equation, and if you are seeing too little failure, you are actually probably not taking enough risks ~ Peter Barris

"The seeming safest path can be dangerous if it's outside of God's Will for you-The seeming dangerous path is safe if it's the one He's called you to go" ~ Jane Theiler

Difficult times disrupt your conventional ways of thinking and push you to forge better habits of thought, performance and being ~ Robin S. Sharma

Whenever you kill time, you will bury opportunities. Meaning: It was Henry David Thoreau who said in his book, Walden that you cannot "kill time without injuring eternity. I can't disagree with him. "To kill time" is an idiomatic expression. It means to waste or while away time. It means to use time aimlessly while waiting. But suffice it to say that, every time wasted is opportunity misused. This is because you could use that time to do something important. In fact, time is treasure. Time is opportunity. And it's our most precious opportunity. When you lose money or any material possession, you can have it back. When you lose some time, you can never have it back. What many of us do not realize is that, time is our life. In other words our life is a period of time. And so to waste time is to waste our life. What we call investment is nothing but making the best use of our time. As the saying goes, 'the best preparation for tomorrow is doing your best today'. If you do only what you like to do, you're wasting time. If you do what you need to do, you're maximizing time. Be provident! (Sam Kyeyune)

Proverbs 23:4 - "Labor not to be rich". The meaning is that your priority in this life should not be to be rich. Neither does the Bible condemns being wealthy nor does it say that poverty is a curse. Faith is not synonymous with wealth. You may be rich but condemned or rich but redeemed. Likewise, you may be poor but redeemed or poor but condemned. "Frugality is founded on the principal that all riches have limits." Ordinary riches could be stolen or lost upon death. Certainly, money cannot bribe your way to heaven. Contentment is the greatest wealth. A transformed heart is neither influenced by the riches nor by poverty. Rich or poor, a person with a transformed heart has the noblest deeds aimed at fostering the kingdom of God. The only way to possess the riches of this world permanently is to make heaven your treasure. Surrendering to Christ is giving yourself and everything you have (family/wealth) wholly to serving God.

"Credit reproduces all the fundamental antagonisms of the capitalist world. It accentuates them. It precipitates their development and thus pushes the capitalist world forward to its own destruction" - Rosa Luxemburg

There is one common thing between faith and money. In heaven, we won't need faith because we shall see God face to face. Also, in heaven, we shall not need money. But faith is not synonymous with wealth. Unlike the riches of this world, faith is given to all without limits. "Frugality is founded on the principle that all riches have limits." Ordinary riches can be stolen or lost upon death. The money will not bribe your way to heaven. Contentment is the greatest wealth. A transformed heart is neither influenced by riches nor by poverty. Rich or poor, a person with a transformed heart has the noblest deeds aimed at fostering the kingdom of God. The only way to possess the riches of this world permanently is to make heaven your treasure. Surrendering to Christ is giving yourself and everything you have wholly to serve God.

Poverty regardless of its demerits has some divine merits. I have realized that being poor or slightly poor is a form of having a higher probability to notching longevity. Most of the world's oldest people that get recorded in even the Guinness world book of records (more so those who've passed by octagenarianism and nonagenarianism) and lived for 100 + years are ordinary people from the general hoi polloi not those in affluence and wealth. One can veracious argue that the reason most poor people live longer is the simple diet they feed on that guarantees longevity of humans than the affluent who feed on junk foods full of oil substances that are good at slackening longevity. The former (because poverty) feed on vegetables that lead to their longevity, unknowingly indulge in physical duties like walking, digging and other menial duties that all buttress longevity which is the opposite to money-wielding folks whose money do most of the work they would have done that unconsciously does much to add on one's years in life. (Posted by Ssenyonjo Brain Ushers)

Living a simple life is difficult but not impossible. I have watched people who are diagnosed with the terminal sickness and sent home to die. They downsize their living to a simple life. If they have a big house, they sell it and move into a single bedroom house. If they have many vehicles they are likely to sell them and keep one. If they can do it, everyone can do it.

Leadership

Good employees are irreplaceable. If you are an employer who wants your best employees to stay, you need to think carefully about how you treat them. You need to make them want to work for you. Many times employers make promises to their employees about salary increment, job promotion or even motivational tokens. This usually places you on the fine line that lies between making them very happy and watching them walk out the door.

No matter who you are relationships are critical to your existence as human beings. God created you to have relationships with others, and Him. He wants to be connected to you through His Son Jesus Christ. A relationship with your creator makes Him the overseer of your life and what you do. It implies that your potential is endless. He guides you to do what you were created to do. "We are but workers in His field. He has us working on different parts of His garden doing different activities for Him such as tilling soil, scattering seed, watering the plants, being the shining sun, pulling weeds and removing rocks and other obstacles for growth. He is the master gardener and He knows which plant needs what type of attention and when. All we have to do as good workers is to listen and obey."

Empathy is seeing with the eyes of another, listening with the ears of another, feeling with the heart of another. Whenever you are self-centered you can't experience the presence of God. The reason is that God is other-centered. "Love your neighbor as yourself" – it isn't a contradiction of other-centered love. We love others with a self-love that's defined by God's unconditional love for us. We see ourselves the way God sees us, receiving His affection for us, then reflecting that same love toward others.

Leaders are born leaders, and they prove that they are leaders. They are always inspiring in everything they do. They are pioneers wherever they are. "If your actions inspire others to dream more, learn more, do more and become more, you are a leader."

Promotion doesn't happen to you. It happens because of you. Where you are now is a fortune of your thinking capacity; if you improve on it, you will grow more. "Your confidence goes up when your skills go up."

Promotion is primarily not about increased salary but increased responsibilities. Salary only pays the bills; it doesn't build your career.

Never step on someone's toe in order for you to go to the top. "When you're on your way to the top, resist this monster called greed. Greed will make you impatient or make you steal and seek for shortcuts as you angle yourself to the top, Resist this at all costs irrespective."

"While at the top, beware of this monster called pride. Pride will make you look down upon people who haven't attained your level of success. This monster normally afflicts the bosses. Resist this monster."

Leadership is making quality choices. The choices we make daily make us what we are. Sometimes the way up is in making tough choices. At the end of the day, some of our greatest challenges become our biggest strengths.

It is an act of bravery to feel your feelings but never make important decisions based on your feelings.

The major qualification of a leader is not their education but their ability to work with people. An effective leader must study the people he leads and handle them on individual bases.

Solving problems in time is the mark of quality leadership. Whenever a problem is not solved it is postponed.

Any time you choose to influence the behaviors of someone, you are a leader. "A candle loses nothing by lighting another candle".

"In order to be a successful leader, you must have great EQ (Emotional Quotient), because EQ knows how to work with people. No matter how smart you are, if you never know how to work with people, you will never succeed, it is just a day dream" ~ Jack Ma

"Employees don't need to be best friends, but there does need to be a level of mutual respect and understanding." ~ Kathryn Minshew

The quality of a good job is not determined by just a high pay but a good working environment. Although the poor wages will not make the worker happy, some people say that a comfortable working environment is more important than a good salary because a long time career can be built in a healthy environment and high salary can be achieved with seniority and work performance. A good leader creates a comfortable working environment in order to stimulate productivity. When your employees are comfortable at work they will be able to think properly which will eventually increase the productivity of the company.

An effective leader motivates the people he leads. As one coach said, "The greatest manager has a knack for making ballplayers think they are better than they think they are". Motivating and engaging employees

isn't something that can be done once and then forgotten; it is an all time thing. "If you're not winning over 'hearts and minds', all you're creating is potential losses."

"If you want to achieve your highest aspirations and overcome your greatest challenges, identify and apply the principle that governs the results you seek."

When the going gets tough, leaders get tough. Often, good result is obtained in a hard way. Serving God the hard way makes things easy; serving God the easy way makes things hard.

Efficiency is the trade mark of the effective leaders. Doing the minimum is not enough. Always opt for the maximum.

Leaders talk less and work more. They are resourceful thinkers who are always busy inside expanding their capacity to deliver. They discuss ideas to create idealness.

"You don't have to say something all the time. Sometimes you just need to listen to what others have to say. You don't have to agree but at least understand someone's perspective".

"A sense of humor is part of the art of leadership, of getting along with people, of getting things done." ~ Dwight D. Eisenhower

The way you think determines the way you live. "Life is better when you are happy, but life is at its best when others are happy because of you: Be faithful in touching other's hearts. Be an inspiration. Nothing in nature lives for itself: Rivers do not drink their own water. Trees do not eat their own fruits. The Sun does not shine for itself and Flowers do not spread their fragrance for themselves. Living for others is a rule of nature. We were all born to help each other. No matter how difficult the situation you find yourself in, still do good to others." ~ Alex Mavura

Good communication is the key to an effective management. One of the most powerful means of communicating non-verbally is through piercing, incisive eye contact; it is the ability to stare at others and make them feel as though you're staring directly into their soul. Also, a cheerful smile, the pat on the back, the arm around the shoulder, the praise for what was done right and the sympathetic nod for what wasn't are part of communication. "Do not wait for appraisals or reviews to give praise and appreciation. Do it on a regular basis. Recognize accomplishments and work well done, and show your appreciation."

An effective leader shows no partiality when dealing with employees. If you decide to hug do it to all otherwise don't do it at all. When fairness disappears from the work place, impartiality replaces partiality.

"Thoughtfulness and kindness and love are never sold. They are the priceless things in life for which no one can pay, and the giver finds rich recompense in giving them away." ~ Helen Rice.

It is good to dress well, talk well, carry yourself well in the office but the main thing is to get jobs done well. A job that is well done is like a benchmark. It will help you do a better job the next time. A job well done is the epitaph of mediocrity and the prologue of excellence. Well done.

Doing a good job is not always about impressive innovation. Sometimes it is only about doing something with plain dedication. Doing a job well is like wearing an impeccable suit – the best way to make a great impression. Well done.

"Every job is a self-portrait of the person who did it. Autograph your work with excellence."

"I had a clear vision: if I take up an assignment, I'll do full justice to it; otherwise I'll walk away" ~ Kiran Bedi

Naturally you can't control what you can't measure. Delegate to others who have strengths where you don't.

For every action, there is a reaction. Achievers are not afraid of challenges; rather they relish them and use them profitably.

Sometimes good people make bad choices it doesn't mean that they are bad. It means they're human. "We don't have to make the right choices all

the times but we can always recover from the wrong ones." God believes in the new beginnings.

"Leadership and learning are indispensable to each other" ~ John F. Kennedy

"Without initiative, leaders are simply workers in leadership positions. Initiative is doing the right thing at the right time without being told.

A leader is to enable others to embrace a vision, initiative or assignment in a way that they feel a sense of purpose, ownership, personal engagement, and common cause. "A leader is the one who knows the way, goes the way and shows the way" ~ John Maxwell

A leader must be confident, persuasive but ready to walk alone if it comes down to it!

"I actually think that the most efficacious way of making a difference is to lead by example, and doing random acts of kindness is setting a very good example of how to behave in the world" ~ Misha Collins

Promotion means more responsibility. Leaders are those who take the initiative at work, they do so not out of obligation but because they understand the concept of responsibility.

Success leaves clues. Stay positive, stay fighting, stay brave, stay ambitious, stay strong, and stay focused. They asked Bill Gates and Warren Buffett this question, what they saw as the single most important factor in the journey of life. They both gave the same one-word answer: "FOCUS."

A leader has multiple personalities: He or she is a loyalist, achiever, enthusiastic, investigator, helper and peacemaker. "The Universal Principle says: What is sown shall be reaped. He who waters, he himself shall be watered also."

The chart puts a leader above the people he leads. Humility and humbleness turns the triangle upside down making a leader a servant of the people whom he leads. The greatest trade mark of a great leader is lack of arrogance.

A leader gets involved by participating in doing the work instead of directing from the bench. "Once you learn to pick your own water, you will know the value of every drop."

Prestige depends not in how many people serve you but in how many people you serve.

"I think whether you're having setbacks or not, the role of a leader is to always display a winning attitude" ~ Colin Powell

"The manager accepts the status quo; the leader challenges it" ~ Warren Bennis

"Team work makes a dream work". A leader who can maintain a teamwork spirit flowing becomes virtually indispensable.

"Be the color to someone's grey". When you shine your light on others your own life is made brighter too!

Matthew 26:40 – "Then he returned to his disciples and found them sleeping." Couldn't you men keep watch with me for one hour?" he asked Peter." The disciples had had a very trying day; Peter and John had undergone much bodily fatigue in preparing the last Supper; they were all weary, full of grief, and weighed down by foreboding; it was no wonder that they succumbed to these influences, though we expected them to have done better. Jesus could have said to His disciples who were sleeping at duty that you are fired, and He could have trained others in their place who were more committed. But He did not. Jesus taught us that to lead is to love. We are commissioned to lead others to Christ with the Christ like character.

"The Master was once a servant. People don't want to serve but they want to become leaders. Yet every person is under somebody. Even when you are a leader, you are under someone's authority. We ought to serve those who are over us, not to rule with them. Learn from them in anticipation to do what they are doing. Otherwise, if you want to roar like a lion you'll have to learn from the lions."

There are two times when people criticize you: When you succeed and when you fail. There are two times when people will flatter you: When they want to impress you and when they want something from you. There are two times when people will stop following you: When you refuse to cater to them and when they don't like the direction you are headed. There are two times when people abandon you: When you hurt them and when you need them.

Great leaders state out loud what they intend to do and in doing so, they get things done ~ Simon Sinek

A good leader applies three steps in order to implement his orders: He asks them to do things; he tells them to do things; he enforces his order for things to be done.

Leaders don't tell people what they are doing wrong only but tell people what they're doing right in acknowledgment. In course of correcting errors, affirm what is right.

"You are likely to lose the heat of your passion irrespective of how hot it was when you surrender yourself to a leader with a lukewarm attitude." ~ Israel Ayivor

The Bible says that only a fool loses his temper. If you can't control your temper, you have lost the right to lead people.

"Arrogance, ignorance, and incompetence. Not a pretty cocktail of personality traits in the best of situations. No sir. Not a pretty cocktail in an office-mate and not a pretty cocktail in a head of state. In fact, in a leader, it's a lethal cocktail" ~ Graydon Carter

The leading rule for the leader, as for the man of every calling, is diligence. "He who labors diligently need never despair; for all things are accomplished by diligence and labor."

A leader of integrity isn't wantonly free to have sexual relations with his or her employees. Doctors should not have sex with their patients, teachers should not have sex with their students; the list is endless. "A person who would attempt to use a superior position to obtain sexual favors from a subordinate could be described as a sexual manipulator." The leaders who use their positions to get sex will do whatever it takes to have things their way even when it means compromising the values of the company. "Abuses of a position are possible from either party in unequal relationships: Sometimes the subordinate person may attempt to balance the disparity by initiating a sexual component into the relationship."

"Dignity does not consist in possessing honors, but in deserving them" ~ Aristotle

FEBRUARY FOR ROMANCE

Valentine's Day is knocking at the door. Valentine's Day, also dubbed the Saint Valentine's Day or the feast of Saint Valentine, is celebrated annually on February 14. The celebrations started around the 14 Century as a Western Christian feast day honoring one or more early saints named Valentinus and it has become a globally a recognized ceremony with cultural, religious, and commercial celebration of romance. It is characterized by offering gifts to the loved ones and often people wear red that means already in love for two people. However, several other colors are worn, each with a given meaning or a message. For instance, green means I am waiting, blue means Love applicants invited, Black mean proposal rejected, White meaning sorry, I am already reserved and orange, one is going to propose. Others include pink which means proposal accepted, yellow for those who have broken-up, brown for broken hearts and purple or grey for those who are not interested in relationships. It is a healthy tradition that infiltrated our Christian values, but like any other traditions, it came to us not without thorns attached to it. The day is celebrated worldwide with massive sexual encounters. Among other activities associated with the day is the popular passing out of rose flowers to lovers accompanied with chocolates symbolic of the sweetness and lusciousness of love. Then romantic meals after which the night explodes into the fireworks of sexual encounters. There is nothing wrong with sex if it is not casual sex. Any sexual relationship is validated by the legitimate marital status in place. Girlfriend or boyfriend is not a legitimate marital status.

On February 14, 2018, Christians across the globe are eager to celebrate Ash Wednesday, and on the same day, people will commemorate, along with their loved ones, Valentine's Day. However, this has not happened since the Second World War in 1945, with several scholars anticipating a repetition of the same in the years 2024 and 2029. The collision has drawn several questions for many believers, especially among Catholics, on whether to start with Lent period with fasting or to feast with their loved ones on Valentine's Day. Ash Wednesday is commemorated on a Wednesday, seven weeks to Easter Sunday and that means its mandatory day of fasting for Christians. The day is characterized by one full meal and two small ones with a total ban on consumption of meat during the Lent Period. The Lent period is done to emulate Jesus Christ, who spent 40 days in the wilderness while fasting, endured all temptations by Satan, who are manifested in the Books of Matthew, Mark, and Luke of the New Testament teaching. Ash Wednesday is observed by many Western Christians, including Anglicans, Lutherans, Methodists, Presbyterians, Roman Catholics and some Baptists. It derives its name from the practice of blessing ashes made from palm branches blessed on the previous year's Palm Sunday and placing them on the heads of participants to the accompaniment of the words "Repent, and believe in the Gospel" or "Remember that you are dust, and to dust you shall return." Unlike Catholics, non-Catholics will flock several hangouts with their loved ones to celebrate the Valentine's Day. I predict that in the USA, it will appear to be more Valentine Day than Ash Wednesday, this being a secular culture.

The manner Valentine Day is celebrated in our culture blurs the line between the saved and the unsaved worlds. There are causal relationships within and outside the Christian circles or social settings. We have a situation whereby girlfriends, like concubines during biblical times, demand conjugal rights. Celebrating casual sex as a ritual is not new; the day of lovers predates the Christian era. For example, during the biblical times, Erotes was the god of sexual longing, yearning, and desire. The pagan world had sexual fantasies on the altars of their temples and love-feasts offerings to their deities. Sexual intimacy was a means by which the deities mysteriously interacted with humans. Regardless of how you pack it and label it, sex outside marriage is a sin defiling to your body.

Valentine's Day is here. This year, Americans are expected to spend $19.7 billion on Valentine's Day, according to the National Retail Federation. The facts show that there are lots of people out there who do not want to be alone on Valentine's Day. Many people are looking forward to having their first date on Valentine's Day. Today, people go on date to get married. During biblical times, in a situation where there were arranged marriages, your wedding day happened to be your first date. I am not suggesting that we should follow the biblical time's traditions when arranging our marriages. I suggest that a person should go on date only with a person in whom they see qualities of a future spouse. The intention of dating should be limited within the context of marriage. As for those of you who are already married, you should know that sincere dating begins after the wedding. Never cease to date each other. As for those who are single, walk with your shoulders up; after all, Jesus was single too! Happy Valentine's Day to you all.

Love is not selfish and self-centered. Love can be sacrificial. There is power in redemptive love; power to change and transform the world. Sacrificial redemptive love: This way of love is the way of life. Jesus gave up His life not to get anything out of it but for the sake of others ~ Most Rev. Michael Curry

Psalms 63:3 – "Because your love is better than life, my lips will glorify you." For life without the love of God is nothing BUT death: a man that has no share in the love of God is dead while he lives. "For better is thy kindness, which thou wilt do for the righteous in the world to come, than the life which thou givest the wicked in this world"; my lips shall praise

thee; that is, for thy lovingkindness, and because it is better than life, and any enjoyment of it.

"There is no prison so secure that love cannot free you; No captor so strong that love cannot liberate you; No sin so terrible that love cannot restore you. Love is your secret weapon that the enemy has no answer for. Today, roll love out onto the battlefield, and watch him fall. Love cannot be defeated!"

Love is persistent compared to the ocean that kisses the shore, no matter how many times it is pushed away.

To all ladies - Don't be a woman that needs a man, be a woman a man needs. Happy Valentine's Day!

"If two people can't seem to stay away from each other maybe they aren't supposed to!"

"In the arithmetic of love, one plus one equals everything, and two minus one equals nothing".

"It is Valentine Day. Be mindful who you choose to sleep with. Condoms will not protect you from spiritually transmitted demons!" ~ Enock Ssenyonjo

A woman's heart is like a garden of roses that requires to be watered consistently.

Women are made to be loved not to be understood ~ Oscar Wilde

A man that speaks to your flesh is not the one for you! Wait for the one who can speak to your soul. Anyone can entice your flesh, but not anyone can speak to your soul!

Men must respect women, not as a prize to be won & displayed, but as a treasure & gift from God above, to be loved, cherished & adored, to be protected & respected always, without excuses, without exceptions.

Sex is not all about making children. You must be a different woman to your husband every time. Seduce your husband, don't always allow your husband to ask for Sex, there must be no timetable for sex. Be creative, don't be predictable. Give him what he wants. If you lose influence over your husband, you have lost womanhood. As for men, do not take a woman who does all these for granted! Pamper her, pray for her, cherish her, love her, support her financially, and make her feel like your woman! God bless you and your marriages. (Posted by Chacha Eka)

"The nicest place to be is in someone's thoughts."

In one lifetime, you will love many times but there is that one love that will burn your soul forever!

"When love is not madness, it is not love" ~ Rachel Vicent

"You are the messenger of love. Your personality charms everyone. You stay authentic and true to yourself".

"When you realize that God is all you have, you then realize that He is all you need."

"To have found God and still to pursue Him is the soul's paradox of love." ~ A.W. Tozer

"The Church is the exclusive portion of her Lord; none else may claim a partnership or pretend to share her love. Christ is dear to you in bonds of marriage union, and you are dear to Him; behold, He grasps both of your hands with both of His own, saying, "My bride." Consider how the Lord gets such a double hold of you that He neither can nor will ever let you go. Be not, O beloved, slow to return the hallowed flame of His love.

Jesus, Your church delights to have it so! Lord, I am your bride. Over and over again, just like rain from above, you shower your love over me!"

Romantic love and intimacy in a God-honoring marriage is an important goal for all couples. God presents love as something to be desired: "Many waters cannot quench love; / rivers cannot sweep it away. / If one were to give all the wealth of one's house for love, / it would be utterly scorned" (Song of Solomon 8:7). True love endures. It overcomes adversity. Nothing is worth giving up on godly love. Love is priceless. According the Bible, God has chosen us in Him before the foundation of the world, that we should be holy and without blame before Him in love (Ephesians 1:4). The greatest revelation is to know that God has been with us from eternity, before the foundation of the world. That is what makes this life heavenly. The greatest thing on the earth is to have God on your side because the wisdom and power of God are unbeatable. The world can't cope with us because we have the Spirit of the power and wisdom of God. We are supposed to walk in His power because we are no longer in the bondage of the old life. God calls us into His presence as the groom calls his bride alone to the secret place to spend time with him and to know him. The more we know Him the more we become like Him. The Church is the exclusive portion of her Lord because of the covenant which was made with Christ from everlasting on account of the chosen ones. Our Groom is jealous of our love, He admits of no rival or competitor in worship; he will not give his glory to another god. And we are jealous of His love; no one else other than the bride may claim a partnership or pretend to share the love of our Groom. We are sent to evangelize because part of the Church is still lost in the world delaying the return of our Bridegroom.

Somebody posted the following message: "I am a Jehovah Witness. I don't believe in pagan holidays. I have deleted every person who sent me a Valentine's Day posting." I respect your position but your decision to delete is fanatical. There are many things which we can't change because they have no spiritual effect on our spirituality. For example we read in the Encyclopedia Judaica that "The celebration of birthdays is unknown in traditional Jewish ritual" (vol.4, p.1054). It points out that the only reference to a birthday in the Bible is that of Pharaoh of Egypt. Are you aware that all of the days and the months on our calendar were named after the Roman heathen gods? Paul said regarding eating foods sacrificed to idols that if you abstain from eating the food believing it is defiling to God, you do it out of faith. Also, if you eat believing that an idol is nothing at all; it is nothing in itself but a piece of wood or metal, and it really represents nothing, that there is only one legitimate God, and there is but one Lord, Jesus Christ, through whom all things came and through whom we live, you do it by faith. (1 Corinthians 8:4-12).

February for Spiritual Growth

John 3:3 – "Jesus answered and said unto him, Verily, verily, I say unto thee, Except a man be born again, he cannot see the kingdom of God." "Verily, verily, I say unto you" is a strong asseveration, a way of speaking often used by Jesus, when He solemnly affirms anything, and would assure of the truth of it, as here. This blunt and curt reply was plainly meant to shake the whole edifice of Nicodemus' religion of self-justification, in order to lay a deeper and more enduring foundation on Christ. To be born again is to be born "afresh," "anew", "from above". No one can see (has spiritual sight capabilities to see) the kingdom of God unless he is born again, or regenerated, and quickened by the Spirit of God; renewed in the spirit of his mind; has Christ formed in his heart; becomes a partaker of the divine nature; and in all respects a new creature (Spirit gives birth to Spirit). He must be "born again"; in distinction from, and opposition to his first birth by nature; in which he was vile, polluted, carnal, and corrupt, being conceived in sin, and sharpen in iniquity, and was a transgressor from the womb, and by nature a child of wrath; and in opposition to God. To "see" the kingdom is to experience it now and to enter it. The condition of the spiritual vision which can see this kingdom is spiritual life, and this life is dependent on being born anew. Regeneration awakens the inner man (spirit) and restores the spiritual sight to see the kingdom of God. Regeneration links the inner man to God. It means that the soul and the body have a new master: The spirit is supposed to dominate the soul/body perpetually. The mind is supposed to be renewed by the Word daily in order to serve the spirit effectively.

John 16:15-17 - "Everything that belongs to the Father is Mine. That is why I said that the Spirit will take from what is Mine and disclose it to you. In a little while you will see me no more, and then after a little while you will see me 'because I am going to the Father'." Jesus is not backtracking on His promise which He made that He will never leave us (Matthew 28:20). The saying "And again a little while, and ye shall see me" means that He will be quickly taken from them by death. But the sorrow of the death will be replaced by the joy of His resurrection. 'Because I am going to the Father' (verse 17), meaning the sorrow of His departure will be replaced by the joy of the coming of the Holy Spirit that will be with us forever; not even death or grave will separate us from Him. Jesus is in heaven, seated at the right hand of the Father but His presence is with us by His Spirit (John 14:16-17). To have the Holy Spirit as our Helper—the Paraclete is to have God Himself present with us, in the here and now. The Holy Spirit is God dwelling in the temple of every person that truthfully and sincerely invests their faith in Jesus Christ. The Bible says that "And I will pray to the Father, and he shall give you another Comforter, that he may abide with you forever" (John 14:16). Another one [allos] is the Helper of the same kind as the Father and the Son; He abides (dwells) in us forever to fulfill the promise of Jesus that He will never leave us (Matthew 28:20). He is the Spirit of holiness and adoption (Romans 1:4). He separates us from the rest of the world and marks us as children of God – We are of the same nature and character with God. He is the Spirit of revelation who reveals Christ and the things of Christ (Ephesians 1:17). He dwells in us to convict us – We are supposed to be of the same will with God. He works alongside us to convict the lost world to repent because a non-repented sinner has no Holy Spirit to convict him.

John 1:16 – "And of his fullness have all we received, and grace for grace." A fallen man deserves no favor from God. Everything God has ever done for a fallen man it is because of His grace. By His grace, God found Adam and Eva in hiding due to the shame of sin and He dressed them. By His grace, God picked Noah to be the preacher of righteousness. By His grace, God picked Abram when he was actively worshipping the multiple gods of his father, including the moon god. The Bible says that God chose Israel of all nations not because of her merits (Deuteronomy 7:7). In the Old Testament, God picked a handful of people to whom He temporarily extended His grace in anticipation of His ultimate future provision through Christ. Those, whom God has loved with an everlasting love, were by nature children of wrath as the rest of the world but were chosen in Christ before the world began. "All we received", the "we all" is co-extensive with "as many as believed." The Bible says "But as many as received him, to them gave he power to become the sons of God, even to them that believe on his name" (John 1:12). To them gave He the power to become the sons of God, as such as they were called, in distinction from the children of men, or of the world. The power to become children of God was part of the divine fullness which they received in receiving Him. He is said to be full of grace and truth; the fullness of the Godhead in trim is incommunicable; and the fullness of His fitness, and ability for His office, as Mediator, was for Himself; but His fullness of grace and truth is dispensatory (distributable), and is in Him, on purpose to be communicated unto others. Faith is the hand which receives Christ and His grace from Him. "We received", means that the scripture is written to the already born again believers, the act of receiving being expressed in the past tense, in regard to their first conversion, when faith is first wrought (activated), and along with it, the abundance of grace is received. In this case, a believer has nothing but what is given to him; but what is given belongs to him forever as long as he is faithful to his commitment. Faithfulness is putting to proper use what is received.

In a monarchy, the subjects obey the king. God's system of governance is that of a monarch. He is the King ruling over the kingdom, comprised of the people of faith, who are mandated to build God's kingdom by sharing their faith. Trusting and obedience to our King are the hinges on which the door of faith moves. Faith is like salt. Salt is made up of two mineral substances (sodium/chloride) which are of great importance to the human and animal health. However, when sodium and chloride are separated they are very poisonous to our bodies. Likewise, the saving faith consists of two substances (trusting/obedience) which cannot work in isolation. No wonder Jesus used the metaphor of salt to describe His followers. Faith is doing for others what God has done for you. Faith is exercised into growth; the more you walk by faith the more faith you get. When a potential Christian makes a "decision" to trust, or put their faith in Christ, they embark on the task of growing in faith and they develop the eagerness to share their faith to make other converts; this is the process and journey traveled by all responsible Christians. It means that faith is a journey, but not a destination (2 Peter 1:5-11 and Acts 2:42-47). Faith is a free gift from God but there is a cost of discipleship. When Jesus invited the people to follow Him, He challenged them to weigh the costs of being His followers (Luke 14:28-30).

Hebrews 10:38 "Now the just shall live by faith: but if any man draw back, my soul shall have no pleasure in him." The term "just" is used in the Scriptures in various senses. It means righteousness or holiness when it is used in reference to God but it means perfect (complete) when it is used in reference to man because our perfectness is in Christ. "Faith" conveys the idea of an objective body of truth, in which one must place confidence and to which he must submit (Acts 6:7; Jude 3). Christ is the object of our faith. We are saved by His faithfulness as opposed to our faith. The word of God says we are saved by grace through faith, NOT by faith through grace. Everyone is given a measure of faith to receive salvation. After which, faith becomes the manner of the just man's living. The last part of the scripture says "but if any man draw back, my soul shall have no pleasure in him." We have the responsibility to walk in the light of the gospel delivered to us or to retreat. The righteousness of God which we received by faith must be lived and manifested from start to finish. Living by the Spirit is synonymous to

living by faith. Faith allows His life to become our living. Therefore, the just are those who invested their faith in Christ and are currently faithful to the Lord's word, and as a result, will "live," or have been delivered from the pending wrath of God.

Hebrews 11:6 – "But without faith it is impossible to please him: for he that cometh to God must believe that he is, and that he is a rewarder of them that diligently seek him." This scripture is about the things we do or our duties towards God. God is pleased by our faith because how we approach God matters. Faith is approaching God within the finished works of Jesus Christ. In the old covenant, the sin and trespass offerings, required the unblemished animals to be offered, representing the sinless Christ, and were laden with the sins of the people. Jesus was laden with our sins, and the law claimed His life to justify us. Everything we do outside Christ is not acceptable to God as a sweat favor offering because God never views sin as pleasurable. Faith is a prerequisite for pleasing God. Jesus proved that He loved us by dying on the cross on our behalf. We prove our love for Him by our faith. Faith is trusting in what He did for us and what He can do through us. The last part says that "he is a rewarder of them that diligently seek him". He justifies by grace through our faith, and He rewards those who faithfully seek Him. Rewarding is about the good works. The faith which is not proven by works is a dead faith (James 2:17-18). Our faith in Christ is evidenced by His manifested life through us. Jesus said He always did those things that please the Father (John 8:29), so we should allow Him to do those things pleasing to the Father through us. We, too, can please God by faith in what Jesus can do in us and through us, and of course by submitting to the Gospel ordinances. Rewarding is the evaluation of our works. It is the judgment of the redeemed, not unto condemnation, but by rewarding accordingly.

1 Peter 1:13-16 - "Therefore, prepare your minds for action, keep sober in spirit, fix your hope completely on the grace to be brought to you at

the revelation of Jesus Christ. As obedient children, do not be conformed to the former lusts which were yours in your ignorance, but like the Holy One who called you, be holy yourselves also in all your behavior; because it is written, "YOU SHALL BE HOLY, FOR I AM HOLY." Our feelings follow our thoughts, and our conducts form our characters. When God doesn't form our behaviors, our behaviors form our gods, and we are miserably held by them to do their will. Therefore be careful how you walk, not as unwise men but as wise understanding what the will of the Lord is (Ephesians 5:15-17). God imputes to us His holiness but demands that we manifest it in our righteousness. In the second part of the scripture, Peter advised us how to excel in godliness: "fix your hope completely on the grace to be brought to you at the revelation of Jesus Christ." Peter calls his readers to holiness in light of the coming of Jesus Christ and the holy character of the God who calls us to salvation. He makes three points: To be holy people, we must be focused on Christ's coming, obedient in all of life, and growing in our knowledge of God's holiness. We have such assurance that when we meet the Lord we will be perfectly sanctified, made completely like Him (1 John 3:2). We are saved by the grace, and the grace teaches us obedience all the way to glorification. It means that the Christian journey begins with the grace, continues in the grace, and is finished in the grace. The grace takes us through a metamorphosis, compared to a butterfly that has gone through a metamorphosis, been released from its dark cocoon, embraced its wings, to soar.

Matthew 22:37-39 "Jesus replied: "'Love the Lord your God with all your heart and with all your soul and with all your mind.' This is the first and greatest commandment. 39 And the second is like it: 'Love your neighbor as yourself." The love for God saturates all the faculties of our very being: The heart > will, the mind > understanding, the soul > affections. It does so in the most sincere, upright, and perfect manner, without any dissimulation and hypocrisy. The love of God compels us to love the neighbor. The scripture never commands us to love ourselves; it assumes we already do. In fact, people in their unregenerate condition love themselves too much—that is our problem as opposed to a solution.

It is natural and normal to love yourself—it is our default position. There is no lack of self-love in our world. Unless regenerated, people naturally love themselves more than God. They only go to God when they want something from Him. To love God in order to get what you want from Him is considered to be self-loving. Also, to love only those who love you is self-love. The balanced, biblical view is to love others unconditionally. "Self-love," is self-absorption or selfishness. The Bible warns against such mentality (Philippians 2:3; 1Cor. 13:4-6; Romans 2:8). The healthy self-love begins with an accurate view of who we are. We are God's unique creation, created in His image, loved by God in spite of our sin, and redeemed by Christ. God sees you as you can be and will become – not just as you are now. God loves you more than you love yourself. It is only in His love that we can love others. The bottom line is that it takes a revelation to love God more than yourself and to love your neighbor as you love yourself.

1 Corinthians 12:12-13 – "Just as a body, though one, has many parts, but all its many parts form one body, so it is with Christ. For we were all baptized by[a] one Spirit so as to form one body—whether Jews or Gentiles, slave or free—and we were all given the one Spirit to drink." To be a Christian means nothing less than this expression: we have all drunk deeply of the one Spirit of God. Jesus baptizes us with the Holy Spirit to identify us with His holiness. The Holy Spirit is the seal of God marking us as His permanent possession (Ephesians 1:13-14). We are all repented sinners, saved by grace, standing at a leveled ground at the foot of the cross in the unity of the Holy Spirit. The Bible says that "And if anyone does not have the Spirit of Christ, he does not belong to Christ" (Romans 8:9). God created you to have relationships with Him and others through His Son Jesus. The Holy Spirit implements such relationship, vertically and horizontally. The Holy Spirit abiding in your spirit is the same Spirit abiding in all believers. The unity of the body of Christ is the unit of the Holy Spirit. Our unity does not come from some ten point program out there; it is the unit of the Holy Spirit forming the body of Christ that constitutes the unity. Want to see the unity of the church? Let every one of us be led by the Spirit of God. The Spirit of God uses the Word of God

to make us a people of God with the same mind of Christ. The apparent divisions among us are the reality of the fallen nature (flesh) manifested in us at different degrees or levels. The remedy is when we all walk by the Spirit as opposed to the flesh.

1 Corinthians 1:9 - "God is faithful, who has called you into fellowship with his Son, Jesus Christ our Lord. I appeal to you, brothers, in the name of our Lord Jesus Christ, that all of you agree together, so that there may be no divisions among you and that you may be united in mind and conviction." These words contain arguments, assuring the saints of their completeness in Christ, and of their being preserved blameless to the day of the return of our Lord. We are called to grow in the knowledge of our Lord and Savior Jesus Christ; of His person, office, and grace; nothing is more valuable and preferable to the principal of the grace. Although we are called to grow in the grace, the Christian's position in Christ is not progressive. Our transformation in Christ is a one-time act of regeneration; we do not grow or develop from a small beginning. We are as perfect and complete the instant we are regenerated as we ever will be in the ages to come. The process of sanctification is the daily conversion involving the cleansing of the minds. It is the manifestation of the fullness of the life of Christ in the church. It is a requisite of those who are transformed; this being the evidence of those who are truly born again. The scripture says "You were called into the fellowship of his Son, Jesus Christ our Lord." There are two meanings: The sharing together in the Father and the Son is certainly the case in 1 John 1:3. It is the sharing vertically in the union each of us has in Christ. Then horizontally, the sharing with other believers the common union we have with Christ. This is a Christian position in the body of Christ (Church). Putting both meanings together means that everyone who is in the state of grace possesses God's love and the neighbor's love in their soul. We keep the love of each other close or secure by fellowshipping. The Bible instructed us that "Not forsaking the assembling of ourselves together, as the manner of some is; but exhorting one another: and so much the more, as you see the day approaching." (Hebrews 10:25). Fellowshipping projects in the physical realm the unity

of the unit of the body of Christ (Church) which exists in the spiritual realm. It is impossible for you to be part of the invisible spiritual body of Christ without being part of the visible congregation of believers on the earth. The church on earth is the reflection of the church in heaven, in the same way the physical material body is the proof of the existence of the invisible immaterial soul. We are conquerors in Christ but the Christian fellowship is the prescribed means of perseverance. The spiritual journey is rigid and rough. It is by working together as one body of Christ that we can bounce back from the bumps in the road. "Resilience keeps our failures from becoming our defeat." In our case, resilience isn't in solitary; we need each other.

John 14:17 - "The Spirit of truth. The world cannot accept him, because it neither sees him nor knows him. But you know him, for he lives with you and will be in you." The children of the Father are identified by the presence of the Holy Spirit in them. "The Spirit you received brought about your adoption to sonship. And by him we cry, "Abba, Father" (Romans 8:15). Regeneration (new birth) brings the fullness of the Godhead to dwells in us: "Anyone who loves me will obey my teaching. My Father will love them, and we will come to them and make our home with them." (John 14:23). God dwells in us to work in us and through us. When sincere love to Christ is in the heart, there will be obedience. Love will be a commanding, constraining principle; and where love is, duty follows from a principle of gratitude. The gift of the Holy Ghost is bestowed upon all of the children of God, and not on the world. The Bible says that "He placed his seal of ownership on us, and put his Spirit in our hearts as a deposit, guaranteeing what is to come." (2 Corinthians 1:22). At glorification we shall be fully restored to His likeness.

John 4:32 – "Meanwhile, the disciples urged Him, "Rabbi, eat something." But he said to them, "I have food to eat that you know nothing about." Verse 35 expounds the food Jesus is talking about: "Jesus

explained, "My food is to do the will of Him who sent Me and to finish His work" (John 4:35). The food for the physical bodies is as important as the food for the soul and we ought to allow the one appetite to be satisfied with as little restraint as the other. The difference is in the output. The food we eat sustains life temporality as opposed to eternally. Eating is enjoyable but it is limitable either by the appetite or the stomach. The spiritual food has no limitation. Faith is venturing into the unlimitedness of God. According to Jesus, doing the will of the Father is essentially the reason for His very existence on the earth. He took as much pleasure in it, as a hungry man does in eating and drinking; He wouldn't stop doing it even if it meant staying hungry. Doing the will of His Father was meat unto Him, delightful and refreshing; and His minds and thoughts were so taken up with it, that he had no inclination to any corporeal food. Jesus availed Himself as the food that sustains life eternally. "I am the bread of life. Whoever comes to me will never go hungry, and whoever believes in me will never be thirsty" (John 6:35). Christ, the true bread only gives life, which is conveyed by the Word, and made effectual by the Spirit. Elsewhere, Jesus said concerning the true believers that they are the ones who partake of His body and blood, and they abide in Him: "Whoever eats my flesh and drinks my blood remains in me, and I in them" (John 6:56). It is the same challenge Jesus made to the Samaritan woman: "Everyone who drinks this water will be thirsty again but whoever drinks the water I give them will never thirst. Indeed, the water I give them will become in them a spring of water welling up to eternal life" (John 4:13-14). The water Jesus gives implicates His passion to be in us; the availability of His Spirit and His grace: "The water I give him will become in him a fount of water springing up to eternal life." (John 4:14). We drink or partake of it by receiving Him and obeying Him. Christ is in the body of a believer as God was in His temple at Jerusalem. This being the best of the best that heaven can deliver.

Philippians 1:21 - "For to me, to live is Christ and to die is gain." According to the scripture, Jesus Christ is Paul's life effectively and efficiently. Life is a precious gift from God regardless of where we are (as

for the believers, heaven or earth). God equally loves the departed saints as He loves the saints who are still living on the earth because we are one body (Church). While we are still on the earth, we are called to number our days but God alone can number our lives because the greatest dimension of life is eternal. Although this world is not paradise, heaven begins here on the earth; we can experience heaven on earth the moment we are regenerated by faith. Planning for the end begins now rather than later. In order to finish well, you must start well. Beginning well is responding to the gospel, and then continuing in your convictions by exercising the discipline of the Christian life till our bodies will be glorified. God alone, by His grace, can take you from where you are to where He wants you to be. The sum of our lives is within the frame of His parameter. Christ must be magnified or glorified in our bodies, whether by life or by death. Spiritually, we must live for Him, and die in Him. A person is never ready to live until they are ready to die. Only a person that is ready to die in Him and for His name's sake can say "For to me, to live is Christ and to die is gain."

2 Corinthians 3:3 - "Forasmuch as ye are manifestly declared to be the epistle of Christ ministered by us, written not with ink, but with the Spirit of the living God; not in tables of stone, but in fleshy tables of the heart." We are Living Epistles required to portray God's glory as the written scriptures do. The message of God is written in our hearts for others to read. We are living epistles of Jesus Christ not written in ink but by the very Spirit of the living God. Every grace that is implanted in the soul is wrought there by the Spirit of God; Christ is the author and dictator; yea, He Himself is the very matter, sum, substance, and subject of the epistle; His character is formed in the hearts of His people in conversion, His image is stamped, His grace is implanted, His word, His Gospel dwells richly, His laws and ordinances are written here in the heart. Faith and holiness, hope and love, the spiritual gifts and comfort, knowledge and wisdom are all built within our new nature. There is the impeccability of the glory of God treasured within us. We are responsible to bring His glory

from within us to the outside. It is for His glory alone that we are living. Our confidence is not in our capabilities but in Christ.

Mark 8:23-25 – "So He took the blind man by the hand and led him out of the village. Then He spit on the man's eyes and placed His hands on him. "Can you see anything?" He asked. Then the man looked up and said, "I see people; they look like trees walking around. Once again Jesus placed His hands on the man's eyes, and when he opened them his sight was restored, and he could see everything clearly". The first healing was symbolic of our spiritual sight. Like this man's first experience of seeing, before regeneration we see things upside down. Even with 20/20 vision, we are blind to the things pertaining to God. We have no capability to see beyond our physical capabilities. We need the touch of God in order for us to have illumination so that we can see what God wants us to see. Elsewhere, Jesus said to a man who claimed to see everything on His own (without the help from God) that, "If you were blind, you would not be guilty of sin; but now that you claim you can see, your guilt remains. (John 9:41). His sin is refusing to be conscious of his spiritual blindness so that he seeks for the spiritual light. Jesus is the ultimate light that dispels the ultimate darkness. But this man claims to see; he thought himself to be wise and knowing, and stood in no need of any illumination from Jesus; he was obstinate and hardened in his infidelity, and willfully opposed and shut his eyes against all the light and evidence of truth. The sin of this man will remain until he admits that he can't see and fully acknowledges the great principle and reason, the motive and characteristics, of the mission of Christ. The Bible says that "Without vision, my people perish" (Proverbs 29:18). The vision is life changing sight and wisdom. God's provision does not come without His vision.

Authentic spiritual discernment must begin with Scripture—revealed truth. Without a firm grounding in divine revelation, human reason always degenerates into skepticism (a denial that anything can be known for certain), rationalism (the theory that reason is a *source* of truth), secularism (an approach to life that purposely excludes God), or any number of other anti-Christian philosophies. When the Scripture condemns human wisdom (1 Cor. 3:19), it is not denouncing reason or perceiving, but humanistic ideology divorced from the divinely revealed truth of God's Word. In other words, *reason apart from the Word of* God leads inevitably to unsound ideas, but reason subjected to the Word of God is at the heart of the wise spiritual discernment. God's truth is a precious commodity that must be handled carefully—not diluted with whimsical beliefs or bound up in human traditions. When a church loses its will to discern between sound doctrine and error, between good and evil, between truth and lies, that church is doomed.

"The scriptures spring from God and flow unto Christ, and were given to lead us to Christ. You must therefore go along by the scriptures, as by a line, until you come at Christ, which is the way's end and resting- place" ~ William Tyndale

1 John 4:20 – "Whoever claims to love God yet hates a brother or sister is a liar. For whoever does not love their brother and sister, whom they have seen, cannot love God, whom they have not seen." When regeneration takes place, the remedial dispensation of the gospel is acknowledged as the means. A brother or a sister whose conscience is rectified and whose will and actions are brought under its control represents Christ on the earth. Therefore, to hate a brother or a sister, who is transformed and made in the likeness of Christ, is to hate God. The Bible says that "Whoso rejects you rejects me, and whoso rejects me rejects him that sent me". The proof of the godly character is the co-existence of the love to God and love to the brethren. The absence of the latter is evidence of the absence of the former; where love to God is, brotherly love also cannot be wanting. Brotherly love

is our distinguishing character. Jesus said that by loving each other, the world will know that we are His disciples (John 13:35).

2 Corinthians 8:9 – "For you know the grace of our Lord Jesus Christ, that though he was rich, yet for your sake he became poor, so that you through his poverty might become rich." Jesus, being God, had equal power and glory with the Father, yet He emptied Himself of the heavenly glory and put on the human flesh for our sake. As a man, He emptied Himself of His life at the cross. There is one Mediator, and that Mediator gave Himself as a ransom for all. "In him, we have redemption through his blood, the forgiveness of sins, in accordance with the riches of God's grace" (Ephesians 1:7). He became poor so that we might become rich. It was rich grace for the Father to provide such a surety as His own Son, and freely to deliver Him up. In Christ, the heavenly blessings overtake us, and we can pursue them with reassurance (faith). True riches are eternal. The best of the Christian duties are drawn from the grace and the love of Christ. The gospel invites us into the inexhaustible harmony with God's eternal abundance. By faith, we come to Him the way that He has appointed; which way is Jesus Christ only. The grace teaches us to choose God over the temporary riches and pleasures of this world. The godly legacy is the one which treasure is in heaven. "Christ is our only hope and He is hope enough."

Jeremiah 17:9 - "The heart is deceitful above all things, and desperately wicked: who can know it?" Faith is a passionate intuition but we cannot make intuitive diagnoses of the human heart. God the omniscient, alone, knows the malice of the hearts of all men. He diagnosed the human heart as wicked. The word wicked also means sick and incurable by any natural means. The human heart is the dark room where all kinds of negativity are developed. No matter how calmly you try to adjudicate there are those little things which will eventually produce bizarre behaviors. The corrupt human heart and the corrupt world are bedfellows. The human heart

naturally inclines towards the fallen world. "The world is not dialectical - it is sworn to extremes, not to equilibrium, sworn to radical antagonism, not to reconciliation or synthesis. This is also the principle of evil." The heavenly virtues cannot be permanently implanted into a wicked heart unless God transforms our hearts by His Spirit and transplants his minds into us by His Word.

Galatians 6:7 - "Do not be deceived: God cannot be mocked. A man reaps what he sows." God is not up there watching you and slapping you on the head for every little thing you do. Most times He watches for things to pray out naturally. There is a sowing and reaping law in place. Sowing and reaping is a bail expression and may be applied to all actions, good and bad, and the reward and punishment of them, and particularly to acts of beneficence, and the enjoying of the fruits thereof. Those who, under the guidance and influences of the Holy Spirit, live a life of faith in Christ, and abound in Christian graces, shall of the Spirit reap life everlasting. Concerning the good deeds of righteousness, our present time is seed time; we shall reap as we sow now. In due time we shall reap the fruits of righteousness; either in this world or in the afterlife, sooner or later; in God's own time. Those who perpetually live a carnal, sensual life must expect no other fruit from such a course than misery and ruin: "For to be carnally minded is death, but to be spiritually minded is life and peace" (Romans 8:6-11). It is self-deception to do things endeavored to satisfy your lustful minds, at the expense of the divine will, hoping that God understands your weaknesses. Certainly, God forgives all the times when we repent but at times He does not undo the done things. He lets things play out (naturally evolve) or happen the way we planned them by our poor judgments and decisions so that we learn from our mistakes. Sometimes you must experience a low point in life in order to learn a lesson you wouldn't have learned any other way. Pain is like the high temperature (fever) in the body projecting that something is wrong somewhere. "Never let an old flame to burn you twice".

John 6:63 – "It is the spirit that quickeneth; the flesh profiteth nothing: the words that I speak unto you, they are spirit, and they are life." The word "quickeneth" renders to the birth of a new life within this life. It is a compound word in reference to a believer's experience after they receive Jesus Christ as their Savior. When you respond positively to the gospel, the new life received by faith is spiritual in nature. The gospel extends to us an opportunity to die with Christ so that we can live in Him forever. Those who live by the flesh will die in the flesh. Dying outside Christ means death forever. Those who died in Christ continue to die to their flesh daily and to live by the Spirit daily and forever. Jesus said that "It is the Spirit who gives life; the flesh profits nothing. The words that I speak to you are spirit, and they are life-giving" (John 6:63). The secret to the strong faith and the Spirit-filled life is the strong preference for the Word. His word imparts life when they are engrafted into our hearts. A believer has two natures: the visible physical nature that is subject to death and the invisible spiritual nature that never dies. It doesn't seem to make sense to some. The good news is that when faith doesn't make sense it makes things possible for those who believe. Faith does not exclude logic but it overlaps logic. The motto of the world is that "What you see is what you get". The reality is that what you can't see is more real than what you can see. The unseen spiritual world preceded the visible physical world and is more real than the world we can see.

Ephesians 5:18 - "Do not get drunk on wine, which leads to debauchery. Instead, be filled with the Spirit". Whereas the Bible lists various biblical characters who were filled with the Holy Spirit, this is the only scripture in the Bible that directly instructs us to be filled with the Holy Spirit. Paul used the illustration of the influence of wine to hammer home his point. Alcohol is the loophole through which the pervert climbs into the minds of ordinary men. An intoxicated person acts contrary to authentic ordinariness. A life lived without God's guidance is a mess. It is Him alone, who made our souls that can teach us how to live right. "Be you filled" -The instruction to be filled is given to us; we are not instructed to ask God to fill us. The word "filled" in this case means to be controlled or

driven. What you are filled with controls you. For example, a person that is filled with rage is controlled by anger. During biblical times they used the dhows (ships) which were driven by winds. These ships had sails (rags) designed to trap the wind. When the sails were filled with the winds, the ship was driven in the direction of the wind. To be filled with the Spirit is to allow the Holy Spirit to control your life or to drive you in the direction of God. When a person is born again, the Holy Spirit indwells them in His fullness - This is God's responsibility. But the process of being filled with the Spirit is your responsibility. If you are not filled with the Holy Spirit, it is not because you have less of Him but because He has less of you. The issue is not how much of the Holy Spirit you have but how much of you the Holy Spirit has.

Dying to the flesh perpetually is the key to being filled with the Spirit. Naturally, what you are filled with comes forth out of you: "Now the works of the flesh are manifest, which are these; Adultery, fornication, uncleanness, lasciviousness, idolatry and sorcery; hatred, discord, jealousy, and rage; rivalries, divisions, factions" (Galatians 5:19-20). By "flesh" is meant corrupt nature, as before the new birth, and by the works of it, not only external acts of sin, but inward lusts; for such are here mentioned among its works, as "hatred", "wrath", "envyings", & etc. and both external and internal acts are so called, because they spring from the flesh, or corrupt nature; they are what denominate and show men to be carnal. On the contrary, a Spirit-filled believer is the one in whom God's grace is a well of living water, and out of whose belly flow rivers of it. Christ's words are the chief method of communicating His life-giving Spirit to us. The words of Jesus are written down for us in form of the Scriptures for us to read, to apply and to grow in the grace.

We are called to create the favorable environment for the consummation of the Holy Spirit. Paul warned us not to be influenced by the worldly practices and philosophies but to be influenced by the Spirit. The people of the world seek excessive drinking in order to temporality escape the pain of the world. The steps of the righteous person are ordered by the Lord; he lives in harmony with God and others. Loving God is evidently seen in loving your neighbor. Paul said that: "Speak to one another with psalms, hymns, and spiritual songs. Sing and make music in your hearts to the Lord" (verse 19). The book of Psalms was also called the book of praising (prayers). The word 'psalm' comes from the Greek word *psalmoi*. It suggests the idea of a "praise song," as does the Hebrew word *tehillim*. The hymns were composed of the gospel; they were sung and read in form of scriptures. It is a calling to a continuous process of devotion by praising God and meditating on the Word. By fervent prayer let us seek to be filled with the Spirit. Let us avoid whatever may grieve our gracious Comforter. We are filled with the Holy Spirit after we empty ourselves of the worldliness (anger, bitterness, hatred and etc). The Holy Spirit is vitally and dynamically involved in our sanctification by primarily instilling in us the essential element of love. Jesus said that "If you have a grudge against someone leave your gift there in front of the altar. First go and be reconciled to them; then come and offer your gift" (Matthew 5:24). This is the only scripture in the Bible stopping us to pray. Worshiping is part of praying. Jesus elevated reconciliation above prayer because he who lives in harmony with God lives in harmony with the neighbor. The Holy Spirit cannot thrive in an environment where there is tension, strife, and confusion.

Matthew 14:24-25 - "The boat was already a considerable distance from land, buffeted by the waves because the wind was against it. During the fourth watch of the night, Jesus went out to them, walking on the lake". The miracle of Jesus walking on the water is recorded in three of the Gospels (Matthew, Mark, and John). It happened after the miracle of feeding the 5000. It was the miracle of Jesus walking on the water that, more than any other convinced Jesus' disciples of His divinity. They responded with a confession of faith in Jesus as God: "Truly you are the Son of God" (Matthew 14:32-33). The miracle involved God's defying of the laws of gravity which He put in place to sustain the universe. Mark reports that when the disciples saw Jesus walking on the lake, they thought He was a ghost (Mark 6:48-50). But Jesus immediately spoke up: "Take courage! It is I. Do not be afraid." "Lord, if it's you," Peter replied, "tell me to come to you on the water." "Come," said Jesus. Then Peter got down out of the boat, walked on the water, and came toward Jesus" (Matthew 14:28). Jesus taught His disciples that with their faith in Him they can do

the works He did. Faith begins by acknowledging that we are weak but Jesus is strong; our strength is in Jesus. Jesus said that "If you remain in me and I in you, you will bear much fruit; apart from me you can do nothing. (John 15:5). Faith keeps us in God. Faith separates us from ourselves and sets us apart to be used by God. Christ's life will be in us only as we seek to make His way of life our way of life—to walk as He walked, to live as He lived (1 John 2:6).

Proverbs 25:16 - "If you find honey, eat just enough– too much of it, and you will vomit." The honey is figuratively used in reference to all things that please the senses or the pleasures of life, but the truism is to be extended beyond physical matters. Our physical experiences affect all of our facilities including cogitation (thinking). What goes on in the minds can be digested and assimilated to impact the spiritual nature; injudicious cramming produces satiety and disgust. According to St. Gregory, "To 'find honey, is to taste the sweetness of holy intelligence, which is eaten enough of then when our perception, according to the measure of our faculty, is held tight under control." Morality is having and giving the right measure of everything (not received/given in excess and not less than required). The morality of God is the yardstick that prescribes the exact measure of everything required at a particular time in accordance to the Creator's mind and assesses. The Bible prescribes the right measure, according to the divine will and wisdom of every aspect or joint of life.

1 John 2:19 – "They went out from us, but they did not really belong to us. For if they had belonged to us, they would have remained with us; but their going showed that none of them belonged to us." The clause "but they did not belong to us" means they were not of us or one of us. The ones who belong must be of the same nature, mind and character, and must be in communion with other believers. They will not leave regardless of the inconveniences. Leaving in this case has to do with departing from the faith rather than leaving a particular denomination or congregation.

The ones who left were most probably not truly regenerated by the grace of God, and so apparently were not of the number, of God's elect: in spite of their profession and communion with the church. Salvation is of God but we are required to be committed to our Lord wholly heartedly. Commitment is the key to the lasting relationship. The difference between cohabiting and marriage is commitment. True love is not seasonal but is committed all the way to the end. "The quality of a person's life is in direct proportion to their commitment to excellence, regardless of their chosen field of endeavor." In commitment, there is dedication and passion for what you are doing. Renewing your relationship involves maximizing and prioritizing your commitment by renewing your minds, your zeal, and passion. Those who are truly regenerated are born of an incorruptible seed, and they abide, as does every true grace, faith, hope, and love; and cannot possibly fall into such errors and heresies as those who left did.

Colossians 3:1-4 - "Since, then, you have been raised with Christ, set your hearts on things above, where Christ is seated at the right hand of God. Set your minds on things above, not on earthly things. For you died, and your life is now hidden with Christ in God. When Christ, who is your life, appears, then you also will appear with him in glory" (Col. 3:1–4). The scripture specifically says that "Christ, who is your life–". Elsewhere, the Bible says "Whoever has the Son has life; whoever does not have the Son of God does not have life." (1 John 5:12). Your life is hidden in Christ; by faith you were buried and raised with Him (Romans 6:4). Your new nature in Christ is the real you. You can't discover who you are until you discover whose you are. Faith is the substance (reality) of things which we can't see. The Scripture says, "Set your minds on the things above", not on earthly things." We are called to set our hearts on those things from above which are invisible to our natural eyes. Whenever we are heavenly minded we are heavenly bound. Thoughtfulness for our souls is the best cure of thoughtfulness for the world. Faith connects the soul to the divine. Our faith is perfected by our desires. Therefore we must submit and resign

ourselves to the spiritual needs. We are recipients of God's grace to pass it on to others. But God calls us to Himself before He sends us to others.

Hebrews 11:6 – "And without faith it is impossible to please God, because anyone who comes to him must believe that he exists and that he rewards those who earnestly seek him." God cannot be pleased except by faith because it is His desire for us to be under the Lordship of His Son. It is for the same reason He ordained seeking Him by faith as a divine rule in His kingdom. God is self-sufficient and self- pleasing. He lacks nothing outside Himself. Yet He is overwhelmingly honest about what pleases Him. It is not necessarily what pleases us that is pleasing to Him. But what pleases Him must please us. God cannot be approached casually. Faith establishes in our hearts the sincere fear and love of God. Faith is a gift from God: Only the power that comes from God can go to God. Therefore, it is absolutely faith alone that can connect us to the grace. The grace grids human weakness with the divine strength. Unbelief is the opposite of faith. The genuine believers must be honest and up front about the fact that persistent unbelief displeases God.

Hebrews 11:1 – "Now faith is the substance of things hoped for, the evidence of things not seen." Faith is a spiritual substance on the inside of you that can either grow or wane. God builds His kingdom on trust, deeming it as the absolute condition of all that pleases Him. Faith is not a mere presumption. It is depending on the capability of God to deliver what He promised. It is being inside rather than outside the reality of the situation that has not manifested yet. "Faith is believing in advance what makes sense in reverse".

2 Peter 1:10 - "Therefore, my brothers, be all the more eager to make your calling and election sure. For if you do these things, you will never fall." We are fragile mortals, given to fears of every sort. We have a built-in

insecurity that no amount of whistling in the dark can mollify. We seek assurance concerning the things that frighten us the most but forget about the possibility of not being truly saved. The assurance we need the most is the assurance of salvation. It is possible to have false assurance of salvation. False assurance usually proceeds from a faulty understanding of salvation. Our salvation is given in three stages: Justification; sanctification and glorification. Our justification (past) and glorification (future) are basically locked in our sanctification (present). Sanctification is the proof of justification and the assurance of glorification. Sanctification removes doubts regarding our intended destiny. All who have been born again will see clear evidences of a new life of Christ manifested in them. While we will never become perfect in this life, we will, nevertheless, experience a changed life. It is this inward transformation that provides a strong confirmation of our salvation.

John 14:15 - "If you love me, keep my commands." Loving God is conditioned by loving obedience. Love is the greatest power. God is love; Jesus came from Love (God) to demonstrate love. How? Obedience is the love language of Jesus. Everything we do in obedience to God we do it in God's power. The Jewish religious leaders loved obedience without the relationship. The lukewarm believers want the relationship without obedience. We are instructed to love God with all of our hearts and minds. "To love God with all your heart, soul, mind, and strength is all-consuming and all-encompassing. It is no lukewarm endeavor." It is worshiping Him by our obedience to Him. We obey God by loving others. This is what Jesus meant by the two greatest commandments of loving God and loving neighbor (Luke 10:27). No one will ever love God and his neighbor as God intended, who is not made a partaker of converting grace.

1 John 4:4 – "You, dear children, are from God and have overcome them, because the one who is in you is greater than the one who is in the world." The scripture says that the children of God are from above (God).

Jesus made the same claim concerning Himself: "You are from below; I am from above. You are of this world; I am not of this world" (John 8:23). The "He who is in us" is the Holy Spirit. The "He who is in the world" is Satan. The term "greater than" is used in comparison of two items of completely different kinds; one is the opposite of the other. The one who is greater is the creator who became like us to overcome the adversary on our behalf. Jesus instructed us how to constantly enforce His victory over Satan and the hostile world. It is not we who are called to live the Christian life but to allow God to live it on our behalf. Walking by the Spirit is constantly manifesting the life of Christ in its fullness. It means bearing the fruit of the Spirit. We overcome hate by love; war by peace. Jesus said that "Peace I leave with you; my peace I give you. I do not give to you as the world gives. Do not let your hearts be troubled and do not be afraid." (John 14:27). A consecrated Christian life is resting in Christ. The evidence is ever shedding light and comfort and peace. The peace that Jesus gives begins in the heart and the mind. The peace of the mind which the world cannot give is acquired when the minds are totally under control of God. We need to be armed with the peace of God in our spiritual warfare against Satan. This is the only war where peace is used as a conventional weapon.

Ephesians 6:17 "In addition to all this, take up the shield of faith, with which you can extinguish all the flaming arrows of the evil one. Take the helmet of salvation and the sword of the Spirit, which is the word of God." Although Satan is our archenemy, the biggest battle is against the flesh and the world. The flesh is the ego that fills the emptiness of life with everything except God. The head is the seat of the mind, which, when it has laid hold of the sure Gospel "hope" of eternal life, will resist or not give way to Satan's temptations. The weapons of our warfare are spiritual. We are fighting the good fight of faith, and having good weapons in particularly the sword of the Spirit, which is the word of God. The sword supplied by the Spirit, the Word being inspired by him, and employed by the Spirit; for He enlightens us to know it, applies it to us, and teaches us to use it both defensively and offensively. A Christian is a person who is at

war with the odd desires by the power of the Spirit. Walking by the Spirit is conquering the desires of the flesh.

John 2:23-24 - "While He was in Jerusalem at the Passover Feast, many people saw the signs He was doing and believed in His name. But Jesus would not entrust himself to them, for he knew all people." The particularism of Christ's withdrawing gives the stronger and better explanation of the reserve of Christ in dealing with the half-believers. They confessed Jesus as their Lord because they saw His miracles but in actuality they were not sincere believers. The phony believers have one thing in common: they do not portray the character of God because they have a contradictory version of Christ. They claim to be broken but beneath the shallow surface, there is the unbroken ledge of rock. They are emotionally moved because they are not deeply rooted in the Word. Fake faith results into plastic Christianity; it is seasonal (won't last forever) and it won't change your destiny - Probably compared to the fake news or the fake Chinese products on the market today. Such faith evaporates when they are exposed to pressure. There is one password to Eternity: The password is Jesus. Faith in Jesus Christ is not a fictitious or sacramental, mystic but a relationship. Jesus unveils (reveals) Himself to give Himself wholly to you. By His Spirit, He programs your conscience with the Word, so that your conscience steers and guides you into the right direction and hence to your intended destiny.

1 Timothy 2:5 - "For there is one God and one mediator between God and mankind, the man Christ Jesus". The term 'the man Christ Jesus' stands for the perfect human figure (God alone is perfect) with one hand stretched to the shoulder of God and the other hand resting on the shoulder of man, purposely to make the will of God the will of man. The Bible says "This is the confidence we have in approaching God: that if we ask anything according to his will, he hears us" (1 John 5:14). There is no

such thing as unanswered prayer as long the will of God is the same as the will of man. Jesus came to make the will of God to be done on the earth.

Romans 12:1 - "I beseech you therefore, brethren, by the mercies of God, that you present your bodies a living sacrifice, holy, acceptable unto God, which is your reasonable service." This scripture is primarily about the perfect worshiping of God. The term "reasonable service" means acceptable worshipping. The temple priesthood at Jerusalem offered the guidelines regarding a perfect sacrifice. A living sacrifice must be perfect. The word 'perfect' is in reference to complete or wholly as opposed to partial. The apostle Paul provides a theological framework for what it means to follow Christ totally and the consequential changes it makes in a person's life. The indwelling Spirit of God is the deposit of God's holiness within us. Completeness is when the holiness of God within us is manifested to the outside in our works. In the old covenant, God didn't accept a lame sacrifice (Leviticus 1:1-8; 8-9, 21); and He doesn't accept it now, in the new covenant. It is a demand for total holiness from within to the outside. Outwardly performance (holiness) that does not originate from the transformed heart has all the trappings that would make for a great follower, while, inwardly you are lacking and holding back. God will not accept a partial commitment. The requirement for the perfect sacrifice is imperative and perpetual. Worshiping is the lifestyle of a believer.

Our bodies are His temple, supposedly to be consecrated to the service of Him who gave it. Worship is a reserve of the one who is holy. True worship begins in the temples of our bodies. The instruction to present our bodies as a living sacrifice is an instruction to make Jesus Christ as valuable as He is supposed to be even in our daily lives. Neither does God call us to make Him look good but holy nor does He call us to look good but holy. Worshiping is the displaying of the worthiness of Jesus. It is turning your daily works into doxology. It is living a sacrificial life glorifying to God. In Verse 2 Paul answers how we can turn all of our life into worship: "Be transformed by the renewal of your mind." We must be transformed and consecrated; not just by our external behaviors, but the way we feel and think — our minds. "The root of all steadfastness is in consecration to God". A person cannot be converted without being consecrated to God. Consecration involves the willingness to do what is revealed in the scriptures and to sincerely hate sin.

In Philippians 2:12-13, Paul writes, "Therefore, my dear friends, as you have always obeyed – not only in my presence, but now much more in my absence – continue to work out your salvation with fear and trembling, for it is God who works in you to will and to act according to his purpose." The sense in which we are to work out our salvation in fear and trembling is twofold. First, the Greek verb rendered "work out" means "to continually work to bring something to completion or fruition." Our salvation is complete in Christ. But we are supposed to compliment it by actively pursuing obedience in the process of sanctification, which Paul explains further in the next chapter of Philippians. He describes himself as "straining" and "pressing on" toward the goal of Christlikeness (Philippians 3:13-14). The trembling experience has to do with the attitude of a Christian when pursuing this goal—a healthy fear of offending God through disobedience and an awe and respect for His majesty and holiness. "Trembling" can also refer to a shaking due to weakness, but this is a weakness of higher purpose, one which brings us to a state of dependency on God. Obedience and submission to the God whom we revere and respect is our "reasonable service" (Romans 12:1-2) and brings great joy.

Colossians 2:9 - "For in Him dwells all the fullness of the Godhead bodily." The word 'Godhead' means Deity. The word "Godhead" is found only three times in the entire Bible and all of the three times are in the New Testament: It is found here in Colossians 2:9, in Romans 1:20, and in Acts 17:29. All the fullness of the Father dwells in Christ. Jesus is the manifested fullness of the Godhead in the bodily form. Jesus turned the impossibilities into possibilities. In Christ's work at the cross, the aspect of the divine family in heaven and the aspect of the fallen family on earth are brought together (reconciled). Christ is at the center of reconciliation. In

Him we are fused with the divine: We have been buried, raised and hidden in Christ God (Colossians 3:3). The Spirit of the Father is the Spirit of the Son, and He is the same Spirit that indwelled us. When we received Jesus Christ, we received the fullness of the Godhead (John 14:23). The Bible says that "And this is the testimony: that God has given us eternal life, and this life is in His Son. He who has the Son has life; he who does not have the Son of God does not have life."— (1 John 5:11-12). It means that all of us, by virtue of our relationship with Jesus Christ, have been equally given all power and authority through the power of the eternal Spirit, who dwelt in Christ and is now dwelling in us to do the same works that Jesus did (John 14:12). By faith, we are engraved in the divine family. The saint's "life" is spiritual and eternal; it is a life of grace from Christ, a life of faith in him, and a life of communion with him. Faith is the greatest power in the universe, with unlimited scope.

Galatians 6:9 - "Let us not become weary in doing good, for at the proper time we will reap a harvest if we do not give up." God never get weary or tired. When we let God to work on our behalf, through us, we cannot get weary. This may be understood of as well doing, or doing good works in general, of every sort, which are done in accordance to the will of God, from a principle of love to Him, in faith, and in the name and strength of Christ, and with a view to the glory of God. In essential – let us work for unity. In non-essentials – let us give liberty. In everything – let us arbitrate charity. The Bible says, "—whatever is true, whatever is noble, whatever is right, whatever is pure, whatever is lovely, whatever is admirable—if anything is excellent or praiseworthy—think about such things" (Philippians 4:8). "For in due season we shall reap if we faint not" is a promise of reaping a hundredfold in this world and in the world to come. Eternal life begins now and is fully experienced after this life. Receiving Jesus is the intimate and experimental knowledge of God, that yields to eternal life (1 John 5:12). Righteousness—obedience to God—produces a change both in us and in the world around us. Piety has an effect on the society whose morality is of God. Piety is our commitment to do good; faith is when we trust God to do it in and through us. He leads us through

piety and anchors us in faith to His promises. Then we can say that "His goodness will follow me all the days of my life". Unlike our goodness, His goodness endures continually, and is unchanging, from everlasting to everlasting. When we abide in Him, we do not give up on doing good.

Galatians 6:7 - "Do not be deceived, God is not mocked; for whatever a man sows, that he will also reap". A lot of people have phrased this principle in a lot of ways: "What goes around, comes around." "You get out what you put in." "Chickens come home to roost." But no matter how you say it, the underlying message is still the same. The laws established by God are not arbitrary; they serve to protect us from decisions and actions that would otherwise lead to painful consequences for ourselves and others. Understanding this principle is vital for understanding so many of God's laws. Our Father in heaven wants us to sow seeds that ultimately result in *happiness*, not pain and sorrow. And we're more likely to do that when we realize that God's laws exist to help us to be happy rather than to deter us from happiness. God created life and He knows how life works. "Man did not weave the web of life; he is merely a strand in it."

Galatians 2:20 – "I have been crucified with Christ and I no longer live, but Christ lives in me. The life I now live in the body, I live by faith in the Son of God, who loved me and gave himself for me." Paul absorbed all kinds of abuses because he was a crucified man. A crucified person loses all the rights; they could do to him as they will. The grace disciplines the mind so that it becomes impervious to the intruding worldliness and the corroding influence of intimidation or fear. Paul says that "I no longer live, but Christ lives in me. The life I now live in the body, I live by faith in the Son of God". Paul dies daily to the old nature and its desires; it is no longer his life but Christ's life (new nature) manifested in him. Everywhere in scripture, God is revealed to be a spiritual being who is not subject to the physical law. The resurrected life of Christ is spiritual in nature; it is not subjected to the material or the physical desires and regulations of the

physical nature. It is a resurrected life of Christ in us that overcame death; it is not subject to death because it is not under the condemnation of the Moral Law; it is not subject to the death code that is steering the world into the abyss. The zeal to live for Christ involves mirroring the greatest person ever walked on the universe. Worshiping is becoming like what you worship.

Hebrews 10:25 - "Not forsaking the assembling of ourselves together, as the manner of some is; but exhorting one another: and so much the more, as ye see the day approaching." We are instructed to fellowship with other members of the body of Christ, whether in our sanctuaries or our homes. Going to church does not save us but those who withdraw from fellowshipping with other believers are most likely progressively on their way out of fellowshipping with the Lord. They separate themselves from the ways of the congregation: Like praying and fasting together, exhorting and comforting one another; attending public worshiping, group Bible study and sharing the doctrines of grace. They miss benefiting from the benevolences of the gifts and ministries of the Holy Spirit distributed in the body of Christ. They are most likely not to be ready for the bright day of the return of our Lord. Jesus said that His coming will take us by surprise compared to a thief at night. Abstaining from fellowshipping is the first step to backsliding. To backslide is to underestimate what you were called to do. Occasionally failing to apply the divine wisdom in course of decision making, and resort to worldliness is a process of backtracking. A devoted Christian life does not look backward; you can't go forward and backward at the same time; it must be lived forwards.

"Those who relinquish Christian communion are in a backsliding state and those who backslide are in danger of apostasy" ~ Crint Hughes

John 21:20–21 – "Peter turned and saw the disciple whom Jesus loved following them, the one who also had leaned back against him during the supper — 21 When Peter saw him, he said to Jesus, "Lord, what about this man?" John is called the disciple whom Jesus loved, not because Jesus showed favoritism but because John discovered the love of Christ more than other disciples. We are related to God evenly but our love for Him varies depending on our devotion. We know God by our intimate relationship with Jesus Christ. Spiritual discipline is attained by dedication through devotion. Devotion is not intended just to increase the amount of head knowledge of the scriptures but to enable us to discover the love of Christ availed to all of us equivalently. The enrichment of discovering the love of Christ for you is discovering the love for others in you (1 John 4:20). We are in a covenant relationship that requires our loyalty and submission.

Hosea 4:6 - "My people are destroyed from lack of knowledge." Because you have rejected knowledge, I also reject you as my priests; because you have ignored the law of your God, I also will ignore your children." According to the context, the lack of knowledge is not due to lack of the facts but rejecting the presented facts. Knowledge, in this case, is essential because God will not help you with something you don't know. God communicated to His people His decrees through His prophets. The people communicated with God through the priests. In the new covenant, we are all priests. God made the way for us to be immersed and absorbed in His Word; rejecting the Word means being unfaithful to our vows of the covenant. The Word (Law) became flesh (human) so that we can know God intimately. He is available to whosoever believes. You can't reject something that is not available. The knowledge demanded by God is now accessible to all. You don't have to belong to a particular sect, ethnicity or to get a college degree in order to know God and to know His will. Whosoever is willing to know God can know Him intimately by having the personal relationship with Jesus Christ. The last part of the scripture says that "I also will ignore your children." When you reject knowledge, your children are most likely to follow you in rebellion, and hence they too will be ignored by God. We are supposed to seek knowledge and to

pass it on (impartation) to our children. God requires you to know and to inspire others to know.

Psalm 119:105 - "Your word is a lamp to my feet and a light to my path." Under the old covenant, the Israelites were requires to be righteous by following the written Word (Law) that God gave to them through Moses and the prophets. No-one could say, "Follow me" - not even the greatest prophets like Moses or Elijah or John the Baptist. Jesus was the first person in the Bible to say, "Follow Me" (Mt.4:1; Jn. 21:19; Lk. 9:23). In the old covenant, God's Word alone was the light for their path. Jesus came and initiated a new covenant. The Bible says that "In him was life, and that life was the light of all mankind" (John 1:4). The Son of God was sent in order to reveal his Father's mind to the world. And He gave us not only the Word of God, but His life to manifest and to follow because there is no contradiction between His life and the Word. So in the new covenant, we have both the written Word and also the Word made flesh in Jesus - or in other words, the written word made visible in a human life - to guide us.

The reality of the providence of God is His security to the believers. Jesus at the cross stood as a net to catch every judgment that was supposed to come towards us. In our darkest seasons, nothing has kept us from dispersion but the promises of the Lord. The conscience of a believer is programmed in the Word of God. When you are defined by the clean conscience, you lose your vulnerability. Yes, at times we are vulnerable but our security depends on the conviction of our conscience rather than condemnation. That is when our vulnerability becomes the glue that holds us to our faith rather than a detour. Faith is the glue of our new life. In times of trials, nothing has stood between us and self-destruction but faith in the eternal Word of God.

How do you know that you are saved? It is when your desires have shifted from the things of the world to loving God through obedience to His Word. God's Word is given for instruction and reproof.

"If you want to be a man or woman of God, get in His very presence; and start feeding your spirit. What you feed grows and what you starve dies!" ~ Rose Queener

1 Thessalonians 1:1–7 - "For we know, brothers loved by God, that he has chosen you, 5 because our gospel came to you not only in word, but also in power and in the Holy Spirit and with full conviction. You know what kind of men we proved to be among you for your sake. And you became imitators of us and of the Lord, for you received the word in much affliction, with the joy of the Holy Spirit, so that you became an example to all the believers in Macedonia and in Achaia." Often, you hear preachers saying that "do not do what I do but do what I say." Regardless of the validity of their claim, our actions often rub on our congregations. Paul says in the above scripture that "We not only brought the gospel to you but also ourselves." The excellence of God is when we become a model of the Word for others to follow.

Galatians 5:22-23 – "But the fruit of the Spirit is love, joy, peace, forbearance, kindness, goodness, faithfulness, 23 gentleness and self-control. Against such things there is no law." The fruit is not identical (same) with the tree but it identifies the tree, and the two are not separateable. A fruit does not take the place of a tree but it is part of the tree. Only a mature tree produces a fruit. A fruit is, therefore, the evidence of maturity. Spiritual maturity is measured by your faith and inner peace. It is called the discipline of the Christian living. The transformed heart is the one that has been exposed to the truth and is practicing the Lord's disciplines. Your character is perpetually determined by the renewed minds (2 Corinthians

4:16). There are nine virtues manifested as one fruit of the Spirit. These are not individual "fruits" from which we pick and choose. Rather, the fruit of the Spirit is one ninefold "fruit" that characterizes all who truly walk in the Holy Spirit. The scripture says that "Against such things, there is no law." The Law has no demand on us when we walk in the new nature because the Spirit of Christ in us is as holy as the Word of God (Law).

1 Thessalonians 2:13 - "And we also thank God continually because, when you received the word of God, which you heard from us, you accepted it not as a human word, but as it actually is, the word of God, which is indeed at work in you who believe." The words of men are clothed with the wisdom, eloquence, and oratory of men but without the credit and authority of the apostles. God is the author of the Word; it comes from Him and is ministered by His authority. God takes His truth and plants it in our lives. His grace teaches us to obey. Jesus did not save us so that we go to heaven only, otherwise, He would have taken us out of this world as soon as we are born again. He saved us to live the glorifying life to Him. It pleases God to see us walking in the light of His Son. "For we are God's handiwork, created in Christ Jesus to do good works, which God prepared in advance for us to do" (Ephesians 2:10). Since the fall of man, Jesus is the only one ever to live a sinless perfect life. He lived in perfect dependence on the Father, always obedient to His will. The Bible instructs us to be holy as God is holy (1 Peter 1:16). God makes us holy, and He demands that we stay holy. His grace gives us the ability to do what we couldn't do before we were born again. First and foremost, we must come to know Him as our Lord and Savior, but in addition to that, He is our primary example for godly living. Peter wrote that "For to this you have been called, because Christ also suffered for you, leaving you an example, so that you might follow in his steps." (2 Peter 2:21).

Philippians 4:8 – "Finally, brothers, whatever is true, whatever is honorable, whatever is just, whatever is pure, whatever is lovely, whatever

is commendable, if there is any excellence, if there is anything worthy of praise, think about these things." It is a challenge motivating us to choose to implement only those things which are compatible with morality. These are the things which deserve to occupy a space in your thoughts. In each of us, there are things which draw virtue from us leaving us feeling underserved and unfulfilled. Purge yourself of anyone and anything that is not adding virtue to you. "It is not foolish to give up what you cannot keep to gain what you cannot lose". Search for quality as opposed to quantity. How long you live in this world is not as important as how you live because how you live determines where you are heading.

Romans 5:12 – "Therefore, just as sin entered the world through one man, and death through sin, and in this way death came to all people, because all sinned". The reason why all people (regardless of their races) are sinners is that Adam is the originator of the human race. Adam did not belong to one particular race but all races came from him. Ironically, if Adam belonged to the White race, then only the White people could have been sinners. Likewise, if Adam belonged to the Black race, then only the Black people could have been sinners. The Bible says that "for all have sinned and fall short of the glory of God" (Romans 3:23). The word 'all' is inclusive of all the races we see today (Black, White, and Brown). All are sinners because God created all of the races in one human race of Adam which was corrupted by sin. All need the Savior because all are sinners. Jesus is called the Second Adam because a new race of the redeemed comes from Him. We are in Christ as Eva was in Adam. We are the bride of Christ as Eva was the bride of Adam. We are one human race without barriers. The Bible says that "There is neither Jew nor Gentile, neither slave nor free, nor is there male and female, for you are all one in Christ Jesus." (Galatians 3:28). The cross bridged the gap that separated us from God due to sin. The redeemed human race knows no ranks of superiority because the ground beneath the cross where all of us stand is leveled; nobody stands on a higher ground.

The deception of Satan is effective where there is division. Satan deceived Eva when she was alone without Adam. We are saved individually but we are called to stand together as a unit (Church) against the deception of the world. Satan promised Eva that she will be like God; she ignored the fact that she was created in the likeness of God. Satan twisted the Word of God to deceive Eva. God has given us the abiding place (the unchanging truth) in order to avoid being manipulated by the deception of the ever-changing cultures of the world. Paul said that "Let the message of Christ dwell among you richly as you teach and admonish one another with all wisdom through psalms, hymns, and songs from the Spirit, singing to God with gratitude in your hearts." (Colossians 3:16). Our highest calling is to worship together. Then building each other by the Word, and helping each other to extend the kingdom of God. We are called to put aside our differences and work together as the divine family (Father, Son, and Holy Spirit) work together. There is no division in God. The notion "three persons in one Godhead" does not mean 1+1+1= 3 but 1x1x1=1.

Matthew 12:36 - "But I tell you that everyone will have to give account on the Day of Judgment for every idle (empty) word they have spoken." We live in two worlds: The spirit is the world of faith, and the flesh is the world of deception and corruption. Men's language discovers what country they are of, likewise, what manner of spirit they are of. The heart is the fountain, words are the streams. A troubled fountain and a corrupt spring must send forth muddy and unpleasant streams. God judges every idle word spoken because the words of our mouth are an instrumental power of creating or making things happen on earth. Words honoring to God prosper life. On the contrary, Satan uses the spoken words dishonoring to God to create or cause havoc. Satan has no power to create anything on the earth but he brings evil things into existence by using your mouthpiece.

2 Timothy 2:15 - "Study to shew thyself approved unto God, a workman that needeth not to be ashamed, rightly dividing the word of

truth." The metaphor, "divide rightly," or "handle rightly", means "to cut straight," the Word of truth". It is preserving the true measure of the different portions of the Divine truth. These sacred writings must, in all ages, be the handbook of the Christian teacher. From it he must prove the doctrines he professes; hence, too, he must draw his reproofs for the ignorant and erring. It must be the one source whence he derives those instructions which teach the Christian how to grow in grace. The threat of apostasy is increasingly tremendous and sneaky such that people embrace the false doctrines unaware. For example, Modernism teaches that the truth exists and can be known by the natural minds without the supernatural. Postmodernism teaches that the truth exists but no one can certainly claim to own it. The Emerging Church Movement teaches that the truth must be adjusted to accommodate the people of this generation. All of these beliefs are aimed at changing the message and the method of evangelism by editing the scriptures. Some things should be emphasized than others. It is not a coincidence that Jesus taught most about hell; then next about the angels; then about love in the third place; then money in the fourth place. In today's culture where the reality and the truth are up for grabs, the God-centered theology must emphasize the doctrines which Jesus emphasized within their sequential order.

The dominion of sin ends in Christ. If sin is not killed in Christ, it will kill you. The Christian life is a fight of faith. It is not faith in faith but faith in God. Faith in faith is trusting in self. Ironically, we often trust in self, yet self cannot save self. Eternal life is a free gift from God as a result of the imputed holiness of Jesus Christ. Eternal life is the life of the soul. He, therefore, who neglects the eternal life, casts away the life of the soul. Faith comes by hearing the words of Jesus. But often we neglect to study the Bible, and become preoccupied with investigating other theories that are misleading, hence diverting our minds from the words of Christ to fallacies of human production. The Holy Spirit guides us into all truth;

He brings to our attention the very things we need most and neglect most. He, who refuses to live for God, squanders all he is and all he has.

2 Timothy 4:3 - "For the time will come when people will not put up with sound doctrine. Instead, to suit their own desires, they will gather around them a great number of teachers to say what their itching ears want to hear." This prophecy is timely concerning our generation that is emotionally obsessed with entertaining. When the itch becomes annoying enough, you scratch it. But the people with itching ears are selective. They want a scratch for every itch, and they utterly reject anything into their ears that doesn't itch. They want to hear only what they want regardless of its validity. They are the very people who edit the Scriptures to fit their doctrines. The urge to know the truth is not just a sensational itch but a burning itch at your ears till you relinquish biblical ignorance. The scratching of a burning itch evokes curiosity and affects understanding, sanity, and spiritual growth.

The branches do not fall far from the person pruning them. Also, a fruit does not fall far from the tree. These sayings are in agreement with the law of nature: "You reap what and where you sow". For example, when you are worried, it is because you are trying to depend on your own capability: It is called sowing in the flesh. When you are at peace, it is because you remembered that God is in control: It is called sowing in the Spirit. You cannot rest in peace (here in this life and in the life after) unless you embraced the Prince of Peace. His name is Jesus.

Somebody posted the following message: "God is not interested in obedience and submission. He longs to have an intimate relationship with you." My response: The Law is divided into three groups: 1) Ceremonial laws like sacrifices – we don't need them because they were shadows of which Christ is the substance. 2) Civil laws and diet laws – We don't need them in order to be saved. 3) The Moral Law – Ten Commandments. We need them, not to be justified, but for our sanctification. Remember salvation is given in three stages: Justification by faith in the finished works of Jesus. We are justified by the grace through faith in the finished works of Jesus Christ on the cross. Sanctification is when we join hands with God to clean up our minds of corruption by our obedience. We are sanctified by the Holy Spirit through the Word; Glorification is the future elimination of the corrupt nature and sin from our presence. Salvation is of God but our obedience is the proof that we received it. Jesus said that "If you love me, keep my commands". (John 14:15). Prove that you are saved by obeying. The Ten Commandments (Moral Law) are repeated all over the epistles – like don't worship idols, don't steal, don't commit adultery, and (etc). We know God intimately through Christ and we prove it by submission. The Bible specifically says that "for sin is the transgression of the law" (1 John 3). Paul said "What shall we say, then? Is the law sinful? Certainly not! Nevertheless, I would not have known what sin was had it not been for the law" (Romans 7:7). We are saved by grace alone and we are called to grow in the grace. It is growing into obedience rather than into disobedience to God.

Jesus taught us to love our neighbor as yourself (Matthew 22:39) but many people might wonder just who is a "neighbor". In Luke 10:25-29, Jesus is confronted by an expert in the law: "Teacher," he asked, "what must I do to inherit eternal life?" Jesus asked him what was written in the Law and how did he understand its interpretation. The man being an expert in the Law said: "'Love the Lord your God with all your heart and with all your soul and with all your strength and with all your mind'; and, 'Love your neighbor as yourself.'" Jesus agreed but the man persisted in trying to trick Jesus by asking: "And who is my neighbor?" Jesus gave an answer using a parable, commonly called "The Parable of the Good Samaritan" (Luke 10:30-37). When Jesus spoke of the "Good Samaritan" He was citing an example of a group of people hated most by those in His audience (Jews). According to the message in the story of the Good Samaritan, you can know your neighbor by choosing to be a neighbor

74

to all including the people who hate you. In this case, the neighbor that Jesus talked about is everybody who is around us (family, relative, friend, enemy, stranger and etc.); anybody who lives on our planet who has a need. "Virtue is not left to stand alone. He who practices it will have neighbors".

Romans 12:21 - "Do not be overcome by evil, but overcome evil with good." The trials of life will either lift you up or break you. We cannot avoid the trials of life but how we respond to the trials makes a difference. God instructs us to overcome evil, and He has given to us the abilities to do so: We overcome evil by good. The way of the world is to go up at the expense of others. The way of the kingdom-minded believer is to be the least, living for everybody, serving others because it pleases God.

Romans 6:4 – "We were therefore buried with him through baptism into death in order that, just as Christ was raised from the dead through the glory of the Father, we too may live a new life." Jesus began His earthly ministry by being baptized in water, and He ended His earthly ministry by the baptism of death and resurrection. Jesus was not baptized to become holy because He was already holy. In the same way, we are called to be baptized after we are born again rather than to be born again. Baptism is an external sign symbolic of the internal regeneration that is already in place. Regeneration is a total work of God alone which cannot be added on by any activity of man, including baptism. We are aware that baptism by immersing was an old Jewish tradition for spiritual cleansing in a purification ceremony regarding people in the following category: Women after childbirth or menstruation; a bride before her wedding; priests (in the Temple) before divine service; men on the eve of Yom Kippur (also optionally, before Shabbat); for Gentile converts to Judaism. John the Baptist baptized widely with the baptism of repentance. Of course, Jesus was immersed not in repentance and not in His own death as we do. Therefore, immersing did not begin with the ministry of Jesus. In fact, Jesus never baptized anybody but He ordered us to baptize (Matthew

28:19). Paul used baptism as a metaphor to teach us that when we were immersed it was symbolic of our death and burial with Christ. And when we came out of the water it was symbolic of being raised with Christ. And when we walked out of the water, we followed Jesus Christ's steps out of the water to change the world. The gospel brings death first before it brings life. When we confessed Jesus Christ as our Lord and Savior, we were united with Christ in His death and raised with Him from death.

Matthew 3:11 - "I baptize you with water for repentance. But after me comes one who is more powerful than I, whose sandals I am not worthy to carry. He will baptize you with the Holy Spirit and fire." The baptism of/by/with fire is the central part of Jesus' earthly ministry. Fire is symbolic of the Holy Spirit. The baptism with fire refers to the Holy Spirit's office as an agent of regeneration; also, as the energizer of the believer's service, and the purifier of the heart from within. The Holy Spirit, like fire, can be quenched: "Do not quench the Spirit" (Thessalonians 5:19). It means a believer should not put out the Spirit's fire by suppressing His ministry. The baptism of the Spirit joins every believer to the body of Christ. All believers who experienced a new birth were baptized with the Holy Spirit. The Bible says that: "For we were all baptized by[a] one Spirit so as to form one body—whether Jews or Gentiles, slave or free—and we were all given the one Spirit to drink." (1 Corinthians 12:13). All believers were baptized in the Spirit and are required to be filled with the Holy Spirit.

Romans 2:29 – "But he is a Jew, which is one inwardly; and circumcision is that of the heart, in the spirit, and not in the letter; whose praise is not of men, but of God." Abraham was justified by faith. Faith does not depend upon circumcision, but upon the heart: he that believes not as he should, even if he is circumcised, he is not a Jew; and he that believes as he ought, he indeed is a Jew, even though he is not circumcised. God changed the covenant because the Law does not change. There is a change from physical circumcision to baptism as a symbol of righteousness. Physical

circumcision involves the spilling of the blood of man whereas baptism is symbolic of trusting in the spilled, pure blood of the Lamb of God. God is pleased by our faith. The word 'Jew' has its root from the name Judah which signifies praising. A true Jew must not expect praise from men, who are only taken, with outward things, but from God, who searches and knows the heart.

3 John 1:2 - "Beloved, I wish above all things that you may prosper and be in health, even as your soul prospers". True prosperity involves the total man (spirit, soul, and body). One of Satan's most deceptive and powerful ways of defeating us is to make us focus on the material world. Satan will give you whatever you ask for if it will lead you where he ultimately wants you. On the contrary, God gives us what we need. He wants us to enjoy this life to the maximum, but without focusing on our little selves but on the magnificent Creator of everything we admire. What is true determines what is desirable, not vice versa. Such a perspective puts God in view in all of life, not just in the moments of the trials when things are not easy. To be born again is the life-changer; then a process of living by the spirit by crucifying the old nature (desires of the flesh) daily. It gives you a whole other perspective on why you live. I mean looking beyond yourself for perspective and viewing God as the cause and source of every good thing. "There are two ways to live: you can live as if nothing is a miracle or you can live as if everything is a miracle."

"The Holy Spirit is in me for my sake, but He is upon me for yours" ~ Bill Johnson

"Fear is faith turned upside down. Faith is fear that has said its prayers." ~ Rose Queener

Fear sees what man sees. Faith sees what God sees!

"The first virtue in a soldier is endurance of fatigue; courage is only the second virtue."

2 Timothy 4:7-8 – "I have fought the good fight, I have finished the race, I have kept the faith. From now on the crown of righteousness is laid up for me, which the Lord, the righteous judge, will award to me on that day—and not only to me, but to all who crave His appearing". Paul wrote these words at the end of his ministry. He lost the exotic treasures this world could offer and he discovered the keys to the eternal treasures. Contentment is the discipline of the transformed heart. Paul bragged that "I have kept the faith". Faith discovers and unlocks the treasures of eternal life. Jesus promised to reward those who have lost everything for His name's sake: "— a hundred times in this present age and in the age to come" (Mark 10:29-30). Jesus Himself is the reward to them. He avails Himself to the faithful servants and adorns them to serve more - in this world and the world to come. "The reward for work well done is the opportunity to do more".

Philippians 3:10 - "That I may know him, and the power of his resurrection, and the fellowship of his sufferings, being made conformable unto his death". Paul wrote this epistle to the Christians at Philippi while he was in a prison somewhere (Phil 1:7, 13, 14, 17), indeed in danger of death (Phil 1:20–23). Paul already knew Jesus intimately but he wanted to know the depth of God experientially even in His sufferings. "In the midst of suffering there is nothing worse than the bumper sticker solution to a life-wrecking hardship." Paul introduced the concept of expecting the crisis and afflictions and using them to intensify our bond with Christ. He overcame the depravity of self-pity, self-pride, and self-love. He regarded all of them to be self-delusion. He rejoiced suffering for Christ's namesake

and to follow Him in His afflictions and persecutions in anticipation of receiving the eternal rewards reserved for the faithful ones.

1 Corinthians 2:4-5 – "I came to you in weakness and fear and with much trembling. My message and my preaching were not with persuasive words of wisdom, but with a demonstration of the Spirit's power so that your faith would not rest on men's wisdom, but on God's power—" Although Paul was taught in the strict conformity to the Law by Gamaliel, the most famous scholar of his times, he did not teach Judaism. Paul preached the whole counsel of God. He preached from his point of weakness as opposed to strength, with fear and trembling. He did not bring His theology to the Bible but got his theology from the Bible. He did not expect praises or flatters from his audiences. He did not seek more 'likes' or to add more friends and followers as we do on social media. He had nothing to prove to the world. He decided to know and to preach nothing less than Jesus Christ crucified. To minister is to make yourself available to serve others. This qualifies every person to be a minister. Your feet are your pulpit. The source of authority in the pulpit is neither the human wisdom nor a private revelation granted to us beyond the revelation of Scripture. A credible minister of the gospel must show the people that what he or she is saying was already said or implied in the Bible. If it cannot be shown in the Bible, it has no special authority. And the people don't need it.

Whenever I speak, God speaks. Nevertheless, quite often I am idolized contrary to my will. I am well respected but also the most miserable person on the face of the earth. I have been invited to many homes but at times I end up being ignored. I am open to every person. I have the capabilities and I am willing to help whosoever comes to me. I give generously to all without expecting of returns. I am an inspiration to many, and at the same time, many people are offended by me. They work around the clock to terminate me, most probably because I expose their wrongs. Intriguingly, even the haters don't want to leave me alone. They are ever in my face for wrong reasons. Some openly confess to loving me but practically they denounce me in their actions. They stumble without me, and they come back to me for consultations. Some use me for their selfish interests. I hate it when people put words in my mouth to say what I didn't mean to say. My name is Bible.

Matthew 5:5 - "Blessed are the meek, for they will inherit the earth". The parallel scripture says that "The meek shall possess the land, and delight themselves in abundant prosperity" (Psalms 37:11). In the Greek Old Testament, the words of the Psalmist are almost identical with the words of Jesus. It says, "The meek shall inherit the land." And the word for "land" in Greek and Hebrew also means "earth." But the earth that Jesus is referring to is the one He will rule over when He returns with the saints. The Second Coming of Jesus is divided into two parts: When He returns for the Saints (rapture). The Bible says that "And he will send his angels with a loud trumpet call, and they will gather his elect from the four winds, from one end of the heavens to the other" (Matthew 24:31); And when He returns with the saints (Revelation 20:4; 21:3-5). After Satan, all of his fallen angels, and all of the unsaved humanity have been cast into the Lake of Fire and Brimstone, there will be only one thing left: God will give the saved humanity their final reward – the New Heaven and New Earth. We will receive the final and ultimate end which will be the New Heaven and New Earth – where God the Father Himself will literally be coming down to live with all of us forever and ever.

Who are the meek? Meek people see themselves as servants of God, not thinking more highly of themselves than they ought to think. To be meek is to accept our strengths and limitations for what they truly are, instead of constantly trying to portray ourselves in the best possible light. Meekness is power under control. Power under God's control means two things: (1) refusal to inflate our own self-estimation; and (2) reticence to assert ourselves for ourselves.

"Jesus has no cellphone, but He is my favorite contact. He has no Facebook, but He is my best friend. He has no internet, but we stay connected." ~ Grace Ann

When you squeeze an orange, you should get orange juice...likewise an apple, a lemon, or any other fruit. When you squeeze an orange and take a big gulp and find out you've gotten lemon juice, it's very disturbing... confusing...it just doesn't make sense! That's why the world is confused when they see a Christian being squeezed and something other than Jesus comes out! When a Christian is squeezed, there should be a sweetness that sends up a sweet smelling savor to God and everyone around us. The question is that "What comes forth when you're squeezed, Christians?" (Todd White)

"Faith is not a commodity once attained to own, but a living power kept alive only in its practicing, for faith denied its daily nurturing in grace and truth grows weak and wearied, in the end departing from man as to return to the Giver of its life." ~ Erika Blignaut

A Gallup poll showed that 78 percent of Americans expect to go to heaven when they die. 34 percent of those who call themselves Christians attend church at least once a week. The rest hardly ever pray, read the Bible, or attend church. Heaven is neither a jackpot which a few lucky ones hit nor is it entered by wishful thinking. If heaven means to be with God then heaven begins here on the earth when we are in Christ. If you don't experience God's presence here on the earth, you don't anticipate to experience it even after you leave this world! It would be rude for God to force you to be in His presence forever in heaven when you hated to be in His presence while on earth. If you hate to worship God on the earth, you don't need to go to heaven because heaven is an all times worshipping thing. In the last chapter of Revelation, the two thoughts of being with Christ and of service for Christ are blended. We read of 'those who serve Him, and see His face.' Here the life of contemplation and the life of active service are welded together as being not only compatible but absolutely necessary evidence manifested in the lives of those whose destiny is heaven. Again, you don't have to work your way to heaven because it is by grace alone through faith we are saved. But there must be evidence of eternal life at work in the lives of those who are destined to heaven.

1 John 2:17 – "The world and its desires pass away, but whoever does the will of God lives forever." The world searches for power in money, relationship, politics, and etc. The Church is supposed to drill her power from the incredible kingdom authority. Unfortunately, this objective truth is fading away as materialism and humanism are taking a heavy spiritual toll on some of the children of the kingdom of God. The ambition of many is searching for temporally comfort from this world instead of the lasting peace that God alone can provide. The Bible warns us that everything we crave for in this world is going to fade away compared to the beauty of a sprouting flower that fades away as soon as it is exposed to an extended season of drought. The symptom of the unfulfilled heart is endlessly yearning for a little bit of more favor, more power, more fame and etc. Eventually, such lustful desires become a spiritual grave to rest in.

Did Jesus Christ need to exercise His faith as we do? Jesus, very man and very God, did not need faith because the Father was in Him and He was in the Father. Faith is trusting in somebody's merits other than yours. Jesus said that "Whatever the Father does the Son also does" (John 5:19). Yes, He submitted to the Father and prayed to the Father believing that the Father hears Him (John 11:42). Spiritually, believing is different from faith. Believing involves seeing but faith involves trusting without seeing (Hebrews 11:1). We need faith now because we can't see God with our natural eyes. When we shall go to heaven we shall not need faith because we shall believe in whom we can see. Jesus did not need faith to see His Father. He said that He and the Father are one (John 10:30). Adam, before the fall, did not need faith because he communicated directly with God. Jesus never asked us to have His faith because He never exercised it. He asked us to have faith in Him. He is the object of our faith. Faith is a gift from God that is given to all of us. But our faith must be activated by the Word and must grow into the Word. The Bible says that "So then faith comes by hearing, and hearing by the word of God" (Romans 10:17). Jesus did not need the Word because He is the Word.

2 Timothy 2:14-16 - "Remind the believers of these things, charging them before God to avoid quarreling over words; this is in no way profitable, and leads its listeners to ruin. Make every effort to present yourself approved to God, an unashamed workman who accurately handles the word of truth. But avoid irreverent and empty chatter, which will only lead to more ungodliness". The Scriptures are the main tool handed to us to unify us. Paul instructs us how to avoid quarreling and divisions within the Church. Whenever we wander off the biblical truth, we wander off the path of integrity. The Christian, by a simple choice, can either be controlled by the human psyche or by the Mind of Christ. The Word of God is the mind of Christ. In the sinful world we live in today, it is obvious that our integrity is imperfect unless we embrace the perfect character and integrity found in Jesus Christ. "The biblical virtue of integrity points to a consistency between what is inside and what is outside, between belief and behavior, our words and our ways, our attitudes and our actions, our values and our practice."

Somebody asked "I'm gonna ask this question because I honestly don't know the answer. I am asking in love. Would you please tell me why are there so many people that call themselves Apostles and Prophets/ Prophetess right now in our current age? I'm not talking about the Apostles in the Bible. I'm talking about the people in current churches. Who gives them the titles? Is there a school they attend to get the title? Or is it given to them by God or is it a denomination kind of thing? A cultural thing? And is it biblical? Or is it heresy?" Reply: The subject concerning the spiritual gifts is a deep one requiring deep studying and understanding. In First Epistle to the Corinthians, the apostle Paul addressed the conflicts within the early church of Corinth. One of the problems experienced during Church fellowship was the discipline of the spiritual gifts and the five-fold ministries. In chapter twelve he begins to address this issue and it would take the apostle Paul three chapters to discuss this problem (1 Cor. 12-14). When I was in the Bible College, I was privileged to be tutored by Dr. Lester Sumrall, the man who had such a great revelation on this subject. Dr. Sumrall was a close friend of Howard Carter who was the most respected Charismatic teachers and who helped many people to receive the baptism in the Holy Spirit and to develop various gifts of the Spirit within the body of Christ (Church).

The ministries of the Holy Spirit are different from the gifts of the Holy Spirit. The ministries of the Holy Spirit are individual lifetime (permanent) callings. There are five ministries: "So Christ himself gave the apostles, the prophets, the evangelists, the pastors and teachers" (Ephesians 4:11). All ministries distributed within the congregation are nurtured by the pastor. The word 'pastor' means shepherd. A pastor should, therefore, be a teacher as well in order to feed the sheep. The gifts of the Holy Spirit are called gifts of grace because they are perfect works of Jesus manifested through His body (Church). They are gifts of grace given by Jesus Christ to the Church; they are released to the individual members of the body of Christ to accomplish a given task. There are nine gifts of the Holy Spirit listed: "But the manifestation of the Spirit is given to each one for the profit of all: for to one is given the word of wisdom through the Spirit, to another the word of knowledge through the same Spirit, to another faith by the same Spirit, to another gifts of healings by the same Spirit, to another the working of miracles, to another prophecy, to another discerning of spirits, to another different kinds of tongues, to another the interpretation of tongues. But one and the same Spirit works all these things, distributing to each one individually as He wills." (1 Corinthians 12:7-11). These gifts of the Holy Spirit are not natural gifts or talents.

The Bible tells us that there are 9 gifts of the Holy Spirit (1 Corinthians 12:7-11), as there are 9 fruits of the Holy Spirit (Galatians 5:22). The gifts of the Holy Spirit are accessible to each and every believer that is available to serve. In my book "Growing in the Spirit", I compared it to our uniforms for the church choir. The uniform is available to whosoever is scheduled to minister in the choir, only at the time of ministering. The gifts of the Holy Spirit work through every person that is willing to serve in accordance to the divine will. They are called gifts because they are controlled by the gift-giver (Christ). We can't choose which gift to have and we have no control over them. Again, unlike the ministries, the gifts of the Holy Spirit do not belong to individual members; they belong to the Church. The gifts of the Holy Spirit are perfect works of Christ working directly through the Church (His body) in accordance to the divine will and providence. They manifest in whosoever is available to serve. God gives us the gift we need to work for us at that particular time to meet the need but the gift does not belong to an individual person; it belongs to the body of Christ (Church).

When I just started my Spanish ministry, I prayed for a young Asian girl who had a hearing problem from birth. Some people started calling me into the divine healing ministry. I told them that it was not a ministry of healing but a gift of healing. It was not about me or my calling; God could have used anybody who was available to be used. Just because I prayed for this little girl, it doesn't mean that I can pray for everybody that needs healing and they get healed. This was a gift given for that particular time, and I have no control over it; Jesus heals whosoever He wills. When I am teaching, quite often, God uses me to speak prophetic words. It does not mean that I am a prophet; it is a gift. Whereas it is true that there are people who are specifically called in the ministries of prophets or prophets, most people who call themselves prophets or prophetess are most probably the people who operated in one of the spiritual gifts (prophecy, word of knowledge, and word of wisdom). But this does not mean that they were called into the lifetime ministry of prophets or prophetess. Hopefully, this brief explanation will help.

Somebody asked: "Is a prophet biblically allowed to lead a church? Why is it that there churches led by prophets in Uganda and they are working and performing miracles?" Reply: A prophet's calling in the Old Testament was to speak to the people on behalf of God. They prepared the people for the coming Messiah. In the New Testament, a prophet is called to proclaim the truth and point to the right direction for the church to follow. A prophet normally does not own a church but travels to different places proclaiming the same message. The most effective way of serving is to do what God called you to do. Given the fact, it is possible to be called in more than one ministry. A prophet can be called to be a pastor as well. Paul had multiple ministries. Chiefly, he was an apostle, but he was also a prophet, an evangelist, a pastor, and a teacher. Paul was an apostle in the sense of being directly commissioned by the ascended Lord Jesus Christ as referenced in 1 Corinthians 12:28, Ephesians 2:20, and Ephesians 4:11. But in Acts 13:1-2 Paul is called a "prophet" and a "teacher." He was a prophet in that he spoke on behalf of the God of the Bible. In 1 Corinthians 13:2, he claimed to prophesy. He claimed to be one of the "prophets" and one of the "teachers" as referenced in Ephesians 4:11. He was one of the "prophets" mentioned in 1 Corinthians 12:28 and Ephesians 2:20. In 1 Timothy 2:7, Paul calls himself, "a preacher" (evangelist), "an apostle," and "a teacher of the Gentiles." Jesus had all of the five-fold ministries.

Somebody asked, "Is being slain by the spirit and falling down under the power of God a sign of being filled with the Holy Spirit?" Reply: Terms such as "slain in the Spirit" and "falling under the power" are not found in the Bible. We are not aware of any Scriptures that specifically describe this experience which occurs in some church services, where believers are prayed for and in the process fall to the floor and remain unconscious for a time. However, falling down is biblical except that today it has been dramatized and dogmatized. The best example of falling down in the Bible is at the dedication of the temple when the glory of God came down, the Bible says that "So that the priests could not stand to minister by reason of the cloud: for the glory of the LORD had filled the house of God." (2 Chronicles 5:14). Also, when they came to arrest Jesus, the Bible says that "When Jesus said, "I am he," they drew back and fell to the ground (John 18:6). In this case, they went backward and fell to the ground. Paul on his way to Damascus met Jesus and he was struck on the ground. In all of these cases, the reason for falling down was because the flesh cannot glory in the presence of God. It is the fragile and weak man standing before the overwhelming presence of God. For example in the case of arresting Jesus, His disciples did not fall down because they belonged to the glory; only the intruders (soldiers) fall down because they did not belong. The people who fall down are not the ones who are filled with the Holy Spirit but the ones who are empty and are in need of the filling of the Holy Spirit. In my book, I compared it to a herd of cows or goats whereby there are multiple mothering cows having various little calves. A mother cow does not error breastfeeding a calf that does not belong to her. Whenever a calf goes to a wrong mother to breastfeed, he is kicked away because he does not belong. Those who belong to God are not kicked down. Again, God works mysteriously; it is not appropriate to limit Him. Also, we should not put God in the box saying this is the only way He works. We should not use our personal experience and encounter with God and use it as a dogma to interpret the Scriptures. Paul's conversion was a personal experience and encounter with God, and he never instructed us to have the same experience in order to be converted.

I have watched with concern many activities like pushing people down, blowing people, stepping on people, throwing up in buckets at the altar, and etc, all done to people in the name of being filled with the Holy Spirit. Remember that the Holy Spirit was given for two main reasons: to sanctify us and others. Every manifestation of the works of the Holy Spirit is intended to edify us and to draw the lost souls to Christ. Whenever we manipulate or impostor the works of the Holy Spirit, we end up pushing people away instead of drawing them to Christ. The world watches and people say "I don't want to be part of this phony drama."

February 2<u>nd</u> my birthday: I want to thank all of you who took time from your schedule to wish me a happy birthday. Your thoughtful compliments were not just an afterthought or cliché but an affectionate communication of insight. Thanks for being exclusively generous. You seasoned the day with warm passions intrinsically woven into it. Birthdays are not about attracting attention and blowing candles; they remind us of the incredible gift of life. "The more you praise and celebrate your life, the more there is in life to celebrate." The beauty of celebrating life is that we impact the lives of others. From this once little baby now there exists a chain of other individuals: children, and children's children, brothers, sisters, relatives, in-laws, friends, and mutual friends. Ironically, we are all one clan of humanity. God created us way back before we entered our parents' wombs. The Bible says that "Before I formed you in the womb I knew you, before you were born I set you apart." (Jeremiah 1:5). It means that when God created Adam, he created you and me. We came from one man (Adam) then we were recreated (new creatures) into one body of Christ. After regeneration, we are called to live the beauty of the gospel together. It means to be a mentor to others and to be mentored by others. This is a push in the right direction. Thanks for being part of my life.

Thanks for the massive birthday wishes. I was overwhelmed by your generosity. If wishes were fishes I would be throwing nets. Keep up the spirit of treating all people, regardless of their status with respect, modeling generosity, and showing up with outright love. Humanity without generosity is not a virtue. Generosity is the trademark of the saints. "Generosity is giving more than you can, and pride is taking less than you need."

MARCH FOR APOLOGETIC

The Bible is inspired, inerrant, infallible, and true, and that it is a sure guide to follow for our faith and our lives. In order to believe the Bible, you must believe in the first verse of the Bible: "In the beginning God—" (Genesis 1:1). The Bible begins with God because it is the story about God. The eternal God existed before time and space. The invisible God created all that is visible and invisible. He is the King that created the physical world for His domain. Man was created for God's pleasure and for His glory (Genesis 1:26-28). That was true for Adam and Eve, and it is true for all mankind throughout the centuries. After what He created was corrupted by sin due to the rebellion of man, God initiated His plan B to save His creation. God is omniscient. He knew that Adam would sin, but such fore-knowing should not be translated as being causative. Adam was not vulnerable as long as he obeyed God. It was not necessary for Adam and Eve to disobey God. They chose to do so. God knew that man will sin before He created mankind, and He resolved from eternity, before He created mankind, to solve the problem of evil in order to avert the ceasing of mankind and nature. So, from Genesis three to Revelation, it is a story of God resolving the problem of sin.

Somebody asked that "Science says that this world is much older than what the Bible predicts. Why should we take the story of creation literally?" First, I want to warn against the duplicitousness of secularism and its influence on many elites while interpreting the scriptures. The Bible does not tell us everything about the universe but it is specific regarding the creation, fall, and redemption of man. The message of salvation is inescapable because it is repeated over and over. I decided to be agnostic regarding certain things which do not matter. In this case, the age of the universe has no spiritual significance to me. What matters is that wherever you place the commencement of the world, the self-existence God who created the universe was there to create it. He preceded time, space and matter. The Bible begins with these words: "In the beginning God". As I said, you must believe this first verse of the Bible in order to believe in the whole Bible.

According to the survey, just in the last five years, it is estimated that the ranks of those who claim no religion have grown from about 15% of U.S. adults to just under 20%. There are now more than 13 million self-identified atheists and agnostics, as well as nearly 33 million more who claim no particular religion. Many of them denounce the infallibility of Scriptures or would say the Bible is a fairy tale! Certainly, the truth is absolute, and it does not depend on one's beliefs but on God. The Christian faith is different from the world religions: It is a relationship with God because of what He has done for us through the sacrifice of Jesus Christ. There is no other plan on earth for man to reach God (He has reached out to us—Romans 5:8). There is no pride (all is received by grace—Ephesians 2:8-9).

Somebody posted this message: "Serious question... on the veracity/credibility of the Bible being the word of God and the so-called truth. It is a well know fact of historical evidence that the Authorship and dating of many of the books in the Bible are in serious dispute". Thanks. Reply: The sovereign God who is able to preserve this huge universe in space is able to preserve His Word from pollution using natural men. Look at Israel. God has been able to preserve the Israelites for centuries. No culture has survived for centuries. Israel is the very embodiment of Jewish continuity: It is the only nation on earth that inhabits the same land, bears the same name, speaks the same language, and worships the same God as it did 3,000 years ago. I believe that God anointed men to write the scriptures and to canonize them. The Bible has been 100 percent accurate historically and prophetically. Many religious books claim to be divinely inspired, but only the Bible has evidence of supernatural confirmation. Jesus, being God incarnate, affirms the inspiration of the Bible. Another evidence of supernatural confirmation is the testimony of prophecy. The biblical authors made hundreds of specific prophecies of future events that have come to pass in the manner they were predicted. No book in history can compare to the Bible when it comes to the fulfillment of prophecy. The Bible is not a mixture of tales and fictions; it is historically accurate. Archaeology has helped us to reconstruct the history behind the Bible, both on the level of great kings and kingdoms and in the modes of everyday life. The story of the scriptures fit into the extraordinary history of the people of Israel. Of course, there are going to be skeptics, in the same manner, a big chunk of youth today dispute the story of man walking on the moon, which happened recently in our generation. The Bible is full of unlocked treasures that are applicable to all generations.

Somebody responded to the above posting regarding the credibility of the scriptures: "In Both of these verses one from Luke & one from Mathew, there is a serious error of the father of Joseph...one scripture states it is Jacob the other states it is Heli. Which of these is the truth?" Reply: That is not an error. It is two people reporting the same incidence from a different perspective. One explanation, held by the church historian Eusebius, is that Matthew is tracing the primary, or biological, lineage while Luke is taking into account an occurrence of "levirate marriage. If a man died without having any sons, it was a tradition for the man's brother to marry the widow and have a son who would carry on the deceased man's name. According to Eusebius's theory, Melchi (Luke 3:24) and Matthan (Matthew 1:15) were married at different times to the same woman (tradition names her Estha). This would make Heli (Luke 3:23) and Jacob (Matthew 1:15) half-brothers. Heli then died without a son, and so his (half-) brother Jacob married Heil's widow, who gave birth to Joseph. This would make Joseph the "son of Heli" legally and the "son of Jacob" biologically. Thus, Matthew and Luke are both recording the same genealogy (Joseph's), but Luke follows the legal lineage while Matthew follows the biological.

Somebody said "I don't believe the Bible can be infallible because men have had their hands on it and have translated it according to their worldviews. We have 105 versions of the Bible all translating it according to their worldview. How can it be infallible? Infallible means without error." Reply: The multiple translations are due to the various interpretations of the original languages. The Bible was actually written in three different ancient languages: Hebrew, Aramaic, and Greek. At times the original languages have different words to translate one English word. For example, in English we have one word for different kinds of love but the Greek language (unlike English) has different words for different kinds of love. The translators at times come up with different translations depending on the choice of words they decide to use. That does not mean there is an error in the original manuscripts. God inspired fallible men to write down His infallible Scriptures. There are more than 24,000 partial and complete manuscript copies of the New Testament. These manuscript copies are very ancient and they are available for inspection now. There are also some 86,000 quotations from the early church fathers and several thousand Lectionaries (church-service books containing Scripture quotations used in the early centuries of Christianity). Bottom line: the Bible has an overwhelming amount of evidence supporting its reliability.

Somebody asked that "Why don't the protestant accept the Apocryphal books of the Bible?" Reply: The word Apocryphal means hidden. Seven books of the Bible, all in the Old Testament, are accepted by Roman Catholics and Eastern Orthodox but are not accepted by the Jews or Protestants. These include 1 and 2 Maccabees, Judith, Tobit, Baruch, Sirach, and Wisdom, and additions to the books of Esther and Daniel. These books are called Deuterocanonical by Catholics and Orthodox and Apocryphal by Jews and Protestants. In 1546, the Council of Trent reaffirmed the traditional list of the Catholic Church. These were the last books of the Old Testament written, composed in the last two centuries B.C. Luther said that these books were profitable for historical purposes but they were not inspired. I agree with Luther mainly because these books were written during the 400 years period (between Malachi and the New Testament), which is referred to as the time when God was silent.

Somebody posted that "Since we have the New Testament, the Old Testament is not relevant to us." Reply: There is one Bible consisting of both the Old/New Testaments. Both testaments are equally the Word of God. Except that, the old should be interpreted in the light of the four Gospels. Jesus quoted the Old Testament 78 times, the Pentateuch (first five books of the Law) alone 26 times. The apostles quoted 209 times from the Old Testament and considered it "the oracles of God." If Jesus and the apostles saw the need to read the Old Testament, why not me?

Somebody said that "Historians claim that the Old Testament King Solomon's story has been changed with time. For example, some books indicate that King Solomon was an Egyptian Pharaoh." Reply: As usual, Critics use fallible resources to justify their rebellion and to challenge the truth. I have been to Jerusalem and saw the tomb of David the father of Solomon. Solomon succeeded David and the throne of David is in Jerusalem as opposed to Egypt. In fact, Jerusalem is popularly called the city of David. Josephus clearly identifies the queen who visited Solomon as "the woman who ruled Egypt and Ethiopia," and tells us that her name was Nikaulis. The Bible does not mention her name but calls her the Queen of Sheba (I Kg. 10; II Chr. 9). The queen of Sheba did not visit Solomon in Egypt, the same territory, where she ruled! Read the Bible instead of other sources. If you search for the wrong answers in wrong places for the purpose of criticizing, you will get them! And you will always be biased and it will be impossible to provide a definitive scholarly view of history and faith.

"Archeology findings: Recent discoveries shed light on the life and time of what I called "least-understood yet incredibly-important person in the Bible," Mary Magdalene. As I said back in April, "more people [mistakenly] 'know' that she was a prostitute—which is based on a misreading of Luke, chapters 7 and 8—than the fact that she was the first witness to the Lord's resurrection." An excavation of her home town, Magdala, just five miles from Capernaum, discovered the remains of a synagogue, and even more exciting, a first-century Roman coin bearing the image of Tiberius. As the head of the dig told the New York Times, there was "circumstantial evidence" that Jesus had been at the site. What's more, the evidence shows Magdala to have been a prosperous town, which is in keeping with Luke who tells us that Mary was among the women who "provided for Jesus and His disciples 'out of their resources.'"

Archaeology discovery of the remains of the town of Bethsaida is proof that Christianity is a true story of faith. The Bible is the best-tested book of antiquity.

If you don't believe that the Bible is the infallible Word of God there is no standard from which we can determine the truth. It means that the truth depends on a person as they view it to be right. Which is wrong because without the absolute truth there can be no God with the absolute standard to judge.

As Christians, we affirm the correspondence theory of truth. In other words, truth is that which conforms to reality. In the face of postmodern relativism, we must emphatically resist any suggestion that ultimate, objective truths do not exist. Though we may not accurately perceive or understand the real world at times, the same does not apply to the Almighty. Truth stands, no matter where, when, how, or by whom it is expressed, and it is expressed, everywhere. John wrote: "This is the disciple who testifies of these things and wrote these things. And we know that his testimony is true. And there are also many things, whatever Jesus did, which, if they should be written singly, I suppose the world itself could not contain the books that would be written. Amen" (John 21:24-25).

A Muslim scholar posted that "God made this life as a test, whereby those who perform better are going to pass to enter eternity". My reply: Sin is like poison; a little bit of it is as dangerous as much of it. God demand pure holiness like Him. Such holiness cannot be attained by natural means unless it is granted by God. The grace imputes the holiness of Jesus to us in exchange for our unrighteousness for which Jesus died. God does not receive any soul dented by sin. The only soul that goes to God is the regenerated soul, recreated in God's original image in Jesus Christ.

What about the people who die in the jungles without getting a chance to hear the gospel? All of us deserved to perish. God did not have to save anybody in this universe. When He saves one person, we say it is amazing grace. The native Indian or African who died before getting the Bible will get the justice of God. The Bible says that the wages of sin is death; God cannot be unjust. If God did not send the Savior and decided to destroy the whole universe, God would have been still holy for being just. Remember that at the time of Noah, He saved just the family of Noah. At Sodom, He saved just the family of Rot. Thank God for His grace that put our guilt and condemnation on Christ to save us.

Somebody posted "I heard Minister Louis Farrakhan's anointed message "That My Redeemer Liveth. My Jesus is Alive." Reply: He is a wolf in sheep's skin! It is a reputation of the cults to preach 90% of truth as given by the Scriptures, and then use the 10% to make a sharp curve taking you directly into the gates of hell!

Global warming is a delicate issue that demands scientific evidence rather than speculations. The problem is that the notion of climate change has been politicized. The Liberals use it as an opportunity to launch their globalization agenda. On the conservatives' side, some discredit any efforts to control the climate saying that God alone created the climate, and He alone can preserve it. Whereas I agree that this universe is under the divine surveillance, also I believe that as custodians of the earth, we have the mandate to keep it safe. Most probably in the same way we have to go to the hospitals even when we know that it is appointed for every person to die. The issue of Global warming is a sensitive matter, and it should not be politicized at all. We should trust science to handle it but not at the expense of morality. Science should not only be compatible with spirituality; it should be a profound source of spirituality because science is the beauty of the wisdom given to us by God. Science cannot dictate morality; morality should be the basis of science. Scientists too should cherish the notion of the God who has created everything for their benefit. A good scientist is the one who has learned to believe in justification, by faith, and verification of evidence presented to give the facts as opposed to hoaxes.

"The atheism to worry about is in the departments of religion and not in the areas of science and in the most highly regarded schools."

Did you know that the word "Jesus" occurs 983 times in 942 verses and only in the New Testament? Did you know that the word 'Gentile' is not used in any of the ancient manuscripts, simply because there was no such word in the Hebrew or Greek languages? The word 'Gentile' as used in our modern Bible versions, including the "much, loved" King James Version, in the Old Testament, always comes from the Hebrew word "goy," (singular) and "goyim", (plural). It is translated five different ways in the Old Testament, according to Strong's Exhaustive Concordance of the Bible; "goy or goyim (singular or plural)", a foreign NATION hence GENTILE; (2) HEATHEN; (3) NATION, and (4) PEOPLE, or ANOTHER." Notice that the Hebrew word "goy, or goyim," is NEVER translated to mean "non-Jew." The word "goy" is found in the Old Testament some 557 times. Thirty times it has been translated GENTILE; eleven times as people; 142 times as heathen; 373 times as NATION, and one time as ANOTHER. But not once as "non-Jew." The concept of all nations comes first in the first chapter of the book of Genesis: "God blessed them; and God said to them, "Be fruitful and multiply, and fill the earth..." (Genesis 1:28a). Also, "Abram fell on his face, and God talked with him, saying, 4 "As for Me, behold, My covenant is with you, And you will be the father of a multitude of nations. 5 "No longer shall your name be called Abram, But your name shall be Abraham; For I will make you the father of a multitude of nations" (Genesis 17:4-5).

Somebody asked that, "What is the core belief known as the Apostle creed?" Reply: There is nothing wrong when you read the Apostle creed to understand instead of as a ritual. Ritualism is equally religiosity as ignoring it fanatically. Remember that the people of the early church who read it were stronger believers than many of us who are emotionally excited.

Somebody posted: "I have been studying the teaching that there is one God revealed in three persons but my minds can't simply understand it. Doesn't the Bible say in Deut 6:4 that God is one?" My reply: God is too big to be studied and comprehended. The God that fits in one's brain is an idol. God wants us to trust Him by believing in His Word even when we don't fully understand it as opposed to being indoctrinated. It is not by accident that almost all of the heresies in the history of the Church are centered on the nature of Christ. Some claim that He is man and not God. Others say He is God but not man. Some deny Him to have the Father whereas He came to glorify the Father. He said that "I am not seeking glory for myself; but there is one who seeks it, and he is the judge" (John 8:50). You can't say that you love me much and at the same time you denounce my father!

Somebody asked "There is one God. Where do you get the Father, Son, and Holy Ghost?" My reply: In Genesis, God introduced Himself by the name of Elohim. Elohim means the supreme unique spiritual being. Biblical usage suggests that Elohim reflects a "plural of honor" or "plural of fullness": "And God said, 'Let Us make man in Our image, after Our likeness; and let them have dominion over the fish of the sea, over the fowl of the air, and over the cattle, over all the earth and over every creeping thing that creeps on the earth'" Genesis (1:26). Also "The LORD God said, 'Behold, the man has become like one of US, to know good and evil. And now, lest he put out his hand and take also of the tree of life, and eat, and live forever'" Genesis 3:22 (NKJ). Jesus used a plural pronoun concerning God: "Jesus replied, "Anyone who loves me will obey my teaching. My Father will love them, and We will come to them and make our home with them" (John 14:23). There are three persons of one Godhead. There are two Hebrew words for one: Yachid always means one and ONE ALONE (not a unified one). *Echad* which is a compound unity of one as opposed to *YACHID*, which always means one and ONE ALONE (not a unified one). "Hear, O Israel: The Lord our God, the Lord is one" (Deuteronomy 6:4.) The Holy Spirit chose to use the Hebrew word, "echad" which is used most often as a unified one or a compound unity. *Yachid* is only used to refer to a strict numerical oneness, whereas *Echad* has a wider range of usage that includes composite unities as well. For example *Echad* is used in this scripture: "That is why a man leaves his father and mother and is united to his wife, and they become one flesh (Genesis 2:24). A husband and wife are two individual people becoming one. In the same way, the church is one but made up of multiple individuals. We are one body of Christ. Jesus is coming for one bride called the church. One, in this case, is a compound noun involving more than one element. Most probably in the same way you say a basket of fruits. It is the same word for "one" that was used in Deut 6:4. Use your concordance and check this fact.

Somebody posted: "For unto us a child is born, unto us a son is given: and the government shall be upon his shoulder: and his name shall be called Wonderful, Counselor, The mighty God, The everlasting Father, The Prince of Peace (Isaiah 9:6)" There cannot be two persons all called THE Everlasting Father. There cannot be more than one person called THE Mighty God." My reply: Do you read the Bible blindly? Throughout the four Gospels, the Son is talking to the Father. The Father and the Son are two persons of the same nature and character. The Bible says that God is ever seated on His throne. There is no time when the throne of God was left empty. So when Jesus came to save us the Father was still seated on His throne. Jesus plainly said to the Jews that He was sent by the Father: "Jesus said to them, "If God were your Father, you would love me, for I have come here from God. I have not come on my own; God sent me" (John 8:42). The Father has a will and the Son has the will: "For I have come down from heaven not to do my will but to do the will of him who sent me (John 6:38). Also, "Father, if you are willing, take this cup from me; yet not my will, but yours be done" (Luke 22:42). It implicates two wills: one of the Son and the other of the Father. Jesus became emotionally nervous about the cross and asked the Father if possible to take it away but he submitted, not to His own will, but to the will of the Father. Furthermore, notice that the wills were in opposition. If the oneness you propagate means that Jesus as a man (Jesus' flesh) was at odds with His own presence as the Father in heaven, then again we have no true incarnation. Jesus surrendered His Spirit into the hands of the Father: "Father, into your hands I commit my spirit. When he had said this, he breathed his last." (Luke 23:46). After the resurrection, Jesus said that He is returning to the Father: "Do not hold on to me, for I have not yet ascended to the Father. Go instead to my brothers and tell them, 'I am ascending to my Father and your Father, to my God and your God.'" (John 20:17).

Somebody posted in response to the above teaching that "When Jesus said that not my will but your will be done, He was referring to His will as a man and His will as God; He is the Father that put on human flesh to be man." Reply: All entities (divine/human) have an individual will. The will is central to humanity. The will is what motivates us to make choices. We have to surrender our will to God in order for His will to be done in us. I have deliberately used the word surrender which is a battle term because we are in a spiritual warfare. It implies giving up all rights to the conqueror and living at the mercy of the conqueror. God has a plan for our lives, and surrendering to Him means we set aside our own plans and eagerly seek His. When we surrender our will to God, we surrender the totality of our selves; God wants the whole, not a part. Jesus was truly God and truly man. Through the Incarnation of Christ, the two natures were inseparably united in such a way that there was no mixture or loss of their separate identity and without loss or transfer of any property or attribute of one nature to the other. The union thus consummated is a personal or hypostatic union in that Christ is one person, not two, and is everlasting in keeping with the everlasting character of both the human and divine natures.

Luke 4:18 - "The Spirit of the Lord is on me, because he has anointed me to proclaim good news to the poor. He has sent me to proclaim freedom for the prisoners and recovery of sight for the blind, to set the oppressed free". Peter preached when emphasizing the trinity: "How God anointed Jesus of Nazareth with the Holy Spirit and power, and how he went around doing good and healing all who were under the power of the devil, because God was with him"(Acts 10:38). Jesus was anointed by the Holy Spirit in preparation for His pending ministry on the earth. Although Jesus was divine, He could only be anointed because He was a

genuine human being, with all of the limitations that such an existence entails. Jesus was both fully God and fully man. In the incarnation, these two natures came together in a union which demands that we speak of Christ as one person. He is one Christ as opposed to two (Christ the divine and Christ the man). We cannot split up His two natures and say that as God He did this, and as man, He did that. Everything that Jesus did, He did so as God manifest in the flesh. He slept as God manifest in the flesh. He healed as God manifest in the flesh. When considering Jesus' ministry, then, we must take into account the genuineness of His humanity. Jesus ministered as God, or limited the exercise of His divine prerogatives in order to live within the limitations of every human being and to demonstrate to us how to live a victorious life in the Spirit. Jesus even confessed to the Jews that He was casting out devils by the Spirit of God, not because He was the Spirit of God, even though He was indeed the Spirit of God made flesh (Matthew 12:28). The Father and the Spirit did not die on the cross but Jesus did. The Father planned our salvation; the Son died for our salvation; the Holy Spirit brought salvation to us.

Somebody posted "In the book of Revelation 3:21, Jesus calls the throne of God His throne; He says "On my throne", implying that He is God the Father". My Reply: Stephen saw Jesus sitting at the right hand of the Father: "But Stephen, full of the Holy Spirit, looked up to heaven and saw the glory of God, and Jesus standing at the right hand of God" (Acts 7:55). According to this scripture, there are three persons of the Godhead: The Holy Spirit is dwelling in Stephen, whereas Jesus is standing on the right hand of the Father. Jesus prayed that "And now, Father, glorify me at your side with the glory I had with you before the world was created." (John 17:5). The Bible says that: "Therefore God exalted him to the highest place and gave him the name that is above every name, that at the name of Jesus every knee should bow, in heaven and on earth and under the earth" (Philippians 2:9). In the book of Revelation, Jesus is seen exalted on the throne of God with the Father, and He invites us to rule with Him: "To the one who is victorious, I will give the right to sit with me on my throne, just as I was victorious and sat down with my Father on his throne." (Revelation 3:21).

Somebody posted the following sarcastic statement concerning the Christian God: "I like his condoning sex by also having Mary pregnant". Reply: The Muslims are the perpetrators of that concoction that Christians teach that God had sex with Mary to have a son. It is extreme ignorance of the scriptures. God cannot have sex as we do because God is Spirit, without human organs as we do. The Bible says that the conception of Mary was a result of a divine act of the Holy Spirit. It was a virgin birth without any sexual encounter involved; that is why Jesus is called the begotten Son of God. Jesus' life did not begin in Mary. He pre-existed as the second person of the Godhead. He is called the Son of God because He is of the same nature (spirit) as God. He is of the same character with God (holy). He is in perfect obedience to the first person of the Godhead (Father). In the same way when we are regenerated (born again or born of God) we are called children of God. Not because God had sex with some women out there in order to have us as His children but because we have acquired the new nature of God; we have acquired the character of Christ; by faith, we are in perfect obedience to God.

Why are there many religions? Answer: I can't answer for various religions. Religion is man's way of getting to God. The fact that there are multiple religions is the reality that there is an empty space in man demanding to be filled by the God who created mankind. Man was created to depend on God, and he is restless until he rests in God. Religions portray the emptiness in man; man in search of the divine in their own ways. I think everyone is religious in their own ways even though some people do not admit to giving allegiance to one particular religion. Even atheism is a pagan religion. It takes more faith to be an atheist than a theist. The word God simply means creator. Only a fool can say that things happened the way they are by accident. You can't get something out of nothing; no matter how long you wait, nothing will ever spontaneously become something. By looking at the beauty of nature, you can tell that there is an intelligent designer called the Creator. It is also foolish to believe that somebody created this magnificent universe and decided to stay anonymous. The problem with skeptics is a logical spin on the idea that something that "exists" beyond time and space logically doesn't exist as we as humans define the word existence. Within in the minds of the skeptics, everything that we have knowledge of actually existing can only exist within time and space, therefore God cannot exist in a manner comprehensible to humans if he's beyond time and space. It would be incomprehensible for humans to make positive claims about existences beyond time and space. We believe in the self-existence God who created the universe. The existence of many contradictory religions is a proof of one true way to God. Fake things are made after the genuine. For example, the fake money in circulation is made after the legal currency. You do not reject all money just because there are fake dollars bills in circulation. You just take precaution to avoid the fake ones. The same applies to religions.

Somebody asked that "Didn't Jesus teach against religion?" Jesus was against the traditions of men that were in contradiction to the written scriptures. Every person is religious one way or the other. Meanings of religion: the belief in and worship of a superhuman controlling power, especially a personal God or gods: a particular system of faith and worship; a pursuit or interest to which someone ascribes supreme importance.

He that perverts truth shall soon be incapable of knowing the true from the false. If you persist in wearing glasses that distort, everything will be distorted to you ~ C.H. Spurgeon

Somebody asked "My Sunday school teacher said that Adam had babies in the Garden. What do you say?" Reply: Adam and Eva were

expelled from the Garden immediately after they rebelled in order to purge the evil from the Garden. God created a perfect man with a mandate and a purpose to exercise dominion over all creation and in order to preserve the image of God. Adam and his wife were given the mandate to rule over the earth. They were to reproduce, to "be fruitful and multiply, and fill the earth with God's image (glory)." God's image in man begins at conception. God gave Adam a woman to procreate and fulfill the mandate to multiply and fill the earth. At every point of legitimate need, God created what was needed. Before Adam's fall, the human instincts, behaviors, and decisions were pure because Adam depended on God to know what is good. God instructed everything to produce after its kind: Incorruption produces incorruption. If Adam had a baby before the fall, there would have been an incorrupt human lineage or race somewhere on the face of the earth prior to the coming of Christ, and there would have been no need for God to send His Son to begin a new perfect lineage. God could have expelled Adam and Eva from the Garden purposely to protect a perfect lineage in the Garden. But there is no such a thing as a perfect person outside Jesus Christ. Jesus is called the Second Adam (1 Corinthians 15:45) because the perfect lineage of the redeemed is patterned after Him. He, therefore, who rejects to be recreated (regenerated) loses his soul and casts away his eternal life in the presence of God.

Somebody asked that "If the story of Adam and Eve is true, then how did Adam and Eve populate the planet? How did the children of Adam of Eve produce the rest of mankind? And how did Noah and his small family repopulate the planet? Lots of incest of course!" Reply: Although Noah's family was already a spider-web of close family marriages: the five generations of parents that preceded both Noah and his wife Emzara all descend from just three individuals. It is true Adam's children intermarried but it does not imply that incest is ok. After Adam lost his innocence and was expelled from Eden, he lost God's guidance and did that which was right in his own eyes as his conscience guided and directed him. Mankind became increasingly evil because his conscience was maimed by sin. It caused God to condemn the earth at the time of the Flood which washed all of the living things, except the house of Noah with the flood waters in bid to purge wickedness and evil from the face of the earth. God chose the Israelites, and placed them under the precise discipline of the Law, to show mankind how He expected them to live. The Law's function in relation to Israel was one of disciplinary restriction and correction to hold Israel in check for their own good until Christ should come. The law against incest was not instituted until the time of Moses. It is important to distinguish between incestuous relationships prior to God commanding against them (Leviticus 18:6-18) and incest that occurred after God's commands had been revealed. Until God commanded not to do, it was not incest. Doctors say that inbreeding causes countless genetic problems in families, which get worse per occurrence and leave detectable dents in the genetic makeup of species. The early generations were not affected by it because they lived much longer than we do. Their genetic makeup was not as corrupted as ours. Adam dies, aged 930; Enoch was taken up by God (did not die [Gen5:24]), aged 365; Seth dies, aged 912; Lamech (Noah's father) dies, aged 777; Noah dies at the age of 950; Methuselah dies the same year as the flood comes, aged 969; Enosh dies, aged 905; Kenan dies, aged 910; Mahalaleel dies, aged 895; Jared dies, aged 962 and etc. We no longer live that long because of God's judgment against the human race: Then the LORD said, "My Spirit will not contend with humans forever, for they are mortal; their days will be a hundred and twenty years" (Genesis 6:3). The human genetic code has become so polluted that close intermarriage is no longer safe.

Somebody asked that "Why does God allow the evil people to thrive?" Answer: Evil is the by-product of sin. Evil does not come from outside to us. Evil is already within us. The effect of sin is spiritual blindness. Every human being is born with the corrupt nature because we are all born after Adam. Through Adam, Satan infected the entire human race with the sinful nature. Therefore, every person has evil intents within their hearts. We are vulnerable to satanic attacks because we have the corrupt nature, and we dwell in the corrupt world governed by the corrupt system. Without the transformation of the heart, we have no option but to cope with the internal and external darkness. In the old covenant, the mercy of God restrained evil by the Law. In the new covenant, the grace of God substituted evil with good but we have the responsibility to crucify (kill) the old nature daily in order to suppress evil. Jesus presents to us His grace whenever the gospel is preached. The true gospel either convicts or hardens the heart. God set a day (Judgment Day) to finally get rid of Satan and evil from the face of the universe. Satan will no long influence things on the earth because his system on earth will be destroyed. Judgment Day will thus be the accomplishment of God's purpose to undo all the effects of the original rebellion against God in the Garden of Eden.

Somebody asked, "If Jesus judged Satan on the cross why is Satan still active and powerful?" Jesus said, "In regard to righteousness, because I am going to the Father and you will no longer see Me; and about judgment, because the prince of this world now stands condemned". (John 16:11). The reality of the judgment of the cross is that the saved souls are no longer under the eternal judgment or damnation which was pronounced over Adam. At Calvary, the redeemed were given the power to denounce their loyalty to the prince of this world. Now, everyone can come to the true king, Jesus Christ—revealed to all as the life-giving One—that they may have life. Those who voluntarily choose to abide under the dominion of the prince of this world (Satan) are judged in his judgment. "And the devil, who deceived them, was thrown into the lake of burning sulfur, where the beast and the false prophet had been thrown. They will be tormented day and night for ever and ever" (Revelation 20:7-15). This is to be understood of the judiciary power and authority of Christ, who has "all judgment" committed to Him by the Father, as Mediator; has all power in heaven and in earth; and as He is appointed, so He is a very fit person to judge the world at the last day. The cross is the standard of the future judgment; that it will be universal, reach to all persons and things; that it will be carried on in the most righteous manner, and there will be no escaping it.

Somebody asked that "Do little children go to hell?" Reply: The Bible says "Everyone who practices sin also practices lawlessness; and sin is lawlessness." (1John 3:4). The Children are not guilty of the individual sins mentioned in 1 John 3:4 because they haven't reached the age of accountability. But there is no human being (include little babies) that is innocent or sinless. David said "Surely I was sinful at birth, sinful from the time my mother conceived me" (Psalm 51:5). The Bible says that "For all have sinned, and come short of the glory of God" (Roman 3:23). Also, "As it is written, There is none righteous, no, not one" (Romans 3:10). The word "All" is inclusive of all human beings including babies. Remember that when God judged the world with the floods all people including babies perished except the house of Noah. When God judged Sodom and Gomorrah, all people including babies were killed except Lot and his house. The Bible says that "For the unbelieving husband is sanctified by the wife, and the unbelieving wife is sanctified by the husband: else were your children unclean; but now are they holy" (1 Corinthians 7:14). It means that the parents' righteousness can rub on the children.

Somebody asked that "Will I see my pet that was put to sleep when I go to heaven?" Pre-Millennialism uses Isaiah 11:6-9 to teach that Christ will return and set up a Golden Age on earth for a thousand years where even normally carnivorous animals will become vegetarian. However, I am sure that the animals we have here on earth do not go to heaven when they die. The reason is that death is not the means of going to heaven. Not everything and person that die go to heaven. The Bible specifically says that the corrupt nature (flesh and blood) cannot see the kingdom of heaven: "I declare to you, brothers and sisters, that flesh and blood cannot inherit the kingdom of God, nor does the perishable inherit the imperishable (1 Corinthians 15:50). The corruptible must be changed to incorruptible in order to inherit the kingdom of heaven. The Bible says that "The creation itself will be set free from its bondage to decay and brought into the glorious freedom of the children of God" (Romans 8:21-22). The salvation of man involves regeneration, in the present time, this being the new nature of Christ in us which is spiritual. Our salvation is completed in glorification when we shall be fully restored (inside/outside) into the likeness of Christ. Heaven begins here on the earth. Even if there might be animals in heaven, they won't be the resurrected animals which died on the earth. Therefore, give to your pets all the love and attention while they are still alive because once they die, you will never see them again.

Today, somebody posted that "Science confirms that dogs and cats can see spirits which humans can't see." Reply: The word science means "knowledge." Scientific knowledge applies to the realm of empirical investigation, material knowledge, also, formal truth. In this regard, we must consider mathematics as a genuine science because math in its formal dimension yields to real knowledge. Scientific research must be proven by practical experiments. It is astonishing to see how frequently people engaged in material scientific research glibly pass over the philosophical presuppositions of their own work. Science, like mathematics is about logic. Does logic really count in our attempt to understand reality? Again, if we're going to assume coherency and cosmos, logic has to count not just for something but for everything. There are certain truths that can be known through special revelation that are not discerned from the investigation of the natural world, while at the same time there are certain truths learned from the study of nature that are not found, for example, in the Bible. The bottom line is that science cannot investigate something that does not exist; for science to be possible, there must be a coherent reality that we are seeking to know. Much more is the fact that scientific answers must be based on evidence from practical experiments as opposed to presumptions.

What disturbs me is that most of the animal's right activists or advocates I know are pro-abortion! They care about animals but not about the lives of human beings destroyed in the wombs.

Somebody asked "Is there a scripture against tattoos?" Answer: "Ye shall not make any cuttings in your flesh for the dead, nor print any marks upon you: I am the LORD." (Leviticus 19:28).

Somebody posted: "Yoga is good. Yoga is about concentrating on your minds and keeping your body in shape." Reply: Yoga is not just physical but it is spiritual in nature. They teach that meditation is necessary for spiritual success and illumination. According to their doctrine, meditation is the key which will unlock the door of the supreme abode of Immortal Bliss. The natural tendency of the mind is to go forward and outward. In meditation, it turns backward and inward. He who practices uninterrupted meditation becomes absolutely fearless. The way to unlock the door of intuition is by meditation. According to their teaching, man is at the center of everything; they claim that they can reach the highest form of existence by meditation. They claim that meditation is a spiritual experience that opens us to the highest state of consciousness and inner bliss. Therefore there is no need for either a savior or the scriptures. They say that when you pray or meditate you shut thy doors. It is the door of the senses. During meditation, you are never left without an unseen guide and teacher. He will help you. It is stepping into your enlightened nature that is free from all suffering. Otherwise, you will wander restlessly from forest to forest while the Reality is within your own dwelling. They say that the truth is here! Until you have found God in your own Soul, the whole world will seem meaningless to you. I want to say that all of the above teachings are not biblical meditations. Yoga makes you focus on "self" whereas the biblical meditation involves the Word of God. Denying yourself rather than focusing on yourself is the principal discipline of the Christian faith. Yoga is basically the common heritage of Dharmic religions, Hinduism, Buddhism, and Jainism. All developments within Yoga have come from these traditions. Historically speaking, Hinduism is the religion where Yoga first originates. The earliest Yogic practices go back to the Vedic people, who called their practice "tapasya"; this involved penance and worshiping practices where they imagined the gods, summoned them and yoked with them.

Somebody asked that "Is the Holy Spirit a She or a He?" Answer: God the Father is masculine. God the Son is masculine. The Holy Spirit is neutral. The She is in the He. God created Eva in Adam. Adam defines mankind.

Somebody asked that, "If all of my sins were forgiven can I lose my salvation?" True, when you get saved all of your sins (past, present, and future) are forgiven. It is the responsibility of the Father to protect you from Satan. Jesus said that "My Father, who has given them to me, is greater than all; no one can snatch them out of my Father's hand" (John 10:29). Your hand is firmly in His hand, and Satan cannot snatch you from His grip. However, you must walk within the boundaries of His protection. God respects your free will before and after you are born again. He can, but He will not force you to love Him. You are safe and secure as long as you maintain the perfect communication with Him. If you decide by your actions to walk away, He can, but most probably He will not stop you from walking away. Jesus said that "Many will say to Me on that day, 'Lord, Lord, did we not prophesy in Your name, and in Your name drive out demons and perform many miracles?' Then I will tell them plainly, 'I never knew you; depart from Me, you workers of lawlessness.'" (Matthew 7:22-23). The culprits were believers who were anointed to cast out demons. Elsewhere, Jesus said to His disciples that: "See, I have given you authority to tread on snakes and scorpions, and over all the power of the enemy. Nothing will harm you. However, do not rejoice that the spirits submit to you, but rejoice that your names are written in heaven." (Luke 10:20). The gifts of the Holy Spirit working in the Church are works of Christ (grace) directly manifested through His body (Church). But He demands our own works of obedience. The Bible warns that "For if we sin willfully after that we have received the knowledge of the truth, there remaineth no more sacrifice for sins," (Hebrews 10:26). Also, "'So because you are lukewarm, and neither hot nor cold, I will spit you out of My mouth." (Revelation 3:16).

Somebody asked that "When somebody commits suicide do they go to heaven?" Reply: People end their lives after deciding that it is better to die than to live a hopeless life. But the hopeless life does not end upon death but it intensifies endlessly. Not to ignore the fact that the victims of suicide pass on even more pain to their beloved ones when they die unexpectedly of unnatural causes. Choosing the pass of suicide in order to end your pain is not the end of the journey of your life. The reality is that the soul lingers on after the demise of the body. It is an illusion to think that when someone commits suicide they will find relief in death. People don't generally commit suicide with a clear, logically-discerning mind. It's hasty. A truly born again person in his or her right minds will not commit suicide. If you are in your right minds and you are contemplating on committing suicide, you need to be born again; otherwise, you will end up in hell. However, if somebody was truly born again, and they commit suicide due to mental or psychological disorder, they go to heaven because all of their past, present, and future sins were forgiven. Suicide is not the unforgivable sin. But it is not an option for a believer in their right minds.

I was listening to a talk show involving an interview of a prominent liberal politician. He was asked if a fetus is mere tissues or a human being. He eloquently answered that it depends on a woman to determine what it is. The impact of free speech is apparent. We have sunk so low into relativism such that there's no longer absolute. We have a situation whereby reality does not depend on merits but rather on one's desires. Last year, the news that dominated the media was about a white teenager who said that she believes she is black in spite of her white skin and blonde hair. We have a situation whereby a person's gender depends on a person's desire. Decades ago things like homosexuality were unthinkable. A person is progressively growing until death. A fetus is a human being in the process of growth to maturity regardless of one's view; the validity of its humanity does not depend on a person's opinion. It is unfortunate that today's culture drinks iniquity like water! Yet, critics of the above immoralities are considered to be on the wrong side of history. The truth is that Jesus is coming soon. If you are not in Him, you are on the wrong side of history. He gave us the free will to love Him or to hate Him. Hell is a place for a person that willfully rejects Jesus.

Musajja Wa Kabaka replied to the above posting in this way: "As long as the fetus cannot survive outside of the woman's body, and is, therefore, dependent on the goodwill of the woman, then its logical that a woman has the choice as to whether she wishes to carry the fetus to full term or not, this must be a personal decision, not a societal one. Morals are not sacrosanct or written in stone by higher mysterious order, they are a human construct and they will defer between societies, it's a slippery slope to use morality as a basis for Law." My Reply: The issue of life is a moral issue rather than a social issue because God is the source of life. We were created by God for a purpose. No one has the right to end the life. You said that a fetus has no right because it is a dependant on the goodwill of a woman. Note that every person is a dependant. There is no life that is autonomous. The fetus has its own blood that is separated from the blood of the mother. That is why a mother that is HIV positive can give birth to HIV negative baby. Life begins in the blood. You said that morals are not sacrosanct or written in stone by higher mysterious order. If you were right it would mean that there is no moral standard for morality. Man could do as he wills. Then we would have contradictory moral values and hence no morals! The truth is that our morality is designed after the supreme entity of the higher moral values, to whom all humanity is accountable; violating His morality is what we call sin.

Isaiah 3:9 – "The look on their faces testifies against them; they parade their sin like Sodom; they do not hide it. Woe to them! They have brought disaster upon themselves." God is against calling evil good and proudly infecting the society with evil. Those who participate in evil and those who applaud them are equally guilty of assisting evil to flourish. The gay parades involving half-naked people that are taking place in various cities including Jerusalem is an example. Men fell into an utter shamelessness without fear or shame and boast of it! They have lost the substance of virtue. Again, if you're not in the parade, it is wrong to give moral support to those who participate, like watch the parade passionately. "Men of integrity, by their very existence, rekindle the belief that as a people we can live above the level of moral squalor. We need that belief; a cynical community is a corrupt community".

Somebody asked that, "Why don't we see angels today as the people of the Old Testament did?" It is true that the angels don't appear as often as they did in the Old Testament. However, the angels still appear to some people depending on the divine will. I happen to be one of the few lucky ones. The angels are spirit beings (Hebrews 1:14) without true physical bodies. Although they do not have the physical bodies, they are still personalities. The angels are everywhere but unless they reveal themselves they are not visible to the natural eyes. The angels are created beings and super intelligent but nowhere does the Bible states that the angels were created in the image and likeness of God, as humans are (Genesis 1:26). The word angel simply means messenger. In the Old Testament, God used the angels and the prophets as messengers to reveal God's message to the people. In the New Testament, Jesus equips the saints as messengers. The Bible says that, "God, who at various times and in various ways spoke in time past to the fathers by the prophets, has in these last days spoken to us by His Son, whom He has appointed heir of all things, through whom also He made the worlds" (Hebrews 1:1-2). Jesus is the finality of the revelation of God. The person of Jesus Christ is the prophet par excellence, even greater than Moses and Elijah (Deut. 18:18-19; John 8:28; 12:49-50). Everything that God wanted us to know is revealed in Jesus Christ. It is from this perspective Paul wrote that "But even if we or an angel from heaven should preach a gospel other than the one we preached to you, let them be under God's curse!" (Galatians 1:8).

Somebody asked "We know that the sun does not move around the earth causing day and night but rather the earth revolves around the sun. Why did Joshua address the sun rather than the earth? Did he believe the sun actually moved?" Reply: It is scientifically not possible to stop the sun which is not moving. The language that Joshua uses in addressing the sun and the moon is the language of ordinary observation still used today in the scientific age. His language should not be pressed to construct a "view of the universe" any more than should today's reference to the rising and setting of the sun. The writer of the story, who happens to be Joshua himself, is interested in the miracle of God suspending the night till victory was acquired. God did not reveal to Joshua how the miracle happened but He answered Joshua's prayer that the sun did not set. The term "the sun stood still", therefore is in reference to the fact that the night did not overtake day.

Somebody asked, "Mr. Kyeyune you've said 'the moral God"? The morality of God is questioned as in the Old Testament the moral God condoned 'superior people' to enslave 'weaker ones'. I don't think that's morality. The same God practiced favoritism of one race (Israelites) among the others. One of the myriads of reasons why people in the Middle East fight till today. The moral God is spoken of to have changed his gruesome character in the New Testament?" Reply: Except for the grace, God is not obligated to deal mercifully with a fallen man. First, we must admit that there is nothing like an innocent person that is born after Adam. We say it every day that nobody is perfect, yet we ignore the consequences of not being perfect. The graphic images we see in the Old Testament, like the destroying of the world by the floods, the destroying of Sodom, the killings of the Canaanites and much more the slaughtering of the Son of

God; all project the ugliness of sin. The graphic images justify the reality that Sin is offensive to the Moral God. The morality of God is projected by His holiness. If it was not for the grace God, man would have been removed from the face of the earth because of his sin. Yet mankind has been preserved, awaiting the salvation promised long ago in the Garden of Eden, when God said to the serpent, I will put enmity between you and the woman, and between your seed and her seed; He shall bruise you on the head, And you shall bruise him on the heel" (Genesis 3:15). Satan successfully brought a curse upon Adam and Eve and all of their offspring. Nevertheless, God promised that from the seed of the woman would come One who would bring about man's deliverance and Satan's destruction. That "seed" was our Lord Jesus Christ. His death on Calvary defeated Satan and fully accomplished the salvation of all who would believe in the Savior. Satan was eager to destroy the promised seed of the woman. All the way from Adam, God protected the lineage from which the Savior was going to come. God ordered the Canaanites to be eliminated tactically in order to prevent their immorality from infecting Israel. It was the process of purging sin from the world by the Holy God. God is justified to destroy all of the corrupted souls infected with sin from the face of the earth. When killing is used to suppress evil it becomes moral. God does not practice favoritism. When He chose Israel over all nations, it was for the benefit of the entire human race. God blessed Israel so that Israel can be a blessing to the entire human race by bringing forth the deliverer from the tribe of Judah and the house of David. The Jewish Messiah came to save the entire human race from obliteration.

Somebody called the killings of the Canaanites by the Israelites in the Old Testament genocide. Reply: Ironically, those who were ordered to kill and those who were killed none of them is living today. Because according to God's judgment it is appointed for every man to die. It doesn't matter when you die. What matters is to embrace God's grace which provides immunity to death. It is acquiring a new nature that is not subject to death through Jesus Christ. As by the offense of one, sin and death prevailed to the condemnation of all men, so by the righteousness of one, grace prevailed to the justification of all related to Christ by faith (Romans 5:19).

Somebody asked "But I have to ask the question to my FB friends..... Why did all those millions (not even all Jews) have to suffer so? Some say it was necessary to get the Jewish Nation to be born, to get the Jews to come back home. I am still praying and trying to understand the evil that happened and reconciling it to the good of Israel being born. Any thoughts? Reply: God is in control of the world but we are in charge of this world and everything that goes on in this world. We have stewardship of everything. We naturally suffer from the consequences of our decisions and other people's decisions. All bad things are influenced by the devil. The Bible clearly teaches that God does not cause us to suffer. The Bible teaches that ultimately "the ruler of this world," Satan the Devil, is responsible for human suffering, for "the whole world is lying in the power of the wicked one" (John 12:31, 1 John 5:19). It is Satan—not God—who causes people to suffer. The Bible says that "I form the light, and create darkness: I make peace, and create evil: I the LORD do all these things" (Isaiah 45:7). The word evil, in this case, is not in reference to a vice but it is in reference to the disasters that come to us as consequences of our sins due to the judgment of God. God gives men up and leaves them to suffer the consequences of their willful apostasy; suffer temporal afflictions and distresses resulting from their disobedience; suffer everlasting punishment in the pit of hell. God is the Author of all that is true, holy, and good but misery and sufferings do not come into the world without His permission. So the answer is that God did not plan the death of millions of the Israelites but He stepped in to save a few in order to prevent the extermination of the nation of Israel.

Somebody posted this: "It is not God who placed the Israelites back to Palestine, but the British, who screwed up the Arabs in order to create puppet states they could steal resources from." Reply: God alone is responsible for Israel. God chose the Jews as custodians of the Word and to produce the deliverer. No wonder the eyes of all people all over the world are focused on this tiny nation! The Jews did not choose God but God chose the Jews. History projects that most times the Jews resisted the God who chose them. He chose them not for their own sake but for the whole world's sake. This tradition of rejecting God assumes that chosenness is not an essential characteristic of the Jewish people, but rather a result of the covenantal relationship. Exodus 19:5 captures this view: "Now then, if you will obey Me faithfully and keep My covenant, you shall be My treasured possession among all the peoples." Of course, they failed to keep the covenant, and God retaliated by establishing a new covenant with the entire human race of which He is responsible for keeping.

Somebody posted "The Bible treats ladies like second class citizens." Reply: The Bible respects and honors ladies more than any other religion. There are five women included in the genealogy of Jesus. The first woman named is Tamar who fathered Perez and Zerah by Judah (1:3). Her story is told in Genesis 38. Tamar was the widowed daughter-in-law of Judah who disguised herself as a prostitute in order to trick Judah into impregnating her and giving her a son who would tie her to her dead husband's family. Often, Tamar is described as a prostitute and thus a blot on the family record. The next woman mentioned is Rahab, the wife of Salmon, who is also identified as a prostitute and a Gentile living in Jericho. Her story is found in Joshua 2 and 6. She gave hospitality to the Jewish spies who came to Jericho and hid them from the king of Jericho when he wanted to kill them. Her confession of faith is found in Joshua 2:11, "the Lord your God is God in heaven above and on the earth below." Ruth, a widow, and a Moabite became the daughter-in-law of Rahab. Ruth's story is a beautiful one of loyalty. She is one of the few women in the Bible who have a whole book named after her. Another woman mentioned in Jesus' genealogy is only referred to as "Uriah's wife" (Matthew 1:6), emphasizing the fact that Bathsheba became King David's wife only after committing adultery with David, who then arranged for her husband to be killed in battle to cover up their shame (2 Samuel 11-12). The fifth and final woman listed in Matthew's genealogy is Jesus' mother, Mary. She is depicted as a young woman (perhaps about 14), a virgin, who was engaged to Joseph. As indicated, all of them (apart from Ruth), had no good reputation but they are in Jesus' family tree.

The resurrection of Jesus is central to the Christian faith. Remember that the first person to see the resurrected Jesus and to be sent to preach the gospel of the resurrected Jesus was a woman. Mary Magdalene was a prominent disciple of Jesus who followed him in Galilee and to Jerusalem. She was the very first person to be commissioned to take the good news. Jesus gave Mary Magdalene both commissions, to share her testimony and to give out His word. Jesus sent her in spite of the Jewish culture that did approve and respect the testimonies of women. In fact, this is one of the reasons proving that the story of the resurrection was not made up. Nobody would make up a story and chooses to use an incredible witness!

Somebody asked "I see ladies in churches dressed in miniskirts. Why doesn't your Christianity respect the bodies of the women as Muslims do? Reply: In the Arabic nations, women are treated like subhuman and as commercial commodities. In the Islamic Republic of Iran, it is illegal to execute a woman if she is a virgin. So the government arranges "wedding" ceremonies to be conducted the night before executions, and prisoners are forced to have sexual intercourse with a guard. Raped by her new "husband," a female prisoner is now fit to be put to death. "Female prisoners who are virgins must be raped before execution to prevent them from entering heaven" ~ Ayatollay Khomenie

Mohamed, the founder of Islam instructed his followers to treat ladies like crap. Here are some of the quotations of the laws in the Muslim Quran (holy book) which allow men to oppress and abuse of women: Husbands may hit their wives even if the husbands merely fear highhandedness in their wives (quite apart from whether they actually are highhanded). The Quran in Sura 4:34 says: 4:34… If you fear highhandedness from your wives, remind them [of the teaching of God], then ignore them when you go to bed, then hit them. If they obey you, you have no right to act against them. God is most high and great. (Haleem, emphasis added). The hadith says that Muslim women in the time of Muhammad were suffering from domestic violence in the context of confusing marriage laws: This hadith shows Muhammad hitting his girl—bride, Aisha (see rule no. 1, below), daughter of Abu Bakr, his right—hand Companion: 'He [Muhammad] struck me [Aisha] on the chest which caused me pain.' (Muslim no. 2127). See this article for fuller details on wife—beating. It clarifies many translations of the verse. At the end, it has many links to modern interpretations of Sura 4:34 and to arguments for wife—beating today. This article is a shorter version. This article, though long, offers a clear analysis of wife—beating, examining the hadith and other early source documents, as well as refuting modern Muslim polemics.

A husband may simply get rid of one of his undesirable wives. The Quran in Sura 4:129 says: It is not within your power to be perfectly equitable in your treatment with all your wives, even if you wish to be so; therefore, [in order to satisfy the dictates of Divine Law] do not lean towards one wife so as to leave the other in a state of suspense. (Maududi, vol. 1, p. 381)

A woman's testimony counts half of a man's testimony. The Quran in Sura 2:282 says: And let two men from among you bear witness to all such documents [contracts of loans without interest]. But if two men be not available, there should be one man and two women to bear witness so that if one of the women forgets (anything), the other may remind her. (Maududi, vol. 1, p. 205). The Quran in Sura 4:11 says: The share of the male shall be twice that of a female.... (Maududi, vol. 1, p. 311)

A man may be polygamous with up to four wives. The Quran in Sura 4:3 says: And if you be apprehensive that you will not be able to do justice to the orphans, you may marry two or three or four women whom you choose. But if you apprehend that you might not be able to do justice to them, then marry only one wife, or marry those who have fallen in your possession. (Maududi, vol. 1, p. 305)

Slave—girls are sexual property for their male owners. The Quran in Sura 4:24 says: And forbidden to you are wedded wives of other people except those who have fallen in your hands [as prisoners of war]... (Maududi, vol. 1, p. 319). The hadith demonstrate that Muslims jihadists actually have sex with the captured women, whether or not they are married. In the following hadith passage, Khumus is one—fifth of the spoils of war. This article quotes the Quran and many hadith passages on sex with prisoners of war. It also analyzes modern Islamic scholars on the topic. They support this practice. In Appendix One, the author answers a Muslim charge that the Old Testament allows this practice. This article provides further details on Muhammad's encouragement to his soldiers to 'just do it.' In addition to the two previous links, more information can be found here and here. The clause 'marry those who have fallen in your possession' means slave—girls who were captured after a war. Men may 'marry' them because slaves do not incur very much expense, not as much as free women do. This means that the limit on four wives is artificial. Men could have sex with as many slave—girls as they wanted.

A husband has sex with his wife, as a plow goes into a field. The Quran in Sura (Chapter) 2:223 says: Your women are your fields, so go into your fields whichever way you like…. (MAS Abdel Haleem, The Qur'an, Oxford UP, 2004).

Muhammad's special marriage privileges: Moreover, it seems that Allah gave Muhammad special permission to marry as many women as he desired or take them as slaves or concubines, just as in the pre—Islamic days of ignorance. The Quran in Sura 33:50, a lengthy verse, grants Muhammad wide latitude in his marriages: O Prophet, We have made lawful to you those of your wives, whose dowers you have paid, and those women who come into your possession out of the slave—girls granted by Allah, and the daughters of your paternal uncles and aunts, and of your maternal uncles and aunts, who have migrated with you, and the believing woman who gives herself to the Prophet, if the Prophet may desire her. This privilege is for you only, not for the other believers…. (Maududi vol. 4, p. 111, emphasis added).

This verse says that besides those women whose dowry Muhammad paid, he may marry slave—girls—that is, he may have sex with them (see this article and this one for more information on this Quran—inspired immorality). Maududi references three slave—girls taken during raids, and Mary the Copt, a gift from an Egyptian ruler. Muhammad had sex with her, and there does not seem to be a political need for this. Second, Muhammad may marry his first cousins, and Maududi cites a case in which this happened. Third, if a believing woman offers herself to Muhammad, and he desires her, then he may marry her (Maududi vol. 4, note 88).

This hadith shows that Muhammad was intimate with his slave—girls. But the capstone of these 'special' marriages occurs when Muhammad also marries the ex—wife (Zainab) of his adopted son (Zaid). His son—in—law divorced her with the Prophet standing in the background. In fact, early Islamic sources say that Muhammad catches a glimpse of his daughter—in—law in a state of undress, so he desired her. Once the divorce is final, Allah conveniently reveals to him that this marriage between father—in—law and daughter—in—law is legal and moral in Sura 33:36—44.

This hadith says that Muhammad used to visit nine (or eleven) wives in one night. See the parallel hadith here, here, and here. This article explains why Christians do not accept polygamy. This page in an online index explains polygamy. For a more thorough analysis of polygamy in the Quran, go to this online booklet and click on Chapter 12. See this article on the number of wives and human sexual property Muhammad allowed himself.

Here is yet another article. At the end, it links to more articles on the marriage and divorce of Zainab and Muhammad. A husband may simply get rid of one of his undesirable wives. The Quran in Sura 4:129 says: It is not within your power to be perfectly equitable in your treatment with all your wives, even if you wish to be so; therefore, [in order to satisfy the dictates of Divine Law] do not lean towards one wife so as to leave the other in a state of suspense. (Maududi, vol. 1, p. 381)

Maududi provides an interpretation of the verse (vol. 1, pp. 383—84, note 161). He writes: Allah made it clear that the husband cannot literally keep equality between two or more wives because they themselves cannot be equal in all respects. It is too much to demand from a husband that he should mete out equal treatment to a beautiful wife and to an ugly wife, to a young wife and to an old wife, to a healthy wife and to an invalid wife, and to a good natured wife and to an ill—natured wife. These and like things naturally make a husband more inclined towards one wife than towards the other. This means that wives are the source of a man's inability to treat all of them equally. One is beautiful, while another is ugly. How can Allah demand from a husband super—human strength under changing circumstances in his wives?

Muhammad was betrothed to Aisha when she was six, and he consummated their union when she was only nine. The hadith says: [T]hen he [Muhammad] wrote the marriage (wedding) contract with Aishah when she was a girl of six years of age, and he consumed [sic, consummated] that marriage when she was nine years old. (Bukhari ; since this is a serious issue, see the parallel hadith here, here, here, here, here, here, here, and here). This hadith demonstrates that Muhammad pursued Aisha when she was a little girl. The Prophet asked Abu Bakr for 'Aisha's hand in marriage. Abu Bakr said 'But I am your brother.' The Prophet said, 'You are my brother in Allah's religion and His Book, but she (Aisha) is lawful for me to marry.' (Bukhari; see this hadith that shows Muhammad's dream life in regards to his pursuit of little Aisha, and this one and this one). This hadith recounts the fifty—plus—year—old Muhammad's and the nine—year—old Aisha's first sexual encounter. She was playing on her swing set with her girlfriends when she got the call.

This hadith describes Muhammad's and Aisha's ill—timed sexual encounters: Narrated 'Aisha: The Prophet and I used to take a bath from a single pot while we were Junub. During the menses, he used to order me to put on an Izar (dress worn below the waist) and used to fondle me. While in Itikaf, he used to bring his head near me and I would wash it while I used to be in my periods (menses). (Bukhari)

APRIL – OVERCOMING TEMPTATION

Satan is styled the "accuser of the brethren" (Revelation 12:10). Also, as the one seeking to uphold his influence among men by bringing false charges against Christians, with the view of weakening their influence and injuring the cause with which they are identified (Job 1:6; Zachariah 3:1). He was regarded by the Jews as the accuser of men before God, laying to their charge the violations of the law of which they were guilty, and demanding their punishment. The same Greek word, rendered "accuser," is found in John 8:10 (but omitted in the Revised Version); Acts 23:30, 35, 24:8, 25:18, in all of which places it is used of one who brings a charge against another. The New Testament calls Satan the devil (diabolos), meaning slander, adversary or enemy. This word is rendered "accuser" in the King James Version and "slanderer" in the Revised Version (British and American) and the American Standard Revised Version (2 Timothy 3:3 Titus 2:3). According to the rabbinic teaching Satan, or the devil, was regarded as hostile to God. His desire is to dethrone God by imposing himself as god over the people; by claiming the loyalty of the masses to him.

Every demand that God put on us after the fall of Adam was delivered to us in one package of salvation through Jesus Christ. The life of Jesus during His earthly ministry is a demonstration to us of a life fully lead by the Spirit of God. Jesus was baptized, tempted, meditated on the scriptures, prayed, died on the cross and was raised for our sake. Faith connects a sinner to the finished works of Jesus Christ. I am going to elaborate on His temptation. Jesus allowed Satan to tempt Him in order that by His temptations He might conquer our temptations, just as by

His death He overcame our death. The purpose of Jesus' temptations is understood as designed to enable fully his priestly role of intercession for those in temptation whom He represents before God. An anthropocentric understanding of the purpose of Jesus' temptations makes our devotion easier. "The temptations of the devil assail those principally who are sanctified, for he desires, above all, to overcome the holy."

Ephesians 5:26 - "Just as Christ loved the church and gave Himself up for her to make her holy, cleansing her by the washing with water through the word". Jesus gave up His life to save us. We are His bride bought by His blood. In the Gospel "blood" stands for Jesus' self-sacrifice in death (6:51-58), without which there is no eternal life. The blood of Jesus is the ever-flowing fountain of grace that never dries up. His blood cleanses your sins to the justification, once for all, the moment you receive Jesus Christ as your Lord and Savior. Your objective is then not to sin but in case you fall in sin (after you are saved), you don't have to go back to Jesus and ask for the cleansing of the blood (justification); you have to go to Him to repent. Sincere repentance involves washing in the Word to detect and rationalize what caused you to fall into sin until you see as God sees. The Word in all its searching is the humbling, rebuking, correcting, informing, stimulating, refreshing, consoling power.

We cannot stand still and firm in godliness without falling unless the Lord sustains us. If we had the ability to overcome our weaknesses on our own, we could have overcome those very weaknesses long before we came to Christ. Amen, not our own strength but to His saving grace.

1 John 4:4 - "You, dear children, are from God and have overcome them, because the one who is in you is greater than the one who is in the world." The one in you is the omnipotent God. He is the Son of God and God the Son. In Him, we are directly connected to Yahweh, who is

the source of life and creator of all things. "Have overcome" means it has already happened, although we are still in a spiritual battle. We are still running a race but at the same time, we see ourselves at the finish line. The hindrances in between are to our advantage. We look beyond the present tribulations of this world and focus on our blessed hope (rapture). There is certainty of our future in spite of the current uncertainty. We are fighting from victory to victory. The scripture calls us dear children of the Father. Elsewhere, Jesus taught us to pray to our Father to deliver us from the evil one (Matthew 6:13). The children of God are no longer under the dominion of the evil one because they were delivered from the second death. However, in course of living, sometimes we make bad decisions with dire consequences. God is willing to guide us into making good decisions, honoring to Him, if we sincerely confess to Him that "Not my will but Your will be done." This is how we denounce the lustful desire of the flesh and the world. Just as God is in the believers and they are in God, so the world is in the evil one (1 John 5:19) and the evil one is in it. "The one who is in you is greater than the one who is in the world" therefore means "if the Lord had not been in us"; which render it thus, "If it had not been the Lord who was on our side" we would have been as vulnerable as the unbelievers. Without Christ, the world and its inhabitants is a dead equation!

Romans 6:18 - "You have been set free from sin and have become slaves to righteousness." The gospel presents to us the best offensive advantage to switch from a bad master to a good master. The status of a true believer is not autonomous. A believer was liberated from the spiritual death but not from 'self'. We are being liberated from 'self' daily by surrendering our ego. When you are transformed, you are no longer the center of your own universe. You relinquish that position to your Lord. To receive the spiritual freedom you have to relinquish your freedom of will. Anything you cannot relinquish possesses and controls you, and in this materialistic age, a great many of us are possessed by our possessions. Freedom from sin does not mean freedom from a sinful nature. We have a sinful nature, but a sinful nature does not have us. We are free from the influence of the sinful nature, free from condemnation, free from the guilt of sin and

the desire to sin. The grace deals with our sins when we repent. Without repentance, there is no remission of sins. Faith connects us to the holiness of Christ. Faith, in its most correct form, never removes responsibility. It eradicates the negative fear and instills the fear of God in the transformed heart making us responsible creatures who are consistently yearning to live righteously. A believer keeps an eye on the mortal while focusing on the immortality.

Satisfaction with Divine Providence is having faith that all things work together for good to them that love him. Your life's story was written before the beginning of time. No temptation has overtaken you except what is common to mankind. And God is faithful; he will not let you be tempted beyond what you can bear. But when you are tempted, he will also provide a way out so that you can endure it (1 Corinthians 10:13). Whether the world smiles or frowns, it is an enemy; but believers shall be strengthened to overcome it, with all its terrors and enticements. The fear of the Lord, put into their hearts, will be the great means of safety.

Acts 2:46 - "And they, continuing daily with one accord in the temple, and breaking bread from house to house, did eat their meat with gladness and singleness of heart". The term "with one accord" implicates the unity of one. The word 'Church' means a group of people called out of the world; it is the biblical word for "assembly." We are individually the church because God dwells in each of us. Worship primarily takes place in each of us when we sanctify our bodies. Then we are collectively called the body of Christ (temple) of which Christ is the head. We are called to get together (fellowship) regularly in one place (church), symbolically of one spiritual body in place. Collectively, we belong to Christ, functioning as one body. There is one Spirit of Christ making up one Church of Christ (all saints). The term "they continued" is in the tense implying to a customary act. It means they never ceased to get together (fellowshipping) to share and to love each other. Church is the first place where a believer searches for love

and gives love to others. I know some people have been offended by other churchgoers but you must not forget that to love is to be vulnerable. After all, you will never escape the people you are trying to avoid in case you are truly saved and the people you are trying to avoid are saved because you will be together eternally.

The advantages of fellowshipping outweigh the disadvantages. We are called disciples because we are students being disciplined. A church is a place where we go to be fed on the Word. It is important to choose a good Bible teaching church, and you should be ready to grow. The church is not a daycare taking care of all-time biblical infants. Going to church does not save you but it is impossible to be part of the body of Christ (church) when you are cut off from it. Fellowshipping is rehearsing on earth what we will do in heaven. In the real world the people who rehearsal are most likely to participate in the real event. Obedience to God, even to fellowshipping, is the highest act of worship. The people of the world watch us; they see us different from them whenever we set time aside to get together to worship our Savior. Also, they sniff for our Christ-like characters when we are outside the four walls of the church. The church never walks out of us wherever we are. No wonder the rebels against God justify their immoral behaviors by claiming that they are not churchgoers.

Acts 4:32 – "All the believers were one in heart and mind. No one claimed that any of their possessions was their own, but they shared everything they had". The book of Acts is the birth certificate of the Church. The word 'love' is not mentioned in the book of Acts most probably because there was no need to teach about love since the early Church was filled with the Holy Spirit. When the Holy Spirit moves, love automatically flourishes. The early Church was a scene where joy and life-satisfaction were just flourishing. The people were fulfilled; they flourished in less materialistic ways as human beings, and in a higher way than in a consumer society. When sharing becomes a habit, it brings contentment, soothes the troubled spirit, and it doesn't hurt the untroubled spirit either. In today's culture where we are tied up with the cravings for more stuff instead of sharing what we have, we are yet to have the early

Church experience collectively. If the Church today is filled with the Holy Spirit, as we propose, we need the baptism of love to maintain the unity of the Spirit in place (Ephesians 4:3). I mean the tangible and visible manifestation of the spiritual union between God and his people, and the saints and saints, and the bond of each union is love; it is which knits and cements them together.

1 Timothy 4:7-8 - "But reject irreverent and silly myths. Instead, train yourself for godliness. For bodily exercise profits for a little while: but godliness is profitable unto all things, having promise of the life that now is, and of that which is to come." We are not called to applaud evil or to fantasize on the heathen worldly traditions. Demons come to us in form of pleasurable entertainment, like Halloween rituals, eventually, they become familiar spirits; the more you practice them the more real they become. The Church is supposed to reflect heaven on earth; ours is a life lived from the perspective of the Creator of life. It is the highest blessedness which a person can enjoy in this world–as well as the rich prospect of the endless life in the presence of God in the world to come. A false asceticism crushes out all the joy and gladness of this present life and is an unreal preparation for that which is future. Paul's phrase "train yourself" is a command. It is in reference to the spiritual training and exercising; it is of some value compared to the physical training of the muscles. Faith has muscles demanding constant training and exercising in order to grow in anticipation of our ultimate vocation. "For bodily exercise profits nothing"–More accurately rendered, bodily exercise is profitable for little; for physical training is of some value, but godliness has value for all things. Physical exercises neither have nor induce lasting and consistent benefits. Its durability depends on age and experience. Intermittent practice is of limited value. But spiritual training has lasting impacts on the soul eternally, and it is necessary as long as we are living in this world.

Isaiah 33:22 - "For the LORD is our judge, the LORD is our lawgiver, the LORD is our king; it is he who will save us." The uniqueness of Israel is that it was a theocracy. Israel was a custodian of the ordinances of God, with the mandate to obey the decrees of God. The best method of government is a theocracy. Theocracy is the rule of God (theos kratos = god rule). Theocracy is the same as the Kingdom of God. Kings rule over kingdoms. God is the King of the kingdom of God, so He rules in the Kingdom of God. The Holy Spirit was given to rule in the hearts of the believers where Jesus is revered and reigns. God's kingdom is established on the earth where His will is done as it is done in heaven. To understand what this means, we have to think about how His will is done in heaven. God's will is done in heaven perseveringly. The angelic hosts willingly worship and serve Him day and night in His heavenly temple. They understand that His wisdom and His will are perfect, so for them doing His will is the natural thing to do. It is natural for a believer to obey God and unnatural to disobey. Rebellion is a contradiction to who we are in Christ. We are called to rehearse on earth what we will do in heaven. The scripture says "For the Lord is our Judge" - The Lord Jesus Christ has all judgment committed to Him by the Father, He will judge His people, right their wrongs, and avenge their injuries. "The Lord is our Lawgiver" – God has enacted wholesome laws for His church, writes them on their hearts, and puts His Spirit within them, to enable them to keep them. "The Lord is our King" – Jesus is King of kings, made so by His Father; He is the head of the Church, under His government the Church is safe and secure, not even the gates of hell can prevail against her (Matthew 16:18).

John 8:44 – "You are of your father the devil, and the lusts of your father you will do. He was a murderer from the beginning, and abode not in the truth, because there is no truth in him. When he speaks a lie, he speaks of his own: for he is a liar, and the father of it." The word 'father' in this context is in reference to whom you obey. Children of God obey God, whereas children of Satan obey Satan. From the beginning, Satan used deception to bring the downfall of Adam. The greatest deception men suffer is neither from their own opinions nor from the opinions of others

but from the devil who is the master of the art of deception. He is the father of lies because there is no truth or "truthfulness in him. "The essence of lying is in deception, not in words." It is the spirit which nurtures falsehood in all its forms and manifestations. "When he speaks a lie, he speaks of his own" - This is in contrast to the work of Christ who speaks not of Himself; He came to speak the truth which He heard from God (John 16:13). The Holy Spirit sanctifies us in the likeness of Christ through the Scriptures. The remedy is injecting your minds constantly with the truth.

1 Corinthians 4:15-16 – "Even if you have ten thousand guardians in Christ, you do not have many fathers; for in Christ Jesus I became your father through the gospel. Therefore I urge you to imitate me." Our earthly parents tell us to do what they say but not what they do. But Paul urged his audience to do what he said and what he did. We are called to preach the Word without watering it down or lowering the bar and to strive to live by the same standards. Certainly, none of us can live up to the perfectness of the Word at all times but our target should be to be perfect, and the grace of God will sustain us up there where God wants us to be. Sin should be not an intentional act but an absurd act of missing our intended mark (target) of righteousness. In such unfortunate situation, the Holy Spirit does not condemn us but convicts us of the amazing security we have in Christ. The bottom line is that we are all equally sinners who are saved by the grace. Therefore, whenever we preach, we preach to ourselves as we preach to others because we are an audience of one.

John 14:29- 30 – "And now I have told you before it happens, so that when it does happen, you will believe. I will not speak with you much longer, for the prince of this world is coming, and he has no claim on Me." Jesus is very man and very God but He defeated Satan as a perfect man. Satan tried to tempt Jesus into sinning but failed miserably. He messed with Jesus but he found nothing in Him sinful to help him. "Has nothing in me" means that there is no sin in Jesus demanding the judgment of the

Law. Even when our sins were imputed to Him, He had sin upon Him but He had none in Him. "Has nothing in me" can be read as "has no hold over me." Unlike Adam, Satan has nothing to hold on Jesus. When Satan tempted Jesus in the wilderness, he failed miserably to cause Jesus to sin (Luke 4:1-6). Eventually, Satan stopped the temptation because it was of no purpose to tempt Jesus Christ, who had nothing in Him for the devil's fiery darts to fasten upon. Satan has something in us to perplex us with because Satan infected all humanity with the corrupt nature. The Bible says that all have sinned because all of us are born of the corrupt seed. The old (corrupt) nature in us is a bowling ally of Satan making us vulnerable to his deceptions. The Bible says that if we resist the devil, he will flee from us (James 4:7). We resist Satan by walking in the new nature of Christ, which Satan has no hold over and which the Law has no demand on. The new nature of Christ in us is the only sin-free-zone. Jesus warned that Satan will try to mess with our new nature but will fail because in Jesus Christ there is no corruption. When we walk by the Spirit (in our new nature) we cannot fulfill the lustful desires of the old corrupt nature (flesh) (Galatians 5:16). Walking in the Spirit is walking after the Spirit of God by making the Word of God the standard of our behaviors. Jesus is the Word of God (John 1:1) that was demonstrated practically by His life for us to follow. It does not mean that we are not going to have the lustful desires of the flesh; it means that we should "not fulfill" them. True righteousness comes from inside to outside. The righteousness of Christ is available for our justification and for us to manifest by living; when we walk by the Spirit, we depend on Him for supplies of grace in the discharge of every duty, and the exercise of every grace (sanctification).

Ephesians 6:12 – "For we wrestle not against flesh and blood, but against principalities, against powers, against the rulers of the darkness of this world, against spiritual wickedness in high places." Wrestling implies fighting. It is a fact that there is a struggle, a "battle of life". Inside each of us, there is the seed of both good and evil. It's a constant struggle as to which one will win. Every step of life involves a struggle. Success comes with struggles and is sustained with struggles. When you read the books

of history, 95% of the writings involve combat wars. But ours is not a physical combat but a spiritual one. It is a truce-less war with the spiritual powers of evil themselves. When Satan tempted Jesus, he claimed to own all kingdoms of the world: "I will give you all their authority and splendor; it has been given to me, and I can give it to anyone I want to" (Luke 4:6). The evil spirits are spoken of as wielding the power which the Tempter (Satan) claims for himself. They use the same power to motivate the dark-minded people to act evil. "Principalities" and "powers" describe simply angelic powers, in this case, evil fallen angels. We are fighting "against the spiritual powers of wickedness in the high (heavenly) places" who are ruling this dark world. Satan dwells in the heavenly realm; he is the prince of the air. He influences the corrupt systems admired by the corrupt world and people. It is a spiritual battle of ideas which takes place primarily in the minds. Ideas are not part of human nature; they actually come to us from outside us in particular when we fellowship with the wrong characters or read and watch demonic magazines and shows. Contradictory ideas to civility and morality are the major causes of conflicts and combats.

Somebody asked "Can demons have any power over the activity of a Christian?" Demons cannot possess a born-again believer. Jesus said that "No man can enter into a strong man's house, and spoil his goods, except he will first bind the strong man, and then he will spoil his house." (Mark 3:27). However, demons can torment and influence a lukewarm born-again believer. "And the Lord said, Simon, Simon, behold, Satan hath desired to have you, that he may sift you as wheat; But I have prayed for you, Simon, that your faith will not fail. And when you have turned back, strengthen your brothers."(Luke 22:31-32). It means that Satan has received permission to test all of you, to separate the good from the bad, as a farmer separates the wheat from the chaff. I want to emphasize that torment does not mean possessing. Satan cannot possess a believer unless Jesus surrenders him or her to Satan as in the case of Judas: "Then He dipped the piece of bread and gave it to Judas son of Simon Iscariot. And after the sop Satan entered into him. Then said Jesus unto him, That thou doest, do quickly." (John 13:26-27). After Jesus surrendered Judah, an evil spirit entered into him, which pushed him on to commit this horrid iniquity. Jesus taught us in the Lord's Prayer to pray and ask "our Father which is in heaven" to deliver us from evil, or the evil one (Matthew 6:13). It means we need God's help to overcome temptations and avoid yielding to it, and hence to be dominated by the evil one.

Man-built churches are churches that try to train, educate, and regenerate the flesh; to walk like a Spiritual Man. Yet, even God who is perfect, could not train, educate, or regenerate the flesh. That is why He sent His Son from heaven to begin a new race which is spiritual in nature. The Father sent His Son as the Lamb from heaven to the earth to become a sacrifice for our sins. The cross is the place where the flesh (corrupt nature), which we inherited from Adam is killed. Flesh brings death, and that is why the traditional churches which ignore the guidance of the Holy Spirit are dead. We are the true dwelling place of God (tabernacle). In this tabernacle, we become one with God. Jesus prayed: "That they all may be one; as thou, Father, art in me, and I in thee, that they also may be one in us" (John 17:21). In this Tabernacle, there is no outer court, no inner court; there is only the Most Holy place consisting of the souls of those who are regenerated by the Spirit of God. This being the consummation of the glory!

Mark 9:48 - "And if your eye causes you to fall into sin, pluck it out. It is better for you to enter the kingdom of God with one eye than to have two eyes and be thrown into hell, where 'the worms that eat them do not die, and the fire is not quenched.'" The gravitational force of the corrupt nature keeps us glued to the temporary things of the world. It is a calling to amputate the cravings of the negative pleasures of this world. Self-denial involves pain but healing comes through pain; it is better to undergo all possible pain and hardship here and be happy forever hereafter. It is not worthy to enjoy all kinds of the worldly pleasures for a season, and then be miserable forever. Jesus gives a snapshot of how hell is. It is a place where

the worms eating the bodies never die because the bodies in hell are ever there. The fire is never quenched because the souls fueling the fire in hell are never consumed. It is God's love for His image in us that compelled Him to kindle the flames of hell. The process is designed to get rid of evil from the face of the earth forever and to preserve His image from contamination. Hell is a reserved place where the non-repented sinners stand in the presence of God forever. David lamented that he cannot escape God's presence: "If I make my bed in hell, behold, thou art there" (Psalm 139:8).

Luke 9:3 - "He told them: "Take nothing for the journey—no staff, no bag, no bread, no money, no extra shirt." Neither bread, neither money; gold, silver, or brass, to buy bread with; because they were to have it, wherever they went. Jesus was training the faith of His disciples. A life of faith is not the one which has things in excess but that depends on God for daily provision. In the Lord's Prayer, Jesus taught them to pray for their daily provision of bread (Matthew 6:11). It is a petition made to God asking Him to give to everyone, "what is sufficient for his sustenance", and to everyone's body what it wants. I am not saying that it is a sin to be rich; God values the lives of the rich and the poor equally but He is against accumulating riches for selfish ends (Luke 12:16-21). Whether rich or poor, God abhors selfishness. God's goal is the manifestation of His glory rather than our glory. We ought to be thankful for what we have, without murmuring at His providences, or envying at what He bestows on others. Remember that there is no man who has enough material stuff to fulfill their soul. Fulfillment does not come from what we have but from whom we have (God). Jesus practiced what He preached: Jesus was born in a borrowed manger. He preached from a borrowed boat. He entered Jerusalem on a borrowed donkey. He paid His taxes not from His hidden treasures but with a coin trapped in the head of the fish. He ate the Last Supper in a borrowed upper room. He was buried in a borrowed tomb. Now He asks to borrow the lives of Christians to reach the rest of the world. Respond by putting your resources to proper use by preaching the gospel. His grace is intended to set the sinners free from sin but not to

make us filthy rich. The stewardship responsibility implies that a steward of all things owns not a thing.

Acts 4:34-35 – "There were no needy ones among them, because those who owned lands or houses would sell their property, bring the proceeds from the sales, and laid them down at the apostles' feet: and distribution was made unto every man according as he had need." According to the scripture, they entirely delivered the proceeds from the sale of their properties to the apostles and subjected them to their disposal. The land was the most important property among the Jews of the biblical times. However, in an ultimate sense, in Israel all property belonged to the Lord, as Leviticus 25:23, made clear: "The land is mine and you are but aliens and my tenants." Because Yahweh is the one and only Lord and ultimate king over Israel, He was also Lord of the soil and its products. In the old covenant, God demanded just 10% (tithes) in form of taxation from His people. In the new covenant, God owns everything we have; we have just the stewardship responsibilities. Christ did not make rules demanding His followers to give Him everything; the Christians of the early church did it willingly out of love. The reason is that if you can't trust God with everything, you can't trust Him with anything. Our lesson is that God put the moral standard of the new covenant higher than that of the old covenant. In the old covenant, obedience was dictated by regulations and rules. In the new covenant, obedience is flowing from the established relationship. It is important to note that God does not need any material thing from us. We have a calling transcending the material things of the world. He created us uniquely in order to have relationship and fellowship with us. He saves us individually and relates to us individually but He deals with us as a unit body (church). Our intimate relationship with Jesus brings us into fellowship with God. When we fellowship with God and receive the Grace as God offers it to us, through our Lord Jesus Christ, sin has no mastery over us.

Whenever our own righteousness becomes the guiding factor in our lives, it dulls our spiritual insight. The greatest enemy of the life of faith in God is not sin but good choices which are not quite good enough. The good is always the enemy of the best. God demands that we embrace His perfect will.

April for the Resurrection

Matthew 20:18 - "We are going up to Jerusalem, and the Son of Man will be delivered over to the chief priests and the teachers of the law. They will condemn him to death". Jesus walked on this universe with prior knowledge of His life's journey from point "A" to point "Z". He had the roadmap and He was in control of His schedule. He had definite goals and a set of indisputable time-bound targets, as a blueprint for tackling the challenges of His time. The climax of His time was the time of His death, or of His exaltation and glorification (John 7:6). Unlike Jesus, we live by faith because we don't have a blueprint of the road map of our life's journey. Faith is depending on Jesus for guidance. The navigation of life begins in the human heart. The Bible is like a roadmap that shows us exactly how the choices we make today will affect our future. Man's greatest fear is death. The reason is that the after-life experience is hidden to a natural man. The atheists refuse to know it. The agnostics pretend not know it. We (believers) chose to know it by choosing Jesus.

I have been watching with interest some posted videos for Palm Sunday services whereby at least every person brought with them small bunches of palm tree branches to wave. Some willingly shared their palms with others who didn't bring. It was amazingly peaceful atmosphere projecting the love of Christ. Most probably the reason is partly that the palms are not significantly of substantial value commercially. All people regardless of their wealth were required to wave at least a branch of palm. There was a uniformity of status rather than a show of the worthiness of the mighty dollars; it was green all over! Contemplating on the picture of uniformity and contentment I saw among the people, I came to the following conclusion: All of us stand on a leveled ground beneath the cross. There is no some big shot rock star who is highly favored than others. Real praising happens when we are united regarding our priorities. That is when we die to our egos and materialism, and live a stress-free life of faith. Holding on the power and the material things of the world are the root cause of strife. It is a calling to embrace the spirit of relinquishment, of letting go of that which weighs us down so mightily. Ironically, the very things (material gains) which we fight for are the same things which the enemy uses to fight against us. Spiritual liberty begins with deliverance from the lust of the flesh and worldliness. This holy week let us take our focus from all obstructions and be united to the One who was tied on a cross to be our Savior.

God instructed Abraham to offer his only son of promise to him at the altar. As they drew near the site, Isaac questions Abraham concerning the intended offering: "We have the firewood, where is the lamb?" With great faith and foresight, Abraham responds, "God himself will provide the lamb for the burnt offering, my son" (Genesis 22:1-8). The New Testament tells us that Abraham believed God would raise Isaac from the dead (Hebrews 11:19). Abraham's act of offering Isaac, his only son of the promise, was symbolic of the Father offering His only Son. God saved Isaac by providing a ram. "Jehovah-Jireh" is the KJV's translation of YHWH-Yireh and means "The LORD Will Provide" (Genesis 22:14). It is the name memorialized by Abraham when God provided the ram to be sacrificed in place of Isaac. In this case, Isaac is symbolic of the Church, for which God provided His Son to save. God saved Abraham's son from death but did not save His own Son because the death of His Son made all of us His children.

John 8:56 - "Your father Abraham rejoiced to see my day: and he saw it, and was glad." There are two recorded accounts when Abraham saw the day of our Lord. The first account is when Abraham met Melchizedek (the

high priest and king of Salem) and gave him his tithe. The Bible says that Melchizedek brought out bread and wine and served Abraham (Genesis 14:18). He served Abraham the same substances (bread/wine) which Jesus serves us in communion. It was most probably a Christophany (theophany (theo-phaneia) appearance or manifestation of Christ before He was physically born on the earth. The Bible says concerning Melchizedek: "Without father or mother, without genealogy, without beginning of days or end of life, resembling the Son of God, he remains a priest forever. Just think how great he was: Even the patriarch Abraham gave him a tenth of the plunder!" (Hebrews 7:3-4). The second account is when God instructed Abraham to sacrifice his only son of promise but God intervened by providing a ram to save Isaac. It was the typology of God offering his Son to die in our place (Genesis 22:1-12). Hebrews chapter eleven outlines the heroes of faith beginning with Abraham: These were ordinary people but their faith made them different from other people. Faith is the mode or the manner by which we possess heavenly things on earth. Faith receives from God the blessings He gives even in promises before they are delivered. The people of the Old Testament had faith in God's future provision of the Savior. We look behind (in the past) at Calvary for God's provision of the Savior.

Although Jesus did not die on Friday, we traditionally celebrate Good Friday as the annual celebrations of Jesus' death. In the natural world, people only celebrate the death of their enemies and mourn the death of their beloved ones. However, we are celebrating the death of the One we love most because each one of us has a birthday (new birth) in His death. His cross became a bridge between heaven and the earth. Cavalry is a place where deep affliction is met with deep consolation. Jesus died on the evening of the preparation day of the Shabbat. The idea of preparation is expressed by the Greek name paraskeué, given by Josephus ("Ant." xvi. 6, § 2). The day was the forerunner of Shabbat, it is called "'Ereb Shabbat" (The Eve of Sabbath). This was not the Jewish Sabbath to commemorate the end of the week but the Jewish Sabbath to commemorate the Passover.

The word Sabbath simply means resting or holiday. We celebrate because A.D. 33, the day Jesus died on the cross is the day when death died.

John 11:25-26 – "Jesus said unto her, I am the resurrection, and the life: he that believeth in me, though he were dead, yet shall he live: And whosoever lives and believes in Me shall never die. Believes you this?" The wages of sin are as high as the depravity of man and are measured by the currency in which they are paid or by their power to destroy life. All of us bountifully earned the wages of our sins, which is death. Jesus didn't have to pay the wages of sin because He was sinless. He died on our behalf to put death out of business. In Christ, we are reunited with God: "For you died, and your life is now hidden with Christ in God. When Christ, who is your life, appears, then you also will appear with him in glory." (Colossians 3:3-4). It is not a mystery that the resurrected Christ lives in a believer by His Spirit, and a believer lives to Him in all he does. "Our old story ends at the cross; our new story begins at the resurrection."

Luke 12:5 - "But I will show you whom you should fear: Fear him who, after your body has been killed, has authority to throw you into hell. Yes, I tell you, fear him." God has the right to take any life that is polluted by sin from the face of this earth and destroy it. God is the source of life; He breathed life into the body He made out of dust, and it became a living soul. Physical death is the separation of the soul from the body. Spiritual death is the dismissal of the soul from the presence of God. Jesus said that "Fear Him … Fear Him" — How striking the repetition here! It is emphasizing the fear of God. It is only the positive fear of God (reverence) that can effectually expel the negative fear of death. The only thing that delivers us from the unhealthy fear is to have a healthy fear of the One whose power is not limited to this life but extends through and beyond the physical death. Elsewhere, when Pilate said to Jesus "Do you not know that I have authority to release You and authority to crucify You?" Jesus replied that "You would have no power over me if it were not given to you from

above." Jesus feared the Father rather than Pilate because the Father had the power to raise Him from death. Pilate had no power to do anything to Jesus unless it was given by God. Pirate had no power to keep Jesus in the grave when God called Him to come out of the grave.

John 19:11 - "Therefore the one who handed me over to you is guilty of a greater sin." The betrayer is guilty of a greater sin – In this case, Jesus measured and evaluated guilt, and with the greater guilt and greater responsibility comes the greater judgment. Every sinful act is an abomination to God but every sin has a voice to speak, but some sins cry. Definitely, there will be different rewarding for our good works. The Bible says concerning the pending judgment that: "But he that knew not, and did commit things worthy of stripes, shall be beaten with few stripes. For unto whomsoever much is given, of him shall, much be required: the more knowledge a man has, the more practice is expected from him; and the greater his gifts are, the more useful he ought to be, and diligent in the improvement of them" (Luke 12:48). The position of Pilate was that of a half-conscious agent wielding this power. By condemning Jesus he indeed sinned, for he acted against his own better nature; but not the greater sin, for he did not act against the full light of truth. It is to be observed, that the sin of Judas is greater than the sin of Pilate. The fact that it was prophesized that the Son of man had to be delivered into the hands of the sinful men, does not excuse the sin of the Betrayer.

Matthew 27:5 - "I have sinned by betraying innocent blood," he said. "What is that to us?" they replied. "You bear the responsibility." So Judas threw the money into the temple and left. Then he went away and hanged himself." The kind and manner of his death, as recorded by Luke in Acts 1:18, that "falling headlong, he burst asunder the midst, and all his bowels gushed out"; which account may be reconciled with this, by supposing the rope, with which he hanged himself, to break, when falling; it may be, from a very high place, upon a rock. The problem with Judah is that

he ran away from the blood-money but not from his sin. The innocent blood of the man whom he had betrayed was able to wash away his sins but instead of running to Jesus for the forgiveness of his sins, he decided to run away from Jesus. Jesus calls all of those who are burdened with their sins to come to Him. Jesus is never offended when we confess our sins to Him. In case of sin run to Him. The act of a sinner running away from Jesus is compared to a sick person running away from a doctor. God does not send us to hell; we choose to go to hell when we walk away from Jesus. Running away from Jesus is running directly into hell.

John 19:28 - "After this, Jesus knowing that all things were now accomplished, that the scripture might be fulfilled, said 'I thirst.'" At this hour Jesus carried on Himself the sins of the world (2 Corinthians 5:21). The drought was due to the cup of God's wrath which He had drunk (Matthew 26:39). Spiritually, the thirst could only be quenched by His Spirit. Remember that Jesus told the woman at the well, that the Holy Spirit of God was the living water (John 7:39), whom He could pour into her life so that she would never thirst again (John 4:13-14). The Spirit caters for the natural but there is nothing in the natural man that can cater for the spiritual man. Human goodness is at its best only if it guides you to Christ. Human goodness becomes your worst enemy when it guides you to human recourses, preventing you from embracing God's grace. Think about it!

Matthew 27:46 - "My God, my God, why have you forsaken me?" Jesus' exclamation of Eli, Eli, lama sabachtani is translated, "My God, my God, why have you forsaken me?" Christ expressed anguish and dismay to the circumstances which caused His isolation rather than at the Father. Although the Father turned away His face from the Son, He did not abandon Him because when Jesus carried on Himself the sins of the world, He was walking in the perfect will of the Father. The Bible says "that God was reconciling the world to himself in Christ, not counting people's sins

against them" (2 Corinthians 5:19). There was a scheme of reconciliation drawn in the counsels of God before the world began. This was what He resolved upon from all eternity, that inasmuch as Christ became the surety and substitute of His people, He would not impute their sins to them, or look for satisfaction for them from them; but would reckon and place them to the account of their surety, and expect satisfaction from Him; and accordingly He did. Essentially, God turned His eyes away from Jesus so that He may not turn His eyes away from us. When we sin, God moves closer to us to convict us of His righteousness instead of moving away from us. The born-again believers can sin because they still retain the old nature but they do not aim at sinning; unlike the people of the world, the redeemed of God are not comfortable with sin, and they do not enjoy sinning. Their sins are not unto death because Jesus paid a ransom price by His precious blood for their sins.

Matthew 27:46 - "My God, My God, why hast Thou forsaken Me?" The cry on the cross is a quote from Psalms 22:2. It was not a desperate cry like of a person drowning and seeking someone to save him. It was not the desolation of an isolated individual. Although God turned His face away from the Son, God never forsook Him because at the cross God was in Christ reconciling the world to Himself (2 Corinthians 5:19). The grieving was a revelation of the heart of God face to face with the sin of man. It was a grieving of the holy One because of man's sin and the death it brought. He went to the Cross because it is the only way to defeat death permanently. Jesus does not want us to have pity on Him but to have a heart like His! May we resolve to have a contrite spirit in regard to our own sin. May we weep in particular over the sin of complacency and syncretism.

"The cry on the cross, 'My God, My God, why hast Thou forsaken Me?' is not the desolation of an isolated individual: it is the revelation of the heart of God face to face with the sin of man, and going deeper down than man's sin can ever go in inconceivable heartbreak in order that every sin-stained, hell-deserving sinner might be absolutely redeemed. If the Redemption of Christ cannot go deeper down than hell, it is not redemption at all." ~ Oswald Chambers

Luke 23:46 - "Jesus called out with a loud voice, "Father, into your hands I commit my spirit." When he had said this, he breathed his last." When Jesus was tortured and suffered at the crucifixion and was put to such distressing pains and agonies, He did not threaten His crucifiers with a future judgment, when He would take vengeance, and execute his wrath upon them, but prayed to His Father for the forgiveness of their sins. He committed Himself to Him that judges righteously; He commended His Spirit, to God His Father, and committed His cause to Him, to vindicate it in what way He should think fit, who He knew was the Judge of all the earth that would do right. The ministry of Jesus was that of reconciliation rather than condemnation.

Somebody asked, "Did the penitent thief on the cross go to heaven with Jesus that day?" Reply: "Then one of the criminals who was hanged blasphemed Him, saying, 'If You are the Christ, save Yourself and us.' But the other, answering, rebuked him, saying, 'Do you not even fear God, seeing you are under the same condemnation? And we indeed justly, for we receive the due reward of our deeds; but this Man has done nothing wrong.' Then he said to Jesus, 'Lord, remember me when You come into Your kingdom.' And Jesus said to him, 'Assuredly, I say to you, today you will be with Me in paradise.'" (Luke 23:39-43). Jesus was crucified between two thieves to fulfill the prophetic word that he was numbered among the transgressors (Luke 22:37). The two thieves represented the world which Jesus came to save: Both of them were positioned near to death and near to eternal life. One went to paradise whereas the other went to hell. Likewise, all of us have a choice to make between death and eternal life. Some people are heading to paradise whereas others are heading to hell. In Luke 23:43, we read of Jesus saying, "Today you will be with Me in Paradise." Did paradise mean heaven in the presence of the Father? But in John 20:1-17 we read that Jesus meets Mary in the garden on the first day of the week and says, 'Touch me not; for I am not yet ascended to my Father: but go to my brethren, and say unto them, I ascend unto my Father, and your Father; and to my God, and your God.'" It seems that Jesus had not yet been with the Father. Where is paradise? Paradise is the garden of God, which is in heaven. It is a place of blessing where the righteous go after death. It is the same as Abraham's Bosom. Abraham's Bosom: Unique phrase found in a parable of Jesus describing the place where Lazarus went after death (Luke 16:19-31). It is a figurative phrase that appears to have been drawn from a popular belief that the righteous would rest by Abraham's side in the world to come, an opinion described in Jewish literature at the time of Christ. The word kolpos literally refers to the side or lap of a person. Figuratively, as in this case, it refers to a place of honor reserved for a special guest, similar to its usage in John 13:23. In the case of Lazarus, the reserved place is special because it is beside Abraham, the father of all the righteous. The phrase may be synonymous to the paradise promised to the thief on the cross (Luke 23:43). Together these passages support the conviction that a believer enjoys immediate bliss at the moment of physical death. Elsewhere, Jesus promised to the faithful in the church of Ephesus: "To him who overcomes I will give to eat from the tree of life, which is in the midst of the paradise of God" (Revelation 2:7). So where is the tree of life? The answer to this question will help us know where paradise is. In Revelation 22:1-4, we learn that the tree of life is in the New Jerusalem. So we can know for certain that paradise is not in heaven where the Father is; it is a separate place reserved for the faithful ones where God reigns.

John 20:22 - "And with that he breathed on them and said, "Receive the Holy Spirit." Jesus was glorified by the resurrection; He had a spiritual body. The breathing and receiving of the Holy Spirit were necessary in order for the disciples to know Him and to communicate with Him in their conscience. This was the beginning of the supernatural life which makes the Christian consciousness unique among religious experiences.

This act of breathing on them, and them receiving the Holy Spirit, created the conviction which was sealed on Pentecost. This being the most divine function of the Church and of the Disciples of Christ ever since. In the minds of the Jewish disciples who worshiped in the temple, it was like "the Spirit went from between the wings of the cherubim, and breathed upon them" by the decree, or order of the Lord." Life begins from the nostrils of God. God made man from the materials He already created (clay) and breathed into him life (Genesis 2:7). It means that at creation there was no life in man without the Divine breathing. Unlike the plants and animals, man received his life from a distinct act of Divine breathing. It was not an in-breathing of atmospheric air, but an in-flatus from the Ruach Elohim, or Spirit of God that constituted to the image of God in man. Man became a living soul, not only capable of performing the functions of the animal life, of eating, drinking, walking, But of morally thinking, reasoning, discerning, discoursing rationally as God; Man does not merely exist, He is a living soul. The breathing of Jesus on His disciples was symbolic of the creation of man (Genesis 2:7), the conviction of which was accomplished and realized on Pentecost (the birthday of the Church) when God created a new life in them to dominate the old corrupted life. Regeneration means recreation.

Matthew 27:51 – "At that moment the curtain of the temple was torn in two from top to bottom. The earth shook, the rocks split" It happened when Jesus cried out in a loud voice, and yielded up His spirit. The veil divided the Holy Place from the Holy of Holies (Exodus 26:1). The Veils before the Most Holy Place were 40 cubits (60 feet) long, and 20 (30 feet) wide, of the thickness of palm of the hand, and wrought in 72 squares, which were joined together; and these Veils were so heavy, that, in the exaggerated language of the time, it needed 300 priests to manipulate each. If the Veil was at all such as is described in the Talmud, it could not have been rent in twain by a mere earthquake or the fall of the lintel, although its composition in squares fastened together might explain, how the rent might be as described in the Gospel (online reference). In sum, the statement that the Temple veil was as thick as a man's hand is

found originally in rabbinic literature (the Mishnah), not Scripture. Later rabbinic commentary tags this description as hyperbolic language. Given the context of the original statement, as well as the uncertainty of rabbinic traditions, it is unwise for us to state in an unqualified fashion that the veil was as thick as a man's hand. It would be more accurate to say something like, "Early Jewish tradition stated that the Temple veil was as thick as a man's hand, although this might be an exaggeration."

Somebody asked, "Was there the ark of the covenant in the temple during the times of Jesus' ministry on the earth?" Reply: This is one of the questions of which I have no biblical answer. I understand that the presence of God dwelt in the Holy of holies where there was the ark, first in the Tabernacle and then in Solomon's temple in Jerusalem. God promised to dwell with His people as long as they were faithful to Him, but Israel rebelled. So when did the Ark of the Covenant disappear? It seems that it disappeared sometime immediately prior to the Babylonian Captivity in the 6th century BC. In the eighteenth year of his reign, King Josiah of Judah ordered the caretakers of the Ark of the Covenant to return it to the temple in Jerusalem (2 Chronicles 35:1-6; 2 King 23:21-23). That is the last time the ark's location is mentioned in the Scriptures. Forty years later, King Nebuchadnezzar of Babylon captured Jerusalem and raided the temple. Less than ten years after that, he returned, took what was left in the temple, and then burnt it and the city to the ground.

An account of the plundering of the temple by Antiochus IV Epiphanes in 170 BC, is given in 1 Maccabees 1:20ff and also was described by Josephus. At that time the temple contained at least an altar of incense made of gold, the table of shewbread, the lampstands, many cups, bowls, and incense holders, crowns and gold plating at the wall where the cherubim had been in days of old. Antiochus also took the "hidden treasures" of the temple site. In three days' time, he murdered 40,000 Jews and led an equal number as captives. He then desecrated the temple by sacrificing a pig on the altar. The actual event was in 167 BC, not 170, as the author claims. I believe that it is fair to say that we are not completely sure what was found in the Holy of Holies in the 2nd temple. We have a really good idea what was in the Holy Place (remember there were two rooms, the Holy Place and the Most Holy Place): the altar of incense, the shewbread table, and the menorah. I believe that there was probably some kind of altar in the holy of holies symbolic of the presence of God, but I am not sure. I am prepared to guess that there may have been cherubim in there as well, but almost certainly not the ark. I doubt that there was a replica ark, However, I lean toward the idea that God "dwelt" in this temple as well because Jesus called it His house (Matthew 21:13). The phrase "My house shall be called a house of prayer" means "the house of my sanctuary shall be called a house of prayer". It was no longer the house but a house of prayer. Perhaps it was in a qualitatively different way than in the Tabernacle or Solomon's Temple when the ark was there. My theory for many years has been that God left the (2nd or Herodian) temple when the curtain was ripped in two. For theological reasons, especially using Hebrews 9 as a model, this makes a lot of sense. I cannot prove this theory, however. So, the only correction I would make is that the ripping of the curtain did not just "show" the relative emptiness of Jewish worship, it also marked the actual becoming worthless/empty as God no longer dwelt there in a special way as he had before that.

Luke 24:2 - "And they found the stone rolled away from the sepulchre." When they came to the sepulchre, to their great surprise, they found it rolled away, which was done by an angel, Matthew 28:2. The stone was not rolled away in order for Jesus to come out as in the case of raising Lazarus. The stone was rolled away for them to come in and be witnesses to His resurrection. The resurrected body of Jesus was spiritual in nature that was not restricted by the physical laws of nature. Remember that Jesus appeared to His disciples when they were together, with the doors locked for fear of the Jewish leaders. He appeared and disappeared through the walls without the need of a door. His spiritual resurrection-body, though a continuation of the old life, with signs of its identity, is, nevertheless, emancipated from the ordinary conditions of our material corporeity.

"But give me the resurrection of Christ and all that precedes His coming and all that follows, falls into place" ~ John Burgan

The infinity death of Jesus Christ projects that when He died, all sinners died with Him. The infinity life of Jesus projects that, He is the author of eternal life. He is Devine. God alone can be worshiped. "Then the eleven disciples went to Galilee, to the mountain where Jesus had told them to go. 17 When they saw him, they worshiped him" (Matthew 28:16-18).

1 Corinthians 15:5-7 - "And that He appeared to Cephas and then to the Twelve. After that, he was seen of above five hundred brethren at once; of whom the greater part remain unto this present, but some are fallen asleep. Then He appeared to James, then to all the apostles." In the secular world, it takes just one sincere witness in order for the judge to convict somebody. Judaism demanded just a firsthand testimony of two witnesses be presented in order to convict somebody. But there are over five hundred witnesses who saw the resurrected Jesus. These were people who knew Christ very well, in the days of His flesh, to whom He had preached, and who witnessed His miracles. Also, the twelve apostles saw the resurrected Christ. This is an overwhelming testimony to the resurrection of Jesus Christ.

MAY FOR MEMORIAL

Memorial Day is observed as a holiday today, May 29th, 2017, in the USA. Memorial Day, originally called Decoration Day, is a day of remembrance for those who have died in service of the United States of America. Because of the current peace embraced by all, the past memories of grief are turned into the present memories of joy. Without the sacrifice of the fallen heroes and heroines, there would have been no culture, no civilization, and no freedom. We commemorate in remembrance because a healed memory is not a deleted memory. Spiritually, we celebrate the death of Jesus by which we were liberated from the wrath of God against sin. We were adopted into the divine family through His death and resurrection: "But as many as received him, to them gave he power to become the sons of God, even to them that believe on his name" (John 1:12). Through the humanity of Jesus Christ, God came down to our level to serve us, and to clean all the mess behind us: "Just as the Son of Man did not come to be served, but to serve, and to give his life as a ransom for many." (Matthew 20:28). The uniqueness of the Christian God is that He works for His people. All of the gods of the world are burdens to the people who worship them but our God is a burden carrier for His people. Only the triune God can create, redeem and preserve what He has redeemed. The Father gave the Son; the Son saved; the Holy Spirit sanctifies. God saved us without coming off the throne. He carried the burdens of our sins without becoming a sinner. In Christ we were unburdened of our inequities; we will never meet our sins (Psalm 103:12). The Lord considers the frailty of our bodies and the folly of our souls. In Him, we travel this arid journey of life with hope.

"Hope is like the sun, which, as we journey toward it, casts the shadow of our burden behind us."

John 11:35 - "Jesus wept." Some people think that Jesus wept because he was missing Lazarus, in the same way, we miss our beloved ones when they die. It does not make sense; why would He weep when He said Lazarus was sleeping, and He was going to wake him up? The reality is that Jesus wept at the living. I mean Lazarus' sisters and relatives who did not understand that in Him there is no shadow of death. He was meditating upon the state of His people as opposed to Lazarus. That is why He said to Lazarus' sister: "I am the resurrection and the life. He who believes in Me will live, even though he dies. and whoever lives by believing in me will never die. Do you believe this?" (John 11:26). God is not limited by time; He sees us alive eternally in Christ: "And God raised us up with Christ and seated us with him in the heavenly realms in Christ Jesus" (Ephesians 2:6). The quickening of Jesus in the tomb resulted in the quickening of Jesus in our hearts. Jesus Christ's resurrection is the virtual cause of our resurrection from a death in sin and hence the acquiring of the eternal life. He wants us to focus on His life in us rather than on this physical life. Remember that all of the twelve apostles' lives (apart from John) were cut short by martyrdom. Most probably none of us has more faith than the twelve apostles who physically saw Jesus die and resurrected. But their reward was not in perishable things, including this life.

John 11:35 - "Jesus wept." Jesus sobbed and mourned. We are supposed to mourn but with hope. Jesus mourned because He had emotions like any of us. But unlike us, His were sinless emotions. Our emotions were corrupted by the sinful nature. Guilt, shame, embarrassment, and pride are some of the manifestations of our corrupt emotions, and they are likely to lead to individuals' thinking and feeling aligning with corrupt reactions and practices like stress, bitterness, anger, contempt, resentment, and hostility. We dwell in the corrupt bodies in anticipation of the sinless

bodies of hope. When we put on the incorruptible bodies we will see God because God is accessible only to the immortal man on a face-to-face basis. Then faith will cease because we shall believe in whom we can see. Hope will cease because our blessed hope shall be realized. Love is the only virtue which we take with us to eternity. When we cross over, we shall continue to love God and our love will grow eternally in its purest form without a possibility of hate. It is from this perspective Paul wrote that "And now these three remain: faith, hope and love. But the greatest of these is love" (1 Corinthians 13:13). Charity is as lasting as eternity.

"There is sacredness in tears. They are not the mark of weakness, but of power. They speak more eloquently than ten thousand tongues. They are the messengers of overwhelming grief, of deep contrition, and of unspeakable love" ~ Washington Irving

Isaiah 6:1 – "In the year that King Uzziah died, I saw the Lord, high and exalted, seated on a throne; and the train of his robe filled the temple." Our lesson focuses on one of the most successful Kings of the Southern Kingdom. Traditions say that Isaiah was closely connected to King Uzziah, most probably the only king he has ever known by this time. Uzziah's father was King Amaziah (2 Chron 26:4). Uzziah's name literally means "Jehovah is strength" and his life illustrates the meaning of his name. Uzziah became Judah's eleventh King at age 16 and held the second longest tenure as Judah's monarchy (52 years). NOTE: He is called "Azariah" in the historical record of 2 Kings. His early years were marked by the significant influences surrounding him. There cannot be a better success story than King Uzziah. Tragically his biography does not end on the note of success but of failure. Instead of being buried in the sepulcher of the Kings in Jerusalem, he was buried in a field outside of the city. It is this ironic twist in Uzziah's career that deserves our concentration. One would expect a marvelous accolade to be chiseled into the grave marker of Uzziah. However, the eulogy is stated with four simple words, "He is

a leper." The slippery slope of decline began when Uzziah allowed his father's "heart problem" to interfere with his devotion to God. The King lost consciousness that Jehovah God was responsible for his success. The King's pride blinded him to the need of humility (v. 16a). He entered into the temple to offer incense, the responsibility strictly reserved for the high priest only. God judged him by striking him with leprosy. What caused him to enter into the Temple and offer incense? (v. 16b). We are not told and it is not necessary to know. What we do know is that the King knew he was doing wrong. The priests knew the King was doing wrong. The entire nation knew their King was doing wrong. Pride could not make a wrong action "right"! All of his godly obedience was erased! All of his successes were eclipsed by folly! Great successes, world renown, fantastic prosperity all were lost because Uzziah refused to follow God's commands! Uzziah as a LEPER (2 Chron 26:19-23).

Somebody posted: "In the second death, nothing that pertains to the lost remains; not even their souls! Ezekiel 18:4. Revelation 20:6. So, there are no people suffering in hell! The gospel is supposed to be preached in love because God is not sadistic." My answer: True the gospel must be preached in love but also in truth. God does not send people to hell because that is where everybody is heading unless redeemed. There is nothing wrong with waking up, somebody, who is in deep asleep when his house is on fire and tell him that you are about to roast in the fire. The gospel should not be reinvented; it should be preached as Jesus preached it. The word "hell" appears 54 times in the Holy Bible. Hell is clearly defined in your Bible as a place of torment and burning. Jesus referred to hell at least 46 times. The word Hell in the Christian Scriptures appears frequently in Mark (3 occurrences), Matthew (12), Luke (3), Acts (2), Revelation (4). God does not send people to hell. People choose to go to hell. Hell was prepared for Satan and the fallen angels (Matthew 25:41). The demons and the fallen angels are synonymous. The most biblically consistent explanation for the origin of the demons is that they are the fallen angels, the angels who rebelled against God with Satan. God will certainly purge the demons and the souls contaminated with evil from the face of the universe by dumping them into the pit called hell. The mercy of God made a way of averting hell by the cleansing power of the blood of Jesus. All people have a choice either to accept God's offer or to reject it.

Nothing lasts infinitely long; even hell won't last forever. Jesus said, "fear him who can kill and destroy the soul" (Matthew 10:28). There is one day when the corrupted souls will be no more.

"I look forward to death with great anticipation, to meeting God face to face" ~ Billy Graham

Life is a pilgrimage; we are travelers targeting various resting spots in this world. We physically walk in this world but we are on a spiritual pilgrimage marching directly to the illimitable domain of eternal bliss, our ultimate destination. We enjoy this world because it is our Father's property but it is never given to us to call it home. We experience heaven on earth but the heaven we call home is a place where life is eternal and filled with the benevolence of the glory of Love. It is a place where there is no hate, no sickness and no need whatsoever. A place where there shall be no night; and they need no candle, neither light of the sun; for the Lord God gives them light: and we shall reign forever and ever" (Revelation 22:5). "Yes, away from the toxins of this world, I will journey eagerly, to take up eternal residence, in that place my Jesus prepared for me."

Ecclesiastes 3:11 – "He has made everything beautiful in its time. He has also set eternity in the human heart; yet no one can fathom what God has done from beginning to end." Regeneration is the beauty of our salvation. By His grace, God reversed the curse of sin. He wrapped eternity into time; timeless in time. The unchanging God condensed Himself to

dwell in the changing world, as it has been, is, and will be. Faith is not limited by time; it is timeless. "There is no instinct like that of the heart". God has put the instinct of our eternal destiny into the human kingdom. He has given human beings an awareness of eternity. We can grasp eternity while we are still here on the earth. It's the conviction we have that there is something more to life; there is something bigger than this life. Jesus said radically that, "And everyone who lives and believes in Me will never die. Do you believe this?" (John 11:26). "When you put your faith in Jesus Christ, not only will you have a life that is worth living, not only will you find the meaning of life, but you also will have the hope of life beyond the grave. That is life during life—and life after death."

Somebody asked that "It is biblical to participate in our traditional rituals of cleaning the grave yards?" Reply: It is good to clean the graveyards to honor the departed souls and because they are monuments for Memorial purposes only. The souls of the deceased do not hang around the graves because they are no long here on the earth. What people call Mizimu (haunting spirits of the deceased) are tormenting demons (evil spirits of fallen angels).

Somebody posted that "There is no scripture saying the soul is immortal". Reply: All scriptures should be interpreted in the light of the gospel. Jesus fulfilled the Law in three main ways: 1) By rightly interpreting it for us; 2) By living under the Law without breaking it; 3) By paying the penalty of the broken Law. Jesus interpreted the Law with the authority of the Lawgiver. Every word out of His mouth is a law because He is divine. That is why He is quoted saying: "They said to you—but I say to you—". If the soul of the redeemed is not immortal, was Jesus being sarcastic when He said that "Very truly I tell you, whoever obeys my word will never see death." (John 8:51). Also "Jesus said to her, "I am the resurrection and the life. He who believes in Me will live, even though he dies. And everyone who lives and believes in Me will never die. Do you believe this?" John 11:25-26).

Ecclesiastes 12:7 - "And the dust returns to the ground it came from, and the spirit returns to God who gave it". The body sleeps but the soul never sleeps. The soul is either dead in sin or alive in Christ. The redeemed soul is forever alive and resting in Christ. The new birth involves the new nature (spirit) regenerated after Christ. It is the opposite of the old, corrupt nature which we got from Adam. Once, we are quickened and reunited with Christ, there is no force, not even death that can separate us from Christ. The Bible says that "And God raised us up with Christ and seated us with him in the heavenly realms in Christ Jesus" (Ephesians 2:6).

Jesus gave a story of Lazarus and the rich man (Luke 16:14-31). This a true real-life account as opposed to a parable since two of its characters are named. They both died. Lazarus went to heaven, and the rich man went to hell: "The time came when the beggar died and the angels carried him to Abraham's side. The rich man also died and was buried. In hell, where he was in torment, he looked up and saw Abraham far away, with Lazarus by his side" (Luke 16:22-23). The other account involves Lazarus whom Jesus raised from death. Jesus said concerning Lazarus that he is asleep. The word 'asleep' is used multiple times concerning the dead. Sleeping does not mean the non-existence of the soul; it implies that the body of the believer rests in the soil whereas the soul rests in Christ. According to Jesus, the death of Lazarus was a brief resting of the body because He was going to wake him up by reuniting his body with his spirit. That is why Jesus said to Martha "I am the resurrection and the life." (John 11:25–26) In this particular event, Jesus did not say where the soul went; but the Bible is not silent regarding the whereabouts of the departed souls of the saints. For example, when they stoned Stephen to death he prayed, "Lord Jesus, receive my spirit" (Acts 7:59). The death of Jesus is projected as the separation of the spirit from His body: Jesus called out with a loud voice,

"Father, into your hands I commit my spirit." When he had said this, he breathed his last (Luke 23:46).

Acts 7:55 – "But Stephen, full of the Holy Spirit, looked up to heaven and saw the glory of God, and Jesus standing at the right hand of God". Normally, Jesus is projected to be sitting rather than standing at the right hand of God. However, in the vision of Stephen, Jesus is seen standing. There are several suggestions why He is seen standing. The first reason is that all the glory of what is happening on the earth belongs to the Son. The other probable reason is found in the context of the chapter. Stephen trusted in Jesus in spite of the sufferings: "Lord Jesus, receive my spirit", was a striking acknowledgment of the divinity of Christ. Only He who gave the spirit could receive it back again, and keep it safe unto the resurrection of the body. Jesus, on the cross, said "Father, into thy hands I commend my spirit" (Luke 23:46); because He came from the bosom of the Father, He returned to the Father. Likewise, the Spirit of Stephen came from Jesus and returned to Jesus. Jesus was honored to receive it back. He is seen standing, as rising to welcome His faithful martyr, and to assume the full responsibility of the soul committed into His hands.

Remembering those who passed on or who changed their addresses from earth to heaven:

"Grief, I have learned, is really just love. It is all the love you want to give, but cannot. All that unspent love gathers up in the corner of your eyes, the lump in your throat, and in that hallow part of your chest. Grief is just love with no place to go." ~ Jimmie Anderson

Last week's shooting in the church of Texas has been the most shocking news, not a surprise though to those who understand the end times. Jesus said that if they hated Him, they will hate us, and it will intensify (get worse) at the end times. The tragedy happened in the tiny town of Sutherland Springs, population 400. The dead ranged from 18 months to 77 years old and included multiple members of some families. "The gunman, Devin Patrick Kelley, who killed 26 people, went aisle to aisle looking for victims and shot crying babies at point-blank range", a couple who survived the attack said. No matter how prepared you might be for the death of a loved one, it still comes as a shock, and it still hurts to the core. The common trend is that such tragedies unite us and strengthen us rather than weakening us; disasters bring us together as one nation regardless of our religion or color. For sure we know that the motivation of evil is the devil. But as the law enforcement is still figuring out the motivation of the shooting and the next big trend thereafter, we should be calm. Social media has been saturated with messages suggesting the necessary precaution required in order to avert the same catastrophe to happen in future. Some suggested going to churches armed; they used Nehemiah 4:17 and Luke 22:36 to justify their cause. One conservative editor wrote: "With all the unhinged rhetoric from the left ceaselessly demonizing followers of the Cross, we're at a time where we cannot take the risk of attending church without a means of protecting ourselves, our families, and our fellow church members. As a friend of mine put it, "A Glock for the flock." Bottom line: it's time for God's men to start packing heat to church." I want to say that grieving is necessary because death robs us of our beloved ones but dying in a church while worshipping is worth celebrating. We should deal with our shock as best as we can and move on with life without despair. True faith is revealed by our reactions and aspirations during the tough times of tribulations. "Faith is the bird that feels the light and sings when the dawn is still dark." Evil is apparent because we live in the corrupt bodies and world. There is a universal disturbance of peace to which we all contribute in one way or the other. Given the fact, the degree of evil we saw recently is beyond normality. Yes, we should pick up our weapons but weapons of the spiritual warfare. God armed us with the 66 calibers (66 books of the Bible) to feed our faith. Also, we are armed with the firing power of the Holy Spirit; He is the Paraclete that walks alongside us wherever we go. He is all comforting God; our defender; our refuge in times of tribulations.

"My only success is in being alive" ~ Sgt. Steven Ssempagala (aka Sgt. Kifulugunyu)

Dr. Martin Luther King Jr.: Martin Luther day is celebrated on 1/15/2018. If Martin Luther returned to the earth today, will he admire what this country has become? Martin Luther's nonviolence struggle against oppression earned him a place on the front row of history. He sought equality in liberty. His was a virtuous and moral struggle targeting the oppressors. If the oppressors were blacks and the oppressed were whites, he could have still walked the same path of struggle. His message of true equality means holding everyone accountable in the same way, regardless of race, gender, faith, ethnicity - or political ideology. In the jungle, where there is no law, the most aggressive person dominates others. Martin Luther taught us to be victors rather than victims. In the politics of Postmodernism improved economy is the main thing. As much as the prosperous economy improves the welfare of the people, it is not the main thing. We were created for a higher calling than the material world. We are not mere raw materials to generate profits. True peace begins with God. "God created the moral basis for the universe before He made the heavens and the earth. His concept of right and wrong was not an afterthought that came along with the Ten Commandments." Any policy, therefore, that ignores the morality of God is anti-people. Occasionally, we need to be reminded of the freedom we have in Christ. It is the inner peace that brings real freedom. Freedom is like air. You are most likely to notice it when you run out of it; when you have it, you enjoy it but you don't notice it.

A special tribute to Dr. RC Sproul (February 13, 1939 - December 142017): When he was asked why his favorite subject is teaching the holiness of God, Dr. RC Sproul replied that: "I teach holiness because I am a sinner". When I was at the Bible College, Dr. Lester Sumrall taught us that whatever you choose to teach most is what you become. If you choose to teach healing most, people will be healed; if you choose to teach prosperity most, you will be prosperous; when you choose to teach holiness most, you will strive to live holy. The moment he mentioned holiness, I was filled with excitement and I said emphatically: "That is what I want". I teach holiness not because I am sinless but because I yearn not to sin. Teaching holiness gives me hunger for more of God's holiness! It is imperative to stand in awe, and sin not. Let us fear the Lord's displeasure, hope in His mercy, and walk in His commandments. As Dr. Sproul said "Holiness is a difficult concept for humans to understand and define. It is best understood by experience." Christianity is not about involvement with religious rituals as a tangent. It involves a meeting with a holy God, who forms the center, or core, of human existence. We often hear many talks about how God is love, yet few ever speak of His holiness and justice. The mercies of God to the sinners are made known in a manner well suited to impress all who receive them, with His majesty and holiness. Dr. RC Sproul said: "The justice of God is always and ever an expression of His holy character." The famous Reformed theologian Jonathan Edwards wrote over 200 years ago: "A true love of God must begin with a delight in His holiness, and not with a delight in any other attribute; for no other attribute is truly lovely without this." Dr. Sproul focused on the attribute of God's holiness as central to all of the scriptures; only God's attribute of holiness is repeated three times in a single verse (Isaiah 6:3; Revelation 4:8), giving it a superlative function, setting apart God's holiness from that of the creations, and providing the essential foundation for the Creator-creation distinction. God is God and we are not nor can be on the same ontological plane as God because we are mere creatures. In the Lord's Prayer, Jesus taught the first petition as "hallowed be thy name". Yet, even so, most people are hard-pressed to define what God's holiness precisely is. Dr Sproul insinuated "Access to God never means we dare approach Him in a cavalier way. For the Christian the holy war is over; the peace has been established. Access to the Father is ours. But we still must tremble before our God. He is still holy. Our trembling is the trembling of awe and veneration." He is our God, not only to bring comfort in time of need but to invoke our adoration and praise; His holy presence drives us to our knees in reverential worship.

Dr Livingstone Mpalanyi Nkoyoyo: The retired Church of Uganda archbishop, Dr Livingstone Mpalanyi Nkoyoyo has lost the battle to cancer today 5th January, 2018, at Kampala Hospital in Kololo. Nkoyoyo was the first bishop of Mukono Diocese, which was carved out of Namirembe in 1984. Nkoyoyo always emphasized the virtue of keeping time. He preached hard work, patience and resilience. The former archbishop was a born again clergy; he was praised for being development-minded and down to earth. He always emphasized the virtue of keeping time. Nkoyoyo returned to Uganda in June last year from the UK, where he had been admitted at St. Mary's Hospital Paddington, London since 2016 after he was diagnosed with cancer of the oesophagus (throat). The candle of Arch Bishop, Dr Livingstone Mpalanyi Nkoyoyo burns out this afternoon. His body has been taken to the funeral home. On Sunday evening the body will be taken for a vigil at All Saints Cathedral Nakasero for an overnight. On Monday morning body will be taken to Mukono St. Andrew and Phillips cathedral for a service at 10:00AM. From Nakasero the body will be taken to his home at Nakabago in Mukono for an overnight family vigil. The Main Funeral service will be at Namirembe Cathedral on Tuesday at 9:00AM. There after the body will be taken to be laid to rest at Namugongo Martyrs Shrine at 4:00PM. We celebrate the life and Ministry of the servant of God who has been promoted to glory.

Martin Luther: On October 31, 1517, (500 years ago), Luther nailed the Ninety-five Theses to the door of the Wittenberg Castle church in disputation, expressing his grievances against the Catholic Church that he loved. He did not want to cause schism but he sought for reform. The word "Catholic" means universal church. Due to the influence of the Roman Empire, the universal church (Catholic) turned into the Roman Catholic Church marred with critical doctrinal eras, putting the Pope and the Church above the Scriptures. Martin Luther, a professor of moral theology at the University of Wittenberg, Germany, started the Reformation, a schism in the Catholic Church which profoundly changed Europe. The Reformation also referred to as the Protestant Reformation. These were the principle doctrines emphasized by Luther: Sola Scriptura ("Scripture alone"): The Bible alone is our highest authority. Sola Fide ("faith alone"): We are saved through faith alone in Jesus Christ. Sola Gratia ("grace alone"). Solus Christus ("Christ alone"): Jesus Christ alone is our Lord, Savior, and King. Sola Deo Gloria ("to the glory of God alone"): We live for the glory of God alone. He emphasized that we are saved by the grace of God alone; the Scriptures are our ultimate and trustworthy authority for faith and practice. He quoted Habakkuk 2:4, which is one of the greatest declarations of faith to be found in the entire Bible: "The just shall live by faith". In other words, the righteous man trusts, not in himself, but in God. His faith is directed upward, not inward! It means that our righteousness is of Christ. The only thing that matters is our object of faith (Jesus). The Bible says "No flesh shall glory before God" (1 Corinthians 1:29). No man may attribute his salvation to anything of the creature, but wholly to the sovereign grace. Christianity is the manifested life of Christ in the Church. The Church is a bride that takes on the reputation of the bridegroom (Jesus). Those who are saved must live as Jesus lived in obedience to the Word. When Luther was asked by the Pope to recant his teaching, he replied that "Unless I am convicted by scripture and plain reason - I do not accept the authority of the popes and councils, for they have contradicted each other - my conscience is captive to the Word of God. I cannot and I will not recant anything for to go against conscience is neither right nor safe. God help me. Amen." If I am allowed to paraphrase, he said that "My conscience may be seared by sin, like any other human being but it is against my conscience to recant against the secret Scriptures. I will not elevate the traditions of men above the Scriptures. My conscience has been captured by the Holy Scriptures."

The history of the Church is rich. The Bible has impacted human history throughout the centuries. The Bible consists of historical books: At least twelve books of the Old Testament deal with the history of the nation of Israel; the book of Acts deals with the history of the early church. Martin Luther is not in any of the books of the Bible but he is one of the helloes of faith because he was the pioneer of the Protestant Reformation. As Harry S Truman said "Men make history and not the other way around.

In periods where there is no leadership, society stands still. Progress occurs when courageous, skillful leaders seize the opportunity to change things for the better." Luther was faced with the pressure of opposition from within and outside. The spirit of the reformer was not crushed by the iron hand of opposition from Rome. The Protestant Reformation also occurred in a time of conflict as Christian Europe was threatened by the Muslim Ottoman Empire. Both Martin Luther and John Calvin lived at the time when there was the ongoing tension of a possible invasion of Europe by the Turkish armies. But to them, there was only one thing which is better than living, and that one thing is to die for the sake of the gospel. The reformers taught us that we must have the perennial faith. We must be faithful to our beliefs in seasons and out of seasons, whether there is freedom of religion or not. History is kind to only those who intend to rewrite it. The past (history) is, therefore, the best instruction book for us to reset the future.

In the late medieval period, the Roman Catholic Church sold indulgences, and this was one of the main reasons which motivated Martin Luther to present his "95 Theses." This was the straw that broke the camel's back. The clergies were authorized by the Catholic Church to absolve penitents from the guilt of his sins and from punishment in the hellish inferno of the hereafter, but it did not absolve them from doing penance on earth. We must remember that the substitution of monetary fines for the punishment of a crime was a well-established practice in secular European courts in the Middle Ages. The Catholic Church was following coeval practices. The doctrine of purgatory was introduced by the Catholic Church as a temporary hell that the Catholics must attend in order to work off their sins. It was taught that as soon as the money clinked into the money chest, the soul flew out of purgatory. Luther saw it as a contradiction specifically intended to cleanse the guilt of sins which are already confessed, forgiven and atoned for by the blood of Jesus. Luther rebutted the doctrine and the method: "If the Pope has the power to forgive sins why doesn't he do it for free?" he asked. The Roman Catholic teaching on purgatory was officially proclaimed as dogma in 1438. This means that during the early church, all the way until that year (1438), the belief in the doctrine of purgatory did not exist. Nevertheless, the sin of exchanging cash for the grace is as old as the church. Simon wanted to buy the spiritual gift with money (Acts 8:18). The spiritual gifts are freely given and freely embraced. You cannot bribe them or coerce them or reason them into working for you. The one who sells prayers and the one who pays for prayers are both guilty of the sin of Simon. Intriguingly, the vice of using the gospel for personal enrichment is rampant in the church today. May we abhor all thoughts of making the gospel to serve our selfish ambitions. May God keep us from that subtle poison of spiritual harlotry.

Luther was a monk, and he was part of the system which he later came to oppose. "He went to Rome as a medieval theologian; he returned from Rome as a Protestant". He pondered how far he can go to merit God's favor in order to find the answer to his burdened soul. It is not because he was ignorant of the Scriptures; after all, he was already a theologian. He held a doctor's degree but he was not a member of the learned guild of scholastic theologians. His theology grew out of his anguished quest for a gracious God. For Luther, theology was not simply the academic study of religion. Rather, it was a lifelong process of struggle and temptation. He said that it is only the experience that makes a theologian. "I did not learn my theology all at once," he said, "but I had to search deeper for it, where my temptations took me. ... Not understanding, reading, or speculation, but living—nay, dying and being damned—make a theologian." He was inspired by the following scripture: "For in the gospel the righteousness of God is revealed—a righteousness that is by faith from first to last, just as it is written: "The righteous will live by faith." (Romans 17:1). He was confronted by the truth within the scripture and his eyes were opened to see what the Bible was saying than never before. He acknowledged that every person is born in sin and needs the Savior. Every sinful man is made righteous by the very act of God, which is embraced by faith. Salvation is not found in ourselves but comes to us from God. Justification is God's righteousness imputed to us in exchange for our unrighteousness. Justification by faith involves the sufficiency of Christ; His atoning blood is a one-time act of remission of sins upon confession. Justification is

God's declaration of a sinner to be free, and is made by God at the start of the Christian life; it is not a trophy of merit issued at the end. "There is therefore now no condemnation to them which are in Christ Jesus, who walk not after the flesh, but after the Spirit." (Romans 8:1). It means that God does not count our sins against us because He is counting our sins on Christ. The condemnation which in the present and final judgment of God impends over the sinner is removed by the intervention of Christ, and by the union of the believer with Him. "For he hath made him to be sin for us, who knew no sin; that we might be made the righteousness of God in him" (2 Corinthians 5:21). Jesus became what we are so that we might become what He is; He became what He was not so that we might become what we were not. Luther noted that without sin there is no need for salvation, and without grace, there is no possibility of salvation. In Him, in His blood is the only means of propitiation by which the righteousness of God becomes the righteousness of man. He resolved to fiercely fight the indulgences which were decreed by Pope Leo in 1517. The indulgences were pieces of papers or tickets with the Pope's seal (stamp), issued to those who paid money for the construction of the new St. Peter Basilica, implicating that they are forgiven or pardoned of all their past, present and future sins. Those who bought them were considered to be as pure as Adam was before sinning or as innocent as paradise. Luther realized that there was no salvation down this path. Eventually, he emerged as the most radical of all sixteenth-century reformers.

Ivan Ssemwanga, who was a few months shy of his fortieth birthday, died yesterday on the 24th May 2017, at the Steve Biko Academic Hospital in Pretoria, South Africa. Ssemwanga lived large and departs the world in similar fashion, said family members who converged at the deceased residence in Muyenga Kampala yesterday. He might not be buried in one of his posh cars like some West African moguls, but no expenses will be spared in ensuring him a befitting send-off. Zari, his ex-wife posted "God loves those that are special and that is exactly who you were and I guess that is why he wanted you to himself. You have touched and helped thousands. You did wonders and I remember you telling me 'life is too short Zee, let me live it to the fullest.' In this dark hour, it makes sense why you always said those words to me. To your sons, you were a hero-some kind of Superman. Anyone who has ever been in your presence knows what a charming person you were. You will be missed and remembered in so many ways. You were Ivan the great!" Zari Tlale posted on social media.

Somebody posted: "Ssemwanga, though he lived not as a saint, this he did to keep a heavenly reward... There is a man called Ananias's in the bible who never knew who God was, but his giving reached God's throne, that even God sent a messenger to introduce Himself to Ananias. Now we might not know about God's details of the judgment of Souls, but God will receive some people in heaven not for the life they lived, but for the compassion of their own hearts, even while unaware of who He is. Blessed is the merciful because they shall "OBTAIN MERCY" Heaven can't reject such people..." My reply: Good works are acceptable to God but God will not bring to Himself a soul that is polluted by sin. He provided the way through Jesus Christ for whosoever is willing to purify their souls. All souls after Adam are considered to be dented by sin. The souls that go to God are the ones which are regenerated by the Holy Spirit. They are the ones recreated in Christ. That is why Jesus is called the Second Adam (1 Corinthians 15:45). If God could take people into His presence out of compassion or their own merits why did He send Jesus to be killed brutally?

The news of the death of cancer sufferer Carol Atuhirwe has prompted an outpouring of tributes from thousands of Ugandans, including friends, family, and well-wishers – within and beyond Uganda. Emotional messages of condolence and love have flooded especially social media since the news of the end of her life in India started to trickle in late Thursday. Born on April 7, 1987, Atuhirwe has died at the age of 30 on Thursday, June 1st, 2017. Somebody posted: "The Almighty Allah finally takes Carol's soul. When 'the Save Carol campaign' started, Prof. Mukiibi of St Lawrence Schools, Don Ivan Ssemwanga, Maj. General Oketa, AIG Andrew Felix Kaweesi, Massy Moses Kasule, Maj Kiggundu, Joan Kagezi, Tycoon Kasiwukira, Tycoon Mabirizi, young Aggy Wiliams among other prominent and ordinary Ugandans, they were all living very happily, none of them ever imagined would die before Carol. All of them died before she did. The Almighty God has and knows best all our death calendar. May their souls rest in peace." Reply: When you die you have no advantage over the people who died before you because you are all equally dead. The only life that counts after death is the one which was regenerated by Jesus Christ, prior to the death experience of the body.

HARARE, Zimbabwe — Morgan Tsvangirai, a former labor leader and prime minister of Zimbabwe who once seemed on the cusp of defeating the country's longtime president, Robert G. Mugabe, only to face bloody intimidation that thwarted his ambitions, died on Wednesday night February 14, 2018. He was 65.

My Sun has set- Morgan Tsvangi: Last day when I shed my earthly body. I will cross over to the spiritual realm. My physical body had fought so many battles in the past. Cancer was but one battle too many. I gave it a shot. In fact, I gave it plenty. As cancer ate my insides I could see the toll on my family. The despair, the misery and the agony which they tried to hide. Unfortunately, on earth, you can only control how you live. No one gets to control how they die. Not even why. Sooner or later our spirits will take to the sky. Eventually we all fly.

I've reflected on my life and I'm proud. I managed to inspire lives. I gave hope to husbands and their wives. It was never a plan or target of mine. I did not do it for high fives. I wanted to stand for workers' rights. I thought that would be enough but I would be found fighting a bigger battle from 1999. History will judge me but I like to think I did mighty fine.

I made my mistakes. I lived through them and I learned. I was a political blacksmith who tried to forge a new Zimbabwe and you know what they say. I played with fire and I got burnt. I won some hearts. I won enemies too. Some I earned. There were things I could have done better. There were things I couldn't and those I don't regret. Some seeds I planted in hearts of my people to blossom and fruit years later.

I've been broken hearted, I've broken hearts both alive and now as I depart. I've been human for the most part. I've had controversy but I have also given reason to celebrate. I've been expected to dangle at the end of a rope only to turn the gloom into hope. All while living on the international stage under a microscope. History will judge me. Did I fail to change the status quo? I don't think so. But it depends what those who judge are looking for. I think I did more.

I opened eyes. I let the people believe they could stare at their tormentors and say no. I would believe I made them believe they could refuse bread crumbs and instead demand more. I didn't do everything. But sometimes all people need is a start. A sign. I hope that's what I'm remembered for.

As my sun sets yours rises. Make hay while it shines. Follow your heart, don't waste your single life conforming, forcing your soul to do what it despises. There's a race to be run. There is work to be done. Do your best. I will see you when you join me on the other side. (Morgan Tsvangirai).

21st February 2018: Reverend Billy Graham, the influential Southern preacher who became a spiritual advisor to several US presidents and millions of Americans via their television sets, has died, his family said Wednesday. "Billy Graham is the closest thing to a national pope that we shall ever see," journalist Garry Wills once wrote in The Washington Post.

It is estimated that Billy Graham has preached to over 215 million people in more than 185 countries. Billy Gram is the most respected evangelist of our generation. The secular world and the liberal media have a different view regarding the power behind the greatness of Billy Graham:

"There will never be another Billy Graham, because the world that made him possible is gone.

Benny Hinn prophesized, some years in the past that the death of Billy Gram will God's sign of a sweeping revival across the world. Yesterday, televangelist Benny Hinn recorded an extended Facebook Live video (the comments start around the 9:30 mark), discussing the legacy of Billy Graham, who died yesterday at the age of 99. And, along with talking about Graham's influence on himself and his ministry, Hinn also got surprisingly candid about his philosophy on the so-called "prosperity gospel."

Though he said, "We get attacked for preaching prosperity, well it's in the Bible," he continued, "But I think some have gone to the extreme with it sadly, and it's not God's word what is taught, and I think I'm as guilty as others. Sometimes you go a little farther than you really need to go and then God brings you back to normality and reality."

He explained, "When I was younger I was influenced by the preachers who taught whatever they taught. But as I've lived longer, I'm thinking, 'Wait a minute, you know this doesn't fit totally with the Bible and it doesn't fit with the reality.' So what is prosperity? No lack. I've said this before."

Hinn said, "Did Elijah the prophet have a car? No. Did not even have a bicycle. He had no lack ... Did Jesus drive a car or live in a mansion? No. He had no lack. How about the apostles? None lacked among them. Today, the idea is abundance and palatial homes and cars and bank accounts. The focus is wrong ... It's so wrong."

Hinn went on to say that he no longer flies private jets, and dispelled rumors that he is worth $40 million. "We all sadly make the mistake of thinking that, 'Well this is what God wants,' and God says 'No, that's not what I want.' It's time to live biblically. You know it all comes down to one thing. Do we love Jesus, yes or no? If we love Jesus then it's all about Jesus. If we don't love Jesus then it's about other things."

I respect Benny Hinn for his humility. We are all likely to preach wrong things because we have humanity in us that can be swayed emotionally.

The sign of a false teacher is when they continue misguiding the flocks even after the truth has been revealed to them. I have seen and heard Benny Hinn three times when he comes out to apologize to the masses on the national television. The first time is when his ministry was at the highest rating; he was called to order by the elders of the Assemblies of God Pentecostal Church who saw pride in his actions of swinging his jacket to his audience to be slain in the Spirit. Benny Hinn came to the national television, broken and apologized to the Church, saying that what he has been doing is not biblical. The other time when I saw Benny Hinn broken was when he came on the national television to renounce his popular teaching that with your faith you can make things happen and claim whatever you want. He said faith must be in God to make things happen but not in self. He said he got that doctrine of error from Kenneth Hagin. I want to end by saying that we should pray for each other. The Bible says that "Be alert and of sober mind. Your enemy the devil prowls around like a roaring lion looking for someone to devour." (1 Peter 5:8). We should always be sober, and on guard, because our adversary as a lion runs about here and there, famished with hunger, using insidious methods, wiles, and stratagem to surprise the saints, and get an advantage of them unaware.

On Wednesday, March 14th, 2018, a renowned British physicist Stephen Hawking, whose mental genius and physical disability made him a household name and inspiration across the globe, died at age 76. Hawking defied predictions he would only live for a few years after developing a form of motor neurone disease in 1964 at the age of 22. The illness gradually robbed him of mobility, leaving him confined to a wheelchair, almost completely paralyzed and unable to speak except through his trademark voice synthesizer. He spoke with the wiggle of the cheek which then sends signals to a computer, which is able to pick up each individual letter, then arranged into words, which then miraculously arranges the words into sentences....all coming out into an 80's robot voice! He was regarded by his admirers as the smartest person. His extreme atheistic views, courage, and persistence with humor influenced many people across the world. The British scientist dedicated his life to unlocking the secrets of the

Universe. He was famed for his work with black holes and relativity, and wrote several popular science books including 'A Brief History of Time' which became an unlikely worldwide bestseller and cemented his superstar status. He wrote that "We are each free to believe what we want and it is my view that the simplest explanation is there is no God. No one created the universe and no one directs our fate. This leads me to a profound realization: There is probably no heaven, and no afterlife either." He said emphatically to support his atheistic views that, "I regard the brain as a computer which will stop working when its components fail. There is no heaven or afterlife for broken down computers; that is a fairy story for people afraid of the dark." However, he believed that this world will come to an end due to some natural causes. For years, Hawking has warned that humankind faces extinction from a slew of threats ranging from climate change to destruction from nuclear war and genetically engineered viruses. Hawking recently estimated that humans have 100 years left on Earth – if we're lucky. He saw the need to love and to be loved. He once said, "It would not be much of a universe if it wasn't home to the people you love." We are called to pray for the living as opposed to the dead. I would have said to him that "RIP" but no one rests in peace till they have known the Prince of Peace!

Monday, April 02, 2018: Winnie Mandela, the ex-wife of South African anti-apartheid fighter and former president Nelson Mandela, died on Monday at the age of 81, her spokesman said. She died in a Johannesburg hospital after a long illness, spokesman Victor Dlamini said in a statement. She was undeniably one of the greatest icons of the struggle against white minority rule in the southern African country. "She fought valiantly against the apartheid state and sacrificed her life for the freedom of the country. Her activism and resistance to apartheid landed her in jail on numerous occasions, eventually causing her banishment to the small town of Brandfort in the then Orange Free State. Winnie Mandela, was married to Nelson Mandela for 38 years, but her place in history was also stained by controversy. Most of Winnie's marriage to Nelson was spent apart, with Nelson imprisoned for 27 years, leaving her to raise their two daughters alone and to keep alive his political dream under the repressive white-minority regime. But her reputation came under damaging scrutiny in the twilight years of apartheid rule. In 1986, she was widely linked to "necklacing", when suspected traitors were burnt alive by a petrol-soaked car tire being put over their head and set alight.

Dr. Lwanga: The life of the late Dr. Lwanga of Uganda projects the highs and lows of life, a fairy tale of a genius humanitarian. He was a thinking tank to edify and direct the community. He was a well-educated and successful physician, with many trophies of excellence in the medical field. He counseled many people with great charm and humor. It is because of his advice and wise counsel that I have been able to achieve much of the success recorded. He was calm and his calmness manifested in the fact that he never exhibited anger or offense even when you rubbed him the wrong way. He cried with the afflicted and smiled even when it was hard to. He was a magnanimous person. He helped many young folks to discover their callings of life. Because of his legacy there are many young doctors across the nation who are aspiring to be humanitarians. Geniuses like you are not limited by the physical bodies to impact mankind positively; you will never die in our minds. You will live on for many more generations to come by your real life exhibited. I choose neither to mourn nor to cry, but to celebrate you. Dr., we shall surely live to light your candle and to pass it on. (Read about Dr. Lwanga's life story in my book "The Legacy of a Hero").

Israel Kyeyune: My dad was the chairman of the board of the Anglican Church at Bombo. We lost him to the cruel hand of death after he was abducted by Colonel Juma Ali Butabika, just a couple of days after the archbishop of the Church of Uganda was killed. Dad, it is now over forty years since you were forcibly removed from our sight. You were not a legend but one of the few people who still believe that honesty is worthy to die for. You defined 'authenticity'. It is because of God's grace that I am what I am. But God used you to mold me into godly values. Dad, they brutally got rid of you from the face of this earth, but in heaven, you have the last laugh! I will always miss you immensely; may your soul rest in peace.

Forty years since the slaying of Archbishop of Uganda Janani Luwum by then president Idi Amin, the army officer who the dishonorable duty of burying the man of God was given to, has spoken out about how they went about laying him to rest.

In an exclusive interview with Daily Monitor, Lt Col Yefusa Bananuka, says the burial of the cleric was much more complicated than pulling the trigger at Nile Hotel on the evening of February 16, 1977. According to Lt Col Bananuka, top government security operatives toyed with the idea of dumping the body of the clergyman into River Nile at Karuma to forever conceal the macabre death in the stomachs of the crocodiles. But Amin's vice president, Gen Mustapha Adrisi, opposed the idea and instead assigned Lt Col Bananuka, to oversee the burial of Archbishop Luwum and the former minister of Lands, Housing and Physical Planning, Lt Col Erinayo Wilson Oryema, killed on the same day for the same alleged crime.

Mr Museveni said at the time when Ugandans continued to flee into exile because of the excesses of the Amin's regime, Archbishop Luwum openly criticized the ruthless and arbitrary killings and unexplained disappearances of Ugandans and foreigners alike under Amin. "In Uganda, his [Archbishop Luwum's] legacy stands out as a spiritual leader, voice of the voiceless, a father and a man of compassion who portrayed the image of true Christianity and leadership," Mr. Museveni said. He said Luwum will always be remembered for his principles, aspirations, and values he stood for, adding that he is a gift to Uganda.

Friday, February 16, 2018: Thousands of Christian believers on Friday screamed with joy and made loud ululation after seeing a circular rainbow around the sun in the sky during the 41st anniversary celebration to mark the martyrdom of Archbishop Janani Luwum in Mucwini sub county, Kitgum District. "Today we are witnessing a very great miracle, when you see this sign; it means God is speaking to people of Uganda to listen to what Archbishop Janani Luwum preached about truth, justice," He added that, "this is a very rare happening; it means that God is reminding people about the legacy of Archbishop Luwum". One of the Christians said as he picked his phone to record the moment. Look at how it's hanging over the grave of the archbishop, this is miracle, he added. Archbishop Luwum was the Anglican archbishop of the Church Uganda, Rwanda, Burundi, and Boga Zaire was murdered on February 17 1977 by Idi Amin soldiers for his sharp criticism against the then regime.

Somebody posted a message defending Idi Amin saying that maybe somebody framed Archbishop Luwum unknowingly to Amin. Reply: The Intelligence Department once told President Milton Obote that Bishop Nsubuga was collecting arms to pass them on to Museveni's guerrillas. Obote instructed Rwakasisi to go pick the guns and leave the man of God alone. And he discovered that it was a hoax; there were no guns as reported. Do you see leadership?

Somebody asked that "Why do people say concerning the dead that they kicked the bucket?" Reply: The concept of "kicking the bucket" has been around for a while, though its provenance is uncertain. Some believe it refers to the act of putting a noose around one's neck, standing on a bucket, and then kicking the bucket away, causing death by hanging. Others "suggest that the bucket being kicked is not, as we might imagine, a pail, but a corruption of the Old French word *buquet*, meaning a balance or beam, from which slaughtered animals were suspended."

JUNE FOR FAMILY

Genesis 1:27 - "So God created mankind in his own image, in the image of God he created them; male and female he created them." God made man in His image; God made man in His glory. The word 'man' in the above scripture means male and female. "Male and female created he them; and blessed them, and called their name Adam, in the day when they were created." (Genesis 5:2).

In the first marriage in history, God got a man and put him into the Garden of Eden (Genesis 2:24). The word 'Eden' means the delightful bright spot (God's presence). The first thing God gave to a man (Adam) is not a woman but His presence. Man needs God's presence first before he looks for a woman. Eva met Adam in the Garden of Eden. A woman needs to meet a man in God's presence rather than getting him from the wilderness and try to pull him into God's presence. (Myles Munroe)

A Good relationship involves finding the goodness in you and finding a good person to marry. The standard of 'good' is not relative to the eyes of the beholder but it is the absolute goodness of God; this guideline is necessary in order to avert the unholy alliance.

Somebody asked "Do you believe in love at first sight if so why?" Reply: Not a good idea at all, unless it is a miracle or a divine act. People don't fall in love imminently but grow into it. Avoid the future regrets by avoiding rushing into relationship please.

You choose to love someone. You have all the power when it comes to loving someone. The right way is to make a decision based on their morals, personality and choosing to trust their abilities. If things do not work out, then you also have the power to stop loving them and release them from your life. Being in love is deeper than falling in love with someone. It doesn't happen by coincidence without a warning. And when it happens, it's something you cannot afford to walk away from. Even if you manage to walk away, that feeling will stick with you forever, that is how you know that you're in love with the person.

"A fish and a bird may fall in love but the two cannot build a home together" ~ (African proverb). The meaning/explanation: When it comes to marriage, it's true that love is important but it's also true that love alone is insufficient. Character and compatibility are other essential factors worth considering before marriage. Compatibility comprises medical and faith orientations. Many factors are secondary when considering whom to marry. Issues like height, race, food preference etc can be adjusted to. But something like faith is a foundational issue and cannot be overlooked without facing serious consequences. A controversial person may argue saying that a penguin can marry and live with a fish in water. But the question is: why is it that there is no penguin that is married to a fish? It means even animals know better what or who to marry. And even if a penguin was to marry a fish, they would have to endure their marriage just as we will, if we marry anyone we are not compatible with. The truth is: marriage is not meant to be merely endured; it is meant to be mainly enjoyed. Yes, you cannot have a perfect marriage but you can have a perfect match. Be sensible! (Sam Kyeyune)

A relationship is work in progress. Don't go into a relationship, build a relationship...

Beauty catches the attention but character catches the heart. Marrying a gorgeous woman who has no character equals to disaster.

It works better when you marry your friend. "The word "friend" is a label anyone can try on. You decide who is best suited to wear it." – Carlos Wallace

When a child of God marries a nonbeliever, they will have God as their father and Satan as their father in law.

The quickest way to derail your destiny is to marry the wrong person.

During biblical times, it was arranged marriage. People got married in order to date. Today people date in order to get married. Whereas arranged marriage is not the best way to go, marriage, as opposed to sex should be the only viable reason for dating. Love must be the only reason for marriage as opposed to lust. I suggest that the married couples should continue to go on date regularly after marriage. The prospect of dating someone should never become less appealing just because you are getting older.

Being in a relationship should feel good, not anxious or stressful! Your significant other is someone you can go to for support and to help you to overcome the challenges you're facing. In a healthy relationship, there must be trust. It takes time to build and earn trust but you must build on trust in order to support each other effectively. Where there is trust your partner accepts and loves you for the person you are, and you will do what you say you will do. Healthy relationships are built on trust and mutual respect, not suspicion and background checks. "Trust is the glue of life. It's the most essential ingredient in effective communication. It's the foundational principle that holds all relationships".

"Chains do not hold a marriage together. It is threads, hundreds of tiny threads, which sew people together through the years." ~ Simone Signoret

It doesn't matter how much you know; you are responsible for only what you say. "If you watch what you think, you won't have to watch what you say!" ~ Bill Johnson

"Verbal abuse is just as bad as physical abuse. Cuts and bruises heal, but memories last forever."

"Positive people also have negative thoughts; they just don't let those thoughts control them. Positive attitude helps you in a lot of positive ways, it creates positive results, helps you solve problems and attracts Good and positive vibes" ~ Precious Aniedi Patrick

'Mature love will stay away from making assumptions and judging others' intentions.'

We are supposed to listen twice as much as we talk. We spend at least 45% of our times listening. Many have been rebuked for talking but nobody has ever been rebuked for listening. Good listeners filter what they hear to grasp what is actually said instead of what they think was said. And they talk only when they have to.

Meekness is power under control: Weak people revenge; strong people forgive; intelligent people ignore.

"One of the surest evidences of friendship that one individual can display to another is telling him gently of a fault. If any other can excel it, it is listening to such a disclosure with gratitude, and amending the error" ~ Edward G. Bulwer-Lytton

Watch out whom you lend your ear to. Marriages are in particular broken when the people who claim to be Christians take counseling from the non-believers who do not acknowledge our values or who are not even married. Whenever you have a marital problem, talk to somebody who is spiritually mature than you, and who has been married for a long time.

Spend value time with your spouse, without kids and other obstructions. Spend less time on social media. The danger of technology is that it takes away from personal interactions.

"Sometimes you just need alone time. People in relationships support each other, and sometimes that support means giving your partner space so they can enjoy their hobbies and passions."

Problems in a relationship should be talked out, prayed out but not gossiped out.

"Silence and smile are the two most important tools. Smile is the way to solve many problems and silence is the way to avoid many problems".

"Don't worry when I argue with you; worry when I stop because it means there is nothing left to fight for."

"Love your enemy": This is one of the greatest laws of marriage. The reason is that your spouse may turn into your enemy occasionally.

Conflicts should be avoided by finding the root causes of conflict. Use conflicts as an opportunity to study your spouse. Turn disabilities into possibilities.

Exodus 20:5 – "—for I the LORD thy God am a jealous God". God is love but also, He is described to have the righteous emotions of jealous. Ironically, love is paired with jealous. There is inbuilt jealous within us to guard what we love most. As for those of you who are married, jealous is a healthy dose if it is prescribed in the right measure. Except that, anything given in access becomes sin. Everything in excess is bad including medicine and food. The sin of Jealous involves desiring what does not belong to you. Therefore, being jealous of what belongs to you is not a sin. Jealous is a reaction we put up, out of fear of losing what we have. Jesus described sin in the intents of the heart as opposed to the actions (Matthew 5:28; Matthew 5:21-22). Therefore, fear and jealous can either be positive (moral) or negative (immoral) depending on the intents of the heart. These are some of the examples of positive fear: The fear of defying the physical laws of nature; the fear of a stranger; the fear of going out late in the darkness of the night, the fear of offending your spouse, and etc. "Fear is the guard dog that is protecting the fortress of spiritual prosperity. When the dog starts barking, we know that the treasure he is guarding is near".

The most important intimate act a couple can engage in is not sex but praying together. People who pray together stay together.

<u>Advice to men:</u> Do not take a woman who is the love of your heart for granted! Pamper her, pray for her, cherish her, love her, support her financially, and make her feel like your woman! Saying to her verbally that you love without actions to support your words is not enough.

Ephesians 5:25 – "Husbands love your wives, just as Christ loved the church and gave himself up for her to sanctify her, cleansing her by the washing with water through the word." There are two Greek words for romantic love: Eros is the kind of love that was named after the Greek god of fertility, and it represented the idea of sexual passion and desire. *Ludus* – this was the Greeks' idea of playful love, which referred to the affection between children or young lovers. We've all had a taste of it in the flirting

and teasing in the early stages of a relationship. But we also live out our *ludus* when we sit around in a social manner bantering and laughing with friends, or when we go out dancing. The ultimate *ludic* activity is almost a playful substitute for sex itself. But in the above scripture, Paul used the word 'Agape' or sacrificial love, the kind of love by which Jesus loved the Church. It means that apart from the relationship with Jesus Christ, nothing should matter to a husband more than his wife.

The only definition of love given by the Scriptures is that God is Love. If God is love and Christ is God then Christ is love. When Christ loved the Church, He did not love her in comparison to His body (Himself); by loving the Church (bride), He basically loved His own body because the Church is His own body (body of Christ). The Bible says that when the two get married they become one: "And the two will become one flesh. So they are no longer two, but one flesh" (Mark 10:8). The Church is His bride and spouse, whom He betrothed to Himself from all eternity. The last part of the Scripture says that "cleansing her by the washing with water through the word". This scripture explains what Jesus meant when He said that, ""Very truly I tell you, no one can enter the kingdom of God unless they are born of water and the Spirit." To be born again is to be justified; it means receiving grace in exchange for justice for our sins. Justification is imminent but those who are justified must be sanctified in the righteousness of God by the Holy Spirit through the Word. This is what it means to be born of water and Spirit. Sanctification is a lifetime process that is completed in glorification. Our Lord modifies the last clause and speaks of entering into the kingdom of God, which is the reserve of the regenerated, rather than perceiving or discerning the features of the kingdom, which any natural man can do. The Word informs, and the Spirit transforms. The head knowledge must be translated into the heart knowledge by the Holy Spirit in order to affect our transformation. Entering the kingdom of God is experiencing a new birth, acquiring the new nature, and the new character that is not in contradiction with the divine. It is the metamorphosis act from the domain of the corrupt kingdom of this world to the domain of the Lordship of Christ. It is an irreversible change compared to a caterpillar that changes to a butterfly; it will never be a caterpillar again.

<u>A father's wise counseling to the son who was searching for a wife:</u> My son, I will be very raw and sincere with you. Do not worry about the size of a woman buttock or breast but worry about the size of her heart and brain. Worry about the size of her love and endurance. Because after 5 or 10 years, it will not be about the breast or buttock. As you can see, your mum now has a flat chest and almost flat buttock but we still live together happily, I still love her and she still loves me.

Be careful of a woman that loves money. I mean the woman that talks 'every time' about her hair, clothes, shoes, bags, panties and make-ups. Marriage is not all about these things. Without make-up, clothes, shoes, and panties a good marriage will still stand but without love, no marriage can stand. When I got married to your mum, I didn't have a car or house of my own. I was not even educated. But I had dreams and she appreciated and supported me. Any woman that does not support your dream is not worth thinking a minute about. There are women that will see your dreams better than you, you are lucky if you find one. My son, open your ears very well, there is a kind of woman you should avoid, do not make a mistake to marry this kind of woman or you will regret it. I mean a woman that always has bad things to say about everyone. If you see this kind of woman, run away. One of the worst kinds of woman you can marry is the one that complains about everything. If you buy this, she says you should have bought that, if you do this, she said you should have done that. Please stay away!

Most women enjoy talking but the one who talks for two hours and listens for two minutes is a potential 'bomb'. Be wise. Be very careful of a pretending partner. A pretending woman is not hard to know. She will always know everything about everything, she will be careful. Just close your eyes and open your heart and you will see! No woman is perfect. If you see a woman who believes in your dream, who respects you, who is committed and who is not all about herself alone then don't let her go. But remember, you must not be a wayward man. I have trained you! If you find a good woman when you are a bad man, you won't have a good marriage! I won't pick a wife for you but I have given you my advice. When you find her, bring her for my blessings. May you find a woman that will increase you not decrease you. (Jerry John Rawlings).

<u>Advice to ladies</u>: The relationship is the most valuable commodity we need in a marriage and it can't be bought. True joy is not found in material things. Money can buy you wedding but not the relationship. Money can buy you a house but not a home; money can buy you a bed but not the sleep. "Your love cannot be bought… no scientist on earth can explain what love is and why it is so extremely powerful – more powerful than anything else we know. It is a phenomenon and it is free." Don't marry for the money; else you'll become one of his possessions. Add value to yourself – get a career. Don't be fooled that a man will solve all your problems. Beauty is not everything. If it is all you have, you'll lose your place to someone more beautiful, better and more mature and competent than you.

Let God make a man out of him before you make a husband out of him! "Spiritual Women on fire for God don't look for a man. They pray for a husband but with knowledge that their husband is in their purpose and he will find her."

Seek a relationship that will edify Christ, not your ego. The beauty of a woman must be seen in her eyes because that is the doorway to her heart. The most beautiful women are the ones who have more to offer than looks. A Christian man doesn't need a woman who can slay a dress or slay some heels; he needs a woman who can slay demons. We're in a war; not a fashion show! Marry someone who will break down the doors of hells with you in prayers. Avoid being unequally yoked with someone you will have to force to bend their knees to pray.

Stop calling yourself ugly. When you call yourself ugly you are actually telling God that He is ugly because God created you in His image. Stop telling God he is ugly when out of His infinite wisdom, He always creates the most beautiful masterpieces. Start loving yourself through His eyes.

Counseling which the ladies need during the intimate moment (s): Many young girls think because they are sexually active and experience they will easily be married and have their husbands loving them. And when a man approaches for marriage they think the greatest asset they have to show the man is sex. Others also think once they are giving out their bodies it means they are giving out the best for which reason they will be chosen above all. Sex is an important element in marriage and until there is sexual intercourse between a husband and a wife, the marriage is not yet spiritually recognized but there is much more to bring to table in relationship than sex.

When sex is the reason for marriage your relationship is at stake. You can have sex on the first date & he ends up loving you thereafter and forever. You can also wait for 5yrs before having sex with him & get dumped after sex. You can even wait till after marriage and he may divorce you after sex. God made sex to be enjoyed within the perimeters of marriage but sex should never be the determining factor of marriage.

Sex is not love. Love is not sex. You can have sex and not be in love. You can be in love and not engage in sex. A man may hate you and still have sex with you. Be wise. Using sex to manipulate a man will eventually fail. It is self-deception to think that giving him sex will make him love you. True Love will never force you to engage in sex. A man who doesn't love you will not change his mind because of sex. If he tells you to 'prove your love' by having sex with him; he is only using you. If he is in it for the sex, 'better sex' from somebody else will take him away from you. If he gets married to you because 'the sex is good', it will be fatal to your marriage in future when you can't keep up with the good sex he needs. Making yourself his 'sex slave' is foolish. True love will never shame or degrade you. Let him get married to you because he loves you, honors you, feels a strong emotional, mental and spiritual connection with you and wants you to spend the rest of his life with you.

"My child, keep this precious gift. The gift is like an egg, you must not allow it to break. Keep your virginity for your future husband. Be good to people, be respectful and loyal but never allow men to unlock your special gift. What you're carrying is a good fortune. It's attractive to all but precious to few. The dog does not know the value of a Rosary. Value your virginity and guide it contentiously. It should be presented to your future husband on your wedding day."

How can a woman create a conducive environment for intimacy? Sex starts in the brain. Therefore, start by setting a conducive environment. Text your husband some hot messages as a shadow of the things awaiting him at home. When your husband returns home, do not greet him with household demands like paying bills and expect to have sex. Instead, create a stress-free environment when he returns home so that he feels safe and relaxed. If you have children make sure that they go to bed early before your husband returns home. It will allow you to focus on your husband without interruptions from the kids. A survey shows that as the children grow and leave the house, couples resume having more sex. This is a contradiction to the research that indicates that the frequency of sex declines as people grow old. "It is possible to find a 70-year-old having sex more than once a week since they are now relaxed. Surprise your spouse regularly with something small like a telephone call from work, a touch that is not sexually oriented, a gift and etc. Such small things reaffirm your commitment to the relationship.

Romantic love does not last forever and can end at any moment. According to statistics, almost 50 percent of married couples in the United States end up divorcing each other at some point. That just proves my point that romantic love on its own can end. Once the honeymoon phase in a relationship is over, that is when things get tough. Arguments ensue, differences begin to rise, but if the couple is in love with each other, they will get past these differences. The reason is that you cannot picture a life without each other. True love goes beyond feelings.

Sex is not all about making children. You must be a different woman to your husband every time. Seduce your husband, don't always allow your husband to ask for Sex, there must be no timetable for sex. Be creative, don't be predictable. Give him what he wants. If you lose influence over your husband, you have lost womanhood. Be part of your husband plans. Don't have too many children, you wanna sell them? Allow your husband to check in and out anytime. When a man is sexually satisfied, he is emotionally stable. Stop saying, is it food? Yes, sex is food!!!

As a wife, try to invest in yourself spiritually so you can adequately support him. Build yourself as his prayer warrior so that you will not be forced to pray at the end of your life. Holy wives don't just speak in tongues. They cook super meals, they raise godly kids, and help the husband to stimulate the income. Don't allow your husband to provide all your needs, he is not a money-making machine. Iron sharpens iron, try to reciprocate. You are meant to support each other spiritually, financially, physically and morally through thick and thin. You are a builder. A wise woman builds her home. Women need the wisdom to build their homes. Do not be too outspoken, know when to talk, when to listen and when to be quiet.

Love your husband with all your heart, never tell him, if not because of my children, remember you've known him before the arrival of those children. Be the number one fan of your husband. Support him in all his interest. Ensure you decree greatness in all his endeavors. Don't allow other ladies to do this for you. Be the first and best at this. Don't focus on the competition outside the home and get bitter. You are not the only lady who loves your husband. Focus on your Husband and give him the best of treatment always; especially when you think he doesn't deserve it. You will win.

Everyone needs space. Don't become a prison for your husband. When it gets to the point where he needs space grant it to Him. There is freedom in true love. Over protective love is false and destructive. Use those periods to better yourself. Get the sexiest look. Be your sweetest self when he returns home. You are always the winner.

Find out what love means to your partner and give it. Don't assume a common definition of love. What is love to you may not be for him. Look at your Husband with the lenses of righteousness in Christ Jesus. He may have some wrong doings but do not focus on the wrongdoings but rather focus on the Christ in him. In other words, focus on his positives and not the negatives. Do this in wisdom!

Be the curious and creative type. Don't be shy to initiate lovemaking. Wearing sexy lingerie does not mean you are spoilt or demon possessed. Wear hot dresses (for their husbands), pamper your husband, put his head on your chest and pray for him. Give him an unannounced kiss from the back. Don't be too holy to be romantic in the public. He is your husband for God sake. Be romantic! It is good for the heart. Some people are not happy that you're happy in that marriage, proof them wrong that you love him and he is your crown, always feel good when you hold him. Take care of your body. Don't look 50 while you're still under 40, it drives men crazy. Always keep fit regardless of your age or body.

<u>Counseling from an African prospective (Toro):</u> The Toro people, Tooro people or Batooro are a Bantu ethnic group, native to Tooro Kingdom, a sub-national constitutional monarchy within Uganda. Their language is called Rutooro. It closely resembles Runyoro, spoken in the neighboring kingdom of Bunyoro. A combined language is called Runyoro/Rutooro. Beatrice Kababiito from Tooro Uganda narrates "I have given away more than 20 girls in marriage as *Isenkatimugole* and I always emphasize *omusaija tayangwa* (a wife is not supposed to resist her husband) term to the brides. This mainly introduces them to how best they must

behave while in their relationship or marriages." Here is a summary of her counseling given to the African ladies to prepare them for marriage:

1). A woman is supposed to obey his husband and do what he requests sometimes not because you want to but for the sake of your marriage.

2). Women should always be calm, respect their husbands to the maximum even if your husband shouts at you, keep calm and quiet. Avoid talking or shouting back at him which could cause breakups in your marriage/relationship.

3). A woman should be the first person to know what her husband wants; like the type of dish he loves, clothes to wear not letting the maids to do it all.

4). A man is always a man regardless of tribe, size, religion, rich or poor, once you accept to marry him, he must always be the best and your one and only, love and care about him to the fullest, never compare him to any other.

5). Communication is very crucial in marriages, know what both of you want and always resolve your problems amicably. Avoid 3rd parties in relationships.

6). Know each other's weaknesses and try to overcome them by helping each other. If you want to have a successful marriage, your husband should be your best friend. Don't keep secrets from him because once he finds out from other people, it will be had for you to convince him, and in all, always pray to God to guide you in everything.

Beatrice Kababiito advises Batooro women to keep respecting themselves and continue being faithful to their husbands to prove others wrong. Any Tooro woman must be respectful, very obedient to her husband. She must be submissive to him during the intimate moment(s). However, she adds that girls are always taught to stay faithful to their husbands no matter the situation or changes from his behavior. She told all girls who are planning to get married to always marry the men they love and follow their heart plus her tips for a successful marriage.

Mother's Day

The celebrations of mothers and motherhood can be traced back to the ancient Greeks and Romans, who held festivals in honor of the mother goddesses Rhea, Hilaria and Cybele. But in modern times, Mother's Day got rooted in the early Christian festival known as "Mothering Sunday." In Africa, Mother's Day celebration was copied from the colonial masters, the British, whose celebration was also copied from the Americans. Originally, it was a religious festival in the UK known as Mothering Sunday. It evolved from the 16th-century Christian practice of visiting one's mother church annually on last Sunday of Lent. That way, most mothers were reunited with their children because even women in service were released by their masters for that weekend.

Meanwhile, in the US, Mother's Day evolved differently, first as an isolated celebration by Anna Jarvis in 1908, when she held a memorial for her mother, Ann Reeves Jarvis, at St Andrew's Methodist Church in Grafton, West Virginia. But her campaign to make Mother's Day a recognized holiday in the US began in 1905, the year her mother, died. She had been a peace activist who cared for wounded soldiers on both sides of the American Civil War, and created Mother's Day Work Clubs to address public health issues. In 1908, the US Congress first rejected her proposal joking that even mothers-in-law would ask for their day. However, they later proclaimed it and, thanks to Jarvis efforts, by 1911 all US states were observing the holiday. In 1914, US President Woodrow Wilson signed a proclamation designating Mother's Day on the second Sunday in May, as a national holiday to honor mothers. As a result of the US influence, Mothering Sunday in UK was transformed into the tradition of showing appreciation to one's mother. In 1914, the holiday was still recognized in the original historical sense of religious recognition with attention paid to Mary the mother of Jesus Christ and the concept of the Mother Church. After World War I, Mothering Day customs declined and by World War II, US soldiers brought the American model of Mother's Day to the UK. From then on, the UK adopted Mother's Day as a celebration of motherhood and popularized it throughout the commonwealth, including Uganda. (Story as told by Hilary Bainamigisha).

A mother is the custodian of the souls of her children. The greatest gift a mother can give to her kids is to steer their souls away from hell. Thank God for all godly women. Motherhood means giving up your private life and living others' lives. Her job prescription is to nurture and rebuke. The greatest power of women is not in their muscular vigor but in their persuasive tongue. The persuasion of a mother is extraordinary and staggering. I want to take this opportunity to acknowledge my mother. She is the first lady to me because she is the woman I met first, and whom I will admire forever. My life was not a straight line. But whenever I was off track, she would not let me get run over. She would reset my path to ensure that I am back on the right track. She is my greatest teacher – a teacher of compassion, a teacher of love, a teacher of values & integrity. My prayer is that she finishes well because how we finish validates our past good deeds. Happy Mother's Day to the caring, loving, and virtuous mother of mine.

Mum, from the day you gave birth to me, you have always been by my side through thick and thin. I was not born with a silver spoon in the mouth because our dad passed on before we matured. We did not have much as a family, but you labored, not in the spirit of antagonism, but rather based on your love for us. You did not abandon us. You overcame the odds of life and you managed to take care of your children. You were always there for us. In times of trouble, you provided a shoulder for us to cry on. You sacrificed your happiness for our wellbeing. The same hands that held me first when I was still a baby are still the ones that hold me now during my adulthood. You are a legend because you have secured a legacy for me to remember. Mum, I will forever treasure and cherish these precious memories of you.

We are varied in our physique and personalities. Home training is the basic training which does not merely give us information but prepares us to live in harmony with all existence. If you've ever known kids who are not regularly disciplined by their parents, you've probably seen some very stark examples of why it's important to discipline children. Without discipline, children grow up when lacking the tools necessary to navigate relationships and other challenges of life such as self-discipline, respect for others, and the ability to cooperate with peers. Mothers play a vital role in the development of the good conducts in their kids and hence their behaviors. Education is the ability to know through formal or informal means. Women, in general, are the newborn child's primary caregivers in most societies. The happiness of the community depends on the foundation of the morals within the families. When a mother fails to discipline her kids, there is future consequential damage to the entire community. Mothers should never expect the schools and the churches to take over their duty of training their kids in good behaviors. Whenever the Sunday school teachers are preoccupied with training the kids in good conducts it takes away time from them to teach the Scriptures.

"The Hand That Rocks the Cradle Is the Hand That Rules the World". This poem by William Ross Wallace praises motherhood as the preeminent force for change in the world.

"Motherhood is the most challenging as well as the utmost satisfying vocation in this world" ~ Nita Ambani

"When I made the woman she had to be special. I made her shoulders strong enough to carry the weight of the world, yet gentle enough to give

comfort. I gave her an inner strength to endure childbirth and the rejection that many times comes from her children."

Newly born baby are first attracted to their parents by their smell. Mothers are the fragrance of love to their children.

A biblical parallel is *Exodus" 2:9:* "Pharaoh's daughter said to her, 'Take this child and nurse it for me, and I will give you your wages.' So the woman took the child and nursed it." This story of Moses shows the importance of women in raising a child. The mother of Moses protects her child from hostility, hides him in a basket and asks the infant's sister to watch from afar. The Princess saves and adopts him. These three women are epitomes of the various women that ensure the growth of any child in society. When one in the chain fails her duty, society loses the opportunity to have another Moses, another deliverer, another reformer. What is not stated but implied in this second chapter of *Exodus* is that the mother of Moses knows that it is right to protect her child. The sister of Moses is well brought up to obey her mother. You won't find many girls in today's world "sticking out their necks" for their little brothers. She was unafraid to suggest a nurse to the princess for her little brother. The Princess knew that it was morally right to raise this child against the Pharaoh's edict. Because the women saved this child through their knowledge of what was right and doing it (education), the people of Israel were saved from the Egyptians and God sent to humankind one of the greatest tools of education: "The Ten Commandments."

Father's Day

Age is wisdom. The older you get, the wiser you become. The older you get, the more you appreciate your parents. Fathers are supposed to be legends to help their children to change the course of their lives. I changed and adapted the way I look because of my father. Dad taught me to innovate, and to take things beyond where they've been. He taught me to absorb and to process. He gave me a lifetime legacy. Dad, you are the true definition of a father. It's easy to make babies but it's a lot tougher to take on the responsibility of fathering your children. Children model us to be men of integrity. Whatever decision I make, I put into consideration how I would model before my children because children often grow up to mimic the behavior, beliefs, and attitudes of their parents. On this Father's Day, I want to give kudos to all my children for making me what I am. I know you have come a long way and you have the right to pout. It is a little bit late to put the past wrongs right but it is never late to make a great comeback and breath a new life into tomorrow. Dads are legends who have attained the dignity of age. "Legend remains victorious in spite of history." Happy Father's Day.

From the tree you planted many, many years ago, I have a shade I am under now. You are that covering I needed from the very first day. I go down on my knees to say "thank you." It is because of you now I can see better. You believed in me before I even knew how to believe in myself. You taught me the way of the Lord, you cast the seed and nurtured it, thank you, dad. I love you multi-million times. (Aima Rebecca).

According to Robby Muhumuza, fathers should not do anything whose motive is to "stand out". That would be playing to the gallery. "The driving motive should be to do something that the child finds awesome. This is different from child to child depending on the age, gender, personality, experience, exposure and relationship with the Dad," explains Muhumuza. Adding to stand out for your child, you should know what makes them go gaga and invest in it. Most human beings (including children) love to be given special personal attention; to be fretted over. To be made to feel loved. A case in point is to look at the 'five love languages'; which are words of affirmation, receiving gifts, being spent time with, acts of service and touch. Know the love language of each of the individual child. Invest in actions or activities that communicate in the love language of each of your children. For example, take turns cooking for them. It would be good if you wake up your family to a nice breakfast prepared by you. Celebrate their birthdays. Get interested in their social activities like sports, and etc. You will not go wrong with any of these and to your children; you will be the best dad ever.

This is for the departed fathers to eternity: "If roses grow in Heaven Lord, Please pick a bunch for me. Place them in my dad's arms and tell him they're from me. Tell him that I love and miss him, and when he turns to smile, place a kiss upon his cheek and hold him for awhile... I love you Dad, Happy Father's Day" ~ Grace Ann

Father's Day Thought: My father gave me the greatest gift anyone could give another person - he believed in me and he taught me to believe in myself." Thank you dad for teaching me to be independent; thanks for building me a nest and letting me fly free.

Men who walk with God have a fellowship of which the world knows nothing. Yet from the world's viewpoint they are lonely and unpopular. ~ John Southey

Parents do not live their private lives. Their achievement is a stepping stone to better the lives of others. Fathers carry on the pain of the consequences of the decisions of their children. Given the fact, nobody has a perfect father. That is why we look at God as the perfect Father. "Whether you had a bad earthly father or you did not have an earthly father in your life, we all have in our minds a picture regarding how a good father should be; that is the image of our heavenly Father."

Life after Divorce

Never take things for granted. Pray for your family and with your family because there is a tomorrow you don't know, talk to God that knows everything, everyday. Now that you're married, if you live a bachelor kind of life with your spouse, you are most likely to be single again. Divorce must be resisted at any cost. Divorce can be tormenting due to rejection. Some communities consider the divorced people as outcasts. Paul Nyende, a psychology lecturer at Makerere University says that relationship stigma and rejection in relationships can drive victims into depression. "If one is ostracized by society, they develop a sense of rejection which can lead to depression and withdrawal from the public," he told New Vision.

Divorce robs us of dignity. Don't waste your life into endless worries. Turn your worries into worship. "Those who leave everything in God's hands will eventually see God's hand in everything. Worries end when faith begins."

"Sometimes when something has blocked your way all you need to do is back up, reposition and move forward. Different direction, different approach."

There comes a time in everyone's life, when you have to decide do you hang on to and value what used to be or do you let go and reach for and value more what will be? You can't have your arms around what used to be and expect to receive what will be, that's why the Word of God says it like this: "Brethren, I do not count myself to have apprehended; but one thing I do, forgetting those things which are behind and reaching forward to those things which are ahead, I press toward the goal for the prize of the upward call of God in Christ Jesus. (Philippians 3: 13-14) (posted by Jeniffer Francis).

Don't rush entering into a new relationship. "Find someone who is willing to help you unpack your baggage, a lot of time we get so caught up in wanting the perfect man or woman that we forget we have all been thru some things and our situations may have created baggage that we need to let go and don't really know how to do that. Be patient God will place the right person in your path to help you to be a better you."

When two past lovers can still be friends it means they are either still in love or they never actually loved each other.

Divorce is the only game whereby both teams lose.

There is that tendency of rushing into a new relationship to prove that you are not rejected. Don't rush into a new relationship just to replace the old one. Spend some time dating yourself while putting your life together.

Life is like a moving train with many stops. You will meet many people in your journey of life. There will be many departing never to meet again but there will never be a meeting without departing in life. Every friend ends with END.

There are purposes and time limits for everybody you're meeting in your journey life. Some are blessings, while some will be lessons. Some are for the season while some are for a reason. Some will make you while some will break you. Some are temporary, while some will be part of your life.

Some you wish they never leave and some you cursed the day you meet them in life.

Never find your happiness in people, you will never feel sad when they decide to leave. Never feel bad when a person decides to leave you, it simply means their chapter in your life is over. A lonely life is a painful life; we will all need a shoulder to lean on at some points in our journey of life. Remember we are all something, but none of us is everything.....

In times of crisis, make more bridges to connect and fewer walls to protect. Show love to everyone, but be careful who you bring into your private life. Choose wisely. A wise enemy is better than a foolish friend. Free your heart from hatred, being positive, humble, kind and bold will help you a lot in life but don't be weak. Avoid living a painful life in order to get people's attention and validation. Those who want to be everywhere may end up nowhere in life. To focus on the crowd is to miss the crown. Go with your own flow, many people will roll with you when you grow in life. Be friendly but never try to be everybody's friend. The moment you decide to be everybody's friend, your value starts dropping. Avoid traffic and drama in your life. Fake things don't last avoid fake friends. Seek advice but don't ignorantly expose yourself.

JULY: SPIRITUAL LIBERTY

Genesis 2:18-23 tells us that Adam named the animals before Eva was made. The task of naming the spices was simplified by the limitations of variation. The Bible says that the animals were created according to their kinds, rather than according to their species—the phrase 'after his/their kind' occurs 10 times in this chapter (referring to both plants and animals). The term 'kind' (Hebrew min) most probably corresponds to the various families of the spices. Adam had a responsibility to name everything as God created it and put them in their right category as God created them rather than as he saw fit. All spices were created for Adam's wellbeing. There was nothing potentially harmful to his life except the forbidden tree of Eden. Adam named everything as God classified it, after the kind and purpose it was created for. It is the same sculpt Adam used to name his bride: "Adam said, "This is now bone of my bones and flesh of my flesh; she shall be called 'woman (Ishah),' for she was taken out of man (Ish)" (Genesis 2:23). God put Adam to sleep and opened his side (rib) to bring forth his bride. God put Jesus to sleep, they pierced His side and there came force blood and water symbolically of His bride (Church). The Church is the exclusive portion of her Lord. He covers our nakedness. We live a virtuous life because our virtues come from Him. He holds us accountable in the same way, regardless of race, gender, faith, ethnicity - or political ideology.

John 10:1 – "He said, "I heard the sound of You in the garden, and I was afraid because I was naked; so I hid myself." And he said, "Who told you that you were naked? Have you eaten from the tree that I commanded

you not to eat from?" God asked Adam that "who told you that you were naked?" Before the fall, Adam's nakedness could not evoke the guilt of shame. Adam became conscious of sin, even realizing his nakedness, after partaking of the forbidden tree of knowledge. It means that when Adam and Eve knew sin they lost their innocence and purity. This kind of 'knowing' is not awareness; it is human interaction with evil on a deep level. Most probably as Adam knew Eva sexually and she conceived and bore Cain (Genesis 4:1). Knowing sin implies guilty of sin. Jesus told the Pharisees who denied to be blind that, "If you were blind, you would not be guilty of sin; but now that you claim you can see, your guilt remains" (John 9:41). By claiming to see, the culprits admitted of having the capability to discern good from bad. The Pharisees claimed to see because they had the Law. The Law brings the consciousness of sin. Condemnation makes you aware of your failure and weakness. Shame and guilt are the characteristics of sin. The blood of Jesus brings the consciousness of God's mercy and grace. God covered Adam's nakedness (shame/guilt) by shedding the blood of an animal (Genesis 3: 21). Jesus Christ, the unblemished sacrificial lamb, bore the shame of our nakedness on the cross! His blood atoned (covered) for our sins. We can now approach boldly the throne of God.

John 8:32 – "Then you will know the truth, and the truth will set you free." The truth proclaimed by the gospel is the truth as it is in Jesus who sets a sinner free. The spirit of truth should lead us into all truth, and cause us to grow and increase in knowledge of Jesus himself, who is the way, the truth, and the life. Some people are ever learning but yet they don't come to the knowledge of the liberating truth because the truth is not figured out intellectually but it is revealed. Satan's primary objective is to blind the eyes of the people from the liberating truth. He makes the non-believers to hate the Bible. They end up searching for the truth elsewhere apart from the scriptures because they hoard irresistible hostility towards the scriptures. Ironically, boasted human intellect without a revelation cannot preserve men from folly, infatuation, and darkness (Romans 1:21-23). At times we

are held in bondage by the very things which we are exposed to. It is better to be ignorant of such things than wishing you never knew them.

John 16:27 - "For the Father himself loves you, because you have loved me, and have believed that I came out from God." The phrase "because you have loved me" is not intended to mean that our love to Christ was the cause of the Father's love to us; but, on the contrary, the Father's love to us was the cause of our love to Christ; and therefore as the cause is known by its effect, we might be assured of the Father's love to us by our love to Christ; for if the Father had not loved us, we would have never loved God, nor Christ. Jesus is the standard of the love of God. The world that God loved is the world that Jesus died for and saved (John 3:16). Rejecting Jesus is rejecting God's love. The Bible says that "No power in the sky above or in the earth below—indeed, nothing in all creation will ever be able to separate us from the love of God that is revealed in Christ Jesus our Lord" (Romans 8:39). The love of God, which is in Christ Jesus our Lord, is based on the merits of Jesus Christ. In this scripture, the term "the love of God", is not meant to emphasize the saints' love to God; for though this is sometimes called the love of God, it is the love from Him, as the author of it, and to Him, as the object of it, and in Him. We can never be separated from the union which is made by it between us and God through Christ; we are persuaded that it can never be dissolved as long as we are committed to it. Real freedom comes by setting your love on things from above. Set your affection on Jesus Christ.

1 John 4:4 - "You are of God, little children, and have overcome them, because the He who is in you is greater than He who is in the world." The term "Little children" means "Little Christ". Our objective as Christians is to be like Christ. We have overcome because of Christ, who dwells in our hearts, whom we received by faith; He brings us to a place of liberty. He is able to keep us and to preserve us from all the corruptions of the body and the world. He who is in us is stronger than all the powers of the world

put together. The Spirit of God that is in us is the Spirit of regeneration, sanctification, and adoption; He is the earnest of our inheritance. He is able to carry on the work of grace in us until our glorification. The phrase "he that is in the world" is in reference to Satan and the demons. Before we got the new Master, we used to belong to Satan. Although we acquired the new nature, the devil still has influence over our physical bodies because they are closely connected to the physical corrupt world. The old nature in us is not of us; it must be put to death and kept far away from us daily. The new nature is spiritual and its desires are spiritual. Jesus said that those who belong to Him must abide in Him, and His words abide in them: "If ye continue in my word, then are ye my disciples indeed" (John 8:31). It is a calling to renew our minds daily by the Word. It is a precaution against following the false doctrines. The major cause of apostasy is embracing the wrong doctrines. The more we embrace the pure doctrine, the more godliness we become. True doctrines isolate the spirits of error. We overcome by the Spirit of truth.

1 Corinthians 3:23 - "And ye are Christ's; and Christ is God's." We belong to Christ and Christ belongs to God. This scripture confirms our security in Christ. Quite often we panic because of what we are going through; we forget that in heaven there is no panic! The worst of ours is His, and the best of His is ours. Every victory of Christ is ours, and all of our defeat is His. The only things that belong to us are the things which pertain to God. The greatest bargain ever made on the face of the universe was made at the cross; it made His righteousness to be mine and my sins to be His. We all deserved to be banished. There is only one person whom God treated worse than he deserved; His name is Jesus. Yet Christ does not want us to pity Him; He did everything willingly for our sake so that we might be reunited with God. All blessings and mercies come to us from Him, and through Him. The saints should not glory in men but in God, and in Christ, as of God (very God), who made unto us an easy yoke of wisdom, righteousness, sanctification, and redemption. In Christ, we are more than conquerors (Romans 8:31-39) because we did not do the cross in order to earn our salvation. God is the ultimate end of all, even of Christ,

His co-equal Son. Neither are we called masters; for one is our Master, even Christ. The Bible says that "If we live, we live for the Lord; and if we die, we die for the Lord. So, whether we live or die, we belong to the Lord (Romans 14:8).

Romans 8:1 - "Therefore, there is now no condemnation for those who are in Christ Jesus". Adam lived in Eden, in the perfect environment, before he was corrupted by sin but he was not exempted from condemnation: "— for when you eat from it you will certainly die" (Genesis 2:17). The redeemed Children of God do not live in the second chapter of Genesis. We live in a better environment of favor with God. We live in Romans chapter eight: "Therefore, there is now no condemnation for those who are in Christ Jesus" (Romans 8:1). When Adam lived in the Garden of Eden, he was subject to condemnation in case he sinned. But to those who are in Christ, who love Christ, and who live after the guidance of His Spirit, there is now no condemnation. Jesus said that He did not come to condemn the world because the world was already condemned, and moved towards the summation of condemnation. The same condemnation (which in the present and final judgment of God impends over the sinner) was removed by the intervention of Christ, and by the union of the believers with Him in His death and resurrection (Romans 6:4). The grace is God's highest favor bestowed upon us. Jesus exchanged our filthiness with His righteousness. We can now stand in the presence of God dressed in His very robe of righteousness. In Christ, we are the very righteousness of God. As Christ was raised up from the dead for the glory of the Father, even so, we also should walk in the newness of life.

Malachi 3:6 - "I the LORD do not change." The Lord—Jehovah: a name implying His immutable faithfulness in fulfilling His promises: the covenant name of God to the Jews (Exodus 6:3). We are all spiritual seeds of Abraham. For I am the Lord Or Jehovah; a name peculiar to the Most High, and so a proof of the deity of Christ. Jesus (Yeshua) actually means

Jehovah saves. The Bible says that "Jesus Christ is the same yesterday, and today, and forever" (Hebrews 13:8). It is owing to the unchangeable love, grace, and power of Christ, that none of His perish internally or eternally, but have everlasting life. God changes not in spite of the two covenants. The word "testament" means covenant. The new covenant is an extension of the old. Critics make negatives comments accusing the God of the Old Testament to be ruthless whereas portraying the God of the New Testament as merciful. He is the same God of the old and new covenants that never changes. His attitude towards sin has not changed with time either. God demanded that His people (the Israelites) be holy: "Be you holy for I am holy (Leviticus 11:45). He was not being sarcastic, He meant what He said, and He gave them the temple as a temporally measure to sacrifice for their sins. The blood of the animals was shed to cover the sins of the people. Likewise, He instructs us to be holy as He did to the Israelites (1 Peter 1:16). The major difference between the old and new covenant is the high priesthood. Our Messiah doubles as the high priest and the sacrifice. He shed His blood to save us. We take on His imputed righteousness so that we stand before God, positionally as holy as Jesus. But He demands that we demonstrate the same holiness by our righteous living on the earth; by living a holy life as Jesus did: "Whoever claims to live in him must live as Jesus did." (1 John 2:6). If there is His life in us, it must be lived practically to prove that we are His, and draw others to Him. He is holy, awesome in holiness and His people who are cleaned by His blood must be clean in their acts. It doesn't mean we can't sin. We who are His must strive to be holy, separated from all that is impure, consecrated to His service. In case of sin, we do not have to take animals to sacrifice for our sins; the only sacrifice required is repenting to our Messiah.

John 3:16 – "For God so loved the world that he gave his one and only Son, that whoever believes in him shall not perish but have eternal life." It is a calling to believe, and live. "It is a road so hard that no self-righteous man can ever tread it, but so easy that every sinner who knows himself to be a sinner may by it find his way to heaven. "Believing is not just awareness or head knowledge; it is believing by adhering and

respecting what you believe. For example, if you believe in the existence of gravity, you must see the need of the parachute in order to jump off the plane. Acknowledging the law of gravity without respecting it won't give you protection from gravity. Jumping off the plane without putting on a parachute will end into disaster. Likewise, believing without obedience ends into a disaster.

James 2:17 - "Even so faith, if it hath not works, is dead, being alone." The term "is dead" is best translated as "is dead in its own self." Elsewhere, the Bible says that "As the body without the spirit is dead, so faith without deeds is dead." (James 2:26). The word "without" means "apart from"; it means that the faith that is not proven by works is dead. It is like a lifeless carcass, a body without a soul. The 'dead works' is the graveyard where faith is buried. As the spirit is the life of the body, so are the manifested works of the Spirit the life of faith. Faith is spiritual as opposed to material. The works mentioned here are therefore motivated works by the Spirit; they are the visible external evidence of the invisible internal reality. I want to emphasize that we are not saved by works but the justifying faith must be proven by works. The Bible says that "Was not our father Abraham justified by what he did when he offered his son Isaac on the altar? Abraham believed God, and it was credited to him as righteousness," and he was called a friend of God" (James 2:22-23). Abraham believed God and he followed through by obeying to offer his son (Isaac), and his faith was declared to be sincere, unfeigned, true, and genuine. Paul taught the same message that we are not saved by good works but for good works: "For we are his workmanship, created in Christ Jesus unto good works, which God hath before ordained that we should walk in them." (Ephesians 2:10). Salvation is of God and by God; it was His purpose, to which He prepared us to do His will that we should glorify Him by our living. The will of God is revealed in His Word. Good works are deeds done in conformity to God's Word, this being the evidence of the true children of God.

Proverbs 25:28 - "He that hath no rule over his own spirit is like a city that is broken down, and without walls." He that rules over his own spirit, without the help of God (the Holy Spirit) has no moral control over his emotions, affections, and passions; puts no restraint, unto them. He is like a city without walls of defense to guard against the intruders (enemies). A natural man who is not regenerated has no moral fence to curb his curiosity, to check his pride and vanity, to restrain his wrath and anger and revenge. To be guided by God is to be guided by love because God is Love. A person that rejects God ignores the truth and he is vulnerable to all kinds of deceptions. Satan is not afraid of your education; he is never afraid of your degrees in science, psychology, philosophy, theology, and etc. Satan is afraid of Jesus alone. When Satan checks the heart and finds it empty (void) of the divine, he settles, and it becomes his proper habitation (Luke 11:25). In such a heart there is no immunity to ungodliness. God created this life to be lived from the perspective of the Creator (God). A spiritual man's living is not influenced by external factors, it is lived from inside to the outside. The inner kingdom of God is our everything. A life lived from inside to outside is a cherished living, being an expression of one's clean consciousness. It is a fulfilled life guided by the Holy Spirit and controlled by the Son who overcame sin and death. On the contrary, a corrupt person who has no Spirit of God for guidance is a slave to sin and death.

Galatians 2:20 –"I am crucified with Christ: nevertheless I live; yet not I, but Christ liveth in me: and the life which I now live in the flesh I live by the faith of the Son of God, who loved me, and gave himself for me." "I am crucified" means something more than that of merely "dying with Christ" i.e., imitating the death of Christ by killing the desires of the old nature. It is through the power of the cross, through contemplating the cross and all that is associated with it, that a Christian is enabled to mortify the promptings of sin within him and reduce them to a state of passiveness like that of death. "Nevertheless I live"- The death unto sin, death of one nature (the old nature or the flesh), does not hinder me from thriving (living) in the other nature (spirit or new nature). The fact is that I live in a truer sense than ever before. My body is sanctified by the

Spirit and presented to God as a perfect offering. Salvation is imperative because life is short, sin is abiding, and death is sure. Our salvation comes from beyond us, from God. But true salvation is Christ in me, not Christ out there but Christ in me. His Spirit checks into every repented heart of faith. And when He checks in, He never checks out. What an amazing Savior we have!

Galatians 4:6 - "Because you are his sons, God sent the Spirit of his Son into our hearts, the Spirit who calls out, "Abba, Father." The name "Abba Father" is one of the most significant names of God in understanding how He relates to people and how we relate to Him. The word Abba is an Aramaic word that is translated as "Father". We are adopted into the divine family by the Spirit of the Son dwelling in us. He is the spirit of son-ship and adoption. Nothing matters in the heart of the Father as the Son and nothing is precious in the eyes of the Father as His Son. The joy of the Father is that the Spirit of His Son (Jesus) is crying out to the Father from the heart of the prodigal son (believer) that was lost, and is found. The Father said concerning him that "But we had to celebrate and be glad because this brother of yours was dead and is alive again; he was lost and is found'" (Luke 15:32). We are all prodigals, and God is the Father of the prodigals. The central picture of the Church in the New Testament is that we are one family of God, and children of the Father. The difference between the children of God in the Old and New Testaments is that in the New Testament there is an incorporated relationship of knowing God through Jesus Christ. He is the same Spirit that came on the people of the old covenant, like Isaiah, Jeremiah and etc., but it was a temporary experience of the Holy Spirit. The Holy Spirit came on them in the light of what Christ will do in future. The fullness of the revelation of the heart of God is in Jesus Christ. It is from this perspective Jesus said: "Truly I tell you, among those born of women there has not risen anyone greater than John the Baptist, yet whoever is least in the kingdom of heaven is greater than he" (Matthew 11:11). The least of those born of the Spirit in the kingdom of God is greater than any of the prophets of the Old Testament! Although John the Baptist is found on the pages of New Testament, he

is considered to be the last of the Old Testament prophets because the principle task of all of prophets was to prepare the people for the coming of their Messiah. John the Baptist is the greatest of all prophets because unlike the rest of the prophets who announced the coming of the Jewish Messiah, John the Baptist introduced Him by baptizing Him (John 1:29).

Romans 3:23 - "For all have sinned, and come short of the glory of God". Sin can be defined as an act - the violation of the revealed will of God; a state - absence of righteousness; a nature - enmity toward God. All have sinned basically means that we're all lawbreakers because sin is the violation of God's law (1 John 3:40). We might look different from outside but we are all the same from inside: We are all sinners, and we all need salvation. Salvation is the glory which comes from the favor (grace) and approval of God. The just God gave His Son so that the righteousness of the law might be fulfilled in us (Romans 8:4). To be a Christian means nothing less than we have all drunk deeply of the one Spirit of God and until we all recognize that each person has come to the foot of the Cross as a sinner and each person stands in the unity of the Spirit, there will never be a healing from our past hurts and the sin of division. All have sinned, and all are accepted by God in spite of their sins because of the grace of God.

1 Peter 1:18 - "For you know that it was not with perishable things such as silver or gold that you were redeemed from the empty way of life handed down to you from your ancestors, but with the precious blood of Christ, a lamb without blemish or spot." The redemption of a soul, which is of more worth than anything in the world, requires a greater price than what the world can offer (gold and silver). Jesus redeemed us from corruption by paying the precious price. The incorruptible price was paid for incorruptible things. Jesus paid for the new bodies which are not made out of the deteriorating earthly clay. Remember that all of the germs of the world are found in the dirt. We shall acquire the new bodies which are not

subjected to sickness and death; which are not limited by age and size. We shall be modeled after Jesus Christ who is God's Masterpiece.

2 Corinthians 5:17 - "Therefore if anyone is in Christ, he is a new creation. The old things have passed away. Look, new things have come." The new birth is a more powerful miracle than the beginning of life or the conception of the soul into the womb of the mother. The reason is that what is conceived by the Spirit is eternal and belongs to the divine family. The spiritual nature alone can relate to God and will see God. Therefore a new birth is a necessary birth that a person cannot afford to miss. 'The old has passed away' means that God has reversed the curse of sin. Now you have a new transformed heart to call on God and to discern the truth. You have the spiritual eyes to see God. You have the spiritual ears to hear what the spirit of God is saying instead of the deception of the enemy. You may look the same from outside but there is a radical transformation taking place from within: The heart is inflamed, the mind is renewed and, the will is surrendered to God.

1 Timothy 1:15 - "Christ Jesus came into the world to save sinners, among whom I am chief". First, Timothy presents the most explicit and complete instructions for church leadership and organization in the entire Bible. In this scripture, Paul teaches us humility. "The ego is nothing other than the focus of conscious attention." Everyone at one point in their life has that moment where you can either let your heart guide you or your ego. Humility motivated Paul to drive down the "Memory Lane" of his past, recalling his former sins and the abundant grace of God that transformed him into the apostle to the Gentiles. Paul told his embarrassing story of conversion at least six times in the New Testament (Acts 9, 22, 26; Gal. 1 & 2; Phil. 3; 1 Tim. 1). He emotionally rehearses it here again for Timothy, with tears watering his eyes when he recalls the amazing grace that saved the worst of the sinners. Out of intense humility, He calls himself the foremost of sinners. Paul had a vivid reason to be lofty and proud: He is

the greatest missionary ever walked on the universe. His wrote one-third of the New Testament. In fact, he wrote this epistle to Timothy when he was about to end his ministry, having such colossal accolades and accomplishment under his belt, but he did not brag about it. He focused on the unconditional love of God demonstrated to him by Jesus Christ; the grace that has the power to save a dented sinner like him. The power that raised Jesus from death is the grace working in us, given to forgive and wash away our sins and to help us to grow in the full stature of Christ.

John 1:16-17 – "From His fullness we have all received grace upon grace. For the law was given through Moses; grace and truth came through Jesus Christ." Moses was the mediator of God's mercy to Israel. The mercy was given to reveal the grace. All truth is Christ's truth. Jesus is the truth of every inch of reality that sets us free from searching for the truth. We are sealed and preserved in His glory by His grace. The grace takes away our sins and teaches us to live the sinless life until we all attain to the unity of the faith and of the knowledge of the Son of God, to mature manhood, to the measure of the stature of the fullness of Christ (Eph 4:7, 11-13). Growing in the grace is growing in holiness by drawing from His fullness of grace and truth. The measure of holiness stems from the stature that Christ achieves in us so that by the power of the Holy Spirit, we model our whole life on His.

Matthew 5:11 – "Blessed are ye, when men shall revile you, and persecute you, and shall say all manner of evil against you falsely, for my sake." The seeming tension, conflicts, and antagonism among the believers, within the same denominations and between different denominations, is the result of deceptive plans of Satan. Satan uses this world, including the carnal Christians to antagonize the church. The moment you become serious with the work of the Father, you become the primary target of Satan. Satan does not hang out with the dead in the graveyards. He is radically targeting the living in Christ. I mean the ones who are actively

pursuing their Father's business on the earth. At times Satanic attacks imply that you are doing something right. Count it a blessing when Satan torments you for the Lord's sake. Suffering is not a means of meriting God's love but God will certainly vindicate those who suffer for His name's sake and who are willing to endure. The only truly affluent are those who shun the applauding of the world.

Hebrews 12:24 - "And to Jesus the mediator of the new covenant, and to the blood of sprinkling, that speaketh better things than that of Abel." The blood of Abel cries for judgment but the blood of Jesus cries for mercy and reconciliation. Abel was slain by his own brother, who was punished for it; Christ was put to death by his own nation and people, the Jews, for whom also He died to save. The efficacy of Christ's blood for the procuring pardon, peace, reconciliation, and the redemption and purchase of his Church and people, portrays Him to be the Savior of the entire human race.

John 15:15 – "I no longer call you servants, because a servant does not know his master's business. Instead, I have called you friends, for everything that I learned from my Father I have made known to you." Jesus calls us friends because He paid a price in order for us to know God intimately. The Holy Spirit dwelling in us is the Spirit of the Father and the Son. Through Jesus Christ, God chose us to be His children, and He is asking us to choose Him to be our friend. The friendship emerges from the relationship but there is a higher level of trustworthiness, loyalty, and reliance in a friendship than in a relationship. Elsewhere, Jesus said that "Very truly I tell you, the Son can do nothing by himself; he can do only what he sees his Father doing, because whatever the Father does the Son also does" (John 5:19). The Father and the Son are one but we see the bonds of friendship sprouting from the perfect obedience of the Son to the Father. By His obedience to the Father, Jesus made us know everything that God requires us to know. We know God by our intimate

relationship with Jesus. The rewards of His obedience were granted to us. Whereas Adam's disobedience brought a penalty, Jesus' obedience brings a reward—for His people. He made it possible for His Father to become our Father (John 20:17).

Romans 7:15 - "I do not understand what I do. For what I want to do I do not do, but what I hate I do." Paul is not bragging about sinning but his new nature in Christ. He sees in himself the conflict between good and evil which used not to exist before he was born again. He used to delight in sinning but now he abhors all of the unrighteousness. There are really two different statements in the scripture - the first, of him doing what he wishes not to do; the second, of him not doing what he wishes to do. He is frustrated whenever he targets doing good and he ends up missing the desired target. The unbelievers have no such conviction. Paul acknowledges this fact: Apart from the grace, man is by nature a sinner, regardless of what he has done or not done; the evil intents are apparently real in every man. We are not good because we are good; we are good because Christ is good. Christ changes us from who we are into who He is.

Romans 8:31-39 – "Who shall separate us from the love of Christ? Shall trouble or hardship or persecution or famine or nakedness or danger or sword? As it is written: "For your sake we face death all day long; we are considered as sheep to be slaughtered." No, in all these things we are more than conquerors through him who loved us. For I am convinced that neither death nor life, neither angels nor demons,[b] neither the present nor the future, nor any powers, neither height nor depth, nor anything else in all creation, will be able to separate us from the love of God that is in Christ Jesus our Lord." We are bragging about the absolute love of God that is irreversible. Christ turned all of the powers that worked against us to work for us. Now, death draws us near to God instead of separating us from God. Christ conquered but we (the beneficiaries) are more than conquerors. The situation is compared to a staying home mother whereby

a husband conquers by working a job but a staying home wife is more than a conqueror when her husband brings home the paycheck and lays it on her lap for her to spend.

Ephesians 4:3 - "Make every effort to keep the unity of the Spirit through the bond of peace." It is a calling to maintain the spiritual union that is already in place, between God and His people, and between saints and saints. The bond of each union is love which knits and cements all, together. At the heart of all ministries lies the work of the Spirit in the divine transaction which initiates and guarantees eternal life and peace to all who believe in the Lord Jesus. It is internal peace and confidence brought about by His presence in us. Such peace surpasses natural understanding and is not terminated by afflictions and persecutions. The believers have peace in Christ in spite of the tribulation of the world. Jesus reconciles us with our past and affirms our future. It gives us the responsibility to practice the virtues of life without liability. We are called to be truthful and to pursue peace with integrity for our conscience's sake. The "world" in its ethical sense is laden with sin and is in need of salvation. In this realm men "loved darkness rather than light, because their deeds were evil" (John 3:19; 1 John 2:15-17). Where sin reigns, spiritual death also reigns, for "the wages of sin is death" (Rom. 6:23). Divided loyalty creates moral ambiguities. We are sent to preach the gospel of peace to the hopeless world to bring about the unity in Christ. Again, our peace does not come to us from outside; It is internal peace radiated from inside to the outside when we respond to the gospel. Our peace does not originate from politicians or any other human resources either. "When you teach people their rights, you get a revolution. When you teach people their responsibility, you get a revival."

Philippians 4:4 - "Rejoice in the Lord always. I will say it again: Rejoice!" Paul wrote this while in jail. He looked back thirty years ago when the Lord met him on the high way to Damascus. Paul focused on the past experience to find the future hope. He rejoices in spite of the

circumstances. It is not rejoicing for the tragedies you are experiencing but rejoicing in the overcoming power of the Lord. It is finding the otherness of you in Christ that has overcome the suffering of the world. The joy of living is the joy of the Lord which is already inside you. It is the delight of the heart that cannot be quenched by any external circumstances. Activated faith restores hope in a hopeless situation.

Philippians 3:8 - "What is more, I consider everything a loss because of the surpassing worth of knowing Christ Jesus my Lord, for whose sake I have lost all things. I consider them garbage that I may gain Christ". Paul takes inventory of his life and comes up with a balance sheet showing that he is never in red. In order for our past experiences to be validated, they must be translated into the present relationship with Christ. What you have done for the kingdom in the past is irrelevant if your relationship with Jesus in the present is not current.

Luke 10:19-20 – "The seventy-two returned with joy and said, "Lord, even the demons submit to us in Your name." So He said to them, "I saw Satan fall like lightning from heaven. See, I have given you authority to tread on snakes and scorpions, and over all the power of the enemy. Nothing will harm you. Nevertheless, do not rejoice that the spirits submit to you, but rejoice that your names are written in heaven." The name of Jesus had the power to demolish Satan even before Jesus died on the cross. Elsewhere, Jesus said that "But if I drive out demons by the finger of God, then the kingdom of God has come upon you" (Luke 11:20). Satan was disarmed and expelled from heaven. Now, by dying on Calvary and rising again on the third day from the grave, Jesus perfected and caused the final collapse of Satan's kingdom but much more is the redemptions of the captives. According to the above scripture, Jesus cautioned His disciples not to rejoice in their success over infernal spirits. Jesus saw Satan's reinforcement falling like lightning from heaven. He instructed them to rejoice that their names are written in the book of life in heaven where

no ordinary power can bolt them out. The victory of the saints is not the defeat of Satan on the earth but their victory over hell. If your name is not recorded or is blotted out of the book of life, your eternal future will be in the lake of fire with the defeated Satan.

"I have given you authority to trample on snakes and scorpions and to overcome all the power of the enemy; nothing will harm you." Snake is figuratively used concerning the devil, and his principalities and powers, and all his emissaries, who, for their craft and cunning, and for their poisonous and hurtful nature and influence, may be compared to serpents and scorpions. We have the legal authority in the name of Jesus to free ourselves and others whom we minister to from the influences of Satan and worldliness. Such as bad habits, generation curses, evil and familiar spirits, witchcraft, sorcery, divination, guilt, shame, condemnation, control, religiosity, manipulation, intimidation, mind control, deception, and false teachings.

A life lived in its fullness is when the Holy Spirit has a monopoly over you. His monopoly helps you to stand on a solid and firm ground. That is when nothing else compels you to move, but the Holy Spirit, and when you move, it is moving forward; no backtracking. In a natural man, every step is a move in a wrong direction. The Holy Spirit is a detour from a one-way dead-end street. The Holy Spirit initiates the change in us (transformation) and manages it inevitably. He gives us the incentive to walk precisely. His monopoly is the antithesis of ego (self). The greatest enemy of a born-again believer is primarily the flesh (old nature) rather than Satan. Satan is a defeated foe, and he would have had no impact on us without the ally of the flesh.

1 John 3:7-10 – "Dear children, do not let anyone lead you astray. The one who does what is right is righteous, just as he is righteous. 8 The one who does what is sinful is of the devil, because the devil has been sinning from the beginning. The reason the Son of God appeared was to destroy

the devil's work. 9 No one who is born of God will continue to sin, because God's seed remains in them; they cannot go on sinning, because they have been born of God." The devil destroyed the works of righteousness in a natural man. Jesus appeared to destroy the works of the devil, which are manifested in sin, by restoring righteousness to us and by paying the penalties of the broken laws on our behalf. Jesus is the expression of God's love and God's grace. He who is born again resists sin by manifesting the righteous works of Jesus. Godliness is the recommended offensive against Satan. The strongest man in the world is the one who has mastered his body (flesh) into obedience to the spirit; anything else is weakness. The mastering of the flesh is not a one-time event but an ongoing daily process that both men and women need to perfect.

Mark 10:30 - "Truly I tell you," said Jesus, "no one who has left home or brothers or sisters or mother or father or children or fields for My sake and for the gospel who will not receive a hundred times as much here in this world—homes, brothers, sisters, mothers, children, and fields, along with persecution—as well as eternal life in the age to come." Your family will either induce you to draw close to Christ or cause you to defect. It is because our earthly families demand loyalty and commitment as Christianity, and when you are committed to a task, you don't want to compromise. It's unrelenting devotion to the Word and absolute loyalty to Christ that makes a difference, hence allowing you to prioritize. The key to prioritizing is ignoring your schedule and allowing God to schedule your priorities. Remember that you are not in your family by chance. You are there by the divine appointment. God gave you the family, and He alone can keep it in place. When you seek the kingdom of God first, the rest of things are added. It is only the shallow minds that choose temporally things over eternal things. It is like deciding to stay in the shallow end of the pool instead of going out in the ocean. The reward of the faithfulness is "a hundred times as much here in this world or now this time and in the age to come". It means eternal life is acquired now, then it is fully realized in the life after (1 John 5:11, 13). Other benevolences of transformation include the love of God, the presence of Christ, the comforts of the Holy

Spirit, and the communion of saints. All of these benevolences begin now and are fully realized later. The joys and pleasures felt in the enjoyment of these things, being a hundred times more and better to those who have abandoned the temporal joy for Christ's sake. And much more is the splendid inheritance in which the blessed shall be heirs of God and joint-heirs with Christ; and so shall possess not only the heaven and the earth, and all things that are in them, but even the throne of God, and all honor, all glory, all joy, not merely as occupiers, but as co-heirs with Christ forever and ever.

Somebody made this comment: "If you want to take away the strength of sin, then remove the law." Reply: The problem is not with the Law but with man. If Adam did not sin there would have been no need of the Law. The Law showed man how much he has fallen from the grace because of the sinful nature inherited from Adam. The Ten Commandments are called the Moral Law because all of them together reveal the morality of God, which man lost and which he cannot reach on his own unless He is helped by the Savior. Without the Savior, the Law simply condemns man because nobody can keep all without a possibility of breaking one during the lifetime. Whenever you break one of the laws (Ten Commandments), you break all of them. Compared to a man hanging on the cliff when sustained by a chain link of ten joints whereby when you cut just one joint off the chain link, he falls down.

Somebody said that "The Law was given to the Jews alone". Reply: You might believe it or not there are just two covenants: The old covenant that man made with God promising to keep God's laws but failed miserably. Then the new covenant when God comes down in form of man to help man to obey. When God chose Adam, He was dealing with the entire human race; in the same manner, when God chose Israel, He was dealing with all ethnic groups (Jews/Gentiles). If the old covenant was prescribed to the Jews only then Jesus could have been sent to save the Jews only.

Somebody said that "God longs to have an intimate relationship with you. He is not interested in obedience and submission." My reply: Jesus said that "If you love me, keep my commands". (John 14:15). Prove that you are saved by obeying. The Ten Commandments (Moral Law) are repeated all over the epistles instructing us what to do and not what to do. For example, don't steal, don't commit adultery, do not worship idols and (etc). The Bible specifically says that "for sin is the transgression of the law." (1 John 3). Paul said "What shall we say, then? Is the law sinful? Certainly not! Nevertheless, I would not have known what sin was had it not been for the law" (Romans 7:7). We know God intimately through Jesus Christ and we prove it by submission. We are saved by grace alone and we are called to grow in the grace; it is growing into obedience rather than into disobedience to God.

Hebrews 13:10 – "We have an altar from which those who minister at the tabernacle have no right to eat." According to the Law, the priests (they. who "serve the Tabernacle," see (Hebrews 8:5) received for themselves a greater or smaller portion of the animals offered as peace-offerings and trespass-offerings; in some cases, also, the flesh of the sin-offerings fell to their lot (Leviticus 4, 5, 7, 23). Now this altar which the saints have and have a right to eat of it is Christ; all that are made priests unto God by Him; all that know him, believe in him, have a spiritual discerning of him, and hunger and thirst after him: to "eat" of it is to believe that Christ is come in the flesh, and is become an offering for sin, and for us that eat; it is to receive, embrace, and possess the blessings procured by it; which is done by faith, with spiritual joy and gladness, and with sincerity and singleness of heart: Christ is our exceeding joy. Before Jesus died on the cross, millions of animals were butchered at the altar, all screaming "Jesus where are you?" Jesus saved all of the animals which would have been

slaughtered to atone (temporary cover) the sins of men. I think if animal activists were sincere, they would all have been Christians!

Galatians 3:1 - "I would like to learn just one thing from you: Did you receive the Spirit by works of the Law, or by hearing with faith?" It is a reproof of the Galatians for Abandoning Faith for Legalism. Paul's teaching is against going back to the Law as a means of getting saved. Our justification comes from the finished works of Jesus Christ alone. The Law cannot save us not because there is something wrong with the Law but because there is everything wrong with man. We are saved by the grace; Jesus' righteousness is imputed to us. It means we are positionally as holy as Jesus. The Holy Spirit guides us into all truth (John 16:13); it is perfect obedience to the Word in order to maintain the perfect communication already established with God. It is the life of obedience as opposed to disobedient. The Word includes the commandments of God and the rewards of obedience (the promises of God). The believers are not going to be judged for their sins because Jesus took care of that but there are rewards for obedience awaiting us at the throne of Judgment. "Behold, I am coming quickly, and My reward is with Me, to render to every man according to what he has done." (Rev. 22:12). The Holy Spirit cannot be separated from the Word. Jesus said that "The words that I speak to you are Spirit" (John 6:63); Also "But the Advocate, the Holy Spirit, whom the Father will send in my name, will teach you all things and will remind you of everything I have said to you." (John 14:26). Everything that Jesus spoke is written down in the Scriptures (Word). The process of obedience is called sanctification. James wrote that faith without works is dead. We prove our faith by the manifested good works of obedience. Again, the works are not intended to save us but to maintain the perfect communication with God. We are called to manifest the sinless life of Jesus Christ.

Ephesians 2:1-2 - "As for you, you were dead in your transgressions and sins, in which you used to walk when you conformed to the ways of this

world and of the ruler of the power of the air, the spirit who is now at work in the sons of disobedience." No man is called a living man, but he who is in the way of truth in this world. Jesus is the way and the truth (John 14:6). And a wicked man who does not go in the way of truth is called, "a dead man". He is dead in his trespasses and sins. But the living man's life is in contradiction to the ways of the world. He loves to obey the ordinances of God. The law is no longer a distance from him; it has entered into his heart and conscience. Now that we are saved there is no hostility between us and the Law because, through Christ, we are as holy (even) as the Law.

Titus 3:3-8 – "At one time we too were foolish, disobedient, deceived and enslaved by all kinds of passions and pleasures. We lived in malice and envy, being hated and hating one another. 4 But when the kindness and love of God our Savior appeared, 5 he saved us, not because of righteous things we had done, but because of his mercy. He saved us through the washing of rebirth and renewal by the Holy Spirit, 6 whom he poured out on us generously through Jesus Christ our Savior, 7 so that, having been justified by his grace, we might become heirs having the hope of eternal life. 8 This is a trustworthy saying. And I want you to stress these things, so that those who have trusted in God may be careful to devote themselves to doing what is good. These things are excellent and profitable for everyone." In a parallel scripture, Paul said that "For we are God's handiwork, created in Christ Jesus to do good works, which God prepared in advance for us to do (Ephesians 2:8). Paul clearly says that we are not saved by good works but for good works. Know what you believe, and live what you believe!

Somebody asked that "Why do our political leaders still preach "An eye for an eye?". Reply: This is one of the civil laws which were given to the nation of Israel (when she was still a theocracy) to administer the social justice (Exodus 21:24). Israel had no political king but God. God demanded that absolute justice be prescribed. When somebody plucked out somebody's eye, he paid back by his eye as opposed to both eyes because it would be considered to be injustice. Israel's hope for the defaulters was in the future coming of their Messiah who is sent to decree the year of Jubilee. "Jubilee"- from the Hebrew word "yobel" (a ram's horn/trumpet—signifying a "trumpet blast of liberty"). Jesus announced that He had come to "proclaim the year of the Lord's favor" (Luke 4:19)—the Year of Jubilee. The grace is God's favor rendered to the guilty. The grace decrees the lifespan as one long year of jubilee. I am concerned that people have not been properly taught the difference between the civil law, ceremonial laws, dietary laws and Moral Law (Ten Commandments). Whenever the Bible teaches about the law, it is important to rightly divide the scriptures in order to know which set of law it is addressing. The Law is divided into three groups: 1) Ceremonial laws (like animal sacrifices/food offerings) – we don't need them because they were shadows of which Christ is the substance. 2) Civil laws and diet laws – We don't need them in order to be saved. 3) The Moral Law – Ten Commandments. We need them for our sanctification. Remember salvation is given in three stages: Justification by faith in the finished works of Jesus; Sanctification is when we join hands with God to clean up our minds of the corruption of sin through obedience; Glorification is the future elimination of the corrupt nature and sin from our presence. The politicians and the secular world may adopt "An eye for an eye" to prescribe justice but it is not given to us as patent truth in the new covenant. The Moral Law (Ten Commandments), revealing the morality of God, is the only piece of the Law given to us to implement.

John 15:10 – "If you keep my commands, you will remain in my love, just as I have kept my Father's commands and remain in his love."

"You will never glory in God till first of all God has killed your glorying in yourself." ~ Charles Spurgeon

Somebody asked that, "Is Christianity a religion?" James 1:27 - "Pure religion and undefiled before God and the Father is this, To visit the fatherless and widows in their affliction, and to keep himself unspotted from the world." Jesus is the everlasting dialogue between humanity and God. Religion cannot save. However, Jesus was not against religion as such; He was against the religiosity spirit that resisted the transformation which Jesus alone can give, and trusted in the merits of man to reach God. Religion is defined as a belief in and worship of a superhuman controlling power, especially a personal God or gods. Religion is a belief in a set of ideas, worship, creed, a particular system of faith and worship. It is a pursuit or interest to which someone ascribes supreme importance. True religion teaches us to do everything as in the presence of God. An unspotted life must go with unfeigned love and charity. Our true religion is equal to the measure in which these things have a place in our hearts and conduct. The uniqueness of Christianity is that it is made up of the redeemed people who invested their faith in Christ for the salvation of their souls and are led by the Spirit of God. But Christianity is also an organized religion based on beliefs taught from the Scriptures. Such systems of beliefs encourage the moral behaviors of the believers toward each other. Jesus is the only way to God whereas religion is a system of beliefs that encourage the moral behaviors of the believers toward each other (James 1:27). Religion without charity is blind and charity without religion is lame.

John 16:13 - "But when he, the Spirit of truth, comes, he will guide you into all the truth. He will not speak on his own; he will speak only what he hears, and he will tell you what is yet to come." The Holy Spirit cannot be separated from the truth (Word). Everything that Jesus said and will say must be in line with the scriptures.

Romans 7:15- 24 – "I don't really understand myself, for I want to do what is right, but I don't do it. Instead, I do what I hate...... So I find this law at work: Although I want to do good, evil is right there with me. For

in my inner being I delight in God's law; but I see another law at work in me, waging war against the law of my mind and making me a prisoner of the law of sin at work within me. What a wretched man I am!" After we are born again, we are wired to pursue excellence but we still retain the old nature that is hostile to godliness. The parallel scripture: "For my thoughts are not your thoughts, neither are your ways my ways," declares the LORD. (Isaiah 55:8).

1 John 4:18 – "There is no fear in love. But perfect love drives out fear, because fear has to do with punishment. The one who fears is not made perfect in love." Doubt and fear are the signs that our love is far from perfect. None of us has the perfect love because none of us is perfect. The redeemed are not worried of the consequences of not being perfect because by investing their faith in Jesus Christ, they reached the perfectness demanded by God. The perfect love that casts out fear comes from the divine. Those who are guided by love, who live charity to the full, are guided by God because God is love. We can count on the perfect love of God that in spite of our failures, everything is going to be ok. Fear brings uncertainty but faith brings absolute certainty. Paul wrote that "For God has not given us the spirit of fear; but of power, and of love, and of a sound mind." For the Spirit God gave us does not make us timid, but gives us power, love and self-discipline." (2 Timothy 1:7). The fear of God and the presence of the Holy Spirit eradicate the negative fear. The Holy Spirit is not the author of a timid or cowardly disposition, or of slavish fears. "Fear is the darkroom where the Devil develops his negatives to counteract our faith."

The gracious Savior purchased our liberty with His precious blood that He may freely bestow it on everyone that believes in Him. Liberty does not necessarily mean happiness. God's primary concern is our holiness as opposed to our happiness. The things pertaining to godliness, most times do not appeal to our emotions. The reason is that the needs of the body are different from the needs of the soul. The comfort of the body does not necessarily cater for the comfort of the soul. For example, sleeping is good for the resting of the body but it does not help when it's your soul that is tired. The body needs clean air to breathe but the soul needs the spirit. When the body takes its last breath, upon death, the soul takes its first breath in eternity.

Somebody asked, "Isn't keeping the Sabbath one of the Ten Commandments?" Reply: There are ten commandants, all equally constitute of the Moral Law. Keeping the Sabbath was given to the Israelites in form of remembrance: "Remember the Sabbath day, to keep it holy" (Exodus 20:8). The Sabbath began at creation when God separated the seventh day from the rest of the days to honor His resting after creating everything. The Law was given to Moses to remind him of the tradition that was already in practice. The Israelites observed it by abstaining from all servile work and business, and from all pleasures and recreations lawful on other days, and by spending it in religious exercises (Exodus 16:23). The early church observed the Sabbath as a resting day and celebrated the first day of the week (Sunday) in honor of the resurrection of Jesus. They partook of the Lord's Supper (communion) every first day (John 20:19, 26; 1 Corinthians 16:2). However, we are also told that the disciples met daily (Acts 2:46), and that Paul preached daily (Acts 19:9). Given the fact, this is not an excuse for not honoring the Sabbath Day.

"Sunday morning my youngest daughter was questioning why we go to church on Sunday when the Sabbath is supposed to be the seventh day of the week. Instead of just giving her answers, I encouraged her to seek this out. I asked her if she had looked deeper into the meaning of the words found in Exodus, "Keep the Sabbath." She hadn't. When she sought out the meaning of the word "keep," she found that it meant to hedge or guard. Immediately, I started sharing this picture of the Garden of Eden in my mind with her... Sometime back, the Lord had shown me that the garden was a fenced place...it was hedged by God and protected...a place where God could commune with man. Next, a memory of Job popped into my mind, as he was hedged by God, as well, because of his unshakeable integrity. And Noah...God shut the door of that ark to protect Noah, the one who found grace in His eyes, along with his family. As we talked, we were getting this picture of what it looks like to "keep" something of such great value" (posted by Gina Green).

Somebody asked, "Isn't tithing an Old Testament law?" True, tithing is rooted in the old covenant. In the old covenant, people gave out of obligation when they were motivated by the Law. In the new covenant, we give cheerfully with an attitude of gratitude when we are motivated by the grace. Intriguingly, the people who have a problem with tithing in the new covenant say it to justify giving less. The Bible says that from everyone to whom much has been given, much will be required; and to whom they entrusted much, of him they will ask all the more (Luke 12:48). We are by far given much favor than the people of the old covenant who were under the Law. Therefore, we need to be more generous than the people of the old covenant.

July for Social Liberty – Politics

4th July is Independence Day. Our colors of freedom are flying high to commemorate the birthday of our great country. Total liberation involves the mindset. There's a mindset of flexibility and adaptability that comes with us. This nation has proudly positioned itself as an ethnic melting pot. America has also become a melting pot in which all kinds of ideas melt; accommodating all viewpoints without a flittering mechanism in place results in suppressing the glory of God. Our country is faced with disintegration instead of integration because we have exchanged the glory of God with the glory of man. To counter the threat, our tree of liberty should be refreshed with moderate reformers, thinkers and moral apologetics. Whereas there is a need for good legislation, true change is going to be experienced when all Christians regardless of their political allegiance embrace the biblical worldviews. I mean the mindset based on the biblical values. Politics is a dirty game. And our politicians have proved beyond doubt to be dirty players. People are fed up with the status quo, and they have expressed their readiness to overthrow it. No wonder businessmen and celebrities are having massive landslide victories in most recent elections. The riskiest thing is to underestimate the size of the problems we face, the strength of the status quo and the urgency of the people's desire for change. I want to specifically say that the real power to change our culture is in the Word. And the Word is in us (Church).

"With liberty and justice for all." These words are echoed daily whenever we recite the Pledge of Allegiance with hands pressed over our hearts. These principles were embraced by our forefathers and are the foundation of our country. We naturally want to live our lives in freedom and expect to be treated with fairness. Webster's dictionary defines "justice" as the administration of reward or penalty as deserved. Justice is served when someone receives what he deserves, whether it is a paycheck for a job well done or a jail sentence for a crime committed. Justice goes hand in hand with the law. The role of justice is basically to satisfy the law. There cannot be justice without the laws. Ironically, most people want justice but hate the laws. Spiritually, when we are saved, we get what we don't deserve. However, the grace does not elude the justice. In order for the grace to be ours, the justice of God was put on an innocent man called Jesus Christ. There is a fine line between innocent and just: We are innocent because of the blood of the just man that justifies us. The grace alone has the power to make the innocent guilty and to make the guilty innocent.

God created mankind and gave us dominion over all creations. I think the term "all creations" includes other human beings as well. Although we have God-given dominion over all creation, nature resists being dominated by man. For example, we have to subdue animals in order to bring them into subjection. The situation is not different regarding humanity. We naturally resist being dominated by others. Resisting oppression is a positive reaction which is an emanation from our own nature and faculties. But there is a negative way of resisting democratically elected leaders. Democracy is not perfect and it is not supposed to make everyone happy. But it is a fair political system that secures the happiness of the greatest number. The best results of democracy can be attained when every individual is the center of a democratic system. In a situation where there emerges a democratically elected leader, we should rally behind him, regardless of our political alliances. We should shun the notion that human beings are naturally competitive, rather than cooperative. The blossoming dictatorship we see and the hysteria thereof are inflamed by opportunists who believe that there should be no ultimate winner unless they are the winners. Such politicians may have been formerly activists and advocates of democracy, but selfishness converted them into opportunists and hence enemies of peace. The worst dictators are the ones who rule in the name of democracy. Inventively, oppression is extended to the people they rule in the guise of fighting for justice. "There is no crueler tyranny than that which is perpetuated under the shield of law and in the name of justice."

The state can be a force for good. Justice is one of the long arms of the state. The Rule of law is absolutely essential to a good life. God instituted the governments and the leaders throughout history and throughout the Biblical narrative for the sake of enforcing the civil laws. Both the state and the government stand for peace and justice. However, the state is growing precisely as the church is fading as a force for good, and this does not seem to be a good trend. Given the fact, I want to mention that the decline we see in church, for example, the decline in church attendance is due to the end time sifting. The church is shaking off the fake and the lukewarm in preparation to meet her bridegroom. The true Church is growing stronger every time, and cannot be stopped by any natural forces.

Revelation 1:14 - "The hair on his head was white like wool, as white as snow, and his eyes were like blazing fire." Jesus' hair appeared as white as wool symbolic of the righteousness of God and His mission to execute justice. White hair is symbolic of a mature person of respect and honor regardless of their race. In this case, Jesus represents the God of ancient days, of heaven and earth. The color of the hair is the point of comparison; signifying purity and glory in which image we were created. During colonial times all judges were required to wear the white wool-like hair coverings over their heads while they were behind their benches symbolic of their responsibility to deliver the righteous judging. Unfortunately, the judges of today are apolitical. There are judges who ground their rulings on logical, unbiased interpretations of our Constitution, our laws and our place in history, but for the most part, the ideal has been killed. Most times, the rulings regarding most cases depend on whether a judge is a liberal or a conservative. On the contrary, the courts were designed and expected to be at least somewhat free of the politics that plague the other branches of government.

Proverbs 22:28 - "Do not move an ancient boundary stone set up by your ancestors." To remove the ancient landmark which your fathers have set was always reckoned a very heinous crime in early times. It is contrary to the law, and a curse is pronounced upon those that did it (Deuteronomy 19:14). In a political sense, the founding fathers of this nation were fallible men, and guilty of many errors and mistakes but among some of the good things they did is to establish the foundation of this nation on the fear of God. They came in search of a place where they can have freedom of worship. Real freedom begins with the spirit without which we are free in mere name only. We are in a free country but freedom does not mean free to do as you will. Freedom is loving what you do when what you do is what you ought to do. We are people of the covenant with a mandate to live the holy life pleasing to God. Our motto is "In God, we trust" because God is the hub of America. Our beliefs form our practices as much as our practices form our beliefs. Happy birthday America.

God places value on life because He created man in His image. There is a need to educate people to respect life and to love and to protect what is virtuous and honorable in life. In this case, education is the knowledge, not of facts, but of the values that sustain life. Our beliefs are the expression of our values and aspirations. When your values are clear to you, making decisions becomes easier. God is the greatest liberator, and He liberates life. When God liberated the Israelites from captivity He liberated them to Himself. He directed them to go to a place of His choice to worship Him, and He gave them the Ten Moral Commandments projecting His character (values). The two tablets of stones handed to Moses were a transcript of the nature and will of God as it was inscribed on Adam's heart in the times of his innocence. The first four commandments instruct mankind how to love and honor God. The last six commandments instruct mankind how to love and respect their neighbor. America is the most peaceful nation today because our constitution was drafted from the Ten Commandments. But America is slowly slipping away from God. The secular world admires it and accepts it; it is the responsibility of the Church to challenge the status quo by staying true to our core values. The ordinances of God were transferred to our hearts (Hebrews 8:10) so that we may practice them, and walk in them. It is an internal experience of the grace and the truth received with affection so that we become the written epistle of Christ for the world to read.

John 18:36 – "Jesus said, "My kingdom is not of this world. If it were, my servants would fight to prevent my arrest by the Jewish leaders. But now my kingdom is from another place." Jesus came to establish His kingdom on the earth. He hereby declares that He had a kingdom from another place; by which He means not His domain, as God, and the Sovereign Creator of all things; but His perfect kingdom, already in place in heaven and which is being established on the earth. The kingdom is currently spiritual in nature. It does not appear in worldly pomp and splendor, nor is it supported by worldly force, nor administered by worldly laws. Christ's kingdom is not of this world: It is not recycled from this world, and the subjects of His kingdom are not of the world. "If my kingdom were of this

world, then would my servants fight that I should not be delivered to the Jews". Jesus was referring to His followers who had ironically abandoned Him because He did not satisfy their political agenda; if He was political, they would have fought for Him. Elsewhere, Jesus said that "Think you that I cannot now pray to my Father, and he shall presently give me more than twelve legions of angels?" (Matthew 26:53). The angels are His creatures and ministering servants from the kingdom of heaven, of whom He has the command. The First Coming of Jesus is not intended to unseat the bad politicians like Caesar. In fact, Jesus demanded submission to Caesar: "Render to Caesar the things that are Caesar's, and to God the things that are God's" (Mark 12:17). So His followers have obligations to God and to Caesar—that is, the secular government. Jesus resolutely refused to get involved in the politics of His homeland. Jesus knew that the solution to mankind's problems, including politics, lay elsewhere—not in human governments. The pastors have the responsibility of educating the people to elect the politicians who embrace our Judeo-Christian values but our hope is not in the politicians.

No idea is more fundamental to Americans' sense of ourselves as individuals and as a nation than freedom. But freedom, when abused, has severe consequences. The Sexual Revolution, also known as a time of Sexual Liberation, was a social movement that challenged the traditional codes of behavior related to sexuality and interpersonal relationships throughout the Western world from the 1960s to the 1980s. The Sexual Revolution marked a time that involved the rejection of typical gender roles. Acceptance for intercourse outside of monogamous, heterosexual, marriages increased which gave individuals more freedom as well as a feeling of being less deviant. Sex became the motivation and the determining factor of everything people did: In order for something to be appealing, it had to be sexual! The so-called sexual revolution is defiance against morality in the name of freedom. The situation was accelerated when the new contraceptives and later condoms hit the market. Of course, people readily admit that today one of the greatest challenges to the sanctity of family is homosexuality. However, the real threat to morality within the church is not homosexuality because the majority of believers acknowledge that it is a sin. The greatest threat to morality is the skyrocketing number of heterosexual people claiming to be Christians cohabiting. Casual sex outside marriage is the silent killer that has been normalized in the name of boyfriend and girlfriend. Lust dethrones God by putting human desires above God's will. The first step to overcome the lust of the flesh and the lust of the world is to acknowledge that the problem is within you; don't pass on a buck. Our propensity for evil and our lack of desire to recognize this within ourselves is the sum of the problems we face.

Isaiah 45:7- "I form the light, and create darkness: I make peace, and create evil: I the LORD do all these things." The word evil, in this case, is not in reference to a vice but it is in reference to the disasters that come to us as consequences of our sins due to the judgment of God. God gives men up and leaves them to suffer the consequences of their willful apostasy; suffer temporal afflictions and distresses resulting from their disobedience; suffer everlasting punishment in the pit of hell. God is the Author of all that is true, holy, and good but misery and sufferings do not come into the world without His permission.

Galatians 5:1 - "It is for freedom that Christ has set us free. Stand firm, then, and do not let yourselves be burdened again by a yoke of slavery." Life demands freedom. There is no liberty without Christ. We are free when God freely comes to help us and we joyfully trust His help; His grace helps us to obey. The key to freedom is whether God comes down to help us do what he requires and whether we live by faith in that work of grace.

When you teach people their rights, you get a revolution. When you teach people their responsibility, you get a revival.

"There should be a sympathy with freedom, a desire to give it scope, founded not upon visionary ideas, but upon the long experience of many generations within the shores of this happy isle, that in freedom you lay the firmest foundations both of loyalty and order" ~ William E. Gladstone

"When the power of love overcomes the love of power the world will know peace" ~ Jimi Hendrix

"Politics is the art of looking for trouble, finding it everywhere, diagnosing it incorrectly and applying the wrong remedies." ~ Groucho Marx

When being stupid is the only means of survival, then intelligence becomes useless!

"Each generation must out of relative obscurity discover its mission, fulfill it, or betray it." ~ Frantz Fanon.

The word parliament comes from a French word, Parler— to speak; with your mouth. Members of Parliament are, therefore, supposed to talk. A legislator who is not vocal articulates in terms of advocacy. To legislate is supposed to be the key output.

Ephesians 5:11 – "And have no fellowship with the unfruitful works of darkness, but rather reprove [them]." An omission is a failure to do

something one can and ought to do. If this happens deliberately and freely, it is considered a sin. One of the sins of omission is that of an enabler. It is a person that enables a sinner to be himself. At times God tests us by allowing evil to flourish before our eyes. In such a situation, God expects us to respond accordingly by restraining sin to prevail. We fail to comply by either applauding evil or keeping silent instead of rebuking it. This is true in particular when politics is involved. The term political correctness in modern usage is used to describe language, policies, or measures that are intended to avoid offense or disadvantage to members of particular groups in society. Some culprits opt to silence rather than holding the bull by its horns. A silence instead of a well-deserved and honest rebuke is a compliment. "May God in his mercy enable us without obstinacy to perceive our errors."

"Today, right now in America, we have lost the ability to disagree in an agreeable manner. If facts supporting opposing opinions are there we should not shout down, verbally bum rush, castigate, and demonize anyone that has a different opinion. We are doomed" ~ Mario Sims

A bill to eliminate marriage licenses in Alabama and set up a process under which probate judges accept affidavits from couples as official records of marriage has passed the Alabama Senate. The requirement of a ceremony to solemnize the marriage would be eliminated. The supporters of the elimination of marriage licenses say it will institute marriage equality. In reality, the law is strategically intended to make it easier for people of the same sex to get married by simply signing an affidavit instead of going to the churches and to some judges who say that it is against their conscience to marry people of the same sex. It is apparently clear that the gay rights' hidden agenda is to dismantle the marriage institution piece by piece. Also, to impose their values on us; it has nothing to do with the equal rights but has everything to do with assimilation by constraint of freedoms enjoyed by the heterosexuals.

"Racism is man's gravest threat to man - the maximum of hatred for a minimum of reason" ~ Abraham Joshua Heschel

The people thought that Barack Obama is the first black President of the United States. Wrong. 1. John Hanson (a Moor) was actually the 1st President of the United States, he served from 1781 – 1782 and he was black.

January 16, 2017, is Martin Luther King's Day. More than forty years ago, on August 28, 1963, a quarter million people gathered in front of the Lincoln Memorial. They marched here for the cause of civil rights. And that day they heard Martin Luther King Jr. deliver his famous "I Have a Dream" speech, a speech in which he challenged America to fulfill her promise.

"I have a dream," he said, "that one day this nation will rise up and live out the true meaning of its creed. 'We hold these truths to be self-evident that all men are created equal.'" While we know of the speech, most people are unaware that King also penned one of the most eloquent defenses of the moral law: the law that formed the basis for his speech, for the civil rights movement, and for all of the law, for that matter.

In the spring of 1963, King was arrested for leading a series of massive non-violent protests against the segregated lunch counters and discriminatory hiring practices rampant in Birmingham, Alabama. While in jail, King received a letter from eight Alabama ministers. They agreed with his goals, but they thought that he should call off the demonstrations and obey the law.

King explained why he disagreed in his famous Letter from a Birmingham Jail. "One might well ask," he wrote, "how can you advocate breaking some laws and obeying others?" The answer "is found in the fact that there are two kinds of laws: just laws ... and unjust laws. One has not only a legal but a moral responsibility to obey the just laws," King said, "but conversely, one has a moral responsibility to disobey the unjust laws." (References: Chuck Colson commentary)

According to Eric Metaxas, many think of King as a liberal firebrand, waging war on traditional values. Nothing could be further from the truth. King was a great conservative on this central issue, and he stood on the shoulders of Augustine and Aquinas, striving to restore our heritage of justice rooted in the law of God.

From the time of Emperor Nero, who declared Christianity illegal, to the days of the American slave trade, from the civil rights struggle of the sixties to our current battles against abortion, euthanasia, cloning, and same-sex "marriage," Christians have always maintained exactly what King maintained.

"The question is not whether we will be extremists, but what kind of extremists we will be... The nation and the world are in dire need of creative extremists" ~ Martin Luther King. Jr.

Tuesday marks the 40th anniversary of the Roe v. Wade Supreme Court decision. In a 7-2 ruling on January 22, 1973, the justices declared laws stating that prohibiting abortion violated a woman's constitutional right to privacy. They also said states could regulate abortion procedures in the interest of a woman's health or in protecting a potential human life starting at the end of the pregnancy's first trimester. Sad day! The history of a fallen man projects a disposable culture wrapped in selfishness. Virtually, throughout history, societies survived by the tactical purging of others, in which case, the powerful ones survived at the expense of the weak ones. In a disposable culture, it's easier to throw things out than to fix them. Unfortunate people, like the disabled, who are viewed as a liability are treated as outcasts. The pro-abortion's main argument is that the unborn babies are disposable cells. In which case, a person is considered to be a person or not a person, depending on their size. Scientists say that our bodies involve a process of continuous cells growth. When the cells throughout our bodies stop duplicating, we stop growing which would mean demise. Although we grow into death, there is no stage of life when we do not grow. When the pro-abortionists call a fetus a cell in the womb they mean life in the making or in progress until birth. In actuality, a fetus is a life inside the life of the mother progressively living as a dependant to the mother. We are all dependants in one way or the other. The unborn babies must be protected. "The right to life is the first among human rights." It is cold hearted and selfish for a person in sound minds to support abortion. As Ronald Reagan said, "I've noticed that everyone who is for abortion has already been born."

The public inauguration of our new political leaders is tomorrow. It will be accompanied by prayers. This is in line with our pledge of allegiance: "One Nation Under God". It is a commitment to fight for justice that is "rooted in the eternal law." The Bible instructs us to obey the commandments of God and the laws of our countries. The commandments make us accountable to the higher authorities. At no point of time and stage of life was mankind created to be autonomous. God created a perfect man (Adam) and put him in a perfect environment (Garden) but still, He gave him a law regarding which tree to touch and not to touch. Any law demands submission. Jesus was truly God and truly man but He submitted to the Father. At every stage of life, there are rules demanding submission: Family rules in accordance to Ephesians 5:22-23; Civil rules - "Let everyone be subject to the governing authorities, for there is no authority except that which God has established. The authorities that exist have been established by God" (Romans 13:1).

President Trump takes over a divided nation bleeding to death because of the irrational quantum disputes. Homicide, drugs, violence, racism are no longer a whisper but a shouted calumny. Now that we have a legitimate government in place, the partisan election politics should be put to rest. Let us consecrate this country to God through prayers. The loudest calling to duty is this: Put your finger on the Biblical passage 2 Chronicles, 7:14, believing God for the healing of our country. Let us rally behind our new leaders and give them a chance to rebuild our nation. Let us allow the long arms of the law to creep the long fingers of lawlessness. Again, our hope does not come by Air Force One; but by the grace of God.

Obama's election was historic because he was the first African-American to become president. It is not a surprise for the massive people who showed up at his inauguration; bigger crowds than those who attended Trump's inauguration. The media have been sarcastic portraying Trump as less popular. They ignore the fact that six million African-American who voted for Obama never voted for either Trump or Hillary. They simply stayed home. No wonder they didn't even show up for Trump's inauguration. They are simply not interested. The good news is that God is interested and that is how Mr. Trump won the election. God made them stay home!

Why would a person who claims to be a born again believer votes for homosexuality and abortion? The answer is that Liberalism is thicker than their faith. They would rather violate God's commandments than being disloyal to their political affiliations!

The news media are obsessed with demonstrations. It is impossible to flip the cable news channels without bouncing into clips of videos showing demonstrators against President Trump. The demonstrations we see are planned to express everything mankind wants apart from God. It is evidently seen by the messages written on their posts. The majority of them project feminism and atheistic views. The beauty of democracy is the freedom of speech. We should not take the same freedom for granted. But our freedom of expression must uphold the sovereignty of God. It means He owns everything, and we are mere stewards. Definitely, our free-will is not absolute because there are consequences of our choices. For our convenience and safety, we are free to do as God wills: Dare not defraud the Lord, by applying your freedom to any other purpose other than His intended purpose for you. In fact, the reason we have the free-will is that there is a need in each one of us demanding fulfillment. Therefore, our free-will is limited in the context of the divine provision. We are given a choice either to embrace or to reject God's supremacy to meet our needs eternally. Whenever we drop the transcendent values and rules, we add sorrow to our lives, and we are left with no moral code. The freedom to express our feelings should never be a substitute for the freedom to think. Any legitimate thinking begins with God. In politics, there are no impeccable rules. There are imprescriptible rules which any person may violate at their will. There is an old adage "History repeats itself". It is the admission of recycling outdated ideas; yesterday's junk can be as well today's treasure! Without the morality of the Moral God, political thinking is vitiated in the same corrupt ways whereby people can envision the future only when it coincides with their own selfish wishes. Yes, the demonstrators may be angry women but they should be thinking ladies of integrity too!

The latest national survey indicates that the resentment against the Evangelicals has risen sharply since the Republican Party had a sweeping victory in the recent elections. I think the negativity is partly due to insecurity. We (Christians) overcame fear by the virtue of our relationship with God. The Bible says that there is the positive fear of God: "The fear of the LORD is the beginning of wisdom, and knowledge of the Holy One is understanding" (Proverbs 9:10). Fear (also used as an infinitive) is in reference to dreadful or exceedingly fearfulness, causing trembling, and resulting in having moral reverence. Such fear drives us to respect the oracles of God. The Psalmist refers to the Word as revered (Psalm 19-10). Without reverence, there cannot be a reproof. We need to be taught the basic principles of the oracles of God in order to make good choices honoring to God. "The fear of the Lord" is essentially a lifestyle of worshiping. The commencement of wisdom is the fear of Jehovah. Whenever the fear of God is not converted into worshiping or fails to draw us towards God to bow down, it drives us away from God with resentment towards everything that is associated with the holiness of God. Without Jesus, life is governed by an endless cycle of resentment. On the other hand, Christians are not surprised by the escalating rejection because they don't belong to the world; they expect rejection rather than comfort from the people of the world.

Somebody posted that "President Trump hates Obama. Mr. Obama watches mostly in silence as his successor takes a political sledgehammer to his legacy." Reply: True, President Donald Trump has the power to rip Barack Obama's legacy out by its roots, brick by brick, in a bid to tear down what Mr. Obama built, but I don't think that it is a personal fight; it is rather a conflict of ideas. Obama was far left whereas Trump is far right. Obama was a loyal cadre of the Democratic Party whereas Trump is a loyal cadre of the Republican Party. What we see is a difference between pure liberalism and pure conservatism. The two are like water and oil; they will never mix!

Somebody posted "We are ashamed of having a president who is accused to have an affair with Daniel, the porn star in the past". My reply: I don't believe the authenticity of Daniel's story, but what if it is true, and Trump repented. Is he worse than Paul who slaughtered a number of Christians but was accepted by Jesus? Christians should discard their political cards and pick their spiritual cards. A true Christian will not bring up the past and use it against somebody. Even God decided not to remember our past when we repent.

My message posted on President Trump's home page: "Mr. President, I am praying for the divine guidance, wisdom, and favor. The liberals are there to pick on you in search for faults but the sincere American people who have America on their hearts are there not to pick on you in search for the faults but to pick from you the fruits."

"Now, one evening at Oxford during dinner, one young man asked me if I would marry an English girl. I looked at him sharply and he apologized. The way I looked at him, he knew I didn't like what he had asked. His colleague, a boy who was also a friend of mine laughed and said, "You don't ask Mayanja Nkangi such a question." He explains, "I know there were beautiful girls. Let me tell you something, they are all God's people, alright. But my mother was a Muganda woman of the lion clan, so I had also to marry a Muganda girl and I did so. This is not to say the other people weren't beautiful, I thought this was what should be done. If we go on marrying other people all the time, there will be no more Africans." ~ Mayanja Nkangi

The elect President of France, Emmanuel Macron is 39 years and married to a 64-year-old wife. He is 25 years younger than his wife. That is called commitment! He becomes the youngest president of France since Napoleon Bonaparte - which is a difference of about 200 years. "In a patriarchal world where it is old men who marry younger women, many have been left agog. The story gets juicier because he first met Brigitte as a 15-year-old schoolboy and she was his teacher. They started an affair. Brigitte was married then. The fact that the difference in age between 70-year-old US president Donald Trump and his wife Melanie, who is 47, is nearly 24 years, didn't raise eyebrows because, well, again, men get to marry younger women. Since time past, the cut off age for men has been much higher than for women. The evolutionary success of humans needed older men to marry younger women. The argument, of course, is how young."

"Emmanuel Macron's success can be traced to being visionary and sacrificially sticking to what he has determined to achieve. Therefore, it takes a vision and unwavering devotion to succeed. God never spoon-feed those He intends to succeed!" ~ Godfery E N Nsubuga

"This police force is big enough for all of us to shine and serve our country. One doesn't have to fall first for me to shine." ~ Ferix Kawesi

"The economy is the start and end of everything. You can't have successful education reform or any other reform if you don't have a strong economy." ~ David Cameron

"Africa's greatest need is the decolonizing of the minds. Mental enslavement lingers on way after the physical one."

"Once weapons were manufactured to fight wars; now wars are manufactured to sell weapons."

"Men must be ruled by God or they will be ruled by tyrants" ~ William Penny

Father Lokodo is a clergy and Uganda minister of Ethics. He complained that his Anti-Pornography law was being violated by even some of his colleagues yet they are supposed to be on the forefront to implement it. He promised to examine the recent leaked sex videotapes of the celebrity

to see if she should be prosecuted. Nyanjura Doreen responded to him in this way: "So father Lokodo also watches the leaked sex videos! Is he not guilty of viewing pornographic content?"

Somebody made the following comment in reference to Idi Amin: "Uganda needs such a leader today to sweep all the financial, military, political, religious and social immorality like the "Kifeesi" community". Reply: The Bible says "As a dog returns to its vomit, so fools repeat their folly" (Proverbs 26:11). Who being sick with what he has eaten, casts it up again, and afterward returns unto it and licks it up? Why should we look into trash cans to refresh ourselves? The young generations of today who watches Idi Amin on big screens, dramatized by Hollywood view him as an African hero. But Idi Amin was a notorious dictator and murderer just next to Adolf Hitler. Those of us who lived during his regime and lost our beloved ones shiver whenever his name is mentioned.

Somebody posted that "It is unbelievable that Idi Amin Dada is the most developmental Ugandan president so far." Reply: In a culture where truth is relative, absolutes cease. Morality becomes a matter of opinion as opposed to reality. One can say cannibalism is good, and the other condemns it; everything is relative depending on personal opinions. This is how one can have guts to applaud a brutal regime that killed and caused the disappearance of scores of people. Amnesty International puts the number of people killed by Idi Amin to 500,000 out of the 12 million Ugandans at the time during his eight-year rule in Uganda. I remember when I was in high school, dead bodies littered the swamps on the outskirts of Kampala like Namanve, Kisenyi just to mention a few. There are idle youths who took advantage of the situation and made money by selling the watches/shoes snapped from the dumped corpses. During Amin's regime, buying a new car was like signing your death sentence, unless you were a soldier. When a soldier admired your wife you were a dead meat. Not to mention other evils like pork was outlawed to be sold on the main streets because it was offensive to Muslims. The non-Muslim who violated the decree were forced to eat raw uncooked pork. Col. Nasur Abdullah, who was the governor of the central region, outlawed wearing sandals in the city. The poor people who could not afford the shoes were punished by ordering them to chew on their sandals (slippers). This was done in broad daylight in our capital city. During the economic war, essentials commodities like sugar, salt, soap and etc were a rare commodity. You had to line up for days in order to get a kilo (a half pound) of sugar. Ordinary peasants often washed their clothes when using pawpaw leaves because of the scarcity of soap. But the Muslims were privileged to get the same essential commodities (sugar, salt, and soap) in their mosques every Friday after their Juma prayers. The ordinary peasant had to buy such commodities on Black Market, four times the original price. The economic war was intended to turn over the businesses formerly owned by the foreigners to the indigenous people. But Idi Amin ended up handing over almost all of the Asians' businesses to his tribesmen most notably the Anyanyas and the Nubians from Sudan, and some loyal senior army officers and Muslims who had no experience at all to operate them. History can tell that black imperialists are worse than white imperialists. Within a couple of months after expelling the Asians, goats were being reared in textile and spare parts stores!

When very senior military officers smile, they etch subtle curves on their faces and show very little, if anything, of their teeth. Facial emotional expression is partly an art form, and Idi Amin used to master it. But remember that when a lion exposes its teeth, it is not smiling!

In his hour-long speech, Robert Mugabe the soon to be 92-year-old leader said he would lead Zimbabwe until God called him. "I will be there until God says come, but as long as am alive I will head the country, forward ever, backward never," he said. That was then, but this is now;

it is not the divine that called him home but the military that has called him to step down.

Convincing Mugabe to step down was essential since the military had insisted that this wasn't a coup, but rather a way to settle a factional battle within the ruling ZANU-PF, they had to either get Mugabe to resign or face a protracted impeachment battle in Parliament to give the power transfer a constitutional flavor.

Fidelis Mukonori became lead negotiator because both Mugabe and the military trusted him. The 70-year-old Jesuit priest from Zimbabwe said he's mediated between bitter political rivals in the past. As a young priest, the Rev. Fidelis Mukonori collected evidence of atrocities during Zimbabwe's brutal civil war. The reports filtered to Robert Mugabe, then a leading figure in the liberation struggles. Decades later, Mukonori helped persuade Mugabe to relinquish power. Mukonori met daily with Mugabe, who is 93 years old and had been the nation's leader for almost four decades.

Mukonori is a debater, he is a thinker, he argues intelligently, he can philosophize. "I'm a tough nut to crack," he said. "I've done this before." Mukonori said his strategy was never to argue with Mugabe, but rather to listen and convince Mugabe he could exit the political stage with nobility. Mukonori said. "It was a question of making President Mugabe see what was happening in the country economically and politically at that time and what was at stake with regard to issues pertaining to the soldiers moving in."

Mukonori said he repeatedly assured Mugabe of his contribution to Zimbabwe as a liberation hero and father of the nation. Though vilified by much of the world, Mugabe is still revered by the military and ruling party leadership. "The generals always treated him with respect during the discussions, they even saluted him," Mukonori said. "He knew he would love to leave with dignity." He said he still speaks to Mugabe almost every day. He said the former president has offered to give advice to the new president, despite most Zimbabweans wishing for a clean break. "He has not vanished from life, he is not dead," Mukonori said. "But he has vanished from the limelight. His brains are still very sharp and working."

Justice Wadyajena, a Mnangagwa admirer and outspoken ZANU-PF parliamentarian, reminded his Twitter followers of the dangers of personality cults." Those falling all over each other pledging loyalty to President ED are just brutes playing meek," Wadyajena wrote, referring to Mnangagwa by the initials of his first and middle names. "If you really are principled, there's no reason to bootlick, your conduct should speak for itself. We've seen the danger of personalizing governance and gate-keeping a national figure!"

AUGUST FOR EVANGELISM

The Church is the body of Christ. The person of the Church is Christ. The person of the Holy Spirit is the unit, unity and power of the Church. "The church is the testimony of Christ to the world exuding out of us individually or every member in particular. The art of reasoning together begins with putting everything we think we know on God's sacrificial altar and paying close attention to what He alone is teaching. It might be a one on one with Him. It might be through conversation with another Believer. It is also a lesson in humility to finally listen instead of always speaking."

Evangelism is submitting and implementing the greatest command from the highest Commander in chief as given in Matthew 28:16-20. Do whatever God instructed you and called you to do. Swing into action; be proactive. Don't sit around waiting for someone to approach you. Once God gives you a direction, approach the person and explain your mission to them.

Matthew 28:18 - "And Jesus came and spake unto them, saying, All power is given unto me in heaven and in earth." The word 'power' in this scripture is translated as authority (exousia) as opposed to strength, power, or ability (dunamis). Jesus as very God (fully divine) retained the absolute divine sovereignty, and as very man (fully human) submitted to God's eternal counsel. He was not less God and less human. Jesus came to the earth, on our behalf, to recover the dominion (authority) which Adam

lost after the fall. The authority is the legal right to exercise the divine power over all creations on the earth. He got the same authority after He was raised from death. The Father gave all authority to the Son; the Son gave all authority to the Church. Jesus said concerning the Church that even all the powers of hell will not conquer her (Matthew 16:18). Neither the power of death nor the power of the devil shall prevail against the Church. Individually, we have access to the same power by faith. "Truly I tell you, if you have faith and do not doubt, not only can you do what was done to the fig tree, but also you can say to this mountain, 'Go, throw yourself into the sea,' and it will be done" (Matthew 21:21). Jesus used the metaphor of the mountain to show, what great things are done by faith, and that an increase of it should even do greater things. "If you have faith as small as a mustard seed" (Matthew 17:20), implies that faith is a gift which really comes in small measures with capability to grow through active obedience and the experience which is gained through it (Romans 10:17). Jesus commissioned us to change the world by proclaiming His life, death/resurrection (the gospel). The gospel dictates that a sinner applies to be saved from the deserved wrath of God against sin by applying for mercy from the Father, through the atonement of the incarnate Son, and by the sanctification of the Holy Spirit.

John 12:32 - "And I, when I am lifted up from the earth, will draw all people to myself." The words "To be lifted up" are in reference to His death on the cross. The words "all men" are used in hyperbole form. It is in reference to God's elect from all nations, all ethnic groups, all genders, rich and poor. The word "draw" is used in the moral sense in reference to God's elect. Jesus said that "No one can come to me unless the Father who sent me draws them, and I will raise them up at the last day" (John 6:44). Drawing is an act of power, yet not of force. God draws people to Christ. It means that people can emotionally or corporeally come to Him, but not spiritually; because they have no power within themselves; being spiritually dead in trespasses and sins. A dead man (corpse) can do nothing for himself unless something is done to him. We come to Christ by the grace through faith when we confess and believe Him as our Lord and

Savior (Romans 10:9). The grace is of God. Faith is not of a man's self, it is the gift of God. Therefore efficacious grace must be exerted to enable a soul that is dead spiritually to come to Christ. The self-condemned sinner needs not perplex himself how this righteousness may be found. Justification by faith in Christ is a plain doctrine. God draws men to Christ by the Holy Spirit when the gospel is preached; it is man's responsibility to receive the grace offered. Jesus saved us because His righteous living was imputed to us (became ours). Also, by dying on the cross the death we will never die; He paid in full the penalties for our sins. Jesus is God manifested to us in human form to save us from our sins by showing us practically that humans can live righteously. Although we live in a multiculturalism social setting, our lives are divided into only two groups: 1) The righteous living perfected (complete) in Christ. 2) The unrighteous living purely projecting the corrupt human recourses. The cross divides the world into two groups: The saved world and the perishing world.

Matthew 10:32 – "Whosoever therefore shall confess me before men, him will I confess also before my Father which is in heaven." Public confession involves believing in the heart, declaring your faith in Him to others, and subjecting yourself to His ordinances. The phrase "him will I confess also before my Father which is in heaven" means Jesus will confess you also before His Father which is in heaven: He will introduce you into His Father's presence, and recommend you to Him, to be honored, blessed, and glorified by him.

Salvation is personal and it is an inside job that is accomplished by God in our hearts, but it is not a private matter. There is no such a thing as a secret Christian called to testify to himself or to operate undercover or underground without being known by the world. We are called to testify about the goodness of God because there is absolutely nothing in this world that will provide more comfort and happiness and hence liberty than a testimony of the truth. We are saved from something to something.

It means that there is no saved person who doesn't have a testimony. God delivers us from the worst so that He can use our testimonies to win others to Him. He turns our testings into testimonies. Also, our testimonies become our defense to stand against the wiles of the devil, and they are a mighty tool in the hands of each and every believer. It is therefore important, wherever you go, for the people to know that you are a child of God sanctified (set apart) for His glory. This is the most effective way of overcoming temptation. It blocks the people of the contradictory characters from engaging you in their nasty schemes and it opens a way for you to share your testimony, as you interact with the people. God made Jesus the masterpiece. Make your life a masterpiece by placing the value of Christ on your character. "Become the Word in body as well as spirit."

John 13:34 "A new command I give you: Love one another. As I have loved you, so you must love one another." As parents, when they take their leave of their children, in their dying moments, give them proper instructions and orders, and lay their dying injunctions on them, so Christ is about to leave his disciples, He gives them what is considered to be a very important instruction to adhere. It is the law of love. Jesus said that as I have rendered it to you, pass it on to others. It is a new commandment because love has been practically demonstrated in a unique manner. The children of God are instructed to love each other sacrificially. It is the kind of love that is filled with the sense of responsibility for each other's welfare. It is a calling to be sensitive to the needs of others more than your own needs. According to this scripture, love should be a reciprocal flow between God and man. The demonstrated love within the church is supposed to be the true basis of morality. This is the surest way the people of the world will realize the presence of Christ in our midst: "By this everyone will know that you are my disciples, if you love one another" (John 13:35). By our love for each other, for mankind, and for God, it is known or denied that men who call themselves Christians are really Christ's disciples. If you

want to win the lost souls of the children of the world, start by loving the redeemed souls of the children of God.

Luke 7:47 – "Therefore, I tell you, her many sins have been forgiven–as her great love has shown. But whoever has been forgiven little loves little." Her great love was not the cause of the remission of her sins, but the consequence of the forgiveness of her many sins. Often, God uses people who were delivered from the ugly past. Not because God pities them but because they love more. Human love is reciprocal. Whenever they remember how much they were forgiven, their love is stimulated. Given the fact, we are all equally forgiven when we repent because our salvation does not depend on our love for God but on His love for us. There is no such thing as half-saved or half-lost. Justification extends complete forgiveness of all sins including the least ones. The purity of the justified people is received rather than achieved. The justified are sanctified and they will be glorified. They constitute a totally distinct group of people called the saints; they find their identity in Christ.

Matthew 28:18-20 - "And Jesus came and spoke to them, saying, "All authority has been given to Me in heaven and on earth. 19 Go therefore[a] and make disciples of all the nations, baptizing them in the name of the Father and of the Son and of the Holy Spirit, 20 teaching them to observe all things that I have commanded you; and lo, I am with you always, even to the end of the age." This is the first executive order given by our Lord after the resurrection. It is the matching order from our commander-in-chief. The only option we have is to implement it as it is given. It is written in plain language for all to understand: Go preach, teach and baptize the converted in the name of the Father, Son, and Holy Spirit, and then teach the disciples to disciple others. All the demons are here wittingly to resist the Great Commission because it is the divine mission to rescue the fallen souls from the grip of damnation and hence emptying hell of its resources.

In spite of the counteract adversity, the gospel will prevail, and this world will be a heaven, and hell a fable.

John 14:12 - "Very truly I tell you, whoever believes in me will do the works I have been doing, and they will do even greater things than these, because I am going to the Father." According to this Scripture, the reason for our greater works is because Jesus is going to the Father. Why going to the Father is a necessity for us to do greater works? Jesus insinuated that "Nevertheless I tell you the truth; It is expedient for you that I go away: for if I go not away, the Comforter will not come unto you; but if I depart, I will send him unto you." (John 16:7). Jesus went to sit on the heavenly throne so that the Father could send the Holy Spirit to sit on the throne of the hearts of all men where Jesus reigns. The Holy Spirit is to us what Jesus was to His disciples during His earthly ministry. The works the Holy Spirit through us is the ministry of Jesus Christ on the earth. We can do the same works as Jesus did qualitatively because it is Jesus working through us. But greater works quantity wise because the body of Christ (Church) consists of many members at multiple locations but Jesus was one person at one place at a time. The explanation of these greater works should not be sought in the terms of individual instances of miraculous power exercised by the believers through the gifts (charisma) but much more important are the souls saved. There is no greater miracle than the salvation of the soul.

Matthew 4:19 - "And he said to them, Follow me, and I will make you fishers of men." Simon and Andrew had followed Jesus Christ before, as common disciples, John 1:37; now they must leave their vocations to pursue their calling. The method of winning the lost soul is similar to fishing. Fishermen go after fishes. Preachers go after souls. Fishing is the knack of tracking down of what is elusive but attainable. During the biblical times, the fishermen used nets to catch fishes. Evangelism is a net of love by which you can catch the lost souls. The gospel is the power that drags the soul out of hell. The gospel initiates faith. Water is the life

to the fishes in the same way faith is the life of the soul. Whereas fishing is pulling the fishes out of life (water) to death, evangelism is pulling the souls from death to life.

John 13:11-15 - "You call me 'Teacher' and 'Lord,' and rightly so, for that is what I am. Now that I, your Lord and Teacher, have washed your feet, you also should wash one another's feet. I have set you an example that you should do as I have done for you." Jesus said if you call me your teacher, then be good students by learning from me. Jesus took on the responsibility of a hired house servant to wash the feet of His disciples. He then asked them to do as He has done (not what He has done). He asked them to have the same attitude of serving one another. Serving does not expect payback. After washing their feet, Jesus did not ask them to wash His feet as well. It was not a kind of 'scratch my back, I scratch your back.' He did what He did sacrificially without expectation of returns, and He asked His disciples to do the same. The highlight is on the attitude rather than the act of washing feet. Jesus was practically explaining His saving work of grace. That is why He told Peter that, "You do not realize now what I am doing, but later you will understand" (John 13:7). When God works in your life it is the grace at work. Jesus cleaned our filthiness when we were helpless; most probably compared to a mother that changes the diaper of her little baby. He saved us at the expense of His life. Grace is the unmerited favor at the expense of Christ.

John 5:39 - "You study the Scriptures diligently because you think that in them you have eternal life. These are the very Scriptures that testify about me, yet you refuse to come to me to have life." There are three witnesses testifying to the deity of Christ. At baptism, the Father testified that Jesus is the Son of God (God in the flesh) (Matthew 3:17). Jehovah the Father took infinite delight and pleasure in Him as His own Son, who lay in His bosom eternally. The works of Jesus testified that He is divine (John 5:36; John 10:30). Jesus said that the works He did, bear witness

of Him, that He was in the Father, and the Father in Him; they were one in nature, and equal in power and glory. In the above scripture, Jesus said that the Scriptures testify to His deity. Jesus basically said to His disciples that "You have a third great testimony to my claim, and yet you are not prepared to accept it." In the last part of the scripture, Jesus claimed to be the source of eternal life.

The writings of Moses and the prophets are of divine inspiration and authority. According to the traditions, the Jews were required to begin to read in the book of the law by reciting the following words: "Blessed be he that has chosen us above all nations, and hath given us his law." And they were required to finish reading the book of the law with the following words: "Blessed is he who hath given us his law, the law of truth, and has planted "eternal life" in the midst of us." Jesus claimed that He is the eternal life: "Now this is eternal life: that they know you, the only true God, and Jesus Christ, whom you have sent" (John 17:3). Jesus is behind each and every moral story in the Bible. You have not read and understood a moral story in the Bible until you find the moral God (Jesus) behind the story. Jesus was not making a mere initiative just to create the awareness of His presence in the scriptures but His purpose too. The Scriptures testify of Christ and point at Him as the way of life so that we could come to Him. Jesus said that "I am the way, the truth, and the life: no man cometh unto the Father, but by me" (John 14:6). He wants us to discover Him in the scriptures, to know Him as the Lord and Savior and to fellowship with Him daily.

God is more glorified in us when we are fulfilled in Him. We are called to preach the Word in season and out of season without lowering the bar. Our lives must not contradict what we preach. Also, we should never use our life's experience as the standard of righteousness. Definitely, people will be swayed by what we do more than what we say. But our priority is to introduce to the people the greatest teacher (Holy Spirit). We are not the light but the reflectors of the light. The greatest mistake is for a preacher to try to become an ultimate icon of the Word. It is a matter of time when people will see some shadows in the light of your life because there is humanity (the fallen nature) behind your spirituality. Therefore, it is healthy to confess that we are fragile and capable of making errors. The surest way to corrupt your calling is to attract people to yourself rather than to the Lord.

Matthew 5:13 - "You are the salt of the earth. But if the salt loses its saltiness, how can it be made salty again? It is no longer good for anything, except to be thrown out and trampled underfoot." Virtually no natural reaction can cause salt to turn into any other compound. In the same way, we never cease to be the children of God. The metaphor "If the salt loses its saltiness," is used to warn us of the danger of ignoring our God-given mandate. It is a warning against double-dipping into heaven and the world. When you follow Jesus and begin to associate with the world, you will definitely lose your saltiness. We are planted in the world but there is nothing glorying to God in worldliness. Losing saltiness has serious consequences. Christians are daily tramped down (bashed) by the insensitive people of the world and bureaucracy every day partly because at times the people who call themselves Christians are not worthy the name of Christ. We are partly to blame for the bashing because we have not represented Christ as we are supposed to do. We have made ourselves a good target for the world to mock. Materialism is consuming the professing believers. The petty bickering and fighting from within are causing us to lose our saltiness. For example, the Church is still divided along political allegiances and racial prejudices as the world is. We are supposed to become members of a new race, overcoming petty prejudice, owing our ultimate allegiance not to politicians but to our Lord. Although we are not exempted from persecution, the bashing we see today is mostly self-inflicted; it is a bash and crash. In this case, losing saltiness applies to what is absolutely useless due to incompetence.

Matthew 23:3 - "So you must be careful to do everything they tell you. But do not do what they do, for they do not practice what they preach."

Jesus instructed His followers to do what the Pharisees say but not to do what they do. The Pharisees were hypocrites because they claimed to keep the whole Law. Nobody can wholly observe the Law without the grace. Ironically, even the good doctrine preached becomes a snare when it is taught by the corrupt characters. The good works must be taught and owned by the vessels who proclaim them. Your lifestyle is the mirror, even without speaking, it reveals the secrets of the heart. Expository living is when you live your life in the manner worthy of the gospel. I want to add that people may scorn what you say but no sane person can hate the lifestyle projecting the morality of the scriptures. The same people who resist the gospel won't resist the flavor of godly people. For example, every person likes a drug-free and a violence-free environment. People resist the Bible not because they hate the values of the Scriptures but with prior intention of resisting accountability. A stiff-necked person looks for mistakes in the scriptures as an excuse for not changing. Poignantly, the inerrancy of the scriptures projects that whenever you find a mistake in the Bible, it is because there is a mistake in your life. Look for mistakes in your life rather than in the scriptures. Read the Bible as it is; never put a period where there is a comma.

Whenever God gives you a message never pass it on before you dedicate it to yourself. The right conviction always starts with self; don't pass on a buck. Whether it is a reproof or a rebuke, own the message by saying that, "It is me". God is interested in changing you first before using you to change others. He wants to change you so that you might become a testimony to change others. Preaching the gospel to ourselves is a spiritual discipline that is both proactive and reactive. No one is more influential in your life than you are because no one talks to you more than you do. God would rather speak to you in your conscience than through others because it is easier to hear your inner voices with great clearness and live by what you hear. Responsibility is to respond positively even to your own sermon.

Everyone has the past. The scars of our past lives are not trophies of pride but proof that this life is dented with flaws. It is after we are born again that we can say with certainty that the dark days are behind us rather than before us. The adage goes "It is better to experience the bad days during your early times than during the end of your life". A credible worrier accepts the war he went through and is ennobled by his scars. I am not ashamed of my scars because God turned the scars of my life into testimonies of His amazing grace. On the contrary, Satan strategizes to turn our scars into baits on the hook to fish men. One way Satan hurts us is by hurting the people we love most, in particular, our family members and close relatives. The people who know us best are most likely to swallow the bait of Satan by rejecting the gospel on account of our past lifestyles. Others instead of taking the path of the light of righteousness we are tracking now decide to imitate our ugly past from which we were delivered. God sets before their eyes our past and present lives so that they can choose wisely but they end up embracing the very things we regret doing in the past! The deception of Satan is that it is easier to do what is wrong than to do what is right. But never forget that every action has consequences and victims. It hurts when the victims are our beloved ones. The broken families are not necessarily those who do not live in harmony but those who do not share the same destiny after this life.

Psalm 90:12 – "Teach us to number our days, that we may gain a heart of wisdom." In human affairs, Providence arranges the moment when everything shall happen, the duration of its operation, and the time appropriate thereto. In the earthly economy, to diversify your investment is to invest in different asset classes and in securities of many issuers in an attempt to reduce overall investment risk and to avoid damaging a portfolio's performance by the poor performance of a single security, industry, (or country). In the heavenly economy, God makes everything beautiful in its season, which man obscurely comprehends (Ecclesiastes 3:11). God is not limited by time but He has a time set for everything to be done in the world according to His purposes and timing. Man has his appointed cycle of seasons and vicissitudes, as the sun, wind, and water

(Ecclesiastes 1:5-7), which he cannot change but he has the power to choose his destiny. The Psalmists prayed for wisdom to number his days. He is asking for wisdom to contemplate on his mortality. God would teach us seriously to meditate on, and consider of, the shortness of our days and live wisely. We all share the same natural life but we have different destinations. The question is where you will spend your eternity. When your allegiance is to Christ, your citizenship is in heaven. Hell is walking apart from Christ. Receiving Jesus is the only exit to come out of the pit of hell.

Luke 19:13 - "And he called his ten servants, and delivered them ten pounds, and said unto them, Occupy till I come." The word occupy is the same as colonizing. In the social and political arena, the word 'colonialism' bred an instinctive arrogance. The advent of colonialism ensured the occupation and domination by a foreign country and hence to be dominated by a foreign power. Politically, there is no justification for colonialism because no country wants to be under the banner of another country. Spiritually, God sends us to occupy (colonize) this planate, to establish the colonies under His banner. We should not feel apologetic about it because this universe belongs to God, and we have His mandate to dominate it (Genesis 1:26). We are sent to liberate this world from satanic colonialism, which is a very paternalistic system that controls the full spectrum of humanity. God equips us morally to dislodge the corrupt system of the world that is in contradiction to His values. This is what it means to be in this world and not of this world.

John 10:16 - "And other sheep I have, which are not of this fold: them also I must bring, and they shall hear my voice, and there shall be one fold, and one shepherd." Jesus was sent first to the Jews: ""I was sent only to the lost sheep of Israel" (Matthew 15:24). The sheep of the other sheepfold are the Gentiles. He brings the Jews and the Gentiles into one sheepfold. The sheepfold was a rock wall enclosure of loosely stacked stones, and this

provided protection against "thieves and robbers" (John 10). Jesus is the entrance (door) to the sheepfold. In this beautiful figure reference is made to the place where we are blessed when coming in and going out; a place where we belong and repose. Amidst the trials and the deceptions of the world, He is our peace - Jehovah-shalom!

Outreach is reaching out to the lost world with the gospel. In-reach is growing in the grace.

"Evangelism is just one bagger telling another bagger where to find bread." ~ R.C. Sproul

We have trained people to be touched by God in a service but not changed by Him in life. And that simply is not good enough anymore. ~ Graham Cooke

There are three groups of people: Those who are not saved; those who are saved; those who think they are saved but when they are not. It is only you that can tell in which group you are.

God is always inviting first-love heart responses from us in every season. "If you can look back and see a time that you were more passionate for the Lord than you are now, that means you are backslidden." ~ Keith Miller

Sitting in church and waiting for the non-repented sinners to show up is like a cap sitting at the police station waiting for a criminal to turn himself in.

When Satan cannot defeat the Church, he joins the Church to fight her from within.

Why is the majority of the Church failing? It is because we, the Church, have become satisfied with producing an audience, and not an army of warriors.

"You never have to advertise a fire. Everyone comes running when there's a fire. Likewise, if your church is on fire, you will not have to advertise it. The community will already know it." ~Leonard Ravenhill

"A meditative man should be a talker; otherwise he is a mental miser, a mill which grinds corn only for the miller." ~ C.H. Spurgeon

Superheroes exterminate their foes but Jesus, the Super Star, saved His foes. ~ Ephesians 2:4-10

"The first thing you must do when approaching a lukewarm is to establish trust. Not fake trust. It's a simple tactic to get what you want from that is manipulative and wrong. You need to do away with mockery, judgment, and pride? Do away with self and be others' conscience. Then, continue with this, opening your heart to them and they will open to you and the Word of the Lord! If you are an ambassador of the Lord, be kind and merciful and with legitimate love. That is how you reach the lost."

I was blessed today to listen to this inspiring testimony. It is about two missionaries to a communist country who were incarcerated for preaching the gospel. They were confined to a compartment with other native prisoners. While jail time pulls at the moral heartstrings of the Christian faith, the nasty conditions of the prison became unbearable. Eventually, they were attacked by bevies of lice due to the deteriorated hygiene. One of the missionaries was aggravated. She diagnosed it to be a vicious demonic attack. However, the other missionary disagreed with her. She quoted Paul's words in 1 Thessalonians 5:18 which say "In everything, we should give thanks". She convinced her partner to thank God even for the lice. The situation became worse forcing the prison wardens who supervised all the operations in the prison to stop walking in their compartments out of fear of carrying the lice on their clothes. This became a golden opportunity for the missionaries to turn their prison cell into a powerful ministry of the gospel without being detected by the prison wardens. Consequently, several underground churches were initiated from this prison. "Thank God for the hardship you are going through. For the lice bothering you are God-sent."

Galatians 5:9 - "A little leaven leaveneth the whole lump." A little bit of the traditions of men can pollute the whole truth. The human heart is the darkroom where negativity is developed. It is within our human nature to find loopholes in something that is difficult regardless of its validity and to conveniently discard it in particular when it doesn't resonate with our emotions and personal experience. Satan is sneaky and deceptive. He gives you a little bit of leeway in order to make you believe a lie as the truth; his ultimate goal is to kill and to destroy. A half-truth is not a truth at all. The tragedy is that when falsehood is recycled it eventually appears as if it is the truth. During the biblical times, the true doctrine was threatened by the

Judaizers. Today, we are mauled by the liberal, watered-down, toothless and people-pleasing gospel. The social gospel is the deception of Satan. We are not called to be nice in order to reach God but to allow God to make us good in order to reach Him. Any version of the gospel that doesn't start with the grace is a watered down version.

Just read an article in the news that the government of Uganda is banning all of the healing advertisements for witchdoctors and born again churches. Yes, it is the duty of the government to step in to regulate the vulnerability of the citizens. But it bothers me to put the Church and the witchdoctors in the same category. The most effective way could have been educating the masses regarding the danger and falsehood of witchcraft. The business of witchcraft will continue to boom as long as the people accept and believe in their crap. People will continue to be attracted to it as long as it is financially profitable. I have no sympathetic words for the witchdoctors but as for the born again, there are some activities which appear as if some are commercializing the gospel. Evangelism should be conducted along ideal, charity and devotion rather than for material gains. Given the fact, my advice to the government regarding how to handle the matters pertaining to the Church is in the Bible: "So in the present case, I advise you: Leave these men alone. Let them go! For if their purpose or endeavor is of human origin, it will fail. But if it is from God, you will not be able to stop them. You may even find yourselves fighting against God." (Acts 5:38-39). There is no need to restrict the Church with imposed sanctions because any false doctrine will eventually fail but the genuine doctrine must stand the test of time.

Somebody asked that, "Does God choose us or do we choose God?" God basically chose us because He came from heaven to the earth to save us. Given the fact, this is a kind of question whereby both answers are correct: God chooses us, and we choose Him. The Bible doesn't try to reconcile these two truths but instead presents them side by side. Jesus said that ""No one can come to me unless the Father who sent me draws them, and I will raise them up at the last day." (John 6:44). Also, "But to all who did receive him, who believed in his name, he gave the right to become children of God, who were born, not of blood nor of the will of the flesh nor of the will of man, but of God." (John 1:12-13). God reached out to the lost with the gospel, and those who believed in Jesus made a real choice to really believe in Jesus as the Son of God and received Him as their Lord and Savior according to the will of God. So, if you want God to choose you, choose Him now!

Somebody asked that "Can't I be saved without believing in the Bible?" The Bible does not save us. We are saved by putting our faith in Jesus Christ alone. We are not even supposed to worship the Bible. Given the fact, nobody can be saved without listening and accepting the gospel. The gospel is part of the Bible. The gospel is the good news because there is no better news than the good news. It is the perfect life of Jesus which He lived on our behalf; His death that was supposed to be our death; His resurrected life of which we become partakers. The Bible is the written Word of God concerning our salvation. Sanctification is impossible without the Bible. For example, we cannot know what is righteous and what is sinful without reading the Bible (Romans 7:7). It is not given to me to decide who is saved and who is not, but I have a hard time to believe that somebody can be truly saved when they do not believe in the Bible.

1 Corinthians 2:2 "For I resolved to know nothing while I was with you except Jesus Christ and him crucified". Christ, in His person, and offices, and sufferings, is the sum and substance of the gospel. When nothing but Christ crucified is plainly preached, the success must be entirely from the divine power accompanying the Word, and thus men are brought to believe, to the salvation of their souls. The gospel is complete; it doesn't need to be added on or watered down in order to bring salvation. Without Jesus, life is just an empty cup. Salvation is being catapulted into a

whole new life. I mean a life that is in contradiction to our human nature and instincts. Jesus came in human form to bring to us the consciousness of the spiritual dimension. The very reason for our existence in human form is to bring the consciousness of the spiritual dimension to this world. The world crucifies Him daily; we preach Him crucified!

1 John 3:1 - "See what great love the Father has lavished on us, that we should be called children of God! And that is what we are! The reason the world does not know us is that it did not know him." There is no man so good that if he places all his actions and thoughts under the scrutiny of the laws, he would not deserve banishment. We are sinners but God dressed us in His robes of righteousness. The only way a sinner can be certainly sure of the forgiveness of sins is to stand before God in His imputed righteousness. In Jesus Christ is the fullness of grace. Your hope for redemption does not come from within you but from outside you; it is in Christ. There is no faith outside Christ. Jesus Christ did not come to win the love of the Father for us. It is the love of the Father that sent Jesus to die for us. The scripture says, "The world does not know us because it does not know Him". The highest form of ignorance is when you reject something you don't know anything about. Spiritually, it is called 'lack of insight'. Sin is rejecting the love of God extended to us through Jesus Christ. God will honor your decision of rejecting Him by rejecting you. Again, this is not what I am saying; it is what the Bible says!

Acts 3:6 – "Then Peter said, "Silver or gold I do not have, but what I do have I give you. In the name of Jesus Christ of Nazareth, walk." Peter and John were led by a Divine direction, to perform a miracle on a man who was above forty years old, who had been a cripple from his birth. God sent the simple men of faith as opposed to the millionaires to deliver the maimed man. Peter and John had no money (they were not filthy rich) but they had the required faith for the healing and the deliverance of the soul from the pit of hell. The crippled man had nothing to offer to earn his

deliverance. God healed him by His grace, in the same way, He saves us by His grace (Psalms 103:3). The body finds the melancholy consequences of Adam's offense, it is subject to many infirmities, and the soul also. Christ alone forgives all of our sins and heals all of our infirmities. The totality of our nature and all of the faculties of the world are crippled. Everything we see will gradually mutate and eventually decay. Jesus came to redeem all of the crippled faculties of our fallen nature, beginning with our souls. The name of Jesus is the greatest power at our fingertips to change this world. Every viable charity should, therefore, be aimed at winning the lost souls.

2 Corinthians 12:7-9 - "Therefore, in order to keep me from becoming conceited, I was given a thorn in my flesh, a messenger of Satan, to torment me. Three times I pleaded with the Lord to take it away from me. But he said to me, "My grace is sufficient for you, for my power is made perfect in weakness." God allowed the thorn in order to restrain Paul because of the abundance of revelations he had received when he was caught up to paradise and heard inexpressible things. God disabled his ego so that he couldn't brag about it. No wonder he wrote about his heavenly experience fourteen years later. Paul asked God to remove the thorn but God gave him more revelation of His grace. God preferred to use him when he was disabled by the thorn. God uses us during our inadequacies when we empty ourselves of ego. I have watched God using the disabled enormously. Not because He pities them but because when people feel rejected by the world they tend to lean on God more. The word 'disabled' means incapable, infirmity and inadequacy. All of us are disabled in one way or another. Romans 8:26 says, "The Spirit also helps our infirmities." God shows no partiality; He rewards all who diligently seek Him. But God wants us to depend on Him. God's strength is revealed in our weaknesses. Paul concluded that "Therefore I take pleasure in infirmities, in reproaches, in necessities, in persecutions, in distresses for Christ's sake: for when I am weak, then am I strong" (verse 10).

Being a Christian means that you have to put up with other people's crap in order to win them to Christ; but not necessarily in all situations. If your goal is to win them to the Lord, you should turn the other cheek.

Not everybody in the church is saved. Sleeping in the garage does not make you a car. "Just because a mouse lives in the cookie jar, does not make him a cookie." ~Pastor Carter Conlin

John 17:12 - "While I was with them, I protected them and kept them safe by that name you gave me. None has been lost except the one doomed to destruction so that the Scripture would be fulfilled." Of all the twelve apostles, Judas alone perished. He was included in "them which Thou gavest Me." For him, there was the same preservation and the same guardianship as for those who remained in the fold. This sheep wandered from the flock and got lost by his own will and act. The following saying is true concerning Judah: "Once lost is lost forever." We should never be stressed when we invest all our efforts in our beloved ones to know Jesus but at the end of the day, they decide to walk away from their faith. If you did whatever the Holy Spirit convicted you to do to win them to Christ, never feel guilty when they don't hold on their faith. Just pray for them so that God could break the repression that turned their flaw into pride. Spiritual blindness is the major cause of prejudices against the truth. Choosing the world over Jesus is opting for a temporary solution to a permanent problem. Everything is temporary. Everything is bound to end except the endless immensity of time. Time is simply how you live your life now and where you will spend your eternity.

I've been thinking retrospectively at the scenario of life. I realized that there are a lot of things I could have done differently if only I could turn back the hands of time. My greatest regret is delaying receiving the gift of salvation. I often ask myself, "Why did it take me so long to acknowledge the truth?" The Bible says that there is a way that seems good to man but in the end it is destruction. One thing I don't regret is that I am saved. Two roads diverged in a wood, I took the one least traveled and that has made all the difference. I will never regret that I chose this path...I am glad I did!

There is only one thing I regret ever since I received Jesus Christ as my Lord and Savior. That one thing is the time I wasted sitting on the pews of the so called men of God who fed me on their lies as opposed to the truth.

1 John 2:19 - "They went out from us, but they were not of us; for if they had been of us, they would no doubt have continued with us: but they went out, that they might be made manifest that they were not all of us." 'They were not of us' means even if they were with us physically, they were alien spiritually. They had made a profession of religion, they were numbered among us, they attended church regularly, and they were actively involved in the ministry but they decided to depart from the truth and follow the traditions of men because they had plastic faith (not genuine faith). The renegade may still be physically fellowshipping in the churches and confessing Jesus Christ by their lips but their hearts are far from God. Jesus said concerning them that "These people honor me with their lips, but their hearts are far from me." (Matthew 15:8). They do everything for their own glory, to be seen and to be approved of men, not caring what God (the searcher of hearts) knows concerning them, or what He required of them. When Jesus appears in His glory, He will say to them "I never knew you: depart from me, ye that work iniquity." (Matthew 7:23). "I never knew you" implies that in order to know Jesus He must know you. Otherwise, He will say to your face that "In vain you worshiped me; I have nothing to do with you." Jesus said concerning His own that "My sheep listen to My voice; I know them, and they follow Me. I give them eternal life, and they shall never perish; no one will snatch them out of my hand" (John 10:28). He knows His sheep; they listen to Him and follow Him. God gave His sheep the free will, and He respects their will before and

after salvation. It means that even when we are bound for predestination, we must exercise our free will and choose whether to accept Jesus or to reject Him as our Savior. And after we are saved we have a free will to be committed to Him or not. Christ's sheep are in His hands, being put there by God the Father; they are safe and secure all the way to the end as long as they stay within the sheepfold of Jesus. But when they decide to walk away, God will respect their will.

Human beings are what we are. Being created in God's image, we have the free will that God respects to a certain extent. We have considerable freedom to choose how we live and express ourselves. We even have the freedom to cut ourselves loose from the metaphorical strings that seem to tie us down. Granted, there are false and illusory bonds, from which we really ought to free ourselves, but there are cords of reality too, and if we cut them we will fall. Real freedom is to be who and what God made us to be. Failure to do so is self-deceit, self-deception, self-delusion and succumbing to muted ecstasy and reverie.

"I have but one candle of life to burn, and I would rather burn it out in a land filled with darkness than in a land flooded with light." ~ John Keith Falconer

"The mark of a great church is not its seating capacity, but its sending capacity." ~ Mike Stachura"

"The Great Commission is not an option to be considered; it is a command to be obeyed."

266

"Love is the root of missions; sacrifice is the fruit of missions" ~ Roderick Davis

Today, revivals are intended to gather people in one place to hear the gospel in anticipation for them to respond by receiving the Savior. There is a tendency for the preachers to exaggerate the number of people who attend our revival meetings. "Perhaps the greatest barrier to revival on a large scale is the fact that we are too interested in a great display. We want an exhibition; God is looking for a man who will throw himself entirely on God. Whenever self-effort, self-glory, self-seeking or self-promotion enters into the work of revival, then God leaves us to ourselves." ~ Ted Rendall

The numerous churches sprouting out all over the city of Kampala are called mushroom churches. According to survey, they are partly influenced and promoted by the prosperity gospel. "I also remembered that mushrooms are saprophytic, the last I checked they feed on the dead decaying matter... the analogy also describes the situation of main stream Christianity today". True revival is not emotional excitement but the repented hearts crying out to God for forgiveness.

Christ is our security. "The light of God surrounds us, the love of God enfolds us, the power of God protects us, the presence of God watches over us, wherever we are, God is, and where God is, all is well."

Somebody posted this advertisement: "April 15th – 16th, - Attend a seminar: Raising the dead class. Come and learn how to supernaturally raise the dead". My response: We are sent to preach the gospel as opposed to preach the miracles; the miracles follow those who preach the gospel in accordance to the divine will. God testifies to the gospel preached by the manifestations of miracles. Of course, the greatest miracle is the changed lives.

Somebody posted: "The scriptures teach that there are only twelve apostles whose names will be written on the gates of the city. Only Christ can make one an apostle. When the disciples cast lots and made Mathias an apostle, it was overturned by Christ when he made Paul an apostle." Reply: True, the mission of the twelve apostles who were chosen by Jesus during His earthly ministry is unique. But Jesus called Paul as an apostle after He went to heaven. The five-fold ministries of the Holy Spirit are still in place: "And he gave some, apostles; and some, prophets; and some, evangelists; and some, pastors and teachers (Ephesians 4:11-16). The word apostle simply means sent. I think all ministries (including the apostle) should be under the direct supervision and guidance of a pastor (shepherd). Jesus was a shepherd.

Paul said "I have planted, Apollos watered but God gave the increase (1 Corinthians 3:6-8). God uses one man to plant, then the other person to water. Justification is a onetime event but salvation is also a process of sanctification that is accomplished in glorification. The Bible instructs us that "Wherefore the rather, brethren, give diligence to make your calling and election sure:" (2 Peter 1:10). It is a calling to those who have obtained faith in Christ to stand in it, and to diligently advance in moral excellence; not be satisfied but press on to increase their knowledge of God's will.

SEPTEMBER FOR LABOR DAY

On this Labor Day, make a resolution to do everything unto God. Doing the will of God is the most challenging as well as the utmost satisfying vocation in this world; it is our ordained vocation. The Bible says that "Whatever you do, work at it with all your heart, as working for the Lord, not for human masters" (Colossians 3:23). This scripture is most taken up in displaying the glory of the Divine grace, and magnifying the Lord Jesus, these being the most pressing duties of the Christian life. In whatever we do, we must never separate the privileges and duties of the gospel. Also, submission to each other is the profound duty of all believers. Choose the path of submission in your relationship, at your place of work, and to those whom God has put in leadership to rule over you. We (believers) are not exceptional; we are called to execute the normal duties of life like other people. "It is only through labor and painful effort, by grim energy and resolute courage that we move on to better things." We experience the same challenges as the rest of the people. When it rains we become wet like other people. The difference is that we do everything unto God. As long as we seek God in everything we do, we are not worried about serving the devil. There is no chance, no destiny, and no fate that can circumvent or hinder or control the firm resolve of a determined soul whose rock is Christ. Happy Labor Day.

Your labor is the industry of your well-being and a reflection of your image. The harder you work, the better the impression you set on the people around you. A good impression should have an influence on you and an impact on others. We work hard to have nice things, however, excessive accumulation of stuff can become a vehicle of our destruction instead of a blessing. The Bible says that "One person gives freely, yet gains even more; another withholds unduly, but comes to poverty" (Proverbs 11:24). This scripture applies to the material gains and the spiritual gifts consecutively. He that generously uses the spiritual gifts, and disperses and dispenses the word of God, and spreads the truths of the Gospel, and freely and fully preaches them, increases himself in spiritual knowledge and understanding. Faith increases in the abundance of knowledge. "It is more blessed to give than to receive" (Acts 20:35). Thus liberality, by God's blessing, secures increase, while penuriousness, instead of expected gain, procures poverty. The spirit of deception searches for abundance life in the accumulated abundance stuff. Ironically, the same things we yearn for are the same things which the miserable people of the world possess in excess, and they are not fulfilled! Abundance life does not come from the things we do or possess but from the things we let God do for us.

2 Thessalonians 3:10 - "For even when we were with you, we gave you this rule: "The one who is unwilling to work shall not eat." Labor is the law of God; idleness is the parent of many crimes and is productive of misery. He who has no business allotted to him ought to choose some useful occupation for himself. Communism's policy of redistribution of wealth takes from those who work hard stuff and give them to those who don't work. The government does not own the free stuff they promise to give away. Every free thing given is taken from somebody who worked hard to get it, and it is given to somebody who didn't work for it. "He that labors on the evening of the Sabbath, he shall eat on the Sabbath day". We must never tire in our work. It will be time enough to rest when we go to heaven.

Matthew 6:26 - "Look at the birds of the air; they do not sow or reap or store away in barns, and yet your heavenly Father feeds them. Are you not much more valuable than they?" The birds mentioned in this scripture are not the ones reared and fed by men (pets) but the birds, which fly abroad

in the air, wild; and are not supported by their own, or any human care, but by the care of God. They do not grow food but they never starve. This scripture does not advocate idleness; it encourages us to work without stress and worry. The birds are not worried about tomorrow. Jesus instructed us to pray for our daily bread (Matthew 6:11). It means God will take care of us, "day by day", every day of our lives, to the end thereof. But we must labor, in the same way God feeds the birds but they must go into the fields to pick the food. When God is the reason we do what we are doing, worrying should never be an option because He will bear our burdens, and we shall find no disappointment in Him. We should embrace our problems with hope instead of bitterness. Your character should never change when your circumstances change because your character is the character of the unchanging God. You are bigger than your problems because one who is with God is the majority. Your self-esteem should not come from human recourses but it should be your confidence in God. People should see it and naturally gravitate towards God instead of towards you.

Ephesians 4:28 – "Anyone who has been stealing must steal no longer, but must work, doing something useful with their own hands, that they may have something to share with those in need." The scripture is divided into three parts: Morality, integrity, and generosity.

OCTOBER FOR PRAYING

Luke 11:1-13 - "Lord, teach us to pray, just as John taught his disciples." The disciples realized that prayer played a vital role in John the Baptist's life, and in the life of the Lord, so it should be their own practice as well. They asked Jesus to teach them how to pray. This is the most humble act of the disciples during the earthly ministry of Jesus. Jesus taught them how to pray. I prefer calling it "The Disciples' Prayer" to "The Lord's Prayer". Jesus was ready and willing to teach on this imperative subject of praying, but only when His disciples were eager to learn. The motivation for learning is at its highest peak when the student asks the teacher to teach and when they love what they are learning to do. Jesus began His teaching by emphasizing the need to pray. He said "When you pray" not "If you pray" because He expected them to pray. Will you pray?

Matthew 6:10 - "Your kingdom comes, your will be done, on earth as it is in heaven." The kingdom of God comes where God's will is done. The decisions we make reflect our will. Life and death are within the decisions we make. We live in the world of decisions. "You and I are essentially infinite choice-makers. In every moment of our existence, we are in that field of all possibilities where we have access to infinity of choices." Our earthly choices are not absolute because our free will is influenced by the spiritual realm (good or evil). God is the absolute sovereign of all things. He made all things to function in accordance to His will. He approves some of the things we do and disapproves many of them. God demands nothing less than perfectness from us even though He allows us to choose either obeying or disobeying His will. Certainly, what God sanctions

can never be broken without encountering dire consequences. Therefore, never quit doing God's will no matter what consequences you must endure doing so.

People, in their corrupt nature, with limited perspective cannot make perfect decisions all of the times without depending on God's unlimitedness. Using myself as an example, the utterances of men concerning me will differ widely, since in passing judgment almost everyone is influenced not so much by the truth as by preference. Jesus came to reveal the will of God. The Bible says that Jesus is the great shepherd that equips us with every good thing to do God's will (Hebrews 13: 20-23). Jesus warned us of false believing: "Not everyone who says to me, 'Lord, Lord,' will enter the kingdom of heaven, but only the one who does the will of my Father who is in heaven" (Matthew 7:21). The kingdom of God is established on earth where God's will is done. God made the way for us to know Him as opposed to knowing about Him so that we can precisely do His will. We know the Infinite God by our relationship with Jesus Christ and we prove it by our righteous living. We are called to renew our minds by acquiring the minds of Christ. "Do not conform to the pattern of this world, but be transformed by the renewing of your mind. Then you will be able to test and approve what God's will is–his good, pleasing and perfect will" (Romans 12:2). Our thinking is never right until we are transformed.

Matthew 6:11 - "Give us today our daily bread." Jesus teaches us to pray that God would give us our daily bread. Bread was a powerful symbol of God's provision for His people in the Old Testament to sustain life. Every person regardless of their status depends on God for the daily portion of food. Before the fall, Adam depended on God for knowledge but not for food. He had only to observe God's rule of not touching the tree of knowledge of good and evil. God walked in the garden in the cool of the day or "the wind of that day." He manifested Himself to Adam as a violent wind, perhaps not too different than how He spoke to Job out of the whirlwind (Job 38:1). Remember that the Holy Spirit came at Pentecost with a "rushing mighty wind" (Acts 2:2). In the garden, Adam ate food but he did not sweat to get it. Adam ate to live but without the possibility

of dying because of not eating because he was not under the law of death. He needed God in order to live as opposed to a daily portion of food. By this time everything Adam ate was perfect since it grew from the perfect environment and ground. God judged Adam to die by cursing the ground from which the food that sustained his life came from: "cursed the ground for your sake" [Genesis 3:17-19]. Following the curse, perfection was ruined and every living thing – including plants, animals, and mankind – slowly changed, the living cells, from eternal to mortal (i.e., subject to death). To this day, every descendant of Adam is born to die. Since the fall of man, mankind has to depend on God for the daily provision of food in order to live another day. We eat to live and live to die. This life would be a meaningless existence except for the fact that God has provided the way out by reconciling us to Himself by the death of His Son on the cross. The inherited sin of Adam was forgiven and hence inheriting immortality. The Bible says that man does not live by bread alone but by feeding on every Word from the mouth of God (Matthew 4:4). Jesus (the Word) reverses the curse of death.

Matthew 6:12 - "And forgive us our debts, as we also have forgiven our debtors." Jesus demonstrated his teaching about forgiveness in the parable of the servant's master who owed a debt that he could not pay back but the master took pity on him, canceled the debt and let him go. But when that servant went out, he found one of his fellow servants who owed him a hundred denarii. He grabbed him and began to choke him, saying, 'Pay back what you owe me (Matthew 18:25-28). The master's wonderful clemency projects that the debt of sin is so great, that we are not able to pay it. Then we see the servant's unreasonable severity toward his fellow-servant, notwithstanding his lord's clemency toward him! The parable projects the attitude of some believers whose after-conduct shows that they never entered into the spirit, or experienced the sanctifying grace of the gospel. Again, we are not justified by what we do. We are justified by faith in what Jesus did. But our good works like repenting and forgiving others daily are necessary for our sanctification in order to sustain our smooth communication with God till the day of glorification. Paul wrote that

"And be you kind one to another, tenderhearted, forgiving one another, even as God for Christ's sake hath forgiven you." (Ephesians 4:32). It is forgiving others on condition of how much we have been forgiven. We are never like God until we forgive like God. Whenever we forgive there is the intensity of glorifying the Father.

Matthew 6:13 - "And lead us not into temptation, but deliver us from the evil one." The word temptation has two meanings: trials and testing. God reserves the right to test our loyalty not because He doesn't know it but to prove it to us. Adam was created a perfect man but he had temptation regarding which tree to touch and not to touch. We are ever in the presence of temptation, and it doesn't have to come from outside of us (James 1:14). But the testing mentioned in the above scripture is the one that comes from God to us periodically. God is not the tempter. We know from James 1:13 that God does not tempt us to sin. If God did tempt us to sin, He would have acted contrary to His holy nature, against His desire for us to be holy as He is holy (1 Peter 1:16), and against all other commandments in the Scriptures that tell us to avoid sin and flee temptation. Satan is the tempter. God allows Satan's temptations to come to us as testing. Trials and afflictions, as allowed by God, are designed to draw us closer to Him; they draw out our graces, but not our corruptions. God sent Satan to test (prove) Job's character: "Then the LORD said to Satan, "Have you considered my servant Job?"" (Job 1:8). Job's character as given in 1:1-5, He feared God and he was blameless, meaning that he did whatever God asked him to do. Job eschewed or shunned evil. God bragged about Job's righteousness. He would not succumb to the temptations of Satan. Also, Satan is referred to as "the tempter" when he meets Jesus in the wilderness (Matt. 4.1-10). Jesus was led by the Holy Spirit to be tempted by Satan: "Jesus, full of the Holy Spirit, left the Jordan and was led by the Spirit into the wilderness, where for forty days He was tempted by the devil" (Luke 4:1-2). He was led by the Holy Spirit to be tested to prove that He won't fall. "Lead us not into temptation" is a prayer acknowledging our vulnerability as humans; it is asking God's testing not to come to us when we are not ready for it. Whether we are asking for God to lead us away from sin or from difficult

trials, our goal is found in the second part of verse 13: "Deliver us from the evil one." The Holy Spirit alone has the power to deliver us from the trials and to sustain us in times of trials. Therefore, a believer can stand as much as he or she can pray.

1 Chronicles 29:11 - "Yours, LORD, is the greatness and the power and the glory and the majesty and the splendor, for everything in heaven and earth is yours. Yours, LORD, is the kingdom; you are exalted as head over all." This doxology was added to the end of the Lord's Prayers to exalt the glory of God. The summation of the glory of God is in His power to create and to redeem what He created from obliteration. Because He created everything, He owns everything. Because He redeemed us, we belong to Him. The unsearchable riches of Christ exceed the splendor of all creations put together infinitely; it surpasses the meanest cottage on earth. The uniqueness of God is that He is infinitely great. Sums in numerical numbers, whether in their actuality or probability, however great they are, have limits. Every creation has a beginning and an end; nothing in this world is infinitely long. The grace makes it possible for an unmediated relationship between God and the material world. By the grace, we can experience eternity but God is not just eternal, He is the Absolute Infinite. Infinite is being endless, vast, immeasurable, and universally omnipresent. Infinity is comprehensible but unattainable except by the divine. The infinite nature of God simply means that God exists outside of and is not limited by time or space. God is not confined as we are in our understanding, nor is He bound in any other sense. God says, who am I like? or to whom will you compare me? The answer being, nobody; nobody's like God, nothing's like God. God is like Himself. And He is the measure of what is true.

Acts 2:1 – "When the day of Pentecost came, they were all together in one place." It was the day when the Jews reckoned their feast of weeks, or seven weeks, or fifty days (Exodus 34:22) which measured out the time of

their harvest. On this day, the Jews say the law was given. The day "was come", in a sense that what was anticipated was now being experienced. It was not a ceremonial event, but a life-changing experience. The disciples gathered together in the upper room praying for the pending harvest; but a harvest of a different nature. Praying preceded the Church. Before the Church came into existence, they were people praying. God listens to our prayers because He expects us to pray. The Church has the mandate to change the world through prayers and by testifying to the truth. God chose the Church, and He has no alternative backup in case of incompetency.

John 11:42 – "I knew that you always hear me, but I said this for the benefit of the people standing here, that they may believe that you sent me." Jesus taught us that when we pray we must believe that God always hears our prayers. Harmony is the essence of praying. There is perfect harmony between the Father and the Son because the Spirit of God is the Spirit of Christ. An effective prayer begins in the Spirit. God hears every word of our conscience because the conscience is the voice of the spirit. In the conscience, there is no idle word. Praying is simply singing the melody of your spirit. An effective prayer is like a beautiful melody, the lyrics of which are composed in heaven. The prayer that goes to heaven begins in heaven, not the contrary.

Philippians 4:6-7 - "Be anxious for nothing, but in everything by prayer and supplication, with thanksgiving, let your requests be made known to God; and the peace of God, which surpasses all understanding, will guard your hearts and minds through Christ Jesus". We are people of the covenant. God's unconditional love brought us into union with Him. It means that our concern is His concern. God grants our needs in accordance to His sovereignty and will. He wants us to rely on Him and to trust Him based on His character. We don't have to crave for the very things which He promised to deliver. Craving for something results in exhaustion and exasperation. Craving eludes the peace of minds. It causes

spiritual fatigue because our psychological state of mind highly affects our spiritual condition. Crave for a thing, you lose it. Renounce the craving, the desire of your heart will follow you.

1 John 3:1 - "See what great love the Father has lavished on us, that we should be called children of God! And that is what we are! The reason the world does not know us is that it did not know him." God is Love, and He gave Himself (Love) to us. Before we ask God for what we want, we need to thank Him for what we already have. We have God in us. The Bible says that "He who did not spare his own Son, but gave him up for us all—how will he not also, along with him, graciously give us all things?" (Romans 8:32). God did not spare his Son because he did not withhold Him. His love for us compelled Him to give His best to save us. What else won't He give us?

John 14:13 - "And I will do whatever you ask in my name, so that the Father may be glorified in the Son." This is an instruction for us to come to the Father in the very essence, character, and integrity of the Son. Everything that glorifies the Son glorifies the Father. Praying in His will is when the Holy Spirit finds the desire of the Son and puts it into our hearts for the glory of the Father. When we are in Christ, our needs are different from our wants. That is when we don't need anything outside Christ. Praying is getting God's will done on the earth rather than our will to be done in heaven. Praying brings the humanity and the divine in agreement. Pray out of need and out of intimacy.

Matthew 18:18 - "Truly I tell you, whatever you bind on earth will be bound in heaven, and whatever you loose on earth will be loosed in heaven. Again, I tell you truly that if two of you on the earth agree about anything you ask for, it will be done for you by My Father in heaven...." Within the context, this scripture was specifically given in reference to a

prayer of agreement to restore a brother that has fallen into sin (verse 15-17). It means whatever is bind in heaven is bound to the earth. It is a calling to have insight on what God has bound for you in heaven to bring it on the earth. It is not claiming whatever you want on the earth. It is having what God wants you to have from heaven. "The prayer that goes to heaven comes from heaven". Elsewhere, Jesus said that "Truly, truly, I say to you, whatever you ask of the Father in my name, he will give it to you." (John 16:23-24). The misconception is that we ask whatever we want and then we are disappointed when we don't get it. Jesus is the strength, the subject and the reason for our prayers. We pray to the Father through Him. We pray with His minds (renewed minds). We ask in His character, integrity, and essence. You cannot ask anything in the name of Jesus that is not for the glory of Jesus.

Matthew 6:5-6 "And when you pray, do not be like the hypocrites. For they love to pray standing in the synagogues and on the street corners to be seen by men. Truly I tell you, they already have their reward. But when you pray, go into your room, close the door and pray to your Father, who is unseen. Then your Father, who sees what is done in secret, will reward you." Eight times in the space of this verse is the pronoun used in the singular number and the second person–a thing unique in all Scripture–as though to emphasize the indispensability, importance and value of private prayer. Private prayer is the test of our sincerity, the index to our spirituality, the principal means of growing in grace. Private prayer is the one thing above all others that Satan seeks to prevent, for he knows full well that if he can succeed at this point, the Christian will fail at every other.

I want to clarify that the above scripture encourages private praying but it is not against praying in public. If it was against public praying the cooperative praying in our churches would have been prohibited. In fact, Jesus recommended it: "Again, truly I tell you that if two of you on earth agree about anything they ask for, it will be done for them by my Father in heaven For where two or three gather in my name, there am I with them." (Matthew 18:19-20). Jesus prayed publically several times. The disciples of

Jesus watched Him praying and they were inspired and they asked Him: "Lord, teach us to pray, just as John taught his disciples" (Luke 11:1). Jesus taught them by demonstration. That is why it is called the "The Lord's Prayer". The above scripture is against hypocrites who pray with wrong motives to be seen and recognized by the public.

Isaiah 1:18 - "Come now, and let us reason together, saith the Lord". Taking these words of our Lord seriously transforms our prayer life from a lifeless form to a conversation with our all-powerful Creator. Praying is engaging our Lord into serious conversation. The greatest prayer is saying to God: "You promised". This is not intended to remind Him because God never forgets. Real praying is holding God accountable for His Word. He likes it because it is proof that we are standing on His promises. God still talks to His children, even in prayers. He is willing to talk to us more than we want to talk to Him. But only those who have their spiritual antennas up can receive the signal of God.

Jesus presents our poorly worded prayers to the father—Every sincere prayer is heard in heaven. It may not be fluently expressed; but if the heart is in it, it will ascend to the sanctuary where Jesus ministers and He will present it to the Father without one awkward, stammering word, beautiful and fragrant with the incense of His own perfection.—(The Desire of Ages, 667.)

"Prayer does not change God, but it changes him who prays."

Worry is the sickness, praying is the prescription, faith is the cure.

Psalm 121:1 - "I will lift up my eyes unto the hills, from whence cometh my help." The lifting up of the eyes is a prayer gesture. "If what is ahead scares you.....And what is behind hurts you.... Then just look above." It is not a onetime gaze; it is a calling to fix your eyes constantly to the God of the mountains you are confronted. He is higher than your mountains. His care is timely, calculated, customized, and comprehensive. He watches over you in your trials. In Him there is no darkness; He never slumbers.

Do not let your prayers be all about your own sins, your own desires, your own imperfections, your own trials. Take time to pray for others. Intercessory prayer is making yourself available to serve others by praying for them. There are people out there who are unable to pray for themselves because they won't pray. Others would not pray in particular when they are experiencing great pains or when they are critically ill. We are supposed to step in and pray for them. Intercessory prayer is the shortest route to reach the uttermost parts of the earth even praying for the people whom we do not know. Take the focus from yourself by focusing on eternal things. Be kingdom minded when you pray. Pray that, "Lord, extend the kingdom of Your dear Son." When you fervently present such a petition, it will elevate the spirit of all your devotions. Make sure that you prove the sincerity of your prayer by working to promote the Lord's glory.

Romans 8:34 - "Who then is the one who condemns? No one. Christ Jesus who died—more than that, who was raised to life—is at the right hand of God and is also interceding for us." The ascension of Christ, his entrance into heaven, and session at the right hand of God are a very considerable security of God's elect from condemnation. But much more are His intercessory prayers for us. When the Son of God prays, He is mindful and consciously aware of only His Father. God always hears the prayers of His Son, and if the Son of God has been formed in me (see Galatians 4:19) the Father will always hear my prayers. Praying is the

highest calling. It is the unfinished work on the earth that our Lord is still doing, and we must do it too.

Isaiah 66:1 – "Thus saith the LORD, The heaven is my throne, and the earth is my footstool: where is the house that ye build unto me? and where is the place of my rest?" According to some Hebrew scholars, there were two places where God was worshiped: The Heavenly Throne and the Ark. God is ever seated on His throne in heaven to exercise His sovereignty over the universe. The Ark was indeed a glorious sight, and it was also the Lord's footstool (when He chose to inhabit it). But God was hardly a genie imprisoned in a bottle that was shuttled around merely to do the bidding of his human masters. No place of resting and residence can be found for God. The temple was built as a house of resting for the ark of the Lord, which before was moved from place to place; but then this was merely typical of the church, which God has chosen for His rest, and where He will dwell, as well as of heaven, the resting place of his people with him to all eternity; no place on earth is either His rest or theirs.

Hallelujah an exclamatory expression of praise or adoration. It is the highest praise a human mouth can make. The phrase "Praise the LORD" in the Old Testament is composed of two Hebrew words - halal and YHWH, the Tetragrammaton, to which we add vowels to derive the Name Yahweh which is transliterated as Jehovah. Hallelujah is found 24 times in the Old Testament, but only in the book of Psalms. Praise ye Jehovah, frequently rendered "Praise ye the LORD," stands at the beginning of ten of the psalms (106,111-113,135,146-150), hence called "hallelujah psalms." From its frequent occurrence, it grew into a formula of praise. In the New Testament, the term appears only in one chapter but four times. The Greek form of the word (alleluia) is found in Revelations 19:1, 3, 4&6.

Psalm 150:6 - "Let everything that has breath praise the LORD." Breath, when used in reference to God it means Spirit. But in this case, the Psalmists intended to mean every living creature breathing in and out, specifically mankind. Breathing is the sign of life in all living creatures. All living creatures including plants and animals breathe. The plants breathe in the carbon dioxide that we breathe out, and we breathe in the oxygen which the plants breathe out. The gift of life must be celebrated. God makes it pretty clear that His creation alone speaks enough about Him that even if we didn't have His Word, we would have no excuse of not to know Him! We don't need a revelation to know that God exists but it takes a revelation to dedicate the beauty in nature to the glory of God: For example, assigning the chirping of the birds and the movements of the branches of the trees to the praising of God. Nevertheless, the holiness and the love of our God are more displayed in man's redemption, than in all His other works. Let us praise our God and Savior for it. The air of praises is the only air worth breathing!

Revelations 5:13 - "And every creature which is in heaven, and on the earth, and under the earth, and such as are in the sea, and all that are in them, heard I saying, Blessing, and honor, and glory, and power, be unto him that sits upon the throne, and unto the Lamb forever and ever". Many Christians tend to avoid Revelation because they view it as a somewhat obscure and confusing book. Others think it's simply a code-book for figuring out the significance of end time events. Many students of Revelation seem hesitant about the musical aspect of the book. There are at least twelve songs in the book of Revelation. The praises of the redeemed are saturated with joy and exaltation because of the victory of Christ on their behalf. During the exodus in the wilderness, God instructed Judah to go ahead of the twelve tribes. The word Judah means praise. Praising is our divine assignment that evokes the power to overcome. Praising prepares us to worship. Every living thing can praise God but worshiping God is a reserve for only those whose spirit is regenerated. I mean those with the spiritual capability to approach the throne of God. They are the ones who

have the Spirit of adoption and sonship crying from within "Abba, Father" (Romans 8:15).

Psalm 22:3 - But thou art holy, O thou that inhabitest the praises of Israel. Another translation says "Yet You are holy, O You who are enthroned upon the praises of Israel." The Psalmists uses the phrase "inhabiting the praises of Israel," when recalling the God of Israel who dwells between the Cherubim: "thou that dwellest between the cherubims" (1 Samuel 4:4). The Psalmists has in mind the invisible God of Israel whose presence is noticeable. Our new nature is closely connected to the invisible spiritual world than to the visible world. Salvation is the first step in turning the invisible into the visible reality and experience. God's presence is guaranteed during praising, as long as He is the subject and the motivator of our praising. Praising Jesus is the new song that Yahweh put in our mouth; it is the new kind of song that the world would not sing. We sing in celebration of God's impeccable character (purity) and His integrity that holds all things in place. We sing in celebration of His love and the new covenant established by the shedding of His blood. We sing in celebration of the powerful name of Jesus that changes lives and that precious name by which we can enter into His presence now and for all eternity. At glorification, when our faith will become sight and our hope becomes reality we will rest in His bosom eternally.

Psalms 33:8 – "Let all the earth fear the LORD; let all the inhabitants of the world stand in awe of him!" Worshiping is gazing through the telescope to get a glimpse of how great God is. God's sovereignty relegates human responsibility to adore Him. God designed and controls everything for His sovereign purpose of glorifying His name. And so we should stand in awe of the Sovereign God of all things. True worshiping is when all your surroundings become Oblivious. Ultimate worshiping goes beyond spoken words; it is standing speechless in awe of God.

Exodus 15:1 – "Then Moses and the people of Israel sang this song to the LORD: "I will sing to the LORD, for he has triumphed gloriously; he has hurled both horse and rider into the sea." This is the first song recorded in the Bible. Praising is about redemption. God created the first man, but he sang no song: however, this is the first on record, and is a typical one; Moses the composer of it, and who bore a principal part in it was sent to the delivery of the people of Israel. The Angel of the Lord that went before the Israelites through the Red sea, and fought for them was a type of Christ, the Redeemer of His Church: "This is he that was in the church in the wilderness" (Acts 7:38). Christ is in this song; He is addressed as a divine person, as Lord of all, God over all, blessed forever, the Almighty God, whose sovereignty is over all the creations as His works of creation, providence, and redemption declare Him to be. And Israel (the people who were delivered) joined with Moses in singing it. The deliverance celebrated here bore a great resemblance to the redemption wrought out by Christ. The Bible projects the redeemed of God in heaven singing the same song of praise: "And I saw something like a sea of glass mixed with fire, beside which stood those who had conquered the beast and its image and the number of its name. They were holding harps from God, and sang the song of God's servant Moses and of the Lamb: "Great and marvelous are your deeds, Lord God Almighty. Just and true are your ways, King of the nations. (Revelation 15:2-3).

Psalm 27:4 - "One thing I ask from the LORD, this only do I seek: that I may dwell in the house of the LORD all the days of my life, to gaze on the beauty of the LORD and to seek him in his temple". The Psalmist yearned to be in a place of divine worship all the times where the Lord granted His presence. The grace made it possible for us to be in God's presence forever. Jesus said that true worshipers worship in spirit and truth (John 4:23). We are God's dwelling place (temple). His presence follows us wherever we go. He made it possible for whosoever is willing to worship Him wherever they are. We join the saints in heaven to worship God seated at the throne. The book of Revelation says "After this I looked, and there before me was a great multitude that no one could count, from

every nation, tribe, people and language, standing before the throne and before the Lamb. They were wearing white robes and were holding palm branches in their hands. And they cried out in a loud voice: "Salvation belongs to our God, who sits on the throne, and to the Lamb" (Revelation 7:9-10). Heaven is not about a place, it is about who is there - God/the Lamb. God's dwelling place is called the temple because the Bible says that heaven and earth cannot contain God (1 Kings 8:27). It was amazing condescension for God to put on the human nature to tabernacle with men on earth. In Christ was the fullness of the glory of the Godhead on display (John 2:19). The same Godhead indwells us by His Spirit (John 14:15). Worshiping is whenever the divine glory from within darts through the veil of the flesh (body). True worshiping comes from God (from the Spirit seated on the throne of the heart) and goes to God (to God seated at the heavenly throne).

Somebody asked that "I and my mom went to the church today and I heard something during preaching that just left me uncertain. This huge church that has 5,000 members; the pastor was saying, God doesn't need our worship because he already has thousands of angels doing that and doing a better job than we do. He said we need worship for ourselves in through that God is gratified. .. Is this right or am I not understanding this right?" Reply: God has no need at all that demands satisfaction from outside Him (either from men or from angels) because He is self-sufficient. He does not stand in need of human praising and worshiping but He demands it because He delights in it and He likes to be worshiped. Our worship is the reasonable service to God. The word 'service' means ministering. The Church is supposed to minister to the Lord. C.S. Lewis said that "I think we delight to praise what we enjoy because the praise not merely expresses but completes the enjoyment; it is its appointed consummation." God created us and redeemed us to worship Him. But we are the primary beneficiaries of our worship. God made it possible for us to come with boldness to His throne of grace to worship, and He encourages us to do so. We didn't deserve it but He qualified us to approach His throne deservingly. Worshiping God is the only thing the heavenly creatures do.

Therefore, worshiping God is an availed opportunity and a privilege for us to experience heaven on earth. If you don't worship, you are cheating yourself the blessings of worshiping. But there is "acceptable" worship and "unacceptable" worship, like in the case of Cain and Abel. There is an incident in the biblical record that causes abiding consternation for many of God's people. It is the story of how two of the sons of Aaron, Nadab, and Abihu, who were slain suddenly by God when they offered what the book of Leviticus calls "unauthorized fire or strange fire" (Leviticus 10:1-3). These young priests clearly violated some prescription that God had set forth for the offering of incense in the holy place. It is imperative that we find out from God how He wants us to worship Him.

"Worship is the proper response of all moral, sentient beings to God, ascribing all honor and worth to the Creator-God precisely because he is worthy, delightfully so." In the old covenant, the burnt offerings were totally consumed, which tells us a thing or two about worship. Worship is costly and appears to be wasteful. But, it's what the LORD wants of us. God is altogether self-sufficient and cannot be served by human hands as if He needed anything but He demands our worship. God desires our greatest good because when He gave His Son to us He gave Himself to us; He gave the best of heaven to the worst of the world. We worship Him in Spirit; the divine in us is His Spirit. God is not man-centered, He is God-centered. True worship is God-centered. The Christ-centered worship is empowered by the Spirit. You want God's acceptance of your worship? Then it must be His way of worshiping.

Worshiping is a lifestyle. Going to church on Sunday then living like the devil the rest of the days won't cut it. "God wants full custody of his children, not just weekend visitations."

"The proud man can't worship God any more than a proud devil can. Worship humbles a man." ~ A.W. Tozer

"Doctrine demands doxology, and doxology is determined by doctrine."

There are two main things we are going to do in heaven: Worshiping God and fellowshipping with other saints eternally. If you are allergic to worshiping God here on earth, and if you can't put up with other people here on earth, most probably you are being groomed for another place other than heaven. Fellowshipping is not limited to church buildings, it might be in homes with other believers "Where two or three are gathered in His name" (Matthew 18:29). When we are born again, a sense of fellowshipping with other people of the same new nature to worship God is born into us. God sent His Son from heaven to fellowship with us, and he promised that He will never leave us alone. Spiritually, all believers are in union with God through the Holy Spirit. But God demands our unity physically here on the earth. He sent the Holy Spirit on earth with the responsibility of weaving us together into oneness. Those who are false resist the current work of the Holy Spirit and fall apart from the woven quilt. "Break a thread in the loom, and you will see the effect when the weaving of a lifetime is unraveled."

"The act of prayer teaches us our unworthiness, which is a very salutary lesson for proud people like us. If God gave us favors without constraining us to pray for them, we would never know how poor we are, but a true prayer is an inventory of wants, a catalog of necessities, a revelation of hidden poverty. While prayer is an application to divine wealth, it is also a confession of human emptiness" ~Alistair Begg

Psalm 35:1 "Contend, LORD, with those who contend with me; fight against those who fight against me." By the Spirit of prophecy, David foretells the just judgments of God that would come upon his enemies for their great wickedness. When you finally realize that this world can't help you; you will cry out to the One who can. If God is our Friend, it doesn't matter who is our enemy.

James 5:16: "Therefore confess your sins to each other and pray for each other so that you may be healed. The prayer of a righteous person is powerful and effective." The righteous person is not a perfect person because nobody is perfect. He is somebody that is complete in Christ and who is in perfect harmony with the neighbor. A person who is intimate with Jesus is not ignorant of the Word. He trembles at the Word because when the Bible speaks God speaks. He studies meditates and acts on the truth in Word. Praying is the reality of getting into the Bible and allowing the Bible to get into you.

Whenever you pray for somebody be ready to be part of the answer to their prayers. God might choose to answer their prayers through you. The very mouth that is interceding, ultimately, is the vessel in front of whom the buck stops. Don't pass on the buck.

Praying is our privilege, right, and responsibility. Pray until something happens! (P.U.S.H).

When God opens a door, no man can shut it, and when He closes a door, no man can open it. Don't just pray for God to open doors. Pray for God to close doors in your life that need to be closed.

"Prayer is not a wish. It is the voice of faith directed to God." ~ Billy Graham

The only prayer of the non-repented sinner that God hears is the prayer of repentance.

Praying in the Spirit is praying in agreement with the will of God. Walking in the Spirit is walking in obedience to God's Word.

The branches do not fall far from the person pruning it. When you are worried, it is because you are trying to depend on your own capability. When you are at peace, it is because you remembered that God is in control.

Nothing happens by accident. You don't have to be worried when you are travelling the pilgrimage of life. Take courage and trust God to direct your steps. He is in His holy temple watching over us. Even if the foundation of the earth crumbles, we have a reassurance that the righteous are in God's favor.

You can't stop a person who has learned to trust in God because his worth is in Christ. Whether it be despair or stress, I've have found praying as an accessory clutch. I opened my eyes this morning praising our Creator. "A heart that goes to sleep thanking God is the heart that wakes up praising God".

Pray while believing that everything is possible if it is in accordance to the divine will. Here's the basic claim: God is an Author. The Word is His story. We are His characters. The scripture points in this direction when it tells us that God preached the world into existence. "He spoke, and it came to be; he commanded, and it stood firm" (Ps 33:9). He is the God who "calls into existence the things that do not exist" (Rom 4:17). Is there anything impossible to Him?

Isaiah 40:12 – "Who hath measured the waters in the hollow of his hand, and meted out heaven with the span, and comprehended the dust of the earth in a measure, and weighed the mountains in scales, and the hills in a balance?". God plans and governs all things. He declares the end from the beginning. He declared the things from ancient times, even long before they happened. His counsel shall stand, and He will accomplish all things as He purposed. The span by which God measures the universe is figuratively portrayed as the distance between your thumb and the little finger. He holds the whole universe in the palm of His hand. He meted out heaven with the span; which He has stretched out as a curtain (Isaiah 40:22). God measures the world as easy as man measures a piece of rag (cloth) by a span of his hand, or any measuring rule or yard. Faith is the span by which we measure the universe. Faith rolls the past and the future into the present. "Faith must span the chasm of sense and time." Faith is embracing the whole counsel of God, the whole will of God and the whole purpose of God.

Daniel 10:13 - "But the prince of the kingdom of Persia opposed me for twenty-one days. Then Michael, one of the chief princes, came to help me after I had been left there with the kings of Persia." The prince of the kingdom of Persia is an entity appointed by Satan to resist God in this particular domain. Evil is not a mere force. There is an entity called the devil behind all of the evil activities against humanity. Satan is the invisible powers which rule and influence the world, the nations, and the people. The prince of the kingdom of Persia withstood the manifestation of the already answered prayers for twenty one days, which was just the time Daniel had been mourning, fasting and praying. When you don't have a tangible manifestation of what you prayed for, it does not mean that God has not answered your prayers. At times the manifestation of the answer to your prayers is delayed by Satan. We are in a spiritual warfare; praying is being on the offensive by taking the war to Satan's dining table. We are ambushed at various spots. When we pray, God sends His angels to wrestle and burst our enemy. We are called to pray before and after securing answered prayers. Our confidence is that the will of our Heavenly Father will prevail; He never leads us to a place where His love will not sustain us and where His grace will not protect us.

Writing in National Review Online, Clay Routledge, a professor and psychological scientist, points to "the tested psychological and social benefits of prayer as well as the reality of how most believers turn to faith-based practices in addition to, not instead of, other courses of action." For those who perceive of God as loving instead of as distant and unresponsive, prayer produces psychological benefits. People whose prayers centered on gratitude and care for others had the fewest symptoms of depression. "So the next time someone says you should do more than pray, remember this insight from Adoniram Gordon, the founder of Gordon College: "You can do more than pray, *after* you have prayed, but you can never do more than pray *until* you have prayed." Amen!

Today's prayer: "Lord you rejoiced in spirit, and said, "I thank thee, O Father, Lord of heaven and earth, that thou has hidden these things from the wise and prudent, and has revealed them unto babes: even so, Father;

for so it seemed good in thy sight." (Luke 10:21). I want to be that baby. Grant to me the childlike energy because it is the maturity projecting the required spiritual growth. A childlike experience is the defining spirit of authentic discipleship. Help me to be childlike but not childish because remaining childish is a stagnant state of ignorance. Help me to grow from the neck up. Open my eyes to see, open my ears to listen, open my minds to understand, and soften my heart to implement what I know. Bring out the best in me. In the name of Jesus, I pray."

Today's prayer: "Lord, your word says that: "I appeal to you, brothers and sisters,[a] in the name of our Lord Jesus Christ, that all of you agree with one another in what you say and that there be no divisions among you, but that you be perfectly united in mind and thought." (1Cor. 1:10). According to your word, there is no excuse for divisions among the believers. Yet, at times we do the opposite and end up with dashed hopes. Putting our hopes in earthly things is apostasy and unfulfilling because our problems go beyond our graves. The faith that works is anchored in the victory of the heavenly throne. The dead hope is restored by embracing the living Christ. Help me not to be swayed by the temporal things of the world. Give me the gift of discerning and activate my patience, and love so that I might face the unfinished task in optimism. Stiff-nakedness gives rise to stiff objection. Give me flexibility instead of hardening me. Make me a pliable substance. Soften my heart so that I may bend my neck bowing in brokenness. In Jesus' name, I pray".

Today's prayer: "Lord, the world where we live is alien to the world we are born into by faith. This false world is but transitory, marred by vainglory. The fact that nothing fulfills us in this world is the proof that I was neither created for myself nor for this world. The secret of fulfillment is acknowledging that I was created for your glory. Seeking my own glory ends up in constant frustration. The perfect man (Adam) became imperfect after he lost your glory. When you redeemed me, you redeemed your lost glory. You poured your wrath against all sins of men on the perfect man (Jesus) to redeem your lost glory in me. His glory became my glory. His goodness became my goodness. Lord, you alone is good, and all "knowledge of good" is God's thoughts given to man. Without you, my life story is a pack of lifetime memories of defeat and shame, and I cannot rewrite it. Orchestrate my life for the sake of the beauty of your name. Help me to see with the delicate eye of faith, thriving best in a pure conscience. (1 Timothy 3:9). In Jesus' name, Amen

Today's prayer: "Lord, this life is characterized by endless yearnings. Everything we do is for the purpose of altering consciousness. We yearn for things which we cannot reach by pulling our own boot-straps. We yearn for satisfaction where there is nothing satisfying. We seek for pleasures in wrong places outside the sacred boundaries in spite of the severity of the outcomes. We like to live long but we deny, delay and resist aging. We seek to be good but you said no one is good but God. This world demands for our success but You demand for our faithfulness. The contradictions are indicative that we were not made for this world. Lord, the standard of goodness is the cross. Help me to seek for your goodness. Your goodness is not a private virtue; it is contagious and dispensable. Let me be a signpost portraying your goodness. Help me to grow steadfastly in the grace of our Lord Jesus Christ. In the name of Jesus, I pray."

Today's prayer: "Lord, you are interested in our healing as much as in our deliverance. You can able the disabled limb and use it for your kingdom. Also, you instructed us to cut off a healthy arm that causes us to sin in order to be effective in your kingdom. Sin is contagious. Our behaviors trigger others behaviors, and others behaviors trigger our behaviors. It is my responsibility to choose good and shun evil. A lot of things trigger my inspiration. It can be the most predictable things. Eternity is wrapped up in your Word. Words have the power to influence but your Word has the power to create and to redeem. You sent your Word to save me by delivering me from evil. Lord, I don't want to be in the Word and in the world. Truth is equated with godliness. Inspire me so that I might be an inspiration to somebody. Create in me the godly consciousness so that I may not be a snare to others but a bridge to optimism. I want to be an asset rather than a liability to your kingdom. I want to be a solution instead of a problem. In the name of Jesus, I pray."

Today's prayer: "Lord, you made your Son to be in our image so that we can be restored to your image. Create in me a new heart that I may sin not. Lord, you know the hearts of all men. You know my sins even before I confess them to you. At times I am stubborn and embarrassed to confess my sins to you. Stiffneckedness gives rise to stiff objection. Soften my heart so that I may bend my neck bowing in brokenness. Create in me a tender spirit of uprightness and integrity; a heart fixed, trusting in the Lord, and comfortably assured of your pardoning grace and mercy. Finish the work you started in me by your grace through faith. In the name of Jesus, I pray. "

Today's prayer: "Lord, you created the time of which we have no control. "Time passes irrevocably." The only time we are not limited by time is when we have reached immortality which is not disturbed by anything material. Every moment I live in this mortal body is an opportunity to prepare myself for the immortal body. You gave to me the gift of faith so that I can operate in the spiritual realm of unlimitedness now, in this mortal body. The surging faith is the grip of the Lord's hand; it is the irresistible surge of will and energy to execute the divine assignment and reach the maximum of my potential spiritually. Indeed, salvation is of God; I bring nothing to the table but my sin. "Just as I am, without one plea; But that your blood was shed for me; And that You bid me come to you; O Lamb of God, I come! I come!"

Today's prayer: "Lord, you an Author. The word 'authority' comes directly from the word 'author'. The authority of any work is the authority of the author. You are the author; the World is your story; we are your characters. According to Bible, you preached the world into existence. "You spoke, and it came to be; you commanded, and it stood firm" (Psalms 33:9). You are self-existence; there is no time you did not exist. And you call into existence the things that do not exist (Roman 4:17). The Scriptures testify that my salvation is because of the powerful arm of the Word. By the Word, you created man. By the Word (Jesus the Word), you redeemed man. By the Word, you are reconstructing what you redeemed. By the Word, I walk the pass of righteousness, and I am preserved. Lord, every step I take in the spirit is correlated to my walk with Christ, in whom I am bonded to you. There is no power in this world that can alienate me from your love. I am confident of this very thing, that He who has begun a good work in me will perform it until the day of Jesus Christ. Amen.

Today's prayer: "Lord, whatever I worship becomes my god. I am satisfied with nothing less than your presence. I want to be what you want me to be. I want to reach the unreachable and to teach the unteachable. I acknowledge that I have nothing to give except what you want me to give. Give me a double portion of your anointing, typically a reserve for the first-born's inheritance.

Lord, you proclaimed that "Let everything that has breath praise the LORD" (Psalm 150:6). Your breath in me is the source of praising. I want your glory to impact my five senses. With my body, I worship Thee, with my heart I love Thee, with my life I adore and serve Thee. If there's anything left O Holy God, humbly I offer it to you without reservation. I want to be partaker of your glory because it is your glory that fends off the sensual deception. May my prayer be acceptable unto Thee. In Jesus' name, Amen.

Today's prayer: "Lord, you speak things into existence, and you speak things out of existence. By your breath, we are regenerated and baptized with fire, and by your breathe your enemies are suppressed. You are a consuming fire. Some are destroyed by your fire whereas others are purified and built by your fire. My spiritual fire cannot burn without the fuel of the Spirit and the Word. Every Word that comes from your mouth is a spark of fire required to rekindle my light. I need more of it because I cannot get enough of you. In the name of Jesus, I pray.

Today's prayer: "Lord, your word says that "And because iniquity shall abound, the love of many shall wax cold. But he that shall endure unto the end, the same shall be saved." (Matthew 24:12-13). This is the most scaring scripture in the Bible. Lord, you did what it takes to establish my relationship with you. You did what you ought to do, and there is nothing you would have done you didn't do. You loved me in spite of me. But often, I have let you down. I have not loved you as you expected me to love you but you still love me regardless. Your grace is the divine influence on the human heart. I am kneeling before the only one who can change me and prevent me from stumbling, and I will not let you go. Help me to bless your name day after day, and to keep it on until you call me home. My prayer is that let me finish well.

Today's prayer: "He who was seated on the throne said, "I am making everything new!" (Revelation 21:5). Lord, you are in a process of rolling this heaven and earth away. You are progressively rewinding time back to the pre-Adamic fall. You are swiftly rolling away this hostile environment of error. Things are moving faster in the spiritual realm than we can comprehend them naturally, and we can't control them. We can't stop the future and we can't rewind the past. Everything will happen the way you intended it to happen. As we are anxiously watching things unfold, you are our only escape route. We have nothing to worry about because, in

Christ, we are already new creations. Our prayer is that you said: "Surely I come quickly." Even so, come, Lord Jesus."

Today's prayer: "Lord, you work all things according to the counsel of your will (Ephesians 1:11). And 'all things' means all things pertaining to life including the trials of life. Trials are tests. Yet, they do not come without detours. At times I feel as if I am left alone to the fate of the circumstances. But the reality is that you are always there; you never abandon me. It is like taking a test in a subject, whereby a tutor sits aside in silence with all answers to the test, but he lets you tussle it alone, trusting in your potentiality to pass the test. Lord, you are the Creator, Sustainer, and Governor of all things. Guide me and use my trials to redirect me to even greater things."

Today's prayer: "Lord, praying is a privilege extended to us, to be honest with ourselves before you, the only one who knows the secrets of the hearts of all men. You incline your ear to the prayer of our conscience. Therefore, kneeling before you is carefully listening to my conscience. Praying is slaughtering my egoism at your altar. Praying is the grave where arrogance is buried. Lord, help me to pray for the good purpose, with serenity, sincerity, and delight, with obedience and reverence. My desire is to put God first because when I put God first, I will never be last.

Today's prayer: "Lord, I am the chief of sinners. I crucified you because I am the very reason you were condemned and crucified. But you exchanged my résumé with your résumé. The ugliness of my wrong deeds became the beauty of your good deeds at the cross. Everything I did, I have done, and I will ever do was filtered in the grace so that it flows through your goodness. You gave me the gift of faith to receive your righteousness and to grow into your grace. Faith involves faithfulness and loyalty. It is being a faithful servant and enduring until the end. Lord, you are the God of the living as opposed of the dead. I am the apple of your eye. I am sure that you are watching over me even in dangerous times, and you will never withhold anything good from me." Thank you, Jesus.

Today's prayer: "Lord, the nature of the seed determines the nature of life. When I read the Bible, the Bible is reading me. Your Word is light and health to the sick minds. Education is useful but it is not light - it is intellect over clamped with knowledge. It is when my knowledge is backed with the scriptures in the background, that I am in position to discern good and avoid evil. Lord, I have hidden your word in my heart that I might not sin against you (Psalm 119:11). Wash me with your blood and cleanse me with your Word. In the name of Jesus, I pray."

Today's prayer: "Lord, thanks for the gift of faith. Faith is the wings of the soul that I need to soar with hope in this hopeless world. Faith sharpens my spirit. Faith is my security that guarantees your provision. Faith is not trusting in myself but trusting in you. It is the assurance that you are in control of my life and you know my needs and desires better than me. Faith is putting you first in my life before my family, before my work, before my processions and before my pleasures. In today's world it takes real faith to put God first in our lives all the time. Lord, morality is not negotiable and preference. Help me to adhere with quality unchangeable characteristic. You recommended just a little faith that has capability to grow into great faith. Indeed, great things are done by a series of small things brought together. Life is a journey, and faith is a step in the right direction. Give me that one small step of faith that leads into a giant leap for faith. In Jesus' name I pray."

Today's prayer: "Lord, you left heaven and came to the earth so that we might understand your level of love and mercy. You are defined by your purposes. You are the door where I access eternity. You are the bread that sustains life eternally. You are the rock of ages. Indeed, you are the steady ridge upon which we walk. Your strength is sure, and your hold upon us is certain! The Bible says that my life is hidden in Christ God (Colossians 3:3). It means that my life is spiritual, and is a life of grace from Christ, a life of faith in Him, and a life of communion with Him. The spiritual life of the saints is hidden from the men of the world, who are alienated from the life of God, are ignorant of the Lord of life, and know nothing of the spirit of life; they are strangers to the nature of this life. But I experienced it and I am contented by my relationship with you through Jesus Christ because, in Christ, I am set to develop as I was intended in this incarnation. Christ is in God, the Father is in the Son, and the Son is in the Father; the Father and the Son are dwelling in me through the Holy Spirit (John 14:23). Thanks for this union; it is my security for eternal life."

Today's prayer: "Lord, in the natural world a broken life is akin to shattered dreams. While journeying through this murky life which is characterized by sorrow and affliction, at times I end up with a broken heart. But my faith sustains me and does not let my experience to define me. This one thing I know for sure: you care about everything I care about because you care for me. Your love is defined by the cross. You carried my cross and died in my place. At the cross, you stretched your hands and said: "This is how much I love you". Broken-heartedness is not strange to you. You were tempted like us," bearing grief for us, bearing grief with us, and bearing grief like us." You died of a broken heart because you loved me when there was nothing lovable in me. Your Word instructs me to have a broken and contrite heart in pursuit of godliness. Brokenness is the key to humility and hence self-sacrifice. The pattern of the prodigal is stiff-neckedness and rebellion. Lord, restore in me the durable peace that surpasses understanding. Help me to find an answer in you rather than in a broken unfiltered world that is decaying. I mean a meaningful answer that is beyond natural understanding. Deepen my trust in the timeless God who is beyond natural understanding. In Jesus' name. Amen.

Today's prayer: "Lord, your Word says that "He who seeks to quench his thirst at the fountains of this world will drink only to thirst again. But he who drinks of the living water becomes a fountain of life (John 7:37-39)." Hungry demands eating; thirty demands drinking. "There are two reasons for drinking: one is, when you are thirsty, to cure it; the other, when you are not thirsty, to prevent it." Naturally, there is no amount of water that a person can drink one time and it prevents a lifetime thirsty without a possibility of wanting to drink again. Lord, I am fulfilled because my soul has drunk the living waters that you alone can give. Faith is digging the well inside me before I am thirty. The renewed relationship comes with the renewed appetite of the soul. Drinking is partaking of the grace, the truly infinite for which I am thirsty. I just want to give you all the praises with reverence."

Today's prayer: "Success is an important part of life. We labor to the point of exhaustion because nobody can climb the ladder of success with their hands in their pockets. People fail but nobody starts something with the objective of failing. Lord, you alone made a difference in my life. You made my shadow to shine. You made a difference in my life so that I can make a difference in the lives of others. You blessed me to be a blessing to others. You motivate me to motivate others. Whenever you lift me up I make sure the ladder is down to help others climb up. All I have is yours to give. As for those whom you put in my life to impact, I cannot push anyone up a ladder of success unless they are willing to climb themselves. Eradicate the mentality of failure because nobody can climb the ladder of success when immersed in the mentality of failure. In the name of Jesus, Amen.

Today's prayer: "Lord, you made a way when our backs were against the wall. It looked as if it was over. But it is not over until you say that it is over. When you say yes, no one can say no. We are what we are because of who you are. You made a way in a situation where there was no way! The longing that exists inside the human heart has a God-shape to it, and only the Father of glory can release to us the reality that gives our lives their fullness. Lord, how priceless is your unfailing love! Both high and low among men find refuge in the shadow of your wings. Fill my cup. "

Today's prayer: "Lord, in the real life light naturally comes with shadows. Increased light means increased shadows. But in the spiritual realm, you are the light without a shadow of darkness. Your righteousness is the light that exposes the shadows of darkness (corruption) in our lives. One thing you can't do is to sin. Also, you decided not to see my sins when I am covered with your blood. It is for the same reason that you were hard-pressed and bled to death. You purge me of my inequities. Your purging is at times uncomfortable and strenuous to my feelings but it is necessary for me to thrive. An open rebuke is better than silent love. Above all I am rejuvenated. Renewed minds mean renewed living. Your grace is an opportunity extended to me to rethink my priorities and be intentional about my behaviors. The most beautiful thing in this world is seeing God work in me and in others, knowing He is the author and architect of it all. Lord, you cannot be impressed but you are pleased with my faith. May the words of my mouth, and the meditation of my heart, be acceptable in thy sight, O LORD, my strength, and my redeemer."

Today's prayer: "Lord, faith is a gift that is given to us with a basic adequacy. It means I am not adequate in myself but I glory in your adequacy. The purity of the heart is a prerequisite for those who desire to rise to the divine platform. To stay pure is to pull away from the pollution of worldliness by manifesting the life of Christ by faith. Lord, help me not to succumb to the overpowering weariness of the comfort of the world and slipping into an uneasy slumber, which is a horrendous foggy and befuddled condition. False impressions are emotional and inevitable. My biggest challenge is not the battles outside me but the battles within involving conquering myself. Faith keeps hope alive. Uplift my faith to grow into knowledge, and knowledge into submission, and submission into a testimony. In the name of Jesus, I pray."

Today's prayer: "Lord, your holy Law says that the soul that sins must die. You became death so that I might become immune to death. You became sin so that I might become the righteousness of God. Your life story became my life story. The reign of sin and the dominion of death were replaced by the dominion of the kingdom of God through righteousness and eternal life. You surrendered your life in defiance against death by dying and resurrecting to the life that never dies. Your resurrection authenticates your death on the cross. At the cross, you absorbed the sting of death in your body. Satan did not understand it, for if he had, he would not have crucified the Lord of glory (1 Corinthians 2:8). I understand it pretty well because I am at the receiving end of the cross. I can blow my own horn in defiance saying "O death, where is thy sting? O grave, where is thy victory?" (1 Corinthians 15:55). Thank you, Jesus.

Today's prayer: "Hardship is inevitable because it is part of life. When trouble comes there is desperation. No illusion is more crucial than an illusion that material prosperity and success as defined by the world can buy us immunity from the common ills of life. Hardship is supposed to evoke brokenness and hence self-evaluation. Brokenness is a virtue involving constant cycles of integration and disintegration in which we are humbled and uplifted. Lord, your word says that "A bruised reed shall he not break, and the smoking flax shall he not quench" (Isaiah 42:3). Lay not on me your iron rod, but holds out the golden scepter of your grace to restore me. Uphold me with your right hand of righteousness. Bind up my wounded heart with the olive oil of your Spirit. In the name of Jesus, I pray."

Today's prayer: Lord, you did not speak on your own, but what the Father who sent you commanded you to say (John 12:49). Also, you said that when the Spirit of truth, comes, He will guide us into all the truth, for He will not speak on His own authority, but whatever He hears He will speak, and He will declare to us the things that are to come (John 16:13). The Holy Spirit has no words of His own but of the Son. Likewise, the Son has no words of His own but of the Father. Conclusively, the Holy Spirit has no message and agenda of His own but the message and agenda of the Father and the Son. Lord, your doctrine is not human but divine. You called me in this great ministry of the Word to minister the blessings of the whole counsel of God. The greater the calling, the greater the caller. Guide me by your Spirit into all truth and into all wisdom and knowledge for the glory of the Father and the Son.

Today's prayer: "Lord, we have too much misplaced confidence in ourselves. We think we can come to God on our terms. But our sinfulness affected our thinking such that we cannot find the truth on our own without the help of God. The promise of Jesus is that the Holy Spirit will guide us into all truth. He is a faithful guide. With His guidance truth is knowable; it is not abstract; it objective rather than subjective. Knowing Jesus Christ is coming face to face with God and experiencing his life-changing power. The power brings glory to Christ rather than to me. Lord, you said that "If ye then, being evil, know how to give good gifts unto your children: how much more shall your heavenly Father give the Holy Spirit to them that ask him?" (Luke 11:13). Let me live out the reality of the life empowered by the Holy Spirit. Help me not suppress the guidance of your Spirit. In the name of Jesus, I Pray."

Today's prayer: "Our Father in heaven, hallowed be your name. Lord, you revealed your name to us as the Father, portraying our relationship with you. And you instructed us to revere the God behind the name by our holiness. Your kingdom is relational in nature. To be holy is to take on your nature and character by the intimate relationship with the Son. You plant your desires in my heart and satisfy my heart. We delight in you by taking our minds off the worldly things and focus on the eternal things, where Christ is (Colossians 3:1-4). But we're not naturally prone to follow this obligation because the things which naturally appeal to our emotions are often contrary to what you intended us to have. In spite of the inconsistency, your love never fails us. Your mercies are new every morning (Lamentations 3:22-23). This is the security guaranteeing my salvation, and a challenge to me to renew my relationship every day. May your name be elevated and known from generation to generation and be remembered forever and ever. Amen

Today's prayer: "Lord, we love this life but the reality is that life is a mystery. Life is full of unexpected things, and analyzing life is like making sense out of a senseless situation. We have it, and yet we own it not. We feel the heart beats but we have no control of the heart. We go to bed without assurance that we will see the sunrise the next day. Without you, we are helplessly waiting with bated breath to find answers to the meaning of life. Some resort to addictive beverages to lift off the burdens from their backs. I choose to run to you because everyone who runs to you makes it. There's no one beyond the reach of a loving savior. There's no life so lost that Jesus cannot save. You are the only one who can take all the wrongs of life and make them right. Help me to live in the glory of your grace. In Jesus' name Amen."

Today's prayer: "Lord, you loved the world and gave your only son, of the same kind as you are, so that we might be of the same kind as you are. Agape love is the essence of the cross. You engraved your name not in a stone monument but on the cross. You did not build for yourself a shrine (temple) because your mission is people. Your love is woven into the lives of the people whom you call the Church. The opposite of love is hate. Hatred is the embodiment of evil. In a mortal man, hatred is immortal. We live in the world that is dominated by hate, and we are losing the moral compass, decency, and sense of civility in our social institutions. A difference of opinion in politics, in religion, and in philosophy, can cause hatred even among believers. Just to name a few manifestations of the loveless desert in which we languish. Hatred intensifies discords but love solves problems through dialogue. Lord, the predicament is that we have taken you out of our institutions, yet morality cannot be separated from the moral God. I am kneeling before the only one that changes me. Create in me the will to love. Use me as an instrument of peace so that where there is hatred I should show love. In Jesus' name, I pray."

Today's prayer: "Lord, Life is short, and we cannot get the most out of it. Hastily enjoying the pleasures which this world could offer does not yield to fulfillment because there is the puzzle of the afterlife. Traveling this life without Jesus is like traveling the dark journey alone. This world is a hostile environment even to those who adore it. Evil is stalking good; the indignation surges, when each day passes, evil seems to prevail. In the real life, there is a place for solid answers, and a place with no answers but to mourn. We mourn with those who are mourning but with such awareness that what is being experienced by others can happen to us. This makes life unbearably grim. Nevertheless, it is heartening to know that you are in control. The reality is that we don't own any portion of life in this world. Lord, life belongs to you, and you called us to live your life here on the earth for your glory. You are the ultimate life which sustains my soul. Faith connects me to your life. Faith gives me an inner strength and a sense of balance and a new perspective of life. Lord, give me the courage so that when complexity arises, I am not perplexed or doubtful but I am ready to handle it. Empower me to be all that you created me to be, in Jesus' name, Amen.

Today's prayer: "Lord, this life is a game which trophies are pain and sufferings. But you designed life as bliss as opposed to tension. When you allow tension and hardship it is because you are attracting our attention to you. But quite often, in spite of our wounded memories and past mistakes, we are hardly moved to contend for your attention because we are rebels by nature. The spirit of the world teaches us to pattern ourselves according to our own fancies. The human heart is deceitful, and it is hard to contend against the heart's desire; for whatever it wishes to do it does even at the cost of the soul. We live in a very unreliable world in which public image counts and ego is applauded. And we embrace the values of the darkened world with both hands. Lord, you said that to love the world is to hate you (1 John 2:15; James 4:4). We can certainly hate you and be hateful to you, but your eternal love triumphs even when you hate what we do. Your zeal, the divine arm, the fervency of the infinite selected us (your elects) from eternity as a masterpiece of your skill and power. As for the lost world, you are merciful, patient and long-suffering but there is a time when your long-suffering will end. Man can certainly flee from God... but he cannot escape Him. Lord, the sin of rebellion is as witchcraft. Bolt my name from the book of the rebels, and write my name in the Lamb's book of life. In Jesus' name, I pray.

Today's prayer: "Lord, I magnify your name. To magnify you is to see you in your majesty. Magnifying you make everything, including me, look tiny compared to the One sitting on the throne. You are unlimited, awe-inspiring and eternal. You set your sanctuary in the highest of the heights beyond all creations: beyond the skies and the heavens where the angels of flaming fires are your messengers and are ministering to you. Yet, you are personal because by your grace you dwell in our bodies. You are an intelligent designer. By your hands, you wonderfully created us and knitted us to function as one body, which is your temple. You did it not for us to be witnesses for ourselves but to be witnesses for you because you alone is holy; righteousness and justice are determined by your impeccable character. We are your dwelling place (temple). It is regarding the cleanness of our bodies (temple) you said that the zeal for your house consumes you. Lord, this world is enticing. We are fascinated by a lot of things but nothing pleases you but our faith. Pursuing holiness is putting faith in the sinless Lamb of God where we find atonement, consecration and fellowship. For this reason, I have decided to place my faith in the very place where you put my sins. I put my faith in Jesus Christ."

Today's prayer: "Lord, you said that your people perish due to lack of knowledge. Also, you instructed that "Opponents must be gently instructed, in the hope that God will grant them repentance leading them to a knowledge of the truth, and that they will come to their senses and escape from the trap of the devil, who has taken them captive to do his will." (2 Timothy 2:24-26). There is a massive ignorance of God among people of all classes; elites and illiterates. Ignoring ignorance is ignoring sin, and the repercussion of ignoring sin goes beyond this life. Lord, help me to exchange my ignorance with knowledge and my misunderstanding with understanding. Sin is defeated by knowing Jesus intimately. Let me rest in the revelation that you alone can bring. My Lord, my Jesus, if ever I loved, my Lord, my Jesus, it is now!"

Today's prayer: "Lord, The mind of man has perplexed itself with many hard questions. To whom shall we turn? In our dysfunctional lives, we turn to You for restoration, wisdom, and strength. I prefer staying close to where you are because it is he who lives in harmony with you that overcomes the world. The closest I can be to you is when I walk by the spirit. But my emotions are the most treacherous thing in the world. They are saturated with excitement and sorrow, pride and arrogance, and at times they drive me in crisis. They lift me up and let me plummet. But as long as I am being lifted by hope I am not worried about plummeting. "Love lifted me! Love lifted me! When nothing else could help, Love lifted me! All my heart to Him I give, ever to Him I'll cling in His blessèd presence live, ever His praises sing".

Today's prayer: "In this world, we are strangers and pilgrims who are seeking a country of our own. No matter how far we travel the horizon is way beyond us. Abraham looked forward to the city with foundations, whose architect and builder is God. He did not look for a city that lasts long but which lasts forever (Hebrews 11:10). Such is the city (paradise) where there will be no corruption; there will be no temptation because the tempter will not be there. Lord, I need your guidance while I am on the pilgrim in this world. Spiritual enlightenment is to gaze with undimmed eyes in spite of the darkness of the world. Help me to take my focus off this world and to look to what is next on the horizon (beyond this world). I bring nothing to the table but my faith. "Rock of Ages, cleft for me, Let me hide myself in Thee — Nothing in my hand I bring, Simply to Thy cross I cling. Naked, come to Thee for dress, Helpless, look to Thee for grace".

Today's prayer: "Lord, this corrupt world is enticingly pleasant. It stands as an open arena for our gaze but the more we gaze into it the more we become like it. I don't have to strive valiantly to prevent my face from being marred by the filthiness of this world. You made for me an escape route from this world called the narrow way. You established a new covenant out of your attributes of love and faithfulness. Deepen my trust in you when sailing through the tribulations of this world. Increase my faith to endure and to grow in your likeness – in your attributes of love, joy, peace, patience, kindness, goodness, faithfulness, gentleness, and self-control (Galatians 5:22,23). Lord, unlike man, you are ever faithful to your covenant. And your faithfulness is my fullness. "Great is Thy faithfulness," O God my Father, There is no shadow of turning with Thee; Thou changest not, Thy compassions, they fail not, As Thou hast been Thou forever wilt be."

Today's prayer: "Lord, our corrupt nature is the epitome of the corrupt world. The people owned by this world seek self- aggrandizing because they are cut off from God. They work hard to please other people in order to earn their approval, yet it is impossible to please all people. Lord, you are the opposite of everything the world is. The world focuses on our abilities but you focus on your capability in us. The world focuses on feelings but you focus on faith. The world focuses on the temporal things but you focus on eternal things. The world seeks for or failures but you look for our uplifting. The world seeks for tangible evidence but you seek faith without seeing. Faith is choosing to please you and it is the means of pleasing you. It is choosing to be what the world is not. Choosing to obey you is choosing to be unpopular to the world because what is right before you is unpopular to the world. My existence is not of this world, and sin is no longer my master because I was redeemed. I want to be the true epitome of your grace. "My hope is built on nothing less Than Jesus' blood and righteousness; I dare not trust the sweetest frame, But wholly lean on Jesus' name. On Christ, the solid Rock, I stand; All other ground is sinking sand."

Today's prayer: "Lord, some folks are about as happy as they make up their mind to be and they see no need of you, but they are not exempted from misery and fear. Others know that they need you but they ignore the liberating truth, yet they're scared of what they're ignorant of. Lord, you are ultimately involved in our lives regardless of our views because we are your creations. You are not on the sideline watching us. You send rain to nourish the righteous and the unrighteous on the earth (Matthew 5:45). But your heavenly blessings are bestowed to the redeemed undeservingly by your grace. The best of us are capable of the worst and the worst of us are capable of the best. But there is no sorrow that heaven cannot heal. You turn the impossibility into possibility. No life is so hard that you can't simplify it. No life is so unmanageable that you can't restrain it. I decide to believe in nothing less than your truth. "When peace like a river, attendeth my way; When sorrows like sea billows roll. Whatever my lot, thou hast taught me to say; It is well, it is well, with my soul"

Today's prayer: "I will bless the name of the Lord" (Psalm 34:1). It means when I go to church to worship, I don't go to get something out of the worship but to put something into the worship. Lord, worshiping is magnifying your name. You are infinitely great. Like the circle, your greatness has no beginning and no end. When I look at all creations, I see the wisdom of God who controls heaven and earth from His throne! The vastness of the universe (creation) projects a greater God than the universe (creation) itself. When I consider your majesty, the whole earth which we occupy is nothing but a point in the space, and I am insignificant compared to a thin smoke without flame. In the natural minds, you are way over yonder separated from us. But in my heart, you are as close to me as my breath. Your endless love turned my heart into the greatest treasure in the universe. In the past, You chose to manifest your presence in despicable places: You chose to dwell in a tabernacle built with rags; You chose to be born in a manger; You chose to die on a rugged cross for my sins. "And I love that old Cross where the dearest and best for a world of lost sinners was slain. So I'll cherish the old rugged Cross till my trophies, at last, I lay down. I will cling to the old rugged cross and exchange it some day for a crown."

Today's prayer: "Lord, you have made everything beautiful in its time. You have also set eternity in the human heart (Ecclesiastes 3:11). You created everything good. You designed everything in their own beauty and you made their beauty to appear in their own season in harmony. But you created man in your beauty to outlive all seasons. You made us different (gender/color) to complement each other. When we were flawed by sin, you prescribed your beauty as the supreme dominion in our hearts; not in the minds to be contemplated and pursued beyond our grasp but in the hearts which is the center from where ideas are cultivated and communicated so that we may grow into them even before we understand them. All words and thoughts come out of the void of emptiness but the testimony of the pure heart is the revelation of the divine truth. "Great is Thy faithfulness!" "Great is Thy faithfulness!" Morning by morning new mercies I see; All I have needed Thy hand hath provided— "Great is Thy faithfulness," Lord, unto me!"

Today's prayer: "My sacrifice, O God, is a broken spirit; a broken and contrite heart you, God, will not despise (Psalm 51:17). Naturally, it's hard asking someone with a broken heart to fall in love again. But God builds his kingdom with materials of broken hearts. A broken heart is the one that is humbled under a sense of pain and sin and sees the need to repent. Lord, you approve and accept my sacrifices of sincere repentance. Therefore, it is not the broken heart that kills, but the unbroken pride. You alone can water my desert and cause it to blossom. In the face of oddity and adversity, grant to me the decency to embrace sanity. Indeed, broken things become blessed things when we let God do the mending.

Today's prayer: "Lord, the only definition of love given by the Scriptures is that God is Love. Since God is Love and Christ is God then Christ is Love. We are called to pursue love as our priority. We are not only made for a purpose but for a person that loves us. "We exist for God" (1 Cor. 8:6). It is love that brought me into relationship with the creator, and it is love that brings me in union with others. Faith brings us into oneness with God. Love is a prerequisite of faith. This is a prerequisite for finding a fulfilling purpose for our lives. When we are in fellowship with God, we walk in love with others: This is a strong testimony of our conversion that attracts the world to Christ; a testimony that we need in order to take the whole Word to the whole world; a testimony that we need in order to sail through the storms of this world. So help me God."

Today's prayer: "Lord, the realization of my own flaw is the beginning of sanity. I have one life to live that will determine my life forever and I must live it to the utmost. I am not scared of adversity because no matter how long the night lasts there must be a dawn. Indeed, one is never ready to live until they are ready to die. Jesus Christ is the light that dispels fear, provides assurance and direction, and engenders enduring peace and joy. He is the unchanging power in the ever-changing world. The greatest reward by Christ is more Christ. To be a disciple is to be ever disciplined. I have decided to settle for nothing less than Christ. I want more of Him because I can't get enough of Him. And I am convinced that when everything seems to be falling apart, I am not falling apart. My prayer today is that I must decrease so that He increases."

Today's prayer: "Lord, it's in human nature to find loopholes in something that seems difficult, and to conveniently discard something that we really don't want to be applied to our personal experience. Normally, we save the easy things to ourselves and pass on the difficult tasks which we can barely handle to others. Your Word says that your yoke is easy. You assigned the tough task to your Son and saved the easy task for me. You are pleased by my faith in what your Son did on my behalf. You don't need my good works but you demand them because I need them for my sanctification and because my neighbor needs them. We are humanitarians because we are humans created in your image. I am your image bearer called to discover your image in others rather than competing with them. Lord, you cover every inch of this world with your love. Love means to love even that which is unlovable, or it is no virtue at all. Compassion (kindness) is the favorable environment where virtues flourish. I don't want just to love without knowing your standard of loving. You are the absolute truth and my object of faith. Let my mode of life be relative to the objective truth. In the name of Jesus, I pray."

Today's Prayer: "Lord, your Word says that in this world there will be tribulations (John 16:33). You warned us that in the end times the tribulations will intensify. Tribulations are afflictions of the devil. You are not the source of our problems but the solution to our problems. After you judged the world with the floods, you gave us a sign of the rainbow being a token of a covenant between you and the earth; that is, between God and the creatures of the earth with a promise that you would no more destroy the earth, and cut off the creatures in it by a flood (Genesis 9:13). The saints are the apple of your eye, for whoever touches us touches the apple of your eye. We are the restrainer to your pending wrath; for it won't be poured on the earth unless we are taken away (raptured). Lord, you called us out of the world and sent us into the world that is not free from tribulations. It means we are not exempted from suffering. Your primary objective is to make us in the likeness of Christ, even through sufferings. Therefore, we are not supposed to seek a supernatural remedy from sufferings but a supernatural use of it for our benefit. We are called Christian because we are Christ-like. Jesus came to the earth with the full armor because He was entering a battlefield. We need His armor because Christianity is not a playground but a battleground. Lord, you are the restorer and repairer of the ruins caused by our adversary, Satan, the Devourer. And you gave us the power of praying in the name of Jesus to overcome. Help us to pick up our mantle of praying and praising amidst the storms of life. In the name of Jesus, Amen.

Today's prayer: "Lord, our sins grieve your heart. You descended to the earth, and then all the way to hell to set the captives free. And you ascended to heaven to prepare for us the places so that where you are, we should be. Your Word chronicles how this race of life will end. Your Word says that there is heaven to inherit and hell to inhabit. Heaven and hell are the reality of judgment. Eternal life in the presence of God is the highest reward heaven can give. Eternal death is the highest reward hell can give. Heaven is up, and hell is below, and there is a big gulf between the two. The road to heaven is narrow. The road to hell is broad and gradually easy but it is a slippery slope to a point of no return. And there is no need of signposts to direct people to go there because all people unless redeemed, are heading in that direction. Lord, you prepared hell, a pit, just big enough to accommodate Lucifer and the fallen angels but Hell has enlarged itself because we are naturally proud people who despise the value and highest premium you placed on our souls (Isaiah 5:14). All I need is, "Just a closer walk with Thee, Grant it, Jesus, is my plea, Daily walking close to Thee, Let it be, dear Lord, let it be."

Today's prayer: "Lord, you instructed us that, "Let your conversation be without covetousness; and be content with such things as ye have: for he has said, I will never leave you, nor forsake you" (Hebrews 13:5). According to your Word, contentment is the greatest wealth, and faithfulness is the best medicine of the soul and hence the basis of the lasting relationship. Awareness of the inner abundance is the best antidote for anxiety. Lord, you promised never to leave us. Your promises are yes and amen. You are not like man who makes promises in the shadow, and forget them in the sunshine. I will always rejoice in you. Your precious Name is like nectar on my lips and a peace unto my soul; I am fulfilled by you. "Beautiful Savior, Lord of the nations, Son of God and Son of Man! Glory and honor, Praise, adoration Now and forevermore be Thine!"

Today's prayer: "Lord, my heart is longing for your presence but your presence is not what will happen but what has already happened. Your Word says that "For in him we live and move and have our being" (Acts 17:28). The implications of this are far-reaching. It means that my God is not remote at all! He is part of our very being because in Him we live and move and have our being. Lord, I cannot escape your surveillance; even when I go through hell on earth, you are ever with me. Even when I can't feel your presence, you are there. Even when at times I leave you, I cannot get away from you. You are Emanuel, God with us. I am the very vehicle in which your Spirit cruises. I do not need to go to heaven to bring you down. In fact, you are closer to us than we are to each other. There is no need for me to scream and shout in prayer, for you hear me always. You can even listen to the echo of my conscience in my silence. Faith is neither loud nor quite but it is firm, sure and confident. It is an upright, loyal and sincere heart that can experience your presence. Restore sanity to my troubled heart. In the name of Jesus, I pray.

Today's prayer: "Lord, Trusting is a tonic for mind and body, and the antidote to solitary, yet we are allergic to it. The only one that can truly satisfy the human heart is the One that created it. In every human heart, there is a round hole that can only be filled by the endless love of God. God's love is extravagant for it accommodates the worst of the sinners like me who barely merits it. Receiving Jesus Christ is making Him my sin bearer in exchange for life eternal. Embracing the cross is the maximum enlargement of life. Enormous enlargement of an object gives it a personality it never had before. To be born again is a conviction that life can only be lived in the presence of God, and it continues indefinitely. Changed lives begin with changed hearts. Eternal life is when God, by His grace, puts His life into the human hearts on basis of the human faith. Death is putting the human life in the human hands and trusting in human resources. Lord, relieve me of unbelief because unbelief is the synthesis of crisis. Wash my soul with the joy of your salvation. In the name of Jesus, Amen.

Today's prayer: "Lord, at times I am held hostage of my imaginations and expectations. I plan but others dismantle what I plan; I strategize but others out- strategize me. But I am not blaming others for my setback. The buck stops with me. Often, my minds wander into many things which are not necessarily sinful but which are not in your perfect will. My imaginations have yet to be clobbered into perfect submission. It is only when I hitch my wagon to something larger than myself that I realize my true potential. Lord, the only one thing that matters is You. Without you, I have no clear-cut vision to reach the buoyant shores of the horizon. Obedience to God proves our love for Him (1 John 5:2-3), demonstrates our faithfulness to Him (1 John 2:3-6), glorifies Him in the world (1 Peter 2:12), and opens avenues of blessing for us (John 13:17). Lord, I may not fully understand the why of everything you command me to do; all that you require of me is to obey and leave the consequences of my obedience to you to fathom. There is no shortcut or quick fix to your glory. Revive my faith and relieve me of a painful ordeal as a result of deviating from your instructions. In the name of Jesus, I pray."

Today's prayer: "He that hears let him hear, and he that understands let him understand". Lord, you gave each of us the gift of faith as the spiritual antenna to receive the gospel. The same antenna (faith) guides us throughout our lives on the earth. Listening and heeding are very important portions of faith. The defaulted life lacks listening ears. Naturally, it is impossible to speak and listen at the same time. The disciplined life is when I numb one end to benefit the other. Lord, whenever you speak, I stand still in silence to hear, and whenever I speak in prayers you listen in silence. The love of the world is the unnecessary sound that blocks the echoes of the gospel to penetrate our ears, unseats God from the center of our being, blurring our love for God. True love cannot be divided. Split loyalty is no loyalty at all. To be double-minded is to believe and doubt at the same time; it is to love God and the world at the same time; it is basically to belong nowhere. It is a selfish life lived apart from God. Life without Christ is compared to buoyantly racing on a one-way street that ends in the dead end without a possibility of turning back. It does not matter how long we live, it is a short journey from nothingness to nothingness. It is vanity of vanities. The corruption of the spiritual death is realized in the physical death that cannot be escaped. Lord, help me to put to the right use the faculties you have given me so that I might relinquish the foggy notion regarding my ultimate need for life. I want to be current in all seasons. What you have revealed to me in light, let me not doubt it in times of darkness. In the name of Jesus, I pray."

Today's prayer: "Lord, you loved me unconditionally. You loved me when there was nothing deservingly about me to love. What was true will always be true; you loved me and you will love me always. You love me persistently and you plan the best for me. At times negative excitement blinds me from seeing your purpose for me; I end up resisting your perfect plan for me. In spite of the deficit, you still love me. You provide the inner peace and confidence to cope with my inadequacy. You multiply my joy and unlock the fullness of life. You turn a meal into a feast and set a banquet before me. You are the anchor that stirs me in the right direction and that holds. All blessings flow from you. When everything seems to be falling apart, I am not afraid because I am not falling apart. Help me to recognize this truth about you so that in times of affliction, I array myself with patience, and I do not murmur or be depressed. You watch my steps but I am in charge of my stride. My stride is not perfectly efficient but with your help, I can weather whatever comes and face the future without fear. I am not looking for a new definition of the gospel but a new demonstration of the gospel in my life. In the name of Jesus, I pray.

Today's prayer: "Lord, you are the great I am, meaning that there is no time that you were not, and you will not be. There is no time you have not been on the throne. The circumference of this life is within eternity. You are an infinite entity, the center of which is everywhere, the circumference nowhere. "To be sensuous means to become aware of the circumference; and to be spiritual means to become aware of the center." Ego denies God His rightful place. The real battle in life is between hanging on my ego and letting go of my ego. Faith is the altar where our ego is slain. God is pleased by our faith because faith is switching our trust from 'self' to Christ. A life-changing decision is made out of faith rather than feelings. Lord, you demand that my faith be proven by my works because faith without works is giving God a lip service instead of a life service. Faith without works is like having a book on the table that I can't read or having a song that I can't sing. Faith is the most contagious force in the world. Lord, give me a contagious faith to change my life and the lives of others. In Jesus' name, I pray."

Today's prayer: "People are not born when equipped with knowledge but they are trained into it. Likewise, nobody is born with faith. Both faith and knowledge are acquired and nurtured. Faith is a gift from God, and it comes (grows) by listening to the Word. Although trusting can be blind, faith is not blind. A heart can follow what the mind cannot understand but it cannot follow what the mind rejects. Therefore, it is imperative to train our kids in godless so as to influence their beliefs. The knowledge and traditions passed on to our kids cannot save them but can be a step positioning them to receive the Savior. My prayer today is for the salvation of my children. A number of children who are raised in the discipline of the Church abandon their faith when they hit the teen-age. Lord, you promised to bless me and my seed. Your Word says "For I will pour out water to quench your thirst and to irrigate your parched fields. And I will pour out my Spirit on your descendants, and my blessing on your children" (Isaiah 44:3). I don't want them just to survive but to thrive. Let my children be numbered among the faithful remnants to receive your Spirit and to know you in your fullness. Let them delight in what you are delighted, and take pleasure in what pleases you. In the name of Jesus, I pray."

Today's prayer: "Lord, the single most important desire of every man is to experience your presence. As the deer pants for streams of water, so my soul pants for you, my God (Psalm 42:1). I am longing for your presence as the drowning man longs for air. Without sincere longing, I will never find it. Heaven seems to be far away but you are the nearest thing to my breath, and wherever you are, is where heaven is. You have set eternity in the hearts of men through a desire to make our earthly tents your dwelling place. You are the divine destiny. In order for me to become a man of destiny my life must become the expression of your grace, and the unveiling of your love. Walking righteously makes crooked things straight. Lord, renew my minds with the gospel and purge my conscience from oddity with your blood so that my passions may be your passions. In Jesus' name, I pray."

Today's prayer: "Lord, without faith, life is reduced to the mere assumption, living one day at a time, not knowing what the day will bring and what the future holds. Each season comes with different opportunities and disposition. Happiness is the hub of the good life but happiness is not absolute; it corresponds to other factors like age. The greatest adversity of happiness is time. Time slips away from our hands uncontrollably, and we cannot roll it backward. We say that time is money but money can't buy time. Real happiness is supposed to be contagiously experienced from generation to generation. Yet searching for happiness in this world is at times like searching for feelings in a numb body. The pleasure of the world is negative excitement disguising as happiness; it is intended to blind us from seeing God's purpose for the time. Lord, you redefined what true happiness is. True happiness spontaneously bubbles from a transformed heart; it is inward tranquility rather than mere amusement from outside while I am empty inside; it is neither manufactured nor reasoned into staying. The world defines happiness in the abundance of things but you say happiness is the abundance of sharing; the world teaches self-importance but you demand to die to self; the world seeks self-exaltation but you say that the least is the greatest; the world seeks to boss others but you seek servant-hood. Lord, according to your Word happiness and blessedness are synonymous. True happiness is to live for the glory of God. Let me be sustained by the tranquility of an upright and loyal heart. In Jesus' name, I pray.

Today's prayer: "Lord, your Word is true; your ways are right. All you require of me is to obey without meddling and questioning your Word. But at times I am caught up in giving excuses and imaginary reasons instead of real reasons. There is that hard-edged arrogant side among all humanity, which is attractive to all even though it is contrary to your character. At times I am selfish, arrogant such that I regard myself higher than I should be. Sanity begins by challenging my own assumption and scrubbing them off. The glory of this world is manifested in prestige, pride, and power. But the glory of heaven is in meekness, humility, and humbleness. We are always at the receiving end of the glory of the world until we decide to die to our egos: That is when we exchange our will with your will; that is when we decide to give to others what we desire for ourselves and do to others what we want to be done to us. Everyone was born for a specific influential assignment, but the common assignment to all is to be pure at heart. To love God is to hate evil. This is the safest and most effective way to overcome temptation. Greater intimacy means greater authority and greater capacity to deliver. Lord, infuse my life with humility; grant to me the pure and uncluttered wisdom typically of a little kid that depends on the parents for guidance. In Jesus' name, I pray.

Today's prayer: "Life without God is like gambling. Whatever path we take and whatever turn we make depends on how we roll our dice. But God doesn't play dice; in the economy of heaven, there are no coincidences and chances. How we live determines how and why we die. Lord, life without you is a continuous process of confusion and frustrations; we get ripped off without a possibility of learning a lesson. Success, as defined by the world, is never transforming. It is basically walking a tightrope to minimize disappointment rather than eradicating it. Suffering is primarily the consequence of the bad decisions we make. Yet, no one's life story is void of grey hair. We are all faced with the tough decisions to make, some of which we have no solution. Temptation comes in different shapes and brands. Trouble stalks us and we ignorantly strive to embrace it compared to a butterfly that keeps on bouncing on the glass of a lamp in a bid to touch the flames of fire. The commandments of God are there for our protection in the same manner the glass of the lamp is positioned to protect the butterfly from roasting in the glowing flames of fire. Lord, our liberty comes from beyond us rather than from within; you alone have the answers to the questions pertaining to life. Position me in your Word and guide me by your Spirit. I don't want just your visitation but your habitation. In Jesus' name, I pray."

Today's prayer: "Sovereign LORD, there is nothing too hard for thee or hidden from thee. You are all powerful and sufficient. You made the heavens and the earth by your great power and outstretched arm (Jeremiah 32:17). You are the great I am, who was, who is, and who will be. By grace, I can know what is (the present) in the light of what was (the past) and what will be (the future). You are the God of boundless mercy and of strict justice. By your triune nature, you expressed your love to humanity: The Father loved us and gave the Son to save; the Son loved us and gave His life to save; the Holy Spirit loved us and dwelt in us to save. There is nothing new under the sun but everything is new under the Son. Lord, you alone can regenerate. Without you the history of man is degeneration - there is nothing beneath and beyond the sky but broken hope. But to the regenerated soul, everything is new. It means that if I want to find myself I must find you. If I want to find you, I must get over myself. You alone can turn the thing around to reconcile me to God and to guide me so that I can have the upper hand in this life and in the life to come. The grip of your hand is my security. In your hands, I relax my grip and enter a state of controlled passivity. May the irresistible surge of your will subdue my will so that I can execute your will in everything I do. In the name of Jesus, I pray."

Today's prayer: "The world is slippery, and life is such a slippery slope, yet sweet. What makes life a slippery slope are the people. Whenever we focus on the people of the world and believe in them, we are most likely to slip also. Lord, I choose to believe and to in you. You are consistency; you will never be what you are not. You are the great I am. You have always been, and you will always be. I just want to be like you. You did not create me the way I am but the way you saved me to be. In order to appreciate Jesus, we must understand God. The Son of God became the son of man so that the sons of men should become the sons of God."

Today's prayer: "Lord, life is a great mystery but it doesn't have to remain mysterious because you have revealed how it works. We are in the spiritual warfare. The war is long and the battles are many. The key to fighting any war is good planning, strategizing and agonizing. Good planning is having my priorities right; it is making the main things main. Lord, my priority is You. You lift me up when I fall down. My strategy is to keep fighting in spite of failures. You don't just carry my burdens but you carry me. You don't just change my circumstances but you change me. You love me in spite of me. And you will never leave me. I want to be like you. I want to love as you love. You don't give a gift in anticipation to receive a gift. I want to love people as opposed to making them love me. I don't want to wait for people to love me so that I can love them. Generosity requires the sensitivity of the Holy Spirit in order to do as you will. So help me God."

Today's prayer: "Lord, you are love, and sin is everything against love. It is love that made your Son to come from the heavenly throne to be like one of us. He was born as a stranger in the world that knew Him not. Ashamed, I see myself as the owner of the inn that slammed the door in Joseph's face, saying that there is "no vacancy", pushing Joseph and Mary in the animal shelter behind the guest house. It was love that made Jesus to die in my place. It was love rather than the nails that held Him on the cross until it was accomplished. Ashamed, I hear my mocking voice call out among the scoffers that "Save yourself! Come down from the cross, if you are the Son of God!" He could have easily come off the cross but His Sonship was intended to demonstrate a much greater instance of power, by His resurrection from the dead. He endured the punishment of the wicked men in order to satisfy the justice of God against my sins. No vain and empty boasts of the scoffers could cause Him to change His minds from saving me. He demonstrated to us God's abundant and unconditional love; the love that justifies the ungodly and saves the sinners. My Lord, my Savior, into your hands I commit my life. I want to be the epitome of love. I don't want to be just the recipient of the grace but the demonstration of it. I want to know the person of Jesus Christ and the power of His resurrection.

"How deep the Father's love for us; How vast beyond all measure that He should give His only Son to make a wretch His treasure. I will not boast in anything; No gifts, no power, no wisdom but I will boast in Jesus Christ His death..."

Today's prayer: "True happiness eludes those who are opposed to God because mankind was made for God. Without the divine, our marks of piety can actually be evidence of our impiety. In real life, there is a tendency of crying at random for things although nothing happens around us is random. The grace transforms a random walk into a chase and hence a catch. Putting God in charge of my soul gives me control of myself and the circumstances surrounding me, making me effective in spite of the challenges and failures. Jesus came to seek the lost because the lost would not seek God. Jesus does not just bring peace, He is the peace. He does not just bring love, He is the love. He is our sufficiency for the development of the godly characteristics which is a gym for harmonious living. He works in us by the power of His grace deep within our hearts. "May Him who is able to do exceedingly abundantly above all that we ask or think, according to the power that works in us, be with you, in Jesus' Amen."

Today's prayer: "Lord, you use whatever and whoever you want to display your glory (Romans 2:11). You are not bound to any person by any laws, but acts as a Sovereign; you are not moved by anything in the creature; as your choice is not confined to persons of any particular nation, family, sex, or condition. We, who were not people, are now called people; who were not legitimate but now legitimate and ordained for the highest calling to glorify your name. We are a chosen nation to be a living testimony to your saving grace. It is when we glory in the grace of God that the scope of thrift is limitless. Whether we're having setbacks or not our role is to display the glory of God. Lord, nothing glorifies you like loving your image in us and in others. We are one body depending on you to serve each other; the good of the whole should be the object of all. This is the ultimate calling of all but self-aggrandizing dislodges us from putting the unity of the body of Christ on display. Lord, teach me to reckon all the effects of this life in the light of eternity. Set me aside to display the irresistible beauty of your unconditional love. Leave me not with a dispossessed mindset; In Jesus' name, I pray.

Today's prayer: "Life is what it is. There is always going to be a mountain in our way. There are those mountains which God ordained us to climb; faith takes us to the mountaintop. Then there are those mountains which we are supposed to move out of our way by faith. Doubt creates mountains; faith is a leap towards demolishing them. Faith is God's hand that crushes any hindrance out of our way. Without faith, we are caught up in the contradiction of finding life a rather perplexing puzzle. Lord, you do not call the qualified but you qualify whom you call. My calling is your enablement. You call and use the broken people who are willing to abandon their own human capability and depend on you. Let me be anchored in your expectations rather than philosophical positive confidence. Strengthen and sustain my faith by the loving embrace and all-sufficient support of your eternal arms, to which I will always hold. In Jesus' name, I pray.

Today's prayer: "Lord, the good news is not good news until I know the bad news. It is when I acknowledge that I am a sinner, confess my sins to Jesus Christ and receives Him as my Savior that I am justified. But this is just the first giant step on an eternal journey of intimacy and fellowshipping with you. You saved me to have fellowship with me, here on the earth and in eternity. Fellowship with you is the major way of preparing for your return. Fellowshipping is maintained by obedience and trusting. God cleans up the heart in order to clean the life. Sanctification is a life of faith lived from inside to the outside. Fellowship is keeping my heart with all diligence every day because out of it flows the springs of life. Lord, fellowship with you casts away all fears. Whenever I hit rock bottom, Christ is the only way up. In times of tribulations I can count on your promises because they are without expiration date.

Today's prayer: "Suffering is a matrix that is counter to what is normal and right. Suffering may be the consequence of our bad decisions. "The keenest sorrow is to recognize ourselves as the sole cause of all our adversities." But at times suffering comes to us without our initiation. The bottom line is that nobody opts for suffering and nobody is exempted from it. Spiritually, suffering is not a sign of abandonment by God but a result of loyalty to God. Jesus is called the suffering servant. Suffering disciplines us into submission. The purest form of faith happens when we reach the bottom of our reasoning and find there is nothing that we can do that will make sense out of what we have been through. "Amidst the confusion of the times, the conflicts of conscience, and the turmoil of daily living, an abiding faith becomes an anchor to our lives." Lord, regardless of the cause of my sufferings, your love frees me of all the sufferings and pains in life. You do not rub my nose in my mess. You carry me in your arms and guide me through to start again. You are the anchor that holds my life from surviving to thriving."

Today's prayer: "In the real world, it is an act of bravery to feel our feelings but it is wrong to act on our feelings. The responses of the people of faith are often counter to their actual feelings. In the spiritual realm trusting begins by focusing on the promises of God in spite of our feelings. God's promises are yes and amen without an expiration date. Lord, faith is dying to self and trusting in you. In the real life, there are those things which we take for granted, and those things which we value most and cannot live without; faith is one of those things. Faith is dying to self and trusting in God. In the economy of heaven, there is no 'I', 'me' and 'myself'. The valid 'I' is God Himself. Lord, you are everything I am, and everything I have. Help me to let go the 'I' mentality and acquire the mentality of the 'Great I am'. In the name of Jesus, I pray."

Today's prayer: "Whereas the natural life is a pickle temporally preserving our physical bodies from decay, the spiritual life is marinated to preserving the soul from corruption. We are born again once but we are given the responsibility to nurture the new life born in us into growth; we are called to perfect the established relationship with God daily. We are all at a certain degree obsessed with the cares of this life even though our passion should be eternal things. We end up quenching the Spirit which is counter to piousness. Lord, Salvation is imperative because life is short, sin is abiding, and death is sure. I don't want to drift away from the anchor of the Spirit. Help me to refocus and make an absolute commitment that is not conditional to the circumstances. In the name of Jesus, I pray."

Today's prayer: "Our blessed hope is the future return of our Lord. History is not at a random. All of the days of the past guide us into our blessed hope, which is the Day of our Lord. But we are not alienated from hope because hope is not just in future but it is also in the present within us – Christ in us the hope of all glory. The redeemed heart is as near to heaven as it can be on earth. Heaven is not so much where we stand, as in what direction we are moving. We are shielded by His promises moving with hope to our blessed hope. Christ is our Savior not in the promise but in the Spirit received by faith. He works for us in the present as much as in the future. "The name of the LORD is a strong tower: the righteous runs into it, and is safe." The attributes of God by which He is made known, are the strength and security of His people. The sinners who run into His tower are called righteous because they know the right place where to run from this world. Ours is a race of faith. A ship does not rely on one small anchor but a soul rests on a single ultimate hope, which is Christ. Faith is God's crowning gift to man. My beliefs run through everything I do. When the odds of life try to drag me, as I know they will, it is to that sense of who I am in Christ and what I believe, to which I will always hold. Lord, help me to cash in on the richness of your grace so that I live through the Spirit and wait by faith instead of the manipulation of the flesh, so that at glorification when my faith will become sight and my hope reality, I might rest in your bosom eternally.

Today's prayer: "Lord, the good news is not good news until I know the bad news. It is when I acknowledge that I am a sinner, confess my sins to Jesus Christ and receives Him as my Savior that I am justified. But this is just the first giant step on an eternal journey of intimacy and fellowshipping with you. You saved me to have fellowship with me, here on the earth and in eternity. Fellowship with you is the major way of preparing for your return. Fellowshipping is maintained by obedience and trust. God cleans up the heart in order to clean up the life. Sanctification is a life of faith lived from inside to the outside. Fellowshipping with you is keeping my heart with all diligence every day because out of it flows the springs of life. Lord, fellowship with you casts away all fears. Whenever I hit rock bottom, Christ is the only way up. Tons of troubles are countered by tons of prayers. When God closes a door, He opens a window. Broken things become blessed things when I let God do the mending. Christ is the reason I sing. I sing in celebration of the powerful name of Jesus that changes lives and that precious name by which I can enter into His presence now and for all eternity. Amen.

Today's prayer: "Lord, you made your Son to be in our image so that we can be restored to your image. Create in me a new heart; hide your Word in my heart that I may sin not. Lord, you know the hearts of all men. At times I am stubborn and embarrassed to confess my sins to you. But you know my sins even before I confess them to you. All you need is my brokenness. Stiffneckedness gives rise to stiff objection. Soften my heart so that I may bend my neck bowing in brokenness. Create in me a tender spirit of uprightness and integrity; a heart fixed, trusting in the Lord, and comfortably assured of your pardoning grace and mercy. Finish the work you started in me by your grace through faith. In the name of Jesus, I pray."

Today's prayer: "Lord, praying is a privilege extended to us, to be honest with ourselves before you, the only one who knows the secrets of the hearts of all men. You incline your ear to the prayer of our conscience. Therefore, kneeling before you is carefully listening to my conscience. Praying is slaughtering my egoism at your altar. Praying is the grave where arrogance is buried. Lord, help me to pray for the good purpose, with sincerity and delight, with obedience and reverence. In the name of Jesus, I pray.

NOVEMBER FOR THANKSGIVING

The English Puritans are credited with creating the oldest, continuously inhabited English settlement in what would become the United States. There are several websites with negative information about the English settlers. I believe that the settlers were motivated by spiritual factors. It doesn't mean they didn't have flaws because they are human beings like us. The Bible instructs us to be thankful in every situation because God turns what was intended to be evil into good. Whether the settlers had hidden agenda or bad intents, but God meant it unto good; He designed that good should come by it, and He brought good out of it. Thanksgiving is a virtue and a discipline of love. Positivity is focusing on the beauty of the situation and appreciating it. Appreciating something doesn't mean there is nothing wrong with it; it means sticking with it in spite of the inconsistency. This is true concerning any relationship. Gratitude is a viable defense against the vice attitude. Hating something begins with the exit of appreciation. Negativity is the means of eradicating appreciation. Normally, before people sell to you their ideas, they first bombard you with a lot of negativity about what you like. The trick is to disengage your minds in neutral by the negative information about what you have so that you open up to embrace the deceptions they are trying to sell to you. No wonder most of the perpetrators of the negativity about the settlers are the anti-Christian folks whose objective is to promote communism and liberal theology.

Thursday is Thanksgiving Day. We are thankful for receiving and giving. "When we give cheerfully and accept gratefully, everyone is blessed." We need to be reminded to be thankful because it is possible to focus on the things we want and forget the things we have. Also, there is a predisposition of failing to acknowledge the little we have to offer and to appreciate the little things done to us. "We cannot do great things on this earth, only small things with great love." Finding the proper way to thank others for their generosity or even reminding ourselves just how much we have to be thankful can be rewarding. The attitude of gratitude evokes rationality. It is when you start counting your blessings that your whole life turns around. I want to take this opportunity to thank all of you for being my friends. I want to go an extra mile to appreciate those of you who occasionally engrave a chunk from your treasured time to respond to my postings on Facebook. Thank you for being the reason I smile.

Thanksgiving is not an event but a practice. Jehovah is the author of all our benefits and the song of our lives; therefore, let Him have all our gratitude. The Bible says that "O give thanks unto the LORD; call upon his name: make known his deeds among the people" (Psalm 105:1). Gratitude compels us to be heralds announcing the goodness of God. Silent gratitude isn't good to anyone; it restrains the hand of the giver and cripples the receiving hand. We should express our gratitude by the uttered words supported by the actions of our lives. We should make Him known by our words and the testimonies of our lives. Remember, the greatest gift is not found in a store nor under the tree but in the hearts of the people of the pure heart. "Change your attitude and gain some altitude." Happy Thanksgiving to all of you.

Thanksgiving is the tradition of gratitude. The settlers saw the need to dedicate this day to thank God for the harvest. Without planting a seed there can't be a harvest. There is a physical and spiritual harvest. Jesus invited His followers to harvest by becoming fishers of men. The biography of Christianity is summarized in three "g" - guilty, grace and gratitude. Guilty is in reference to our situation before receiving the grace; grace is in reference to our current situation after receiving God's unmerited favor; gratitude is our response to the grace received. Thanksgiving is our testimony to make God known by what He has done. Jesus is the grace personified. The Holy Spirit is the custodian of the truth. We are the recipients of the grace and the agents of distribution called to dispense the truth. The Holy Spirit was given to the Church to cleanse the world by the washing of the Word. The Church is the custodian of the gospel. We are the ministers of God's grace. The Greek word for thanks is built on the word for grace: *charis* becomes *eucharistian*. This could have been preserved in English by the use of 'grace' and 'gratitude' which show the same original root. Thanksgiving plays a very crucial part in evangelism; it is a tremendous power necessary if the ministry of the gospel is to succeed and people are to be converted and transformed.

"Thinking and thoughtfulness are words of the same family because in order for you to be thankful you must have the memories joy." God has been so good to us, and He never ceases to be good to us. Thanksgiving is giving back to God. It should not be limited to one day; it must be our lifestyle.

"Sometimes you will never know the value of a moment until it becomes a memory. You need to learn to appreciate even the smallest things. Be grateful for every single thing God has blessed you with, remember there's someone out there who has nothing and would do anything to have what you have."

Philippians 4:6 – "Be anxious about nothing, but in everything, by prayer and supplication with thanksgiving, let your requests be made known to God." Thanksgiving is the wrapper in which our prayers are wrapped and presented to God. The term "but in everything" means in

every time whenever we pray, thanksgiving is the necessary accompaniment of prayer; it ought never to be absent from our devotions.

Hebrews 11:4 - "By faith Abel brought God a better offering than Cain did. By faith he was commended as righteous, when God spoke well of his offerings. And by faith Abel still speaks, even though he is dead." The first thanksgiving offering in the Bible was given by Cain and Abel. The writer of Hebrews proceeds to examples of faith, and begins with Abel: it may seem strange that Adam and Eve are not mentioned. Cain was the first baby to be born with an umbilical cord followed by Abel. Abel offered an acceptable sacrifice to God. The superior excellence of Abel's sacrifice to Cain's, lay both in the matter, and in the manner of it; the one of Abel was offered heartily to the Lord, the other only in show. Abel looked through his sacrifice to the sacrifice of Christ, not so Cain. Abel's sacrifice was a lamb, a type of Christ, the Lamb of God. And it was accredited to him as faith.

DECEMBER FOR THE FIRST COMING OF CHRIST

Whether you celebrate Christmas or not there is something of spiritual significance that takes place during this season. I was flipping through the radio channel stations while driving, and it was hard to find a Christian radio station without reading the formatted numbers. The reason is that the majority of the radio stations (including the secular radio stations) played Christmas carols. I know the secular radio stations do it primarily for commercial purposes. Regardless of the oddity of the motivations, there are psychological and spiritual benefits to the listeners. One writer said "I think at first Christmas music is nice, it's nostalgic, and it gets me into the holiday spirit," says the writer from Escondido, Calif. Then, "it gets old, and it can start to feel like a part of a giant sales machine trying to bleed me dry." Music's effect on us in any situation depends on our own psychological state. Christmas season is, therefore, a good ground taking into account that during this season most people are in a jolly mood. Although some of the popular Christmas carols and hymns were sung by secular musicians, they can still be of spiritual significance because they were composed from the four Gospels. The word gospel means the good news involving the birth, life, death, and resurrection of Jesus. At least every carol or hymn has a story of the birth and purpose of the birth of the Savior. Therefore, there is no season when the gospel is openly preached to all like this season. If you don't celebrate the day, concentrate on the music of the day. Where the traditions of men fail, music speaks. Meditate and enjoy the nuggets within the lyrics of the carols and be blessed.

Luke 1:5-6 - "In the time of Herod king of Judea, there was a priest named Zechariah, who belonged to the priestly division of Abijah, and whose wife Elizabeth was a daughter of Aaron. Both of them were righteous in the sight of God, observing all the Lord's commands and decrees blamelessly." The Aaronic Priesthood was hereditary and it was non-transferable to anyone outside the descendants of Levi. Zachariah was doomed for not having a son to continue the priesthood in his house because Elizabeth was barren. God delayed the conception in Elizabeth's womb to fulfill prophecy. "And they were both righteous before God" – The word righteous when used in reference to God, it means holy but when used in reference to a fallen man it means sincere, complete and blameless. God alone, who sees the hearts, can declare a person to be righteous. Not as the Pharisees, who declared themselves to be righteous by their own deeds in accordance to their own interpretations of the law. No man can be justified in the sight of God by their own merits. The Bible clearly teaches that all people have sinned except Jesus (1 Peter 2:22; Romans 3:23). Zechariah and Elizabeth were blameless; not that they were without sin, as any one of us is, but they were justified by the future death of Christ at the cross, so they were without fault before the throne God. Their acts of obedience were counted as faith in the coming Messiah. God accepted them by the imputed righteousness of Christ. They were sinners as all are, and they were justified and saved in the same way as we are saved.

Somebody replied to the above posting in this way: "Not so. They were Righteous because they kept the commandments given to Moses. Within those commandments was a "sin offering" which covered their sins and in YHWH's eyes, they were righteous. If you look to those Scriptures you can see the plan of salvation. We do not take on the righteousness of Messiah solely by accepting the fact that He is Messiah and believing Him to be so. We CONFORM ourselves to His Likeness by practicing Righteousness - which is the doing of the Torah. " My reply: It is true the sin offering covered for their sins, but temporarily. That is why they had to do it over and over. The purpose of the sacrifices was to maintain their daily communication with God but there was no established permanent relationship with God. All went into exile as per God's judgment. And the whole generation that was redeemed from Egypt never entered the Promised Land as per God's judgment. All sacrifices in the old covenant pointed to the ultimate sacrifice at Calvary. The Bible has always, everywhere, taught that there's only one way to God and that way is by faith. In the book of Hebrews in the eleventh chapter, the heroes of faith are listed here in this most marvelous chapter, and there's just one after the other through the whole chapter, they didn't have the Law because the Law was given to Moses; we find that all of them are tied together with something they did in their life that showed that they really believed God and it was accounted to them as faith in God the Savior. The Jews celebrated the Passover in anticipation of the coming Messiah. This is the tradition of having the cup of Elijah at the Passover table. Also, there is a common tradition to designate a seat for Elijah at the Passover and at circumcision. Elijah was believed to be the forerunner who was expected to introduce the Messiah to the people. They believed in the future Savior; we believe in the Savior in the past. Jesus told the Jewish religious leaders that "Your father Abraham rejoiced at the thought of seeing my day; he saw it and was glad." (John 8:56). Abraham obeyed God but he saw the day of His Messiah, with an eye of faith.

Luke 1:60-67 – "And his mother answered and said, Not so; but he shall be called John. And they said unto her, There is none of thy kindred that is called by this name. And they made signs to his father, how he would have him called. And he asked for a writing table, and wrote, saying, His name is John. And they marveled all. And his mouth was opened immediately, and his tongue loosed, and he spake, and praised God. And fear came on all that dwelt round about them: and all these sayings were noised abroad throughout all the hill country of Judaea. And all they that heard them laid them up in their hearts, saying, What manner of child shall this be! And the hand of the Lord was with him. And his father Zacharias was filled with the Holy Ghost, and prophesied, saying blessed be the Lord God of Israel; for he hath visited and redeemed his people". According to the Jewish culture, the matter of the names of children

was very sensitive. "There is none of thy kindred that is called by this name" from whence it appears, that it was usual to give names to children after their relatives and ancestors. But this child was different from other children. This child is not going to follow the norms and natural aptitude of the community. He is going to be filled with the Holy Spirit from his mother's womb. "His name is John" - There is something emphatic in the use of the present tense. It was not a question to be discussed. The name had been given already. "And they marveled all" - They were astonished, not so much at the new name brought into the family, as at the agreement between Elisabeth and Zacharias in this point, when the latter was both deaf and dumb; they knew nothing, as yet, of the angel's message to him. Zacharias was filled with the Holy Ghost, and prophesied, the divine visitation and providence of a redeemer of whom his son is the forerunner.

Luke 1:26-38 – "In the sixth month, God sent the angel Gabriel to Nazareth, a town in Galilee, to a virgin pledged to be married to a man named Joseph, a descendant of David. The virgin's name was Mary. The angel went to her and said, "Greetings, you who are highly favored! The Lord is with you." Mary was greatly troubled at his words and wondered what kind of greeting this might be. But the angel said to her, "Do not be afraid, Mary, you have found favor with God. You will be with child and give birth to a son, and you are to give him the name Jesus. He will be great and will be called the Son of the Most High. The Lord God will give him the throne of his father David, and he will reign over the house of Jacob forever; his kingdom will never end." "How will this be," Mary asked the angel, "since I am a virgin?" The angel answered, "The Holy Spirit will come upon you, and the power of the Most High will overshadow you. So the holy one to be born will be called the Son of God." Mary's faith was demonstrated in her response. Being a young girl who was waiting for her wedding day, she could have asked the angel that "What about my fiancée?" But she asked a logic question regarding how it will be since she was a virgin. Her ambition was about pleasing God. She did not dispute the message but wanted to be resolved by what means it would be brought about. Being pregnant while still a virgin is not normal; she wanted to

know how it will happen because people don't become pregnant by sharing cups. The angel gave her an account of the manner in which what he had said should be affected, for the strengthening of her faith. The moral lesson is that if God called you to go somewhere or to do something never give Him an excuse for not doing it. Not even your family is a valid excuse for not doing what God called you to do.

According to a new Pew Research, nine-in-ten Americans (90%) and 95% of Christians say they celebrate Christmas. The Pew study, based on interviews conducted in recent weeks with 1,503 adults, found that while a vast majority of Americans still celebrate Christmas, most of them do it as a favorite tradition as opposed to a religious obligation. Although Christmas is being secularized, the real threat is not against Christmas but against Christianity which has been undermined by liberalism. The world rejected Jesus from the beginning. Upon His birth, there was no room in the high places except in the manger. Much more, there is no room for Jesus in the hearts of the unbelieving and perishing world. The world will celebrate anything apart from Christ. Jesus said that "Very truly I tell you, you will weep and mourn while the world rejoices. You will grieve, but your grief will turn to joy" (John 16:20). He was prophetically predicting the circumstance surrounding His pending death and resurrection. "Verily, verily, I say unto you" is a strong asseveration, a way of speaking often used by Jesus, when he solemnly affirms anything, and would assure of the truth of it, as here: that you shall weep and lament; meaning an expression of mournful gestures by His disciples upon His death. They will be filled by inward grief, they shall weep and lament when He is taken away from them but the world will rejoice. The joy of the world began when Jesus was crucified. For a little while, the world got its way and succeeded in getting rid of Jesus, rolled a huge stone to His sepulcher to seal His fate, and staged armed soldiers as watchmen to keep Him away forever. But thank God that the power of the grave could not hold Him in the grave. He rose, and He is alive! The joy of the believers does not come from Christmas but from the resurrection of Jesus. "But your sorrow shall be turned into joy" - As it was when He was raised from the dead, which was so wonderful and surprising to His disciples; they could scarcely believe their own eyes when they saw Him alive; the occasion of their sorrow became the foundation of their joy. The joy of our salvation has its roots in the resurrected Christ. It is the joy of the Holy Spirit who is with us forever. Whereas the joy of the world is the absence of Christ in everything including Christmas; our joy is the presence of Jesus in us and in everything we do. It is an eternal joy from within!

Isaiah 9:6 – "For unto us a child is born, unto us a son is given: and the government shall be upon his shoulder: and his name shall be called Wonderful, Counselor, The mighty God, The everlasting Father, The Prince of Peace." The birth of Jesus was unnatural because it involved a virgin birth, without a male partner involved. This makes Jesus exclusively different from any other human being. He is God's only begotten Son. He was announced seven centuries before His birth: "The child is born" - This clause respects His humanity, His incarnation, and birth; it means He is human. "A Son is given" means He is of the same nature as God; He is divine. "Wonderful" means extraordinary magnificent and awesome. "Counselor" means He is the great counselor full of wisdom. He is the truth that guides us to the truth. "The mighty God" means God-the-Mighty-One; it means He is the creator of all things (John 1:2-3). God redeems by rebirth. Regeneration is the new nature of God born in us; it is ascribed to God. Christ is the author of the new creation. The Bible says concerning Him that "The Son is the image of the invisible God, the firstborn over all creation" (Colossians 1:15). He is the firstborn of every creature; not the first of the creation, or the first creature God made; for all things according to Colossians 1:16 are said to be created by him. He is the masterpiece after which all children of God are made (Ephesians 2:10). Everybody that is born of "Everlasting Father" means He is the source of our providence and protection now and eternally. Fatherhood is a recurring depiction, throughout the Bible, of the close relationship between the Creator and His people: "But now, O LORD, thou art our father; we are the clay, and thou our potter; and we all are the work of thy hand" (Isaiah 64:8). "The Prince of peace" means He brings peace to the world which the

world has not known before. He brings harmony and tranquility between God and man, and between man and man by reconciliation.

Matthew 2:9-11 - "After they had heard the king, they went on their way, and the star they had seen when it rose went ahead of them until it stopped over the place where the child was. When they saw the star, they were overjoyed. And when they [the wise men] had come into the HOUSE, they saw the young child with Mary his mother, and fell down and worshipped him". The wise men (Magi) were "from the East" according to verse 1; they are generally thought to be from Persia, which is east of Jerusalem. The star alerted the Magi to the birth of Christ, prompting them to make the long trek to Jerusalem. The star reappeared to the Magi at Jerusalem and led them to the house (not manger) at Bethlehem where Joseph and Mary settled with their little kid (not a baby) Jesus. Curiously, the Magi seem to have been the only ones who saw the star—or at least the only ones who understood its meaning. Unlike the natural stars we have in space, the star that led the Magi moved southwards. This was not an ordinary star but the star. This seems to be one of those incredible acts of God—specially designed and created for a unique purpose. Of course, God can use the natural laws to accomplish His will but this was a supernatural encounter, most probably in the same manner the conception of the King whom they were looking for involved a supernatural encounter. The Virgin Birth itself was a supernatural event that cannot be explained within the context of known natural laws. The Baby born and the circumstances surrounding Him were supernatural. God sent the angels from heaven to announce His birth and to direct the shepherds to the manger where He was born (Luke 2:8-18). The star led the wise men to the manger in the same way the glory of God (the Shekinah), the pillar of cloud by day, and of fire by night led the Israelites in the wilderness guiding them to God's intended destiny (the Promised Land). God guides what He commissions. The Word (gospel) leads us to the cross. The cross guides us vertically and horizontally: By the cross, we reach up to God and across to each

other. The Holy Spirit guides us in all truth. The people of great faith are individuals ready to follow His guidance.

Matthew 2:14-16 – "So he got up, took the child and his mother during the night and left for Egypt, "where he stayed until the death of Herod. This fulfilled what the Lord had spoken through the prophet: "Out of Egypt I called my Son."" Herod, waited for a proper time for the return of the wise men (Magi), and they didn't; he concluded that he was tricked and outwitted by them. He was furious, and he gave orders to kill all the little boys in Bethlehem and its vicinity who were two years old and under, in accordance with the time he had learned from the Magi. When the Magi promised to return, and bring to Herod the information about the kid (Jesus), they were serious. But they changed their minds after they received a divine oracle, were admonished and counseled by God. They thought it most advisable to obey God rather than man (Matthew 2:12). They departed to go to their own country another way. The moral lesson is that when you meet Jesus you don't go back the same way you came. "When they had gone, an angel of the Lord appeared to Joseph in a dream "Get up," he said, "take the child and his mother and escape to Egypt. Stay there until I tell you, for Herod is going to search for the child to kill him" (Matthew 2:13). This time Jesus escaped death because His time to die had not come. He escaped death this time so that He may die at Calvary so that we might escape death forever.

Matthew 2:19: "After Herod died, an angel of the Lord appeared in a dream to Joseph in Egypt. "Get up!" he said. "Take the Child and His mother and go to the land of Israel, for those seeking the Child's life are now dead." This was to fulfill the prophecy "When Israel was a child, then I loved him, and called my son out of Egypt. I loved him, and called my son out of Egypt" (Hosea 11:1). The first part of the verse is in reference to

Israel and the second part typically to the history of Messiah's childhood, in whom Israel reached its completeness.

Some people think that December 25th might have been chosen because the Winter Solstice and the ancient pagan Roman midwinter festivals called 'Saturnalia' and 'Dies Natalis Solis Invicti' took place in December around this date - so it was a time when people already celebrated things. The Roman pagan celebration was actually not carried out on the 25th December but was carried out from 17th to 23rd December.

The Second Coming of Christ

The return of our Lord is divided into two parts: The rapture and Second coming of Christ on earth. The rapture is intended to catch away the saints to meet Jesus in the air. The rapture is imminent. It means that we are not waiting for any sign predicting the rapture; it can happen anytime. Paul thought it would happen during his times (Rom. 13:11-12). He said that we shall be changed and caught up; suddenly, in a moment, in the twinkling of an eye (1 Thessalonians 4:17). The promised signs we see precede the Second Coming of Jesus Christ when He will return to rule over the new heaven and earth for a thousand years (Revelation 20:6-7). We are seeing the hazardous of nature in form of landslides, floods, earthquakes and etc. This summer has been bad for some people, and winter will be worse. God does not cause the weather disasters but He warned that they will happen. If God is not the cause, then the extraordinary weather tragedies are orchestrated works of the Prince of the Air (Satan) and the demons, and we are hurtling towards the worst. We are not supposed to watch on the sidelines helplessly. We must fight back. The Bible says that "For our struggle is not against flesh and blood, but against the rulers, against the authorities, against the powers of this dark world and against the spiritual forces of evil in the heavenly realms" (Ephesians 6:12). We were given the power in the name of Jesus to counteract such tragedies (Mark 16:17). Remember that Jesus rebuked the wind and said to the waves, "Quiet! Be still!", and the wind died down and it was completely calm (Mark 4:39). Jesus in a majestic and authoritative way reproved the wind as if it was a servant that had exceeded his commission. He proved that He is the most high God, who gathers the winds in his fists, and stills the noise of the seas and their waves. He can work for us when we pray. There is nothing impossible to Jesus. He can heal a tumor, in the same way, He heals a pimple. He can eradicate the drought, in the same way, He can stop the floods. But we must pray. The question is why pray when God predicted that the hazardous conditions will happen? We can pray for our spiritual strength and for our safety. Unlike the Great Tribulation, the source of trouble during the Tribulation period is the devil. Jesus warned regarding the tribulation that, "If those days had not been cut short, no one would survive, but for the sake of the elect those days will be shortened" (Matthew 24:22). God has always and will preserve a seed, a remnant, according to the election of grace that should be saved.

2 Corinthians 11:14 - "And no wonder, for Satan himself masquerades as an angel of light." The scripture conveys the idea that Satan is ever transforming himself such that it is easy to mistaken a satanic for an angelic apparition. Satan is incapable of creating anything and he is not omnipotent but he can cause every good thing that God created for us to enjoy to work against us. The real identity of Satan is the angel of darkness. Behind every manifestation of evil, there is a hand of Satan. One of the ways Satan disguises as an angel of the light is by taking credit for the good things done and attributing the bad things to God. For example, recently I read some posted messages falsely accusing God of the menace caused by the storm in Texas. God judged the world before with the floods and He promised that He will not do it again, except in the Great Tribulation after the Church (the restrainer of God's wrath) is taken away. Certainly, Satan is the source of all the problems which we experience in the current period of tribulation. Every good thing comes from God because after He created everything, He gave a benediction that "it is very good" (Genesis 1:31): Very good in itself, and in its use. It means evil was not part of God's creation; evil comes from Satan. The redeemed of Christ overcame Satan but we can still be vulnerable to his wiles, stratagems, and cunning devices

because although we have the power over sin, we are still in the presence of sin. Satan's major ally is the corrupt minds. God renews the minds by the Word after transforming the heart. A clean conscience purged by the blood of Jesus strives to be as holy as God. If the doors of perception were cleansed everything would appear to man as God intended it to be.

Genesis 18:24-25 - "Far be it from you to do such a thing—to kill the righteous with the wicked, treating the righteous and the wicked alike. Far be it from you! Will not the Judge of all the earth do right?" Abraham acknowledged God as the supreme righteous Judge, for there is no unrighteousness in Him, who will judge righteous judgment but also as a Mediator, whose ways and works portray, not strict rigorous justice, but a mixture of mercy with justice because all have sinned and fall sort of the glory of God. Abraham pleaded with God compared to an earthly judge who administers justice but with moderation and clemency. The Judge of all the earth will show mercy, and in the midst of deserved wrath remember it, and not deal according to the rules of inexorable and inflexible justice, and to this sense, the answer of the Lord inclines to Abraham's request. Abraham called it as a thing unbecoming for the divine Majesty, and contrary to the nature and perfections of God to judge the righteous with the unrighteous. The righteous in this case is not perfect because we cannot be perfect by our own merits; they are those who earned God's mercy. Abraham knew that the Judge of all the earth would do right. He does not plead that the wicked ones may be spared for their own sake or because it would be severe to destroy them, but for the sake of the righteous who might be found among them. And righteousness only can be made a plea before God. God replied that for the sake of as little as ten righteous he will not destroy the city. But God did not find even ten righteous people in Sodom. He resorted to evacuating the family of Lot, which found the favor of God, before pouring His wrath on the city. The Church is the preservative preventing God's wrath to be poured on the world. However, God's wrath will be poured over the world, as His judgment, during the Great Tribulation. The tribulations which are currently experienced by all of us (the righteous and the unrighteous) are

attributed to the devil. Remember that the earth was judged when Adam sinned, and it is functioning contrary to the original divine plan. Sin is the cause of our tribulations, and the suffering will intensify during the end times. But God's wrath against the sins of the world will not be poured out equally on the righteous and the unrighteous. The doctrine of rapture projects the catching (taking) away of the Church before the period of the Great Tribulation to save us from the wrath of God.

Luke 12:37 – "Blessed are those servants, whom the lord when he cometh shall find watching: verily I say unto you, that he shall gird himself, and make them to sit down to meat, and will come forth and serve them." The title "blessed," when used by our Lord, is ever a very lofty one, and implies some rare and precious virtue in the one to whom this title to honor is given. It will be a happy moment for those servants whom the Master will find watching. Watching is the opposite of being asleep or dormant; it is a status of alertness, activeness, and readiness. Those who received Him as their Savior upon His First Coming must also be ready and prepared to receive Him upon His Second Coming. They are the ones who serve God wholeheartedly. They are the ones who are about their Father's business because He assigned it to them. We should always be ready because we are uncertain as to the time of His coming to us. The phrase "Will come forth and serve them with food" is an expression of a servant who goes round about the table, whilst others sit. It means that Jesus shall stand to minister unto the faithful servants. "He shall gird himself" is an image in reference to His servanthood attitude. Jesus will appear in His glory, as the King of kings (not in the form of a servant), but He will indeed serve us (His servants) by readily and cheerfully introducing and immersing us into His eternal joy. He will make us partakers of His eternal glory. He will crown the saints with the glory of His victory. And we will worship Him by casting our crowns at His feet, before the throne; signifying that we received them undeservingly by His grace; the One sitting on the throne (Jesus) is the only one worthy to wear them. If we value the beauty of the coming glory, we cannot crave for the luxuries which this world has to

offer. It is in Christ alone that we can enjoy the fullness of life. I mean the cream of this life and the everlasting life in the presence of God.

Question: Who are the two witnesses of Revelation 11:3–12? There are several speculations regarding the identity of the two witnesses. Although there is no foundation, either in this text or elsewhere, some of the ancient Christian fathers, and of the Papists, as Lyra and others, taught that Elijah with Enoch will come before the Day of Judgment, and restore the church of God ruined by the antichrist. Some suggest that it will be Moses and Elijah. Generally, Enoch and Elijah are seen as the possibilities for the two witnesses because they are the two individuals whom God has taken to heaven without experiencing death (Genesis 5:23; 2Kings 2:11). However, the problem is that although Elijah and Enoch never physically died, they can't be in heaven in their mortal bodies. The Bible says that flesh and blood cannot see heaven (1 Corinthians 15:50). In the Jewish writings the phrase "flesh and blood" is a distinguishing mark between what belongs to man from what belongs to God. If they are already in their immortal status it is impossible for them to die unless they put on the mortal bodies. I think if Enoch and Elijah are the two witnesses, God is perfectly capable of taking the two "ordinary" believers, living on the earth today, and put the spirit of Enoch and Elijah over them enabling them to perform the same signs and wonders that Elijah did. Remember that Jesus said concerning John the Baptist that "And if you are willing to accept it, he is the Elijah who was to come" (Matthew 11:14). This same person, "John the Baptist", is Elijah (Elias), which was to come; who was appointed by God to come, and was prophesied of Malachi 4:5 that he should come because the spirit of Elijah was on John the Baptist. John the Baptist's office as forerunner began its 'decrease' and Christ's redemptive mission began to 'increase.' The Bible says concerning Elijah that "And he will go on before the Lord, in the spirit and power of Elijah, to turn the hearts of the parents to their children and the disobedient to the wisdom of the righteous—to make ready a people prepared for the Lord." (Luke 1:17). Elijah was given the ministry to be the forerunner of the Messiah. He is unique because of the particular office he holds as the forerunner of both the First and Second

Coming of Christ to earth. As I said, it is most likely that God will pick two ordinary believers to come in the spirit of Elijah and Enoch as the two witnesses who will be given extraordinary power.

Question: "The recent massive floods are believed to be signs of the end times. Can the evil spirits cause floods? Answer: Yes they can. First, Satan is behind the evil decisions which people make. Demons are the unseen evil powers controlling this dark world including the sea world. I will use the following examples to support my answer: Mark 6:48-50 – "And he saw them toiling in rowing; for the wind was contrary unto them: and about the fourth watch of the night he cometh unto them, walking upon the sea, and would have passed by them. But when they saw him walking upon the sea, they supposed it had been a spirit, and cried out: For they all saw him, and were troubled. And immediately he talked with them, and saith unto them, Be of good cheer: it is I; be not afraid." Much of Jesus' ministry occurred around the Sea of Galilee, and He sometimes used the symbolism of the sea to challenge His disciples and to demonstrate His power. We know that this world (nature), like us (people), is under the curse of Adam; it is groaning for its redemption. During the biblical times, geographically, the sea's location made it subject to sudden and violent storms. Storms often developed when an east wind dropped cool air over the warm air rising from the sea. This sudden change produced surprisingly furious storms in a short time (Matt. 8:24). Understandably, these fierce storms scared ancient people and caused them to avoid large bodies of water. When Jesus walked on the water amidst the storms, His disciples thought it was a ghost. There is a valid reason why the disciples jumped to a false conclusion that it was not Jesus walking on the water but a ghost (evil spirit). Cultural stories depicted the sea as a monstrous beast and a place where Baal would battle other gods. Set amidst this culture, the Jewish people also feared the sea. They were rooted in the wilderness, and they saw the sea as an alien and threatening power. Few could swim, and even fisherman avoided deep water. Not surprisingly, biblical writers often used the sea to describe terror and danger.

Spiritually, in Jesus' day, Jewish people recognized the sea as a symbol of chaos, abyss, and hell. Jesus told His disciples that "Truly I tell you, if anyone says to this mountain, 'Go, throw yourself into the sea,' and does not doubt in their heart but believes that what they say will happen, it will be done for them (Mark 11:23). The mountain represents every troublesome situation including demonic influences; by faith in Christ, they can be cast it into the sea. Another correspondent story is when Jesus was traveling in the hilly region east of the Jordan River, the path of the man who was controlled by demons and lived among the tombs (Matthew 8:28-32). Jesus thereby made known His authority and thwarted whatever evil purpose the demons had over the man. Jesus demonstrated His power over demons by casting them out of the man. In the same way, we have the power to cast them out in the name of Jesus. The evil spirit begged Him to enter a herd of pigs. The demons may have made this strange request because it was their last chance to avoid confinement in the Abyss, the place of confinement to which evil spirits are doomed (Revelation 9:1-6). Jesus gave them permission to enter the pigs. The evil spirits caused the pigs to rush down the steep bank into the lake, and the pigs were drowned. Why did the evil spirit drown the pigs? The lake is the place of influence where evil spirits have dominion. Definitely, the pigs perished in the water but not the evil spirits because water cannot suffocate spirits. In the fallen world, the evil spirits control the waters of the seas. It is not a coincidence that in ancient times, most of the big lakes and rivers were called places of gods. For example in Uganda, Lake Victoria was called 'Nalubaale', the word for place of traditional gods (Lubaale). The "Queen of India's sea" is the head of Marine kingdom, while the "Queen of the Coast" is next in command and resides within the Atlantic Ocean. It is said that both are also among the fallen angels and travel in the form of half humanoid and half fish. In many occult practices, the source of the witchcraft is water base, where these water spirits are contacted for supernatural powers. The word 'sea' is often used in the Bible to describe the ungodly world. The book of Revelation says, "The sea gave up the dead that were in it, and death and Hades gave up the dead that were in them, and each person was judged according to what they had done" (Revelation 20:13).

Jesus said concerning His return that, "But about that day or hour no one knows, not even the angels in heaven, nor the Son, but only the Father. (Matthew 24:36). Jesus used the metaphor of the Jewish wedding to explain His return. According to their customs, the father determines when the groom picks up the bride. It is from the same perspective Jesus said that "Concerning that day and hour no one knows except the father." Christ is the groom; the church is His bride. We are going to look at the Jewish wedding in details in order to understand the pending wedding feast.

The Jewish wedding - The first step, the Ketubah, or Betrothal, was the establishment of the marriage covenant, usually when the prospective bridegroom took the initiative and negotiated the price (mohair) he must pay to purchase her. Once the bridegroom paid the purchase price, the marriage covenant was established, and the young man and woman were regarded as husband and wife. From that moment on, the bride was declared to be consecrated or sanctified - set apart - exclusively for her bridegroom. In the same way, Jesus purchased us by His blood and sanctified us by His spirit, to set us apart for Himself.

As a symbol of the covenant relationship that had been established, the groom and bride drank from a cup of wine over which the betrothal had been pronounced. After the marriage covenant was established, the groom left his bride at her home and returned to his father's house, where he remained separated from his bride for a period of time, sometimes up to approximately 12 months. This afforded the bride time to gather her trousseau and prepare for married life. During this period of separation, the groom prepared a dwelling place in his father's house to which he would later bring his bride. When I went to Jerusalem, I discovered that most homes were storey houses which appeared as if they were still under construction, ready to add another floor on top. Our guide told us that the tradition has been passed on from generation to generation, for a father to build his house that way in anticipation for his sons to add more floors on top in case they get married. The father of the bride is the only one who had the right to determine that the place is ready and to authorize the groom to go and pick up his bride. The bride had to be ready to be picked up by the groom anytime without notification. Jesus used the metaphor of the Jewish wedding to explain His return.

At the end of the period of separation, the bridegroom came - usually at night - to take his bride to live with him. The groom, the best man, and other male escorts left the father's house and conducted a torch-light procession to the home of the bride. Although the bride was expecting her groom to come for her, she did not know the time of his coming. As a result, the groom's arrival was preceded by a shout, which announced her imminent departure to be gathered with him. After the groom received his bride, together with her female attendants, the enlarged wedding party returned from the bride's home to the groom's father's house, where the wedding guests had assembled. Shortly after their arrival, the bride and groom were escorted by the other members of the wedding party to the bridal chamber (huppah). Prior to entering the chamber, the bride remained veiled so that no one could see her face. While the groomsmen and bridesmaids waited outside, the bride and groom entered the bridal chamber alone. There, in the privacy of that place, they entered into physical union for the first time, thereby consummating the marriage that had been covenanted approximately one year earlier. After the marriage was consummated, the groom came out of the bridal chamber and announced the consummation of the marriage to the members of the wedding party waiting outside. Then, as the groom went back to his bride in the chamber, the members of the wedding party returned to the wedding guests and announced the consummation of the marriage. Upon receiving the good news, the wedding guests remained in the groom's father's house for the next seven days, celebrating with a great wedding feast (part of the story was posted by Brad Piteau).

Hosea 2:19-20 - "And I will betroth you to Me forever; Yes, I will betroth you to Me in righteousness and in justice, In lovingkindness and in compassion, And I will betroth you to Me in faithfulness. Then you will know the Lord". Men and women were betrothed when they were engaged to be married. The Church is the bride prepared for our Bridegroom (Jesus Christ). Until Jesus comes back, we are not actually married to Him, we are betrothed to Him. Betroth is to promise "by one's truth." We are betrothed forever by virtue of the blood of Jesus and the deposited dowry

of the Holy Spirit who indwells every believer. Jesus is coming for the bride (Church) without wrinkle or spot. He is sanctifying her, cleansing her by the washing with water through the Word so as to present her to Himself as a radiant Church, without stain. Like in any marital relationship, Jesus knew prior to our engagement that there are going to be weaknesses in us to fix; and He is not surprised when those weaknesses surface. Also, we cannot perform beyond expectations. It is a continuity relationship of appeasement involving our surrendering. He strips us of the rags of our self-righteousness and dresses us (the bride) in the robes of His very righteousness, then we become as a bride, adorned with ornaments, and so made ready for the nuptials. "Let us rejoice and be glad and give the glory to Him, for the marriage of the Lamb has come and His bride has made herself ready." [8] And it was given to her to clothe herself in fine linen, bright and clean; for the fine linen is the righteous acts of the saints. [9] And he said to me, "Write, 'Blessed are those who are invited to the marriage supper of the Lamb.' "And he said to me, "These are true words of God."(Revelation 19:7-9). We are called by His name, Christians, and partake of His honor; He is King, and we are queen; and a very beneficial relation it is, for all that Christ is, and has, are ours; and a most marvelous and wondrous thing it is that He should betroth us to Himself, when He is the Son of the living God, Himself the true God, God over all blessed forever, the Maker and Ruler of the world, and heir of all things. Right now, we are God's image bearer positioned on the earth to decorate this world with His beauty for His glory. Will you let Him clothe you with His righteousness?

Matthew 24:12 - "And many false prophets will arise and mislead many. And because iniquity shall abound, the love of many shall wax cold. But the one who perseveres to the end will be saved." The abounding iniquity in this scripture means the malice and wickedness due to the errors and heresies of the false teachers, the consequence of which would be a great fall away. This message is written concerning the believers who embraced the Christian dogma of loving God with all their heart, mind and soul. But due to the principles of the false teachers, their love for God

will gradually diminish. According to the scripture, the agape love will grow cold, even though there may still be brotherly love, kindness, and human affection. The Bible says that agape love is shown to God through our obedience— so when disobedience increases, agape love grows cold. In the book of Revelation, Jesus wrote a letter to Ephesus saying that: "Yet I hold this against you: You have forsaken the love you had at first. Therefore, keep in mind how far you have fallen. Repent and perform the deeds you did at first." (Revelation 2:4-5). When there is a compromise or the setting aside of God's standard of righteousness and holiness, then the submissive love toward God and the sacrificial love toward man will begin to grow cold. It is a simple cause-and-effect relationship. The love for God can only be substituted with the love for 'self'. Self-love is the after product of the lack of fear of God. Self-love is automatically attracted to the love of the world, and the carnal ease that comes in with the pleasures of this life. "But the one who perseveres to the end will be saved." There is hope because the remnant (God's elect), in whom He is well pleased, who were chosen in Christ, before the foundation of the world will endure to the end. It is a calling to us to give the diligence to make our calling and election sure by discerning truthfulness from falsehood; the Spirit of God from the spirit of the age.

Matthew 7:22-23 – "Many will say to Me on that day, 'Lord, Lord, did we not prophesy in Your name, and in Your name drive out demons and perform many miracles? Then I will tell them plainly, 'I never knew you. Depart from me, ye workers of iniquity." He will say to them "Away from me, you evildoers!'" this being the punishment of loss, and being sent to the everlasting fire. "I never knew you" means that to know Christ is to be known by Him. 'Works of inequities' expression may be in reference to people in two categories: 1) Those who confessed Christ but lived the contradictory lives. 2) Those who confessed Christ, and were neither adulterers, nor murderers, nor drunkards, or involved any other openly profane sinners; but in as much as they did the work of the Lord deceitfully for their own glory; sought their own things, what they did, they did with a wicked mind, and not with a view to his glory. The grace does not sanction

us to do as we will. To be born again is to acquire the new nature, the character, and the will of Christ. I want to emphasize that this scripture does not mean that salvation is merited by our good works. It means that those who are truly saved must have evidence of the characters of the Savior. Hell is going to be filled with people who were baptized, went to church regularly, exercised the gifts of the Holy Spirit, and gave money to the work of God but who were not truly born again. Good works cannot earn us salvation even when they are done in the name of Jesus. Jesus approves only the works He does in and through us because even the best of our good works are like filthy rags before God. This is what Paul meant when he said: "Every man's work shall be made manifest: for the day shall declare it, because it shall be revealed by fire; and the fire shall try every man's work of what sort it is" (1 Corinthians 3:13). It is the testing fire of the Day of the Lord that will flitter and separate His works in and through us from the works of the flesh.

While exiled on the island of Patmos, the apostle John received a revelation from Jesus Christ that we now call the book of Revelation. In this vision, Christ gave John seven messages for seven first-century churches in Asia Minor. The church of Ephesus had many positive qualities; Christ commended them in five specific ways—they were dynamic, dedicated, determined, disciplined, and discerning (Revelation 2:2-3). But verse 4 reveals where they went wrong. "Nevertheless, I have this against you, that you have left your first love." The ancient church in Smyrna. They suffered because of pressure, poverty, and persecution (Revelation 2:9). Pergamos was nicknamed "Satan's City." The Christians in Pergamos were surrounded by pagan beliefs and practices. In spite of their faithfulness in some areas, the Christians in Pergamos had compromised their faith in others. They had allowed idolatry to creep into their congregation. The ancient church in Thyatira allowed an immoral individual to lead many others away from Christ (Revelation 2:20). Like the church in Thyatira, there are Christians and churches today who feel a need to be relevant and all-inclusive when it comes to spiritual and moral boundaries. With the church of Sardis there are no commendations; Christ begins immediately with a denunciation: "I know your works, that you have a name that you are alive, but you are dead." The church was full of what we today would call "nominal Christians"—Christians in name only. Christ gives specific directions for the church that is dead. Then Christ recommended the church in Philadelphia for four things: they have an open door, they have a little strength, they have kept the Word of God, and they have not denied the Lord. The church in Philadelphia is the model of the congregation we are supposed to imitate. The church in Laodicea was lacking in every way. It was a compromising, conceited, and Christless church and Christ said that it made Him sick (Revelation 3:16). The messages to the seven churches represent the qualities and nature of our congregations today.

Turkey: In the New Testament, three churches in the Lycus River valley in Asia Minor sounded forth the word of God. Paul wrote an epistle to the church at Colosse and mentioned the brethren at Laodicea and Hierapolis. Laodicea was also one of the "seven churches of Asia" mentioned by John in the book of Revelation.

Matthew 13:30 – "'No,' he said, 'if you pull the weeds now, you might uproot the wheat with them. Let both grow together until the harvest. At that time I will tell the harvesters: First collect the weeds and tie them in bundles to be burned; then gather the wheat and bring it into my barn.'" Jesus gave to us a sample of the kind of congregations we are going to have in our churches; it includes the fake and genuine believers. There is no such thing as a perfect local church made up of perfect people. The "wheat" or true believers are repented-sinners under the grace. They grow in the exercise of grace, as of faith, hope, love, humility, and in spiritual knowledge of the will of God, of the doctrines of grace, and of Christ; which growth is owing to the dews of divine grace. The tares are not God's own plantation. They confess Christ without sincere repentance and the leap of faith to practice what they believe. Whenever there is the proclamation of the truth there are those who fake to live it but in actuality,

their lives are intoxicated with false faith and are guided by the spirit of the age instead of the Holy Spirit. Today, the false doctrine of quick material gains for selfish reasons has attracted tares to Christianity. Faith is not self-centered but others-centered. The last part of the scripture says, "Let both grow together until the harvest". It is not our duty to sort the tares out. Jesus will do that at the end of the harvest. The rapture and the end time judgment are called times of the harvest. It means the separation of good from the corrupt world. "At that time I will tell the harvesters", the harvesters are the angels. Jesus will return with a visible cloud of angels to affect the gathering together of all the elect (harvest) to him. "And he will send his angels and gather his elect from the four winds, from the ends of the earth to the ends of the heavens." (Mark 13:27).

In the end times, Satan will make one last (and almost successful) attempt to consolidate religion around himself, and to rule in God's stead. The satanic trinity consists of: (1) Satan himself (2) A man called Antichrist (3) A figure called The False Prophet. The false god is symbolized by a dragon; the false christ is symbolized by a beast out of the sea; the false spirit is symbolized by a beast out of the earth. The book of Revelation describes towards the end, when the unholy false trinity are destroyed. The serpent, the dragon and the beast and the false prophet and the city that man has built in his self-centered, anthropocentric adoration and worship will be destroyed. Fallen is Babylon, and then comes down from heaven that new Jerusalem, the city of God, the garden expanded into the whole world where John tells us in the book of Revelation, there was no temple. And the reason there was no temple is because there, everything will be temple. The people of God serving Him, lost in wonder and love and praise. Every saint will be a temple where worship is made and from where it comes forth, the choir director of which is Christ. Then the glory of God will fill this earth as the waters of the seas.

The Antichrist is called by many names: The incarnation of sin; the embodiment of evil; the son of perdition; the abomination and desolation; the Beast.

1 John 3:2 - "Dear friends, now we are children of God, and what we will be has not yet been made known. But we know that when Christ appears, we shall be like him, for we shall see him as he is." Children of God are supposed to be of the same nature and essence as God, their Father. We have a conception of what we shall be. Now we are walking like Christ but at glorification, the Christians will ultimately be like Christ. The transfiguration of Jesus was a preview of what we may look like when Jesus returns (Matthew 17:1-2). The scriptures states that "We know that when He shall appear" that is, Jesus Christ, who is now in heaven, and out of sight, to whom we are intimately related by His Spirit, but will appear a second time: the time when is not known, but this one thing is certain: we shall be like Him; in body, fashioned like to His glorious body, in immortality and incorruption, in power, in glory, and spirituality, in a freedom from all imperfections, sorrows, afflictions, and death; and in soul, which likeness will lie in perfect knowledge of divine things, and in complete holiness. At glorification, God will be seen as He is in Christ; and Christ will be seen as He is in Himself, both in His divine and human natures, as much as can be, or can be desired to be seen and known of Him. We now have power over Satan in the name of Jesus but in future, we shall be like Christ and rule with Him over Satan. Satan knows it and he hates it. Satan lost the war against Jesus but he is still fighting the believers purposely to delay the return of our Lord; he is basically resisting his designated place, which is being under the control of the believers. Satan is resisting the revelation of the ultimate image of Christ in us.

Revelation 1:14 - "The hair on his head was white like wool, as white as snow, and his eyes were like blazing fire." Jesus' hair appeared as white as wool symbolic of the righteousness of God and His mission to execute

justice. White hair is symbolic of a mature person of respect and honor regardless of their race. In this case, Jesus represents the God of ancient days, of heaven and earth. The color of the hair is the point of comparison; signifying purity and glory in which image we were created. During colonial times all judges were required to wear the white wool-like hair coverings over their heads while they were behind their benches symbolic of their responsibility to deliver the righteous judging. Unfortunately, the judges of today are apolitical. There are judges who ground their rulings on logical, unbiased interpretations of our Constitution, our laws and our place in history, but for the most part, the ideal has been killed. Most times, the rulings regarding most cases depend on whether a judge is a liberal or a conservative. On the contrary, the courts were designed and expected to be at least somewhat free of the politics that plague the other branches of government. Justice is synonymous with righteousness. Jesus is the righteous Judge that executes justice without bias.

God seats on the throne but the throne does not make Him God. God is infinite who is actually not limited by His own creation (matter, space and time); He can exist independently of it. The Bible says that the heaven and earth cannot contain God (2 Chronicles 2:6; 1 Kings 8:27); wherever God is, His throne is there also. God said that "Heaven is My throne, and earth is My footstool." (Isaiah 66:1). The transcendent god existing beyond the physical universe chose the Ark in the tabernacle as His footstool where He can meet with His people. Certainly, God has the throne but the Bible projects several other thrones established by God. Jesus said to His disciples that, "Assuredly I say to you, that in the regeneration, when the Son of Man sits on the throne of His glory, you who have followed Me will also sit on twelve thrones, judging the twelve tribes of Israel" (Matthew 19:28). The Book of Revelation talks about "thrones". Revelation 4:4 speaks of "twenty-four thrones". The book of Revelation specifically says that there are two thrones of the end time's judgment: The Judgment Seat of Christ, which occurs at the Marriage Supper of the Lamb in Heaven. At the judgment seat of Christ (Bema), the believers are rewarded based on how faithfully they served Christ (Revelation 22:12). The judgment seat of Christ does not determine salvation; that was determined by Christ's sacrifice on our behalf (1 John 2:2) and our faith in Him (John 3:16). All of our sins were forgiven when we received Jesus Christ as our Lord and Savior, and we will never be condemned for them (Romans 8:1). The other throne is the great white throne judgment; it is for those who are resurrected unto death. It is a throne of condemnation set up for all unrighteous souls who do not have the righteousness of God through Christ. It is not going to be in heaven because non-repented sinners will not go to heaven. The white throne judgment is described in Revelations 20:11-15, and it is the final judgment prior to the lost being cast into the lake of fire. We know that this judgment will take place after the millennium (about 1000 years later) and after Satan, the beast, and the false prophet are thrown into the lake of fire (Revelation 20:7-15).

"Iran's Supreme Leader says Israel 'will not exist in 25 years' Benjamin Netanyahu warns Iran Israel is a 'tiger, not a rabbit' after latest threat". Prophetic: Zechariah 12:2 - "Behold, I will make Jerusalem a cup of trembling unto all the people round about, when they shall be in the siege both against Judah and against Jerusalem." The phrase "a cup of trembling" also translated as "a vessel full of inebriating liquor;" which intoxicates and makes giddy, and causes to tremble, stagger, and fall like a drunken man. The phrase denotes the punishment inflicted by the Lord upon the enemies of Israel. Calvin with the Septuagint translates, "threshold of destruction," on which they shall stumble and be crushed when they attempt to cross it.

Wisdom

James 1:5 - "If any of you lack wisdom, let him ask of God, that giveth to all men liberally, and upbraideth not; and it shall be given him." Wisdom is the ability to apply the truth to knowledge. The search for wisdom is forever as long as you are living. There is no college to graduate in wisdom. The English Standard Version says that if any of you lacks wisdom, let him ask God, who gives generously to all without reproach, and it will be given. He will not rebuke you for asking, and there is no tuition required.

Wisdom is knowing the right path to take. Integrity is taking it.

"The door to your mind is always open. Do not be a careless doorkeeper! Keep watch over the thoughts that enter..."

Unless people are educated, there is no medicine for stupidity!

Happiness is the greatest deception if you are ignorant of the causes of true happiness!

Feeling gratitude and not expressing it is like wrapping a present and not giving it. ~ William Arthur Ward

Maybe it's time you become selfish, unapologetic and blatantly honest; stop trying to make people happy at your expense. Some people are not and will never be grateful. They will still treat you bad no matter how hard you try. The "selfish beast in them will always be ungrateful." Help in anticipation of no return. At times, just walk away and focus on being the best you can be.

Noise pollution is a public nuisance, a health hazard. It can kill. I vowed never to be a noise pollution offender.

"Don't kill people with your kindness because everybody deserves your kindness. Kill people with your silence because not everyone deserves your attention"

The best pill to swallow is your pride. "There's no shame in admitting what you don't know. The only shame is pretending you know all the answers."

The only reason pride lifts you higher is to let you hit the flour harder!

"If you have to hesitate choosing between me, and someone else, pick them."

The love of beauty is taste. The creation of beauty is art ~ Ralph Waldo Emerson

"The things I have seen have taught me to trust the creator for the things I haven't seen." ~ Ralph Waldo Emerson

The world is a book, and those who don't travel only read one page ~ St Augustine

"Don't drain yourself trying to satisfy people who only love you when it benefits them."

"A great man [woman] is always willing to be little." ~ Emerson

Getting your mind right and getting your mouth right means getting your life right. Changing your perception means changing your position. Real change begins with the transformation of the heart by God.

Unless you will change, adjust and improve, it is better not to tamper with change.

Some silences are heavy sagging under the weight of the words unsaid.

Not knowing is better than regretting that you wish you never knew.

"If you have nothing nice to say don't say anything at all."

"Knowing when to be silent is a very wise thing. Quiet people have the loudest minds."

A wise man's ears are the grave yard where gossip dies and is buried.

"Two things to remember in Life: Take care of your thoughts when you are alone, and take care of your words when you are with people." ~ Sam Kyeyune

When someone's words cut like a knife, forgiveness stops the bleeding and puts in the stitches.

Matthew 12:36 – "But I say unto you, that every idle word that men shall speak, they shall give account thereof in the Day of Judgment." Idle words are careless words spoken about others. They might be false accusation spoken out of malice or truth spoken with bad intents to hurt others.

"You are the Gardner of your own soul. Plant your own garden and decorate your own soul instead of letting someone else to do it and leave you with wilted flowers".

If it ain't ok with God; it ain't ok with me.

"Worrying is like paying a debt that may never come due." ~ Victor Torres

Nothing is more beautiful than a confident woman who doesn't pretend to be something she's not.

"Affairs are easier of entrance than of exit, and it is but common prudence to see our way out before we venture in". ~ Aesop

"The truth is that everybody is going to hurt you: you just gotta find the ones worth suffering for" ~ Bob Marley

If you aim at nothing, you will always hit the target!

"Anyone who has ever struggled with poverty knows how extremely expensive is to be poor". ~ James Baldwin

Good things come the hard way. "Often the prickly thorn produces tender roses".

It is not the man who has too little, but the man who craves more that is poor!

"A man with a reputation of giving makes more enemies when he is broke than a stingy man!" ~ David Mukisa

Inconsistent people are like unpaved roads; full of unseen bumps and lots of wrong turns.

"Sincerity and competence is a strong combination. In politics, it is everything." ~ Peggy Noonan

"Once you hit rock bottom, that's where you perfectly stand; that's your chance of restarting, but restarting the right way." ~ Justin Kanayurak

"Education is what remains after one has forgotten what one has learned in school." ~ Albert Einstein

I'll always choose the man who taught me something over the one who bought me something.

Whenever the people of the world reject you, never have disappointments; remember that you don't belong to the world. "I believe that rejection is a blessing because it's the universe's way of telling you that there's something better out there." ~ Michelle Phan

"Sometimes I feel my whole life has been one big rejection." Rejection is part of life. I have been rejected plenty of times that I no longer flinch a bit when it happens.

Intelligent people are easily annoyed by people in general but tend to say nothing in an attempt to avoid meaningless arguments.

Virtues can be faked. Depravities are real.

Self is your greatest enemy. "If you can't change your Attitude, you simply become your own Demon!"

"You can't soar with the eagles as long as you're pecking around with the chicken."

A fear faced is a fear erased!

The "invisible" is just as important as "visible"… Hence a battle is first won or lost in the mind before it was ever fought.

"Nobody cares how much you know until they know how much you care." A friend is the one who increases your joy by subtracting your sorrow; one who moves in when everyone is moving out.

Proverbs:

Proverbs 4:23 - "Above all else, guard your heart, for everything you do flows from it."

\# The good head plans but only the heart truly binds. Faith is the key that fits the lock of everybody's heart to unlock the benevolence of life.

Proverbs 24:17 – 18 – "Rejoice not when thine enemy falleth, and let not thine heart be glad when he stumbleth: Lest the LORD see [it], and it displeases him, and he turns away his wrath from him."

\# Vengeance is of God. "Allow your enemies their space to hate; they will destroy themselves in the process".

Proverbs 27:5 - "Better is open rebuke than hidden love."

\# I'd rather be "hurt" with the truth any day than kissed with a lie! (Of course, rebuke done in love, is preferred, rather than not.) As iron sharpens iron...

Proverbs 16:28 - "A perverse person stirs up conflict, and a gossip separates close friends."

\# The apathy of the sycophant is compared to a horde of hungry hyenas aimed not to keep you on a pedestal, but to isolate you in a cage.

Proverbs 16:9 – "A man's heart plans his way, But the Lord directs his steps".

\# Your life isn't an accident. You have a destiny. Faith is allowing God to direct your steps to your intended destiny.

Proverbs 22:2 - "The rich and poor meet together: the LORD is the maker of them all."

Hold on to God and He will hold on to you. "He causes his sun to rise on the evil and the good, and sends rain on the righteous and the unrighteous" (Matthew 5:45).

Proverbs 9:17 – "Stolen waters are sweet, and bread eaten in secret is pleasant."

Satan always gives the best first and the worst last. The sweet morsel of sin ends up into a disaster.

Proverbs 18:24 - "One who has unreliable friends soon comes to ruin, but there is a friend who sticks closer than a brother."

A true friend will show respect to you even when you don't deserve it; not as a reflection of your character but a reflection of his character.

Proverbs 12:26 – "One who is righteous is a guide to his neighbor, but the way of the wicked leads them astray."

Be a blessing rather than a snare to someone. Bless others in anticipation for your blessing.

Proverbs 27:21 - "The crucible for silver and the furnace for gold, but people are tested by their praise."

As the crucible brings all impurities to the surface, so public opinion drags forth all that is bad in a man, and he who stands this test is generally esteemed.

Proverbs 14:34 – "Righteousness exalts a nation, but sin condemns any people."

The prosperity of the nation depends on the spiritual prosperity of the people. God uses the righteous people to change the course of the nation.

Proverbs 26:5 – "Answer a fool according to his folly, lest he be wise in his own conceit."

You need to use wisdom in order to get wisdom. There is time to say nothing in the presence of a fool. Hold your words in and wait for the right time to speak them to the people who will benefit.

Proverbs 24:16 - "For though the righteous fall seven times, they rise again, but the wicked stumble when calamity strikes."

The difference between a wise man and a fool is not the absence or presence of mistakes but the lessons learned; a wise man learns from his mistakes but a fool just keeps on repeating them!

Proverbs 13:18 - "Poverty and shame shall be to him that refuseth instruction: but he that regardeth reproof shall be honored."

People prefer to give reproof to others than to receive it. Yet, wisdom begins with reproof. Tough love is true love in spite of our faults. "The rod and reproof give wisdom, but a child left to himself bringeth his mother to shame"

Proverbs 31:9 – "Speak up and judge fairly; defend the rights of the poor and needy."

Speak against all of the social injustices. There may be times when we are powerless to prevent injustice, but there must never be a time when

we fail to protest. "Silence grants consent; you ought to have spoken when you were able to."

Proverbs 10:13-14 – "Smart people speak wisely, but people without wisdom should be punished. The wise don't tell everything they know, but the foolish talk too much and are ruined."

\# Great men are always wise. Wise men speak wisely. They speak because they have something to say; Fools speak without limitations for the sake of speaking.

Proverbs 22:9 – "The generous will themselves be blessed, for they share their food with the poor."

\# Nothing in nature lives for itself. Rivers don't drink their own water, Trees don't eat their own fruit. The sun doesn't produce heat for itself and the moon never goes on a honeymoon. Living for others is the rule of nature. Be each other's keepers and God will reward you abundantly.

Proverbs 22:7 – "The rich ruleth over the poor, and the borrower is servant to the lender."

\#This shows how important it is for every man to keep out of debt. The poor often have a slave mentality, which makes the rich their savior and the solver of each of their problems. It only makes them dependent on the rich. He becomes the oppressor. He can do anything he wants to them without fear because they can't resist him. Their capacity to resist was mortgaged monetarily.

Proverbs 22:6 – "Train up a child in the way he should go, And when he is old he will not depart from it."

\# May what happens in the life of this young one ever magnify the greatness, worth, sufficiency, and saving power of our God. An apple never falls far from the tree.

Proverbs 16:2 – "All the ways of a man are clean in his own sight, But the LORD weighs the motives."

\# Anyone can count the number of seeds in an apple, but only God can count the number of apples in a seed.

Proverbs 3:3-4 – "Never let go of loyalty and faithfulness. Tie them around your neck; write them on your heart. If you do this, both God and people will be pleased with you."

\# Many people just mouth loyalty, but it's not a reality in their life. If you don't understand the value of loyalty, you will never understand the damage of betrayal.

African Proverbs

If you close your eyes to facts you will learn from accidents.

\# "A prudent man sees danger and takes refuge, but the simple keep going and suffer for it". (Proverbs 22:3).

Old men sit in the shade because they planted trees many years before.

\# The values you stand for in your youth shape or determine the outlook of your adult life and consequently, your old age. Please don't waste your youth! ~ Sam Kyeyune

A legend plants a tree which shade they will never enjoy.

Legends plan things not necessarily to benefit them but for the future generations to enjoy. The seed we plant today is a victory for someone tomorrow.

He who eats alone vomits alone.

He who pays the piper calls the tune. The person who is paying someone to do something can decide how it should be done. And hence suffers the consequences of his decisions alone.

Gonorrhea does not infect an umbilical cord but the responsible genital.

The person responsible for the crime should pay the prize for their crimes.

A monkey will not favor burning the forest.

In humanity there is an inherent built-in conflict of interest. It is a situation that has the potential to undermine the impartiality of a person because of the possibility of a clash between the person's self-interest and professional interest or public interest. "Rights can be considered wrongs, depending on who is judging."

A smooth sea does not make a skillful sailor.

Life is like the sea: sometimes we get a gentle sea, at other times we get a stormy sea. But a gentle sea never made a great sailor. It's like a boot-camp. Good soldiers are not made at playgrounds; they can only be produced at boot-camps. (Sam Kyeyune)

A lion does not seek the counsel of a sheep on how to be king of the jungle.

"It is not the wisest choice to consult someone for advice that has never done what you're trying to do or has never been where you're trying to go".

Under every wolf dressed in sheep clothing is the story of a dead sheep.

Satan never takes vacations. Sin lurks at the door waiting for the moment of doctrinal or moral carelessness. The command for the elders, therefore, is: Stay awake. Be alert. Watch.

You don't miss the water until the well runs dry.

God can move people out of your life faster than He moves them into your life. You don't miss people until God takes them out of your life. ~ Joy Marie

A curved tree or plantation that is never straightened up as a seedling will never be straightened up at the later age after it matures and blossoms. Efforts to straighten it at the later stage will result into breaking.

Nab the bad habit out of a child in the bud (at the earliest time possible) before it blossoms. Waiting too long might be too late. "Train up a child in the way he should go: and when he is old, he will not depart from it" (Proverbs 22:6).

The reward of cutting down a dead tree stump is a handful of blisters.
Arguing with a fool makes you look like one.

The fall of a dry leaf is a warning to a green one!

\# Learn from the bad experiences of others, knowing that you are not exempted from them; it is a matter of time. Sometimes you will never know the value of the moment until it becomes a memory.

Never test the depth of water with both feet.

\# It is risky to put all eggs in one basket. The only safe basket to put in all of your eggs is God.

If you want to enjoy eating a fowl, ignore what it eats and focus on the meat.

\# African hens are outdoor creatures that search for food in nasty places. It is possible to lose apatite when you recall what they eat. Ignore what they eat, and focus on the meat. The same thing applies to our relationship – Always there is going to be bad things; ignore the bad and focus on the good.

The educated are many, but the learned are few.

\# Many are educated but not all of them are "well - groomed" and civilized.

"A wise man fills his brains before he empties his mouth"

\# Speak only when you have the right reason to do so. "Speak only when your words are better than your silence". ~ Sam Kyeyune

<u>Humor</u>

One of the things that bind us as a family is a shared sense of humor. Start every day off with a smile. A day without laughter is a day wasted. Never ever lose your sense of humor. It is one of your most valuable resources for good health. Run from toxic people who try to take it from you.

"A person without a sense of humor is like a wagon without springs. It's jolted by every pebble on the road." ~ Henry Ward Beecher

"Everything is funny, as long as it's happening to somebody else." ~ Will Rogers

"The problem with people who have no vices is that generally, you can be pretty sure they're going to have some pretty annoying virtues" ~ Elizabeth Taylor

The problem with close minded people is that their mouth is always opened!

"Books are as useful to a stupid person as a mirror is useful to a blind person" ~ Chanakya

Technically, Moses was the first person with a tablet downloading data.

"When a woman is silent, listen to her very carefully!"

I bet Eva counted Adam's ribs every day to see if another woman had been created.

We wear the crosses around our necks but Jesus wore the cross on His back.

Get to go to heaven on your own strength? Why, you might as well climb to the moon on a rope of sand - Gorge Whitefield

"No man has a good enough memory to be a successful liar." - Abraham Lincoln

I am a human mirror…a reflection of what you actually are…..if you see good you are actually good….if you see bad you are bad…….. Fact.

I would rather accommodate all except that I am an unpleasant experience to a fool.

I asked God to protect me from my enemies. I started losing friends.

"Current relationship status: made dinner for two; Ate both".

It's the people who have an incentive to find the problem who usually find the problem ~ Andrew Ross Sorkin

If the money is not picked from trees why do banks have branches?

It is harder to live through prosperity than through the misery of scarcity.

Through shallow intellect, the mind becomes shallow, and one eats the fly, along with the sweets ~ Guru Nanak

The fastest way to spread the message is to tell it to a woman, and ask her to tell nobody.

Sometimes I wish I could wake up with amnesia to forget about those stupid little things!

For every dollar you give away, you'll get a hundred back. And for every buck you steal, you'll lose a thousand ~ Albert R. Broccoli

"Hearts get infiltrated. Promises get broken. Rules get shattered. Love gets ugly."

They call it the American dream because you have to be asleep to believe it.

Back in primary school in an English class, we were taught the following. A group of cows was a herd. A group of lions was a pride. A group of donkeys was a drove. A group of monkeys was a troop. A group of bees was a swarm.

"No man has a good enough memory to be a successful liar" ~ Abraham Lincoln

Wild animals are very cuddly until they change their mind.

Questions to ponder: Can you cry under water?
Why is it called building when it is already built?
'I love you' is not a question, then why does it need an answer?
If glue sticks everything why doesn't glue stick to its bottle?
If money doesn't grow on trees then why do banks have branches?

Why when post a package by road transportation, it is called shipping, whereas when you ship by water it is called cargo?

Is sand called Sand because it is in between sea and land?

You want your boyfriend to take you out every day; are you a trash can?

Facts of life: The whitest man on earth still has a black shadow.

No mechanic can repair the breaking news.

No matter how tall you are, you can never see tomorrow.

The fish stays in water yet it stinks because it will not take a shower.

"You said all women are equal? I totally disagree, women are not the same. If we were the same, men would be faithful" ~ Nyanjula Doreen.

What is the past tense of 'She is pregnant'? Answer: She had sex.

Being single gets lonely whenever you miss that feeling of being taken.

"Virginity is the best wedding gift any man would receive from his newlywed wife but lately, there's nothing as such any longer because it'll have already been given out as a birthday gift, token of appreciation, job assurance, church collection, examination marking schemes & for lorry fares!"

"A pastor married a jealous woman. One day, the woman was in the kitchen cooking when she overheard her husband praying in the living room saying; Thank you Lord for bringing Mercy, Joy and Grace into my life….she ran quickly with a cooking pan, hit him on the head and said, I knew you were a player and a fake pastor. You have just prayed for all your girlfriends... you think I didn't hear you? Who is Mercy, Joy, and Grace?"

"If you marry a good wife, you will be happy; if you marry a bad one, you will be a philosopher" ~ Varltrude Mujawumukisa

Somebody asked an old man that, "Even at ninety years old, you still call your wife Darling. What is the secret?" The old man answered, "I forgot her name ten years ago and I am scared to ask her".

"Women who start out as ugly ducklings don't become beautiful swans. What they mainly become is confident ducks. They take charge of their lives." ~ Maeve Binchy

"I'm always relieved when someone is delivering a eulogy and I realize I'm listening to it" ~ George Carlin

Somebody said that "Temptations are everywhere". I replied that "So is God".

They say don't put all your eggs in one basket; I did put all my eggs in one basket, and I handed it to God.

"There are no non-believers in hell." Every nonbeliever will believe that there is God when they are languishing in hell.

The older you get, the more you realize that no one has a clue what they are doing.

I am not lazy. I just enjoy doing nothing!

Politicians and diapers have one thing in common; they both should be changed for the same reason.

"I do not want people to be very agreeable, as it saves me the trouble of liking them a great deal."

"I have gone through an anger management training course, but as far as overthrowing M7 is concerned, Ugandans need an anger enhancement course." ~ Nyanjula Dorren

"Keep rolling your eyes, maybe you will find a brain back there."

Mirrors don't lie; I am grateful that they don't laugh!

I wanted to go jogging this morning but Proverbs 28:1 says "The wicked run when no one is chasing them". I decided to abstain.

"So you expect your boyfriend to be rich in his 20s, while your father is still broke in his 60's, my sister what you are smoking is not good for you." ~Robert Mugabe.

"Believing yourself is one of the worst things you can do because you've been telling yourself lies your whole life."

"The fault-finder will find faults even in paradise" ~ Henry David Thoureah

Printed in the United States
By Bookmasters